WHATEVER HAPPENED TO MINORITY ECONOMIC DEVELOPMENT?

READINGS AND CASES

WHATEVER HAPPENED
TO MINORITY
ECONOMIC DEVELOPMENT?
READINGS AND CASES

Edited by
SAMUEL I. DOCTORS

with the assistance of
David Banner
Susan Doctors
Sharon Lockwood

The Dryden Press
Hinsdale, Illinois

To my students, past, present and future

ABOUT THE AUTHORS

Samuel I. Doctors is Professor of Business Administration, Graduate School of Business, University of Pittsburgh. He was a member of the United States Office of Education Task Force on Minority Business Education and Training and a consultant to the Opportunity Funding Corporation in Washington. Professor Doctors holds a Bachelor of Science degree from the University of Miami with majors in Mathematics and Physics. He has done graduate work in mathematics and history and holds a Doctor of Jurisprudence degree from the Harvard Law School and a Doctor of Business Administration degree from the Harvard Business School.

He has been a consultant for the Urban Training Center for the Christian Mission, Associate Director of the President's Advisory Council on Minority Business Enterprise (PACMBE) for National Strategy and Goals, a consultant to the Office of Economic Opportunity and a consultant to various private firms in management education and fair employment practice. He was the principal author of the final report of PACMBE.

He has authored such books as *The Role of Federal Agencies in Technology Transfer* (MIT Press, 1969); *The Management of Technological Change* (The American Management Association, 1970); *The NASA Technology Transfer Program: An Evaluation* (Praeger, 1971); and *Minority Enterprise and the President's Council* (Cambridge: Ballinger, 1973). His articles have appeared in such journals as the *Minnesota Law Review*, the *MSU Business Review*, the *Journal of Law and Contemporary Problems*, the *Business and Society Review*, the *Urban Affairs Quarterly*, the *Urban and Social Change Review, Business Perspectives*, and similar journals.

David K. Banner is Assistant Professor of Business Administration at the University of New Brunswick.

Susan Doctors was a Research Assistant at the Graduate School of Management, Northwestern University.

Sharon Lockwood was the Economic Advisor to the President's Council on Minority Enterprise.

ACKNOWLEDGEMENTS

The only new minority development initiative of the Nixon Administration has been that of "minority capitalism." It therefore appears important to explore the nature of this initiative as well as some of programmatic development that was initiated prior to January 1969. This book aims to explore the pattern this minority capitalism initiative has taken in the context of one urban setting, that of Chicago.

My first involvement in minority economic development was as a research assistant and legal counsel to the Program on Technology and Society, Harvard University in 1968. Since that time I have been actively involved in minority economic development both in Washington and Chicago.

In Washington I worked closely with the President's Council on Minority Business Enterprise and the HEW/OMBE Task Force on Minority Business Education and Training. In Chicago, I have offered courses in minority economic development and business environment which required that I develop materials for use in the classroom and for special programs for community developers, businessmen and public officials. As a result of this teaching, I have felt that there has been an important need for a book of empirically based case studies and readings in the area of minority enterprise development. This book was written in response to that need.

No single book of this size could possibly encompass as much detail about minority enterprise development as the interested reader might want. Also, practical considerations of space limitations have required that we select only the more illustrative readings that have been developed.

Many of my M.B.A. and Ph.D. students played a major role in the development of this book. Some wrote course reports which were later expanded and developed, eventually being incorporated into this book. Others worked on articles or case studies, which while quite good, were discarded because of space limitations but which provided important insights and background.

I would especially like to mention two M.B.A. students for special praise, Robert Donath and Tracy Russell. Both of these men were diligent students and assisted materially in the development of this book.

I will generally refrain from mentioning for especial praise students whose papers are included in this book. The inclusion of their papers bears testimony to their diligence and hard work. However, I must single out two Ph.D. students, Anne Huff and Robert Yancy. Anne not only wrote one of the case studies included in this volume ("United Distributors"), but also helped in the initial editing and gathering of materials. Bob, in addition to coauthoring one of the included articles ("The National Alliance of Businessmen"), helped gather data for several others.

Veta Appel, my research assistant, has provided substantial help in editing the final version of the manuscript. She also proofread the copy edited manuscript and has provided numerous helpful suggestions.

I owe a debt of gratitude for assistance to many community leaders in Chicago, including Garland Guice (Chicago Economic Development Corporation), Cecil Butler (North Lawndale Economic Development Corporation), John Vinzant (Vinzant's Coalition), John Linton (Talent Assistance Program), George Johnson (Johnson Products), Chester Robinson (Westside Organization) and Al Boutte (Independence Bank).

Also at the national level a number of people were most helpful, Congressman Alan Steelman, John Topping (OMBE), Art McZeir (SBA) and Theodore Cross (Attorney, Editor of *Business and Society Review/Innovation*). The staff of the President's Council on Minority Enterprise were most helpful and provided good materials and leads for articles.

My colleagues at the Graduate School of Management, Northwestern University, were most helpful in providing articles and cases. Raymond Mack, the Vice President for Academic Affairs, was most supportive and provided financial assistance for several doctoral students who worked on the manuscript as did the Research Committee of the University. Lou Masotti and John McKnight, Director and Associate Director of the Northwestern Center for Urban Affairs were also most helpful.

A number of very patient people helped in the typing and retyping of this manuscript including Debbie Silver, Martha Rappaport, Ginnie Churchill, Ellen Schechet, and Joanne McGovern.

Vera Chatz deserves special praise for her work in editing all of the readings and case studies. Vera labored long and hard and many of the positive aspects of the book are due in no small way to her diligence and incisive editorial assistance.

George November, a candidate for the Masters of Management degree (Northwestern University, 1974), helped in up-dating and revising many of the cases and readings and was most important in the final revision of the book.

I am grateful to a number of journals for permission to reprint articles or portions of articles previously published by them—*Journal of Law and Contemporary Problems*, "New Directions for Minority Enterprise," (July 1971); *Business Perspectives*, "Creative Inducements to Private Investment in the Minority Community" (Winter 1973); 2nd, *Business and Society Review/ Innovation*, "Nixon's Minority Capitalism: Full Steam to Where?"

I am responsible for any omissions or mistakes in this manuscript. I only hope that it will provide a stimulus for students, scholars and policy makers to step back and view minority economic development more objectively and thus move more rapidly to realize the very significant potential of the beginning that has been made.

CONTENTS

AN OVERVIEW

The riots of the mid-1960s shattered Lyndon Johnson's "Great Society"; the nation's social ills, which had been hidden beneath a facade of unprecédented national prosperity, exploded and forced themselves on the American conscience. The urban riots have only hinted at the extent to which minority Americans in this day, more than 100 years after emancipation, are alienated, distrustful of a society that has not provided equality of opportunity. Minorities are determined to remake a society, which has not provided equality of opportunity in areas such as housing, education, health care, employment, and business development.

If solutions to this continuing problem in America were simple, the problem would no longer exist; however, the problems of the minority communities continue to grow in the ghettos, barrios, and reservations, and finding solutions is anything but simple.

Referring to the reports of commissions that had investigated riots throughout U. S. history, Dr. Kenneth B. Clark, a distinguished and perceptive scholar, said:

I read that report . . . of the 1919 riot in Chicago, and it is as if I were reading the report of the investigating committee on the Harlem riot of '35, the report of the investigating committee on the Harlem riot of '43, the report of the McCone Commission on the Watts riot.

I must again in candor say to you members of this Commission—it is a kind of Alice in Wonderland—with the same moving picture reshown over and over again, the same analysis, the same recommendations, and the same inaction.

(Testimony before the Kerner Commission, 1967)

Moreover, the early seventies have seen a growing sense of apathy by most Americans to the continuing social, political, and economic inequities of minorities. Some gains have been made, but in fiscal 1973 the Nixon administration decided to hold the line or to cut back funding in all domestic areas save (1) law enforcement, (2) environmental protection, and (3) small business development, including minority enterprise development. Each of these areas receives relatively modest expenditures compared to the Great Society programs initiated under the Johnson administration. This book concentrates on one of these three domestic growth areas: minority enterprise development.

Only a few tentative strategies for minority enterprise development have been advanced. One of them concerns the role of private enterprise in minority communities. Many large corporations produce voluminous literature portraying their programs for the present and future development of minority group employees. These program descriptions outline the hiring, training, and development of minority managerial as well as blue-collar talent. More recently, business involvement in minority enterprise development has received some publicity in the media. Unfortunately, these efforts have actually been relatively modest. Minorities have been sidestepped all along the way throughout the history of the United States. During most periods of American economic growth they have made modest progress, but during economic downturns they usually have lost many of their modest gains. They have been the last to be admitted into the system and the first to be turned out; for example, during World War II minority unemployment statistics were quite low but they grew again to the historical rate (twice that of nonminority unemployment) shortly after the end of the war.

Relatively few minority individuals have been fortunate enough to overcome the many obstacles between them and managerial and professional careers. Minority representation on the boards of directors of the 500 largest U. S. corporations has grown since 1969, but representation remains small; minorities still occupy less than 3.0 percent of all managerial and professional positions in these major corporations. Most of the managerial positions held are far from the sources of power and corporate decision making.

Similarly, minority Americans have fared badly in the control of economic resources. Although minorities represent about 17 percent of America's total population, little more than 4 percent of American business (with less than 0.3 percent of the business assets) is owned by minorities, and even those businesses all too often are marginal enterprises; few offer any hope for growth and development and many are simply doomed to failure. These businesses appeal mainly to the ghetto consumer, an underdeveloped, impoverished market. Minority alienation from business has been compounded further by a long-standing distrust of creditors, insurance companies, banks, and other symbols of white economic power.

Prior to the 1960s, the ghettos were relatively quiet and inactive. But the experiences of New York, Detroit, Chicago, Los Angeles, and many other urban centers have proved that minority Americans are willing to seek full citizenship and equal power in this nation at any cost. But what is this cost? Specifically, what is the cost to business and government now? Are present and planned expenditures on economic development sufficient to help minority groups participate as full partners in American life during the seventies? Is the business community sufficiently imbued with the desire to make minority enterprise succeed?

A major theme of this book is that the interface between America's business society and disenfranchised minorities could prove to be the focus for many important solutions to America's problems. Potential elements of change were introduced in the sixties in such programs as the Department of Labor's JOBS program, the Small Business Administration's (SBA) minority lending program, the SBA's minority enterprise small investment companies (MESBICs), the new Office of Economic Opportunity (OEO) capital market experiments (Opportunity Funding Corporation—OFC), and various local community development corporations (CDCs).

SCOPE AND PROGRESS TO DATE

In recent years progressive business managers have demonstrated the social responsibility of business by showing greater interest in the ghetto and barrios. But what are the forms that this interest should take? In fact, can the present economic structure accommodate minority demands for full partnership? Would blacks and other minorities be better off developing their own economic system in a separatist society rather than attempting to integrate their development into that of white society?

Furthermore, will the present administration and those that follow during the seventies and eighties actively pursue President Nixon's promise to "get private enterprise into the ghetto and get the people of the ghetto into private enterprise"? Have the minority capitalist theorists gone wrong? Why have employment programs such as the Labor Department's JOBS program failed to live up to the expectations of both minority and nonminority communities?

Each of the above questions—and many others—have been seriously and vociferously debated both in the ghetto and on Wall Street. Hopefully, those who seek answers will find some empirical data, meaningful perspectives, and tentative solutions in the studies presented here.

Although many oft-cited statistics "prove" that minorities have significantly improved their lot in America, one study presented in this book illustrates that, relatively speaking, minority Americans may be falling further behind the white American majority in a number of important economic areas (see "Economic Causes of Social Unrest" by James H. Weaver). Other studies indicate that small minority businesses are making painfully slow progress in becoming viable, growing organizations. Clearly, studies such as these challenge the common saying that "all is being done that can reasonably be done," and even more important, they challenge examinations of social indicator data such as that in Daniel Moynihan's "Benign Neglect" memorandum or in Edward Banfield's notion that our race problems are simply a matter of expectations outracing performance.

By the date that this book reaches publication, the impact of our domestic policy (or lack of impact) will be felt more fully. Little has occurred during the Nixon administration to encourage anyone, poor and/or minority, that the government has a continuing interest in playing a leadership role in minority social, political, and economic development. The Johnson years at least gave us something to study—money, manpower, and new programs directed at alleviating some of the problems of the minority urban poor. Although these programs weren't able to achieve all of the advertised benefits, they were far better than a policy of benign neglect. This new policy of neglect has allowed other issues (in some ways far less rending of our national fabric) to become more dominant. The economy, Vietnam, ecology, crime, and consumer protection have become perceived as more pressing national issues. These issues are far less guilt-producing, as they do not continually remind us of our lack of empathy for our less fortunate citizens or of very difficult social issues that must be faced.

We haven't even begun to tackle the problems of educating and training minorities and providing new capital bases in minority communities, both urban and rural. What little has been accomplished in the desegregation of our educational system is being threatened by increasing negative sentiment and direct federal action against bussing. Are we going to go back to a policy of separate but equal, a concept that has long been discredited? The present actions of the Nixon administration go against the thrust of much in the Supreme Court rulings that provided the impetus for national policy in the sixties directed toward more equality of opportunity for minorities. The Nixon administration has not enacted any spectacular new program, yet massive new efforts are desperately needed if we are to achieve some parity of opportunity before the end of the twentieth century.

The concept of minority economic development is not new. Booker T. Washington was an outspoken advocate of such a program at the turn of the century. What is new is federal and nonminority business involvement in minority economic development and the concept of economic development initiated and operated by community corporations as well as by individual entrepreneurs.

This change directs our attention to the focus of this book: What is going on in minority economic development? The enterprises detailed in this book are not all successes, but they have an importance beyond their profit and loss statements: they are examples of the only minority-focused program which has grown and is projected to grow substantially during the two terms of the Nixon administration.

Many of the cases presented are Chicago-based because Chicago is representative of the problems and opportunities seen nationwide. Moreover, Chicago has been the subject of a number of important social science studies including those by Edward Banfield (*Political Influence*) and St. Clair Drake and Horace R. Clayton (*Black Metropolis*). Chicago has also been an important arena for the development of black consciousness and power. It is the home of Operation PUSH—People United to Save Humanity. (In December, 1971, most of the leadership of Operation Breadbasket in Chicago, the economic arm of the Southern Christian Leadership Council, branched off to form PUSH—a Chicago-based national economic-social development organization for the disadvantaged.)

The 1970 census indicated that about 40 percent of Chicago's population was minority, and this percentage is expected to grow to over 50 percent within the next 20 years. Thus political power in the nation's second largest city is likely to be in minority hands before the end of this century. This easily forecast result, as much as any other motivating factor, has caused the nonminority business community that must remain in the city to become actively involved in a variety of community development activities.

There are literally dozens of important political, social, and economic leaders in the Chicago minority community, including two of the nation's most successful black businessmen, George Johnson of Johnson Products (sales in 1972 of over $12 million) and John Johnson of Johnson Publications (sales in 1972 of over $23 million, including *Ebony* and *Jet* magazines). The Reverend Jesse Jackson, President of PUSH and Edwin C. (Bill) Berry, director of the Johnson Foundation and former director of the Chicago Urban League, are only two of the nationally known black leaders whose home base is Chicago.

A recent book by Philip Drotning and Wesley South (*Up from the Ghetto*. New York: Cowles, 1970) presents brief biographies of blacks who have risen from ghetto backgrounds to positions of prominence in a variety of fields. Eight of the 14 reside in Chicago. These illustrations are merely meant to indicate the importance of Chicago to minority development.

This city provides an excellent focus for a book that attempts to provide an in-depth look at a major new thrust of minority development, that of enterprise development. We could conclude that some minority group members do "make it" in our system, but they are the exceptions to the rule. Individual blacks, Mexican Americans, and Puerto Ricans have made it all along. There has been a small black upper middle class population since shortly after the Civil War. Individual black-owned enterprise is only an incidental result of federal minority economic development programs—they might have made it anyway.

This account is depressing, but the truth it speaks is real—something needs to be done *NOW*, on a large scale, with enough power behind it to transform the economics of ghetto life before another generation is lost.

This book is divided into five sections as follows.

Section One. The first section discusses the overall problem of economic disparities between the minority and nonminority populations and the questions as to the extent to which these disparities have decreased during the past decade. Then three proposed solutions are considered—Jobs; Minority Capitalism; and, Community Economic Development.

Section Two. The second section builds on the discussion of the "Case for Jobs" in Section I and provides several specific examples of private and public sector involvement in the development of job opportunities. The section also provides a detailed discussion of job disparities in the Chicago labor market.

Section Three. In this section, the whole question of minority capitalism is discussed, using a number of essays and case studies to raise the major issues that have been debated by businessmen, government agency spokesmen, and minority community leaders. These debates have often been acrimonious and filled with accusations of bad faith and an attempt is made to present as much of the substance of these disagreements as possible without the rhetoric. Some examples of unsuccessful, but conceptually important, projects are presented along with one example of a very successful minority entrepreneur and several examples of businesses are presented whose success is still indeterminate.

Section Four. This section attempts to present some of the major areas of nonminority business involvement in both the jobs and capitalism areas and to suggest the multiplicity of ways in which business has become involved in this area of pressing national concern. This section also presents areas of potential business involvement which appear likely to provide more effective means for such involvement in the years ahead.

Section Five. Section five presents articles and a case study illustrating some of the problems and opportunities inherent in community based economic development. Some of the problems of such development at a national level are also discussed.

SECTION ONE:
THE PROBLEM AND
ALTERNATIVE APPROACHES

INTRODUCTION

The purpose of the first section of this book is to impart an understanding of the substantial social and economic differences between minority and nonminority communities and to present three approaches to the solution of these problems. Each of these approaches then will be dealt with in depth in the following sections. Although the editors of this book have their own bias, they have attempted to present alternative viewpoints for consideration by the reader. Two distinctly different views about the dimensions of the problems have been viewed in debates concerning the state of the nation. One school of thought holds that while a disparity exists and is a serious problem, the relative disparity between minority and nonminority communities has decreased substantially since World War II and will decrease still further in the years immediately ahead. In line with such thinking, present expressions of discontent by minorities are caused primarily by the liberal establishment's public and private pronouncements that have caused minority expectations to outrace the very substantial progress being made to close the economic gap. The exponents of this view hold that what is needed for the immediate future is not so much new and greatly expanded national programs, but rather a period of "benign neglect" during which present programs, such as the various training and employment programs, the newer minority capitalism program, and various community development programs can be further strengthened and implemented.

Those who espouse this viewpoint feel that a variety of demographic, technical, and political factors, about which very little can be done in the short run, have caused the present problems. They feel, however, that these problems have been substantially exacerbated by the media and by the angry rhetoric of militant groups that have convinced Americans that they have an impending Armageddon if they do not mount a huge, new multibillion dollar public program to immediately seek to reduce the disparity. They argue that what is really needed is the maintenance of a low profile by government and the establishment of a cooling-off period. This period may have to extend over several decades until substantial numbers of minorities are enrolled in the middle class and the disproportionately large number of lower class youths is reduced by a lower birthrate among the disadvantaged.

The other school of thought is of the opinion that we are in a desperate situation, that we are in effect rapidly moving toward two distinct societies—one white and one black (probably this view would include Spanish-surnamed individuals and American Indians)—separate and unequal. In accordance with this view, it is primarily "white racism" that prevents progress toward the economic and social integration of our society. Further, if we continue to ignore the legitimate aspirations of our minority citizens for an equal share in the action, the result will be the destruction of our society. The civil disorders of the 1960s are seen by these observers as the result of a number of interrelated factors such as the failure to move rapidly enough to provide economic opportunities for our minority communities, an increased concentration of minorities in our inner cities, frustrations caused by lack of access to power, and pervasive discrimination in education and housing.

This view acknowledges that some economic progress has been made during the late 1960s, particularly during the war years. But, with the end of the war in Vietnam, it is feared that considerable economic backsliding will result, as has happened after other wars. The rapid rise in minority unemployment to more than 10 percent in 1971 is seen as an indication of the backsliding. Another indication is the number of present cutbacks in the area of social programs by the federal government.

Two of the leading academic exponents of the "benign neglect" view are Professors Edward Banfield and Daniel Moynihan, both of whom have served as urban affairs advisors to the Nixon administration.[1] Their argument includes an enumeration of the substantial economic gains made by minorities, including the fact that between 1960 and 1970, nonwhite family income rose dramatically with almost one-third of all such families (28 percent) earning $10,000 or more compared with 11 percent in 1960.[2] Also unemployment for nonwhite heads of families dropped from 7.9 percent in 1962 to 3.9 percent in 1971.[3]

Banfield argues further that our problems today are largely ones of perception; that is, too many unrealistic promises have raised minority expectations beyond any realistic level. In fact, he says that we have made substantial progress in all economic and social areas, and with the passage of time, we can expect additional progress.

Banfield contends that a major portion of our urban problem is not so much a racial as a class problem because lower class characteristics such as a present-oriented life style, a need for action, a lack of self-esteem, and a taste for risktaking are at the core of the problem.

A recent economic analysis of the causes of minority discontent investigates the same data that Banfield and Moynihan have analyzed and concludes that many economic indicators show minority gains to be very uneven. Conducted by Professor James Weaver, this analysis argues that blacks are, in a number of ways, worse off today than they were a decade ago. Although black family income rose from 51 percent of white family income in 1947 to 63.7 percent in 1970, this may be a misleading comparison. Weaver notes that the absolute dollar gap stood at $2,402 in 1947 and at $3,770 in 1970; that nonwhite families are significantly larger than white families; that these income figures do not include other types of income such as rent, dividends, or interest; and that minority purchasing power is smaller than that of whites.

Several trends are working against continued economic gains for minorities during the 1970s. These include the increasing exodus of industry to the suburbs, coupled with increasing housing segregation, an increasing need for highly skilled workers and a growing period of economic downturn in the early 1970s. One may thus conclude from Weaver's essay that the Nixon administration's policy of benign neglect may well result in a further period of civil strife.

Many observers of the contemporary scene have concluded that minorities lack a sufficient economic stake in the system and that this fact contributes in no small measure to frustration, angry rhetoric, and, at times, violence. Even those observers who feel that minority frustrations arise from a failure to perceive the great strides that have been made in the last few decades (a failure resulting from what these critics view as slanted coverage of these inequities by the mass media) conclude that further reduction of the economic gap between the races would be beneficial to society.

THREE PROPOSED APPROACHES

Even if we substantially lessen the economic gap between the communities, this will not of itself solve all the social, educational, and political problems that cause continuing feelings of hostility between the minority and nonminority communities. The Kerner Report, published in 1968, recognized the need for a comprehensive coordinated attack on many fronts—education, employment, health care, housing and community economic development. It is the purpose of this book to concentrate largely on economic development.

Three general approaches have been suggested to help reduce the economic gap: jobs, minority capitalism, and community economic development. The jobs approach was in special vogue with the advent of a variety of government-sponsored job training programs during the Johnson administration and with the initiation of the Alliance of Businessmen JOBS program in 1967. The second approach, minority enterprise, was well publicized during the 1968 presidential race when Richard M. Nixon urged that minorities be directly involved in business as owners and managers. The last approach, community development, has had a somewhat less publicized introduction under Title I-D, the Special Impact program of OEO. It has received some recent publicity following congressional introduction of the Community Self-Determination Act of 1968 and 1970 (neither act has thus far received congressional approval; nor is there any indication of early passage of such an act).

These three interrelated strategies also are related to various socio-political ideologies that achieved some prominence during the 1960s. Integration has long been the ideology espoused by various liberal groups, particularly after the Supreme Court decision on school integration in 1954 (*Brown V. the Little Rock Board of Education*). While economic integration or at least economic parity has become an important goal of all factions today, many minority leaders have moved away from social integration and toward other ideologies such as separatism or liberation. However, one of the highest ranking minority members in the federal government, Andrew Brimmer, a governor of the Federal Reserve System, has become a leading advocate of the ideology of integration. Brimmer has stated that only through a strategy of integration into the American mainstream can minorities hope to change their deprived status. In particular, the integrationists argue against any strategy that primarily depends on the development of a capital base in the ghettos or barrios. They feel that such a strategy will tend to institutionalize the present dual society and will in effect lock minorities into the deprived economy of the ghettos and barrios. Brimmer feels that, given the present status of our economy, the only real opportunities for economic development lie in expanded employment opportunities for minorities outside the ghettos. He specifically argues that minority businesses have traditionally been concentrated in areas of low profit: and growth-potential and that the probability of success has been and will continue to be unacceptably low. He also argues that minority enterprise development will provide very few employment opportunities. Section II of this book is devoted to the jobs approach to bridging the economic gap in our society.

On the other hand, separatists and black power advocates such as Stokely Carmichael and Roy Innis argue that minorities must first consolidate their power base in their existing communities before they can deal with the "other society"[4] on a basis of equality. Thus they favor the development of a capital base that would allow minorities to own and to manage the businesses in their own communities and generally to control the flow of capital to and from the community. Without this control over their own economy, they feel that they will remain in a colonial status in respect to the larger society.

Arguing that black capitalism is a necessary corollary of the black power movement, Professor Fred Allvine contends that blacks have been systematically deprived of the opportunity to develop viable businesses in their own communities and that our entire progress as a nation will be retarded unless we provide greater opportunities for minority business development. He feels the black community has undergone a transformation during the 1960s: pride in blackness and a belief in the ability of blacks to manage and control their own economy has grown considerably. Allvine says that the time is ripe for the development of substantial new businesses in the minority community. However, Allvine notes that there is considerable disagreement about the definition of "black capitalism." Brimmer defines black capitalism as small business developments serving an impoverished clientele in ghetto areas. Some proponents of black capitalism feel that such development must not be exclusively in the ghettos and barrios; it must have access to wider markets outside the ghetto and involvement in newer, higher growth-potential businesses than the traditional small retail or service business.

Beginning in February, 1964, when the Small Business Administration (SBA) made experimental "six by six" loans to ghetto businessmen of $6,000 for six years with little or no collateral, early federal government programs were all focussed on small loans to small businessmen.[5] Using the "six by six" program as a model, Congress enacted Title IV of the Economic Opportunity Act of 1966, which provided the equal opportunity loans (EOLs) up to $25,000 (as of 1972 a $50,000 maximum is permitted) could be provided to small business firms located in areas of substantial unemployment or to low-income individuals either in business or wishing to enter business. Both the model "six by six" program and the later EOL program provided a small amount of management and technical assistance for disadvantaged entrepreneurs.[6] In the summer of 1968, a major thrust to provide loans to minority businessmen was initiated under the direction of SBA Administrator Howard Samuels.[7] This new SBA initiative now includes both the EOL program and an adaptation of the more usual SBA loan programs for minority entrepreneurs.[8] These SBA loan programs together with the other portion of the minority enterprise program are the fastest growing federal domestic programs, aside from law enforcement, with a projected spending rate of $1.6 billion for fiscal 1974 (up from $150 million in fiscal 1969).

A recent survey of SBA loans to minority entrepreneurs indicates that the average loan to minority entrepreneurs in fiscal 1970 averaged about $24,000, versus $56,000 for nonminority entrepreneurs,[9] although there is some indication that average loan size has moved up in the fiscal years from 1971 to 1973. Section III presents case studies and essays about minority enterprise.

The federal government claims that it has changed its notion of minority capitalism to place major emphasis on assistance to larger, more viable minority enterprises and to provide more assistance for the development of facilities needed for major economic development programs such as shopping centers and industrial parks.[10] However, the government has not yet initiated a comprehensive capital base development program in our urban ghettos and barrios such as that outlined by Theodore Cross in his book, *Black Capitalism.*[11] Cross calls for an end to "philanthropy" and an end to the "crash programs," "task forces," "target areas," and "business involvement" that do not deal with the "basic wealth-forbidding deficits of American slums." To Cross, the ghetto economy can not be strengthened solely by government-run and government-directed programs, and ways and means must be found to employ the expertise and financial wherewithal of the private sector to move on a broad front to create a viable economy in the ghettos and barrios of the nation. He feels that the government must provide a variety of incentives to induce private sector investment and involvement in ghetto development. Government alone cannot accomplish this goal, because it has neither the expertise nor the necessary financial resources. Therefore, government must induce private involvement and must use its own resources as leverage for private sector investment.

Cross has been influential in the development of the federal minority capitalism program and his concept of the need for capital base building in minority communities is being tried in the OEO sponsored Opportunity Funding Corporation (OFC). OFC is the only attempt thus far to implement an experimental program in the minority enterprise area and is discussed in detail in "The OFC Approach" by David Banner and Samuel Doctors.

The government has initiated a limited experimental program to test some of these ideas in the form of an OEO grant of $7.4 million (for fiscal 1971 and 1972) to a nonprofit corporation, the Opportunity Funding Corporation.[12]

To make good on his "Bridges to Human Dignity" speech during the 1968 presidential campaign, Mr. Nixon established in March, 1969, by Executive Order 11458, the Office of Minority Business Enterprise (OMBE) in the Department of Commerce and a President's Advisory Council on Minority Business Enterprise (PACMBE). OMBE was given the operational mandate to help develop and coordinate all public and private programs designed to encourage the development of minority enterprise. The advisory council was slated to design a national strategy for the 1970s and was composed of 84 representatives of the business, university, and minorities communities, including Sam Wyly as chairman and Berkeley Burrell as vice-chairman.[13]

The council made its report to the president and the secretary of commerce in February, 1971. The report held that minority enterprise development must be made a "national priority" for the 1970s. The rationale for the council's more than 100 recommendations is included in this volume to provide an indication of present strategic thinking on the subject of minority economic development. The council was reconstituted (1972) under a new chairman, Robert Keeler (chairman of the board of Phillips Petroleum), to provide a continuing advisory input. But Mr. Keeler resigned the chairmanship early in 1973 and no new chairman or executive director has been named as of September 1973.

The council called for a broad new program including an emphasis on management education, capital base development, technical assistance, and expanded ownership. The council report states that many forms of economic ownership must be encouraged including business development, community ownership and development, increased stock ownership in nonminority businesses, and development of credit unions and cooperatives to provide credit, goods, and services on more reasonable terms in ghetto areas. The council decision to include recommendations in the community development area is indicative of a growing interest in this form of economic development. Thus far, little action has been taken on many of the council recommendations.

About seventy-five distinct community development corporations (CDCs) were identified by the Twentieth Century Fund Task Force for Community Development in urban areas that were controlled by the community and were planning on operating development projects.[14] These projects range in size from the very large to the very small: the comprehensive program of the Bedford-Stuyvesant Restoration Corporation includes a special impact area population of four hundred thousand and has had total Special Impact (OEO Act 7 1966) funding of over $33 million (between 1967 and 1972); on the other hand, the rather small program of the East Central Citizens Organization in Columbus, Ohio, has a target area population of only about seven thousand and has had minimal funding.[15] These CDCs are largely supported by OEO grants under Title I-D, which amounted to $30 million in fiscal 1973 and are projected to reach $39 million in fiscal 1974. Other sources of funds have been provided by foundations, church groups, and private business. The number of CDCs is still growing and they are engaged in a variety of projects ranging from housing to electronics manufacturing. Some function as not-for-profit corporations; some control their various enterprises directly; others own stock but do not control operations; still others merely assist in establishing enterprises or expanding existing ones.

The War on Poverty, initiated early in the Johnson administration, created a number of new community organizations under the auspices of the OEO Act and the Model Cities program of the Housing and Urban Development Department (HUD).[16] Some experts on economic development, such as Stewart Perry, Professor Richard Rosenbloom, and Geoffrey Faux, think that the community development corporation concept is timely and provides the most meaningful vehicle for comprehensive community development. These experts agree that the CDCs provide a missing and vital ingredient of poverty area community control and management of the development process.

A recent report prepared by a panel of economic development experts for the Twentieth Century Fund Task Force for Community Development found that the twin strategies of dispersal and community development as recommended by the Kerner Report were no longer realistic for the immediate future, and thus the major thrust of minority economic development should be internal.[17] They concluded the "minority capitalism," while a viable strategy for small scale business development, was simply not a viable strategy when applied to community development. Geoffrey Faux, the principal draftsman of the Twentieth Century Fund Report of CDCs, feels the vital distinction between CDCs and other corporations to be that the "primary objective of the CDCs is not to make a profit but to enhance the economic power of poor communities."[18]

Another proponent of the broadly based community development concept is Elliott Sclar, who is of the opinion that minority enterprise as presently supported by the Nixon administration is not a viable approach to solving the problems of our urban ghettos and barrios. Because of the declining demand for unskilled labor in the cities, Sclar sees little opportunity for capital accumulation by blacks in contrast to the immigrant experience.[19]

In Stewart Perry's brief essay on CDCs, the focus is on the fact that "CDCs are not inherently a part of the federally sponsored poverty program"; they are initiated independently and are the product of local community pressures for a vehicle with which to achieve their aspirations for a better society. Perry sees the CDC as a means for the community to "seize" real power in its own neighborhoods—"the economic muscle of business development." Examples of private sector involvement in minority economic development are presented in Section IV, while a number of brief case histories and a longer case study of a CDC is provided in Section V. The readings in this book should enable the reader to judge for himself the validity of the varying hypotheses concerning the best methods for developing the economies of minority communities.

FOOTNOTES

[1] Professor Moynihan's memorandum to President Nixon concerning the status of American Negroes is included in this volume. Professor Banfield's views are most explicitly stated in his book, *The Unheavenly City* (Boston: Little, Brown and Co., 1970).

[2] "Nonwhite" apparently does not include most Spanish surnamed individuals, since the category is 92 percent black and Spanish surnamed individuals number well over 9 million in 1973.

[3] U.S. Department of Labor, *Black Americans: A Chartbook* (Washington, D.C.: U.S. Government Printing Office, 1971), p. 24. The Labor Department reported that *overall* nonwhite unemployment went from 9.0 percent in 1950 to 10.2 percent in 1971.

[4] See Stokely Carmichael and Charles Hamilton, *Black Power* (New York: Vintage, 1967); Roy Innis, "Separatist Economics: A New Social Contract," in *Black Economic Development*, eds. William Haddad and Douglas Pugh (Englewood Cliffs, N.J.: Prentice-Hall, 1969), pp. 50-59.

[5] The "six-by-six" program was initiated under the leadership of SBA administrator Eugene Foley, who discusses the program in his book, *The Achieving Ghetto* (Washington, D.C.: The National Press, 1968), pp. 106ff.

[6] The EOL program was initially administered by OEO, which experienced a loss rate in excess of 20 percent; it was later transferred to SBA. Loss rates at SBA are as yet unreported, but they may be higher than 20 percent.

[7] Initially the project was named "Project Own" and later was changed to "Operation Mainstream." See James Hund, *Black Entrepreneurship* (Belmont, Calif.: Wadsworth, 1970), pp. 46-47.

[8] SBA loans to minorities increased from 2,235 in fiscal 1968 to 4,654 in 1969 and to 6,262 in 1970 and in value from $41.3 million in fiscal 1968 to $297 million in FY 1972 to an estimated $450 million in FY 1973. Data was supplied by SBA, February 1973.

[9] This study was performed for the President's Advisory Council on Minority Business Enterprise by Sharon Lockwood, the economic advisor to the council, in the fall of 1971, and made use of SBA-supplied data.

[10] This impression was gained from discussions with SBA and EDA officials as part of the author's work on the National Advisory Council, 1970; also see the report of the Twentieth Century Fund Task Force on Community Development Corporations, *CDC's: New Hope for the Inner City* (New York: The Twentieth Century Fund, 1971), p. 45.

[11] Theodore Cross, *Black Capitalism* (New York: Atheneum, 1969).

[12] A paper analyzing this new governmental approach to minority enterprise development is included in this volume in the article by Banner and Doctors.

[13] Mr. Wyly is chairman of the board of University Computing Corporation and Berkeley Burrell is a leading Washington black businessman and president of the National Business League. The work of the Council is analyzed in Samuel Doctors and Ann Huff, *Minority Enterprise and the President's Council* (Boston: Ballinger Press, 1973).

[14] Report of the Twentieth Century Fund Task Force on Community Development Corporations, p. 5.

[15] *Center for Community Economic Development Newsletter* (August 1973), pp. 4, 5. "Special impact" or "target area" refers to the language in the OEO Act of 1966, Title I, designating the poverty areas where CDC's money must be spent.

[16] See sections 121 and 123 of OEO Act which provide for OEO support of community action agencies (CAAs), and see Title I of the Demonstration Cities and Metropolitan Development Act of 1966.

[17] See Report of the Twentieth Century Fund, *op. cit.*

[18] Twentieth Century Report, p. 29. Mr. Faux was formerly Acting Director of Economic Development for OEO and considered by many to be a principal architect of the CDC concept in government.

[19] Professor Banfield contends that "automation and technical change are not creating a serious unemployment problem and are not likely to; that the unskilled, far from facing a hopeless future, will probably maintain and improve their position relative to the skilled. . . . " *Unheavenly City*, pp. 89ff.

Edward C. Banfield*

EXCERPTS FROM *THE UNHEAVENLY CITY*[1]

In many important respects, conditions in the large cities have been getting better. There is less poverty in the cities now than there has ever been. Housing, including that of the poor, is improving rapidly: one study predicts that substandard housing will have been eliminated by 1980.[2] In the last decade alone the improvement in housing has been marked. At the turn of the century only one child in fifteen went beyond elementary school; now most children finish high school. The treatment of racial and other minority groups is conspicuously better than it was. When, in 1964, a carefully drawn sample of Negroes was asked whether, in general, things were getting better or worse for Negroes in this country, approximately eight out of ten respondents said "better."[3]

If the situation is improving, why, it may be asked, is there so much talk of urban crisis? The answer is that the improvements in performance, great as they have been, have not kept pace with rising expectations. In other words, although things have been getting better absolutely, they have been getting worse relative to what we think they should be. And this is because, as a people, we seem to act on the advice of the old jingle:

Good, better, best,
Never let it rest
Until your good is better
And your better best.

To a large extent, then, our urban problems are like the mechanical rabbit at the racetrack, which is set to keep just ahead of the dogs no matter how fast they may run. Our performance is better and better, but because we set our standards and expectations to keep ahead of performance, the problems are never any nearer to solution. Indeed, if standards and expectations rise faster than performance, the problems may get (relatively) worse as they get (absolutely) better.

That government cannot solve the problems of the cities and is likely to make them worse by trying does not necessarily mean that calamity impends. Powerful accidental (by which is meant, non-governmental and, more generally, non-organizational) forces are at work that tend to alleviate and even to eliminate the problems. Hard as it may be for a nation of inveterate problem solvers to believe, social problems sometimes disappear in the normal course of events.

*Edward Banfield is a Professor of Political Science at Harvard University and he has been a special Urban Affairs Advisor to President Nixon.

Although it is easy to exaggerate the importance, either for good or ill, of the measures that government has adopted or might adopt, there does appear to be a danger to the good health of the society in the tendency of the public to define so many situations as "critical problems"—a definition that implies (1) that "solutions" exist or can be found and (2) that unless they are found and applied at once, disaster will befall. The import of what has been said in this book is that although there are many difficulties to be coped with, dilemmas to be faced, and afflictions to be endured, there are very few problems that can be solved; it is also that although much is seriously wrong with the city, no disaster impends unless it be one that results from public misconceptions that are in the nature of self-fulfilling prophecies.

FOOTNOTES

[1] Edward Banfield, *The Unheavenly City*, (Boston: Little, Brown and Co., 1970), pp. 19, 21, 257, 259. Permission by Little, Brown and Company.

[2] William G. Grigsby, *Housing Markets and Public Policy* (Philadelphia: University of Pennsylvania Press, 1963), p. 322.

[3] Gary T. Marx, *Protest and Prejudice* (New York: Harper & Row, 1967), p. 6.

Following is the text of a "Memorandum for the President" by Daniel P. Moynihan, counselor to President Nixon, on the position of Negroes: [*]

TEXT OF THE MOYNIHAN MEMORANDUM ON THE STATUS OF NEGROES

As the new year begins, it occurs to me that you might find useful a general assessment of the position of Negroes at the end of the first year of your Administration, and of the decade in which their position has been the central domestic political issue.

In quantitative terms, which are reliable, the American Negro is making extraordinary progress. In political terms, somewhat less reliable, this would also appear to be true. In each case, however, there would seem to be counter-

*Memorandum to President Nixon, January 16, 1970. Material in brackets has been added by the editors.

currents that pose a serious threat to the welfare of the blacks and the stability of the society, white and black.

1. EMPLOYMENT AND INCOME

The nineteen-sixties saw the great breakthrough for blacks. A third (32 percent) of all families of Negro and other races earned $8,000 or more in 1968 [34 percent in 1971 and 20 percent earned less than $1000] [1] compared, in constant dollars, with 15 percent in 1960.

The South is still a problem. Slightly more than half (52 percent) of the Negro population lived in the South in 1969. There, only 19 percent of families of Negro and other races earned over $8,000.

Young Negro families are achieving income parity with young white families. Outside the South, young husband-wife Negro families have 99 percent the income of whites! For families headed by a male age 25 to 34, the proportion was 87 percent. Thus, it may be this ancient gap is finally closing.

Income reflects employment, and this changed dramatically in the nineteen-sixties. Blacks continued to have twice the unemployment rates of whites, but these were down for both groups. In 1969, the rate for married men of Negro and other races was only 2.5 percent. Teenagers, on the other hand, continued their appalling rates: 24.4 percent in 1969.

Black occupations improved dramatically. The number of professional and technical employes doubled in the period 1960-63. This was two and a half times the increase for whites. In 1969, Negro and other races provide 10 percent of the other-than-college teachers. This is roughly their proportion of the population. (11 percent.)

2. EDUCATION

In 1968, 19 percent of Negro children 3 and 4 years old were enrolled in school, compared to 15 percent of white children. [In 1971 both Negro and white enrollment was 21 percent.] [2] Forty five percent [47% in 1971] of Negroes 18 and 19 years old were in school, almost the equal or the white proportion of 51 percent [49% in 1971]. Negro college enrollment rose 85 percent between 1964 and 1968, by which time there were 434,000 Negro college students. (The total full time university population of Great Britain is 200,000.)

Educational achievement should not be exaggerated. Only 16 percent of Negro high school seniors have verbal test scores at or above grade level. But blacks are staying in school.

3. FEMALE-HEADED FAMILIES

This problem does not get better, it gets worse. In 1969, the proportion of husband-wife families of Negro and other races declined once again, this time to

68.7 percent [65.7 percent in 1972].[3] The illegitimacy ratio rose once again, this time to 29.4 percent of all live births. (The white ratio rose more sharply, but was still only 4.9 percent).

Increasingly, the problem of Negro poverty is the problem of the female-headed family. In 1968, 56 percent of Negro families with incomes under $3,000 were female-headed. In 1968, for the first time, the number of poor Negro children in female-headed families [2,241,000] was greater than the number in male-headed families [1,947,000].

4. SOCIAL PATHOLOGY

The incidence of antisocial behavior among young black males continues to be extraordinarily high. Apart from white racial attitudes, this is the biggest problem black Americans face, and in part it helps shape white racial attitudes. Black Americans injure one another. Because blacks live in de facto segregated neighborhoods and go to de facto segregated schools, the socially stable elements of the black population cannot escape the socially pathological ones. Routinely, their children get caught up in the antisocial patterns of the others.

You are familiar with the problem of crime. Let me draw your attention to another phenomenon, exactly parallel, and originating in exactly the same social circumstances: Fire. Unless I mistake the trends, we are heading for a genuinely serious fire problem in American cities. In New York, for example, between 1956 and 1969 the over-all fire alarm rate more than tripled, from 69,000 alarms to 240,000. These alarms are concentrated in slum neighborhoods, primarily black. In 1968, one slum area had an alarm rate per square mile thirteen times that of the city as a whole. In another, the number of alarms has, on average, increased 44 percent per year for seven years.

Many of these fires are the result of population density. But a great many are more or less deliberately set. (Thus, on Monday, welfare protestors set two fires in the New York State Capitol.) Fires are in fact a "leading indicator" of social pathology for a neighborhood. They come first. Crime, and the rest, follows. The psychiatric interpretation of fire-setting is complex, but it relates to the types of personalities which slums produce. (A point of possible interest: Fires in the black slums peak in July and August. The urban riots of 1964-1968 could be thought of as epidemic conditions of an epidemic situation.)

5. SOCIAL ALIENATION

With no real evidence, I would nonetheless suggest that a great deal of the crime, the fire-setting, the rampant school violence, and other such phenomenon in the black community have become quasi-politicized. Hatred—revenge—against whites is now an acceptable excuse for doing what might have been done anyway. This is bad news for any society, especially when it takes forms which the Black Panthers seem to have adopted.

This social alienation among the black lower classes is matched, and probably enhanced, by a virulent form of antiwhite feeling among portions of the large and prospering black middle class. It would be difficult to overestimate the degree to which young, well-educated blacks detest white America.

THE NIXON ADMINISTRATION

As you have candidly acknowledged, the relation of the Administration to the black population is a problem. I think it ought also to be acknowledged that we are a long way from solving it. During the past year, intense efforts have been made by the Administration to develop programs that will be of help to the blacks. I dare say, as much or more time and attention goes into this effort in this Administration than any in history. But little has come of it. There has been a great deal of political ineptness in some departments, and you have been the loser.

I don't know what you can do about this. Perhaps nothing. But I do have four suggestions.

First. Sometime early in the year, I would gather the Administration officials who are most involved with these matters and talk out the subject a bit. There really is a need for a more coherent Administration approach to a number of issues. Which I can list for you, if you like.

Second. The time may have come when the issue of race could benefit from a period of "benign neglect." The subject has been too much talked about. The forum has been too much taken over to hysterics, paranoids, and boodlers on all sides. We may need a period in which Negro progress continues and racial rhetoric fades. The Administration can help bring this about by paying close attention to such progress—as we are doing—while seeking to avoid situations in which extremists of either race are given opportunities for martyrdom, heroics, histrionics or whatever. Greater attention to Indians, Mexican-Americans, and Puerto Ricans would be useful. A tendency to ignore provocations from groups such as the Black Panthers might also be useful. (The Panthers were apparently almost defunct until the Chicago police raided one of their headquarters and transformed them into culture heroes for the white-and-black-middle class. You perhaps did not note on the society page of yesterday's Times that Mrs. Leonard Bernstein gave a cocktail party on Wednesday to raise money for the Panthers. Mrs. W. Vincent Astor was among the guests. Mrs. Peter Duchin, "the rich blonde wife of the orchestra leader," was thrilled. "I've never met a Panther," she said, "this is a first for me.")

Third. We really ought to be getting on with research on crime. We just don't know enough. It is a year now since the Administration came to office committed to doing something about crime in the streets. But frankly, in that year I don't see that we have advanced either our understanding of the problem or that of the public at large. (This of course may only reveal my ignorance of what is going on.)

At the risk of indiscretion, may I put it that lawyers are not professionally well equipped to do much to prevent crime. Lawyers are not managers, and they are not researchers. The logistics, the ecology, the strategy and tactics of reducing the incidence of certain types of behavior in large urban populations simply are not things lawyers think about often.

We are never going to "learn" about crime in a laboratory sense. But we almost certainly could profit from limited, carefully done studies. I don't think these will be done unless you express a personal interest.

Fourth. There is a silent black majority as well as a white one. It is mostly working class, as against lower middle class. It is politically moderate (on issues other than racial equality) and shares most of the concerns of its white counterpart. This group has been generally ignored by the Government and the media. The more recognition we can give to it, the better off we shall all be. (I would take it, for example, that Ambassador [Jerome H.] Holland is a natural leader of this segment of the black community. There are others like him.)

FOOTNOTES

[1] U.S. Bureau of the Census, *Current Population Reports, Income in 1970 of Families and Persons in the United States* Series P-60, No. 80 (Washington, D.C.: U.S. Government Printing Office, 1971), pp. 59-60.

[2] U.S. Bureau of the Census, *Current Population Reports, The Social and Economic Status of the Black Population in the United States, 1971*, Series P-23, No. 42 (Washington, D.C.: U.S. Government Printing Office, 1972), 79.

[3] *Ibid.*, p. 100.

James H. Weaver*

ECONOMIC CAUSES OF SOCIAL UNREST

James Weaver, in "Economic Causes of Unrest," analyzes some of the same indicators described by Moynihan and Banfield, but he arrives at much different conclusions. Weaver seriously questions the "social progress" that blacks have

*James Weaver is a Professor in the Economics Department at American University, Washington, D. C. The article presents statistical excerpts from his full article, "Economic Causes of Social Unrest." James Weaver was assisted by Edward Lehwald and Suzanne Hof.
**About 92 percent of nonwhites are blacks.

achieved and are achieving. Four specific economic and social indicators are considered:

(1) The family income gap between whites and nonwhites—Is the disparity between white and nonwhite income lessening?

(2) Purchasing Power—Do nonwhites get the same value for their consumer dollar as do white people?

(3) Distribution of income—What income level groups among nonwhites are making advancement?

(4) Employment—Are nonwhites making it in the work force?

FAMILY INCOME

Table I presents data on the income received by nonwhites** during the period 1947 to 1970, expressed in constant 1970 dollars. We can see that giant strides were made during World War II. By 1947, blacks were earning 51 percent of white family income as compared to slightly more than 33 1/3 percent prior to the war.

At least two interpretations of these data are possible. If one looks at the absolute income—the income received by nonwhite families compared to that of white families—one sees that the growth rate of nonwhite family income has been far greater than that of white families, and nonwhite family income as a percentage of white family income rose from 51.2 percent in 1947 to 63.7 percent in 1970. With this data, one can show that the incomes of nonwhites rose significantly, both absolutely and relative to white incomes.

But could there be another interpretation? One other interpretation comes from looking at the absolute dollar gap between white and nonwhite family income. This gap stood at $2,671 in 1947 and had increased to $3,720 in 1970. During a period of maximum effort to obtain equal opportunity for blacks, the gap narrowed from $3,784 in 1964 to $3,720 in 1970. This is a decline of $64 in 6 years, or $10.66 per year. At this rate it would take 349 years to close the gap! If we can continue the maximum effort we have been making during the past years—War on Poverty, Fair Employment Practices, and so on—black families can look forward to having the same incomes as white families in the year 2319. Why indeed are blacks so impatient?

A more pessimistic picture also becomes apparent when we look behind the data. First, nonwhite families are significantly larger than white families. In 1972, the average nonwhite family size was 3.48, whereas the average white family size was 3.01.[1] Thus, family income statistics are misleading. In 1970, nonwhite families had 64 percent of white family income but only 55 percent of white family income per capita. Thus, the use of family income data overstates nonwhites' relative economic status by 9 percent.

Table I

1947-1970 Income of Families by Color of Head, in Constant 1970 Dollars

	1947	1950	1958	1959	1960	1961	1962	1963	1964	1965	1966	1967	1968	1969	1970
White	5478	5601	7118	7517	7664	7783	8009	8307	8590	8925	9341	9628	9972	10362	10236
Nonwhite	2807	3014	3645	3883	4236	4142	4273	4401	4806	4930	5591	5978	6249	6568	6516
Gap	2671	2587	3473	3634	3428	3641	3736	3906	3784	3995	3750	3650	3723	3794	3720
Dollar Increase Over Previous Year:															
White		+123	+1517	+399	+147	+119	+226	+298	+283	+335	+416	+287	+344	+390	−126
Nonwhite		+207	+631	+238	+353	−94	+131	+170	+405	+124	+661	+387	+271	+319	−52
Percent Increase Over Previous Year:															
White		+2.25	+27.08	+5.61	+1.96	+1.55	+2.90	+3.72	+3.41	+3.90	+4.66	+3.07	+3.57	+3.91	−1.22
Nonwhite		+7.37	+20.94	+6.53	+9.09	−2.22	+3.16	+3.98	+9.20	+2.58	+13.41	+6.92	+4.53	+5.10	−.79
Nonwhite as a Percentage of White	51.24	53.81	51.21	51.66	55.27	53.22	53.35	52.98	55.95	55.24	59.85	62.09	62.67	63.39	63.66

Source: U.S. Bureau of Census, Current Population Reports, Series P-60, No. 80, "Income in 1970 of Families and Persons in the United States" (Washington: U.S. Government Printing Office, 1971), p. 23.

PURCHASING POWER

Real purchasing power of blacks is also less than that of whites. David Caplovitz has demonstrated beyond any doubt that *The Poor Pay More*. They get less housing for their money. They pay more for inferior goods at the grocery store, the furniture store, the clothing store, and their financing costs for these goods are significantly higher. Black tax dollars buy poorer schools, less frequent garbage collections, and less police protection than white tax dollars. It has been estimated that a markup of 5 to 10 percent on black housing still exists in urban areas.[2] Henry Terrell has estimated that nonwhite income should be deflated 3 to 5 percent to account for higher prices paid for all consumable items.[3]

Two additional factors that lower nonwhites' real income relative to whites' have been pointed out by Andrew Brimmer and Henry Terrell.[4] The first is the lower net worth of nonwhite families. They do not have the welfare-generating assets—such as consumer durables—that white families have. The Survey of Economic Opportunity revealed that the average white family has total assets of $25,444 and total debts of $5,832. This leaves net assets of $19,612. The average nonwhite family has total assets of $5,825 and total debts of $2,427, leaving it with net assets of only $3,398. Nonwhite families have only 17 percent, or one-sixth, of the net assets held by white families.

Terrell points out that the nonwhite family housing is valued significantly lower than white family housing.[5] Owner-occupied housing yields real welfare to the owners, and white families derive greater welfare from their homes. The average nonwhite family has housing equity of $2,134, whereas white families have average housing equities of $6,490. Assuming the customary 10 percent rate of return, this difference means that whites receive $649 per year in nonmonetary income from their housing compared to only $213 received by nonwhites.

Terrell has attempted to compute the impact of all the factors that make nonwhites' real income less than the official government figures. His conclusion is that nonwhite family income is overstated by about 10 percent. Thus in 1970 the average nonwhite family actually received only about 54 percent of an average white family's real income. The same overstatement can be assumed to hold true for earlier years as well, nor is there much evidence that his 46 percent gap will be closed very rapidly.

INCOME DISTRIBUTION

It can be seen from Table II that distribution of nonwhite family income is more unequal than white family income distribution. Thus, the assertion that nonwhite family income increased during this period is misleading. The increase only reflects the fact that *some blacks* have experienced improvement and pulled the average up, but these gains are very unevenly distributed.

Table III shows the gap between white and nonwhite family income by

Table II
Distribution of Income among White and Nonwhite Families in the United States
Selected Years 1947-1970

		1947	1950	1958	1959	1961	1963	1965	1966	1967	1968	1969	1970
White	Lowest Fifth	5.4	4.8	5.6	5.5	5.2	5.5	5.6	5.8	5.8	6.0	5.9	5.8
	Second Fifth	12.1	12.2	12.8	12.6	12.1	12.5	12.5	12.7	12.5	12.7	12.6	12.3
	Third Fifth	16.9	17.3	17.9	17.8	17.3	17.7	17.7	17.7	17.5	17.7	17.6	17.4
	Fourth Fifth	22.7	23.1	23.4	23.4	23.2	23.6	23.4	23.4	23.5	23.4	23.3	23.4
	Highest Fifth	42.8	42.5	40.2	40.8	42.2	40.7	40.8	40.4	40.7	40.3	40.6	41.1
	Top 5 Percent	17.7	17.6	15.6	16.1	17.3	15.7	15.5	14.5	14.9	14.0	13.8	14.2
Nonwhite	Lowest Fifth	4.3	3.5	3.8	3.9	4.0	4.3	4.6	4.7	4.4	4.8	4.7	4.5
	Second Fifth	10.3	10.2	9.9	9.6	9.7	10.3	10.7	10.7	10.4	10.5	10.8	10.4
	Third Fifth	16.0	17.6	16.4	16.5	15.9	16.1	16.5	16.8	16.4	16.5	16.8	16.5
	Fourth Fifth	23.7	25.2	24.9	25.1	24.3	24.5	24.7	24.9	24.1	24.6	24.4	24.5
	Highest Fifth	45.7	43.5	44.9	44.9	46.0	44.7	43.5	42.9	44.7	43.6	43.2	44.0
	Top 5 Percent	17.1	16.6	17.0	16.4	17.4	17.2	15.5	15.4	17.5	16.1	15.5	15.4

Source: U.S. Bureau of the Census, *Current Population Reports*, Series P-60, No. 80, "Income in 1970 of Families and Persons in the United States" (Washington, D.C.: U.S. Government Printing Office, 1971), p. 28.

Table III

Percentage Distributions of Mean Family Income by Color, Percentage of White Family Income Received by Nonwhites, and Gap between White and Nonwhite Family Income 1947, 1960 and 1970.

	1947				1960				1970			
	White	Non-white	Percent	Gap	White	Non-white	Percent	Gap	White	Non-white	Percent	Gap
Income of All Families	3,718	2,016	54.2	1,702	6,674	3,921	58.8	2,753	11,586	7,807	67.4	3,779
Lowest Fifth	1,022	484	47.4	538	1,769	764	43.2	1,005	3,385	1,789	52.9	1,596
Second Fifth	2,268	1,029	45.4	761	4,138	1,882	45.5	2,256	7,233	4,138	57.2	3,095
Middle Fifth	3,142	1,538	50.4	1,559	5,840	3,216	55.1	2,624	10,253	6,560	64.0	3,693
Fourth Fifth	4,238	2,380	56.2	1,858	7,715	4,980	64.1	2,800	13,840	9,769	70.6	4,071
Highest Fifth	7,919	4,619	58.3	3,300	13,815	8,766	63.5	5,049	23,219	16,779	72.3	6,440
Top 5 Percent	12,938	6,558	53.0	6,080	22,293	12,677	56.9	9,616	30,006	21,047	70.1	8,959

Source: Derived from U.S. Bureau of the Census, *Current Population Reports*, Series P. 60, No. 80, "Income in 1970 of Families and Persons in the United States," (Washington, D.C.: U.S. Government Printing Office, 1971) pp. 59-60.

quintile for the years 1947, 1960, and 1970. We see lower-income nonwhite families have fared far worse than their white counterparts. The poorest 20 percent of nonwhite families had 47 percent of the income of the poorest 20 percent of white families in 1947, while the average nonwhite family had 54 percent of white family income in 1947. Thus, the income of these poorest nonwhite families was 7 percent lower (as a percentage of poorest white incomes) than the average income of nonwhite families (as a percentage of average white family incomes). By 1960, the poorest nonwhite families had fallen to only 43 percent of the poorest white family income. The average nonwhite family had 59 percent of white family income in 1960. Thus, the poorest nonwhites' income was 16 percent below the average nonwhite family. In 1970, the average nonwhite family had achieved 67 percent of white family income, but the poorest nonwhite families had only 53 percent of the poorest white family income. Thus, the poorest nonwhites were 14 percent below the average nonwhite family. Clearly, even compared to the poorest white families, the poorest portion of the nonwhite population remains far outside the economic mainstream after a decade of very rapid national growth.

In comparing these income figures we should also bear in mind that *nonwhite family incomes are only as high as they are because the wife often works*; that is, 43 percent of white women were in the labor force in 1971, but 49 percent of nonwhite women were working and they work more hours on average than their white counterparts.[6] Thus, the comparison of family incomes is again a somewhat misleading indicator.

Many analysts of the economic status of blacks point to the fact that between 1947 and 1970, black family income rose by 132 percent, whereas white family income increased only 87 percent. These numbers are impressive but deceptive. *It is not surprising that the percentage increase for nonwhites is greater, since any slight increase over a low income will be a higher percentage than that same increase over a higher income.* The increase in income for nonwhites is also misleading in that it does not reveal the sources of income. The increase included all transfer payments such as unemployment benefits and welfare. Although the nonwhite family income has risen as far as it has in part because of these transfer payments, we must assume that the family morale has been lowered because they are accepting welfare and unemployment benefits rather than income from employment.

Another factor to consider is that real income for nonwhites probably fell when they moved to the cities. Although money incomes were obviously higher, the cost of living in cities was also significantly greater.

EMPLOYMENT AND UNEMPLOYMENT

Hiestand has constructed an index which measures the occupational status of black men relative to white men. His work indicates that the index was virtually unchanged (around 77.5) between 1910 and 1940. Between 1940 and 1950, significant improvement was made, and the index climbed from 77.5 to 81.4. Between 1950 and 1960 the index was again virtually unchanged, moving from 81.4 to 82.1.[7]

In 1940, 16.8 percent of the nonwhite experienced labor force was unemployed. In 1950, the percentage was 7.8, in 1960 it was 8.7, and in 1970 it was 8.3. The corresponding percentages for whites were 14.2 percent in 1940, 4.5 percent in 1950, 4.7 percent in 1960, and 4.5 percent in 1970. The ratios between nonwhite and white rates were 1.18 in 1940, 1.73 in 1950, 1.83 in 1960, and 1.84 in 1970. Thus, *for experienced workers, nonwhites' unemployment rates have consistently increased relative to whites' since 1940.*[8]

Table IV reflects the percent unemployed in the civilian labor force—experienced and inexperienced combined. Unemployment for nonwhites has fluctu-

Table IV
Unemployment Rates, 1947-1971

Year	Nonwhite	White	Ratio: Nonwhite to White
1947	3.0	4.7	1.6
1948	5.2	3.2	1.6
1949	8.9	5.6	1.6
1950	9.0	4.9	1.8
1951	5.3	3.1	1.7
1952	5.4	2.8	1.7
1953	4.5	2.7	1.7
1954	9.9	5.0	2.0
1955	8.7	3.9	2.2
1956	8.3	3.6	2.3
1957	7.9	3.8	2.1
1958	12.6	6.1	2.1
1959	10.7	4.8	2.2
1960	10.2	4.9	2.1
1961	12.4	6.0	2.1
1962	10.9	4.9	2.2
1963	10.8	5.0	2.2
1964	9.6	4.6	2.1
1965	8.1	4.1	2.0
1966	7.3	3.3	2.2
1967	7.4	3.4	2.2
1968	6.7	3.2	2.1
1969	6.4	3.1	2.1
1970	8.2	4.5	1.8
1971	9.9	5.4	1.8

Source: U.S. Bureau of the Census, *The Social and Economic Status of the Black Population in the United States, 1971, Current Population Reports,* Series P-23, No. 42 (Washington, D.C.: U.S. Government Printing Office, 1972), p. 52.

ated from 3.0 percent in 1947 to 12.6 percent in 1958. However, if one looks at the nonwhite rate in relation to the white rate, the picture is not one of fluctuations. There is a trend and the trend has been upward. The nonwhite rate was 1.6 times the white rate in 1948, but it was 1.8 times the white rate in 1971. The absolute percentage difference also increased between 1947 and 1971. *In 1947, the nonwhite unemployment rate was 1.7 percent greater than the white rate. By 1971 the nonwhite rate was 4.5 percent greater than the white rate.*

Another important indicator is the unemployment rate among the young. Table V reveals that, since 1958, nonwhite unemployment rates for teenagers have been hovering around 25 percent. The peak rate of 31.7 percent was

Table V
Unemployment Rate—Both Sexes, Ages 16-19

Year	White	Nonwhite	Ratio
1954	12.1	16.5	1.4
1955	10.3	15.8	1.5
1956	10.2	18.2	1.8
1957	10.6	19.1	1.8
1958	14.4	27.4	1.9
1959	13.1	26.1	2.0
1960	13.4	24.4	1.8
1961	15.3	27.6	1.8
1962	13.3	25.1	1.9
1963	15.5	30.4	2.0
1964	14.8	27.2	1.8
1965	13.4	26.2	2.0
1966	11.2	25.4	2.3
1967	11.0	26.5	2.4
1968	11.0	25.0	2.3
1969	10.7	24.0	2.2
1970	13.5	29.1	2.2
1971	15.1	31.7	2.1

Source: U.S. Department of Labor, *Manpower Report of the President 1970* (Washington, D.C.: U.S. Government Printing Office, 1970) p. 220, and U.S. Bureau of the Census, *Current Population Reports*, Series P-23, No. 42, "The Social and Economic Status of the Black Population in the United States, 1971" (Washington, D.C.: U.S. Government Printing Office, 1972), p. 53.

reached in 1971. This level of unemployment has not been experienced among white workers since the worst years of the Great Depression.

There are certain understatements in the nonwhite unemployment statistics. The Census Bureau does not count all blacks. It has been estimated that as much as 15 percent of the black population in inner cities is not counted in the decennial census. Many of these uncounted persons are unemployed.

Unemployment statistics for nonwhites also conceal underemployment.

There is a large group of blacks who hold jobs but are underemployed. *In 1968, the U.S. Department of Labor reported a subemployment rate for nonwhites of 21.6 percent compared to a white rate of only 7.6 percent.*[9]

Whatever the percentages of unemployment, underemployment, and so forth, the fact is that there were far more blacks unemployed in 1970 than there were in 1954.

Using a number of economic indicators, we can see that there is some numerical record of gains for nonwhites since World War II. In general the trend has been to higher absolute and relative status. However, the picture is far from being as simple and positive as Professor Moynihan would have us believe.

FOOTNOTES

[1] U.S. Bureau of the Census, "Consumer Incomes" *Current Population Reports*, Series P-60, No. 84 (Washington, D.C.: U.S. Government Printing Office, 1972), p. 16.

[2] John Kain and John McQuigly, "Housing Market Discrimination, Home-Ownership and Savings Behavior" (Paper presented before the American Economic Association, December 29, 1969).

[3] Henry Terrell, "The Non-White Income Ratio Reexamined," mimeographed (Washington, D.C.: Federal Reserve Board, no date).

[4] Andrew Brimmer and Henry Terrell, "The Economic Potential of Black Capitalism" (Paper presented before the American Economic Association, December 29, 1969).

[5] Terrell, *op. cit.*

[6] U.S. Bureau of the Census, "The Social and Economic Status of the Black Population in the United States, 1971," *Current Population Reports*, Series P-23, no. 42 (Washington, D.C.: U.S. Government Printing Office, 1972) 61.

[7] Dale Heistand, *Economic Growth and Employment Opportunities for Minorities* (New York: Columbia University Press, 1964).

[8] Andrew Brimmer, "The Negro in the National Economy," in *Race and Poverty*, John Kain, ed., (Englewood Cliffs, N.J.: Prentice-Hall, 1969). Also, Bureau of the Census, *Black Americans—A Decade of Occupational Change* (Washington: U.S. Government Printing Office, 1972), p. 5.

[9] U.S. Department of Labor, *Manpower Report of the President 1968* (Washington, D.C.: U.S. Government Printing Office, 1965).

THE CASE FOR JOBS

Andrew Brimmer, Henry Terrell*

THE ECONOMIC POTENTIAL FOR BLACK CAPITALISM[1]

The general conclusion from [this] analysis is that the strategy of black capitalism, as we have defined it, offers a very limited potential for economic advancement for the majority of the Negro population.[2] The ghetto economy as we understand it today does not appear to provide profitable opportunities for large scale business investment, and any economic advances made by residents of this marginal sector of the economy in all likelihood will not materially alter the investment prospects. This situation is in large part due to a tendency for affluent Negroes to shop in the more diverse national economy.

The strategy of black capitalism fails, however, for an even more fundamental reason: it is founded on the premise of self-employment. Our research has indicated clearly that self-employment is a rather rapidly declining factor in our modern economy because the rewards of employment in salaried positions are substantially greater. Self-employment may be the path to affluence for the fortunate few who are very successful, but for the great majority of the Negro population it offers a low and rather risky expected payoff.

---

*Andrew Brimmer is a governor of the Federal Reserve Board and Henry Terrell was an economic advisor to the Federal Reserve Board.

At this juncture, we would like to point out that our disenchantment with the strategy of black economic development through black capitalism is not based simply on its limited economic potential. We are also concerned that reliance on such a strategy may be substituted for efforts in vital areas which are of the utmost importance to the Negro population. In the long run, the pursuit of black capitalism may retard the Negro's economic advancement by discouraging many from the full participation in the national economy with its much broader range of challenges and opportunities. A strategy of black capitalism may also prove deleterious to the Negro community because, in the words of two observers, "the programs would place those least capable of accepting risk in the position of accepting large risks."[3] New ghetto enterprises would certainly be more prone to failure than established firms, and their failures would leave a lasting burden on the individuals starting these firms and on those employees who had been induced to work in such enterprises rather than in businesses not dependent on the ghetto economy.

The solution of the economic problems of Negroes and other disadvantaged groups is a complex and difficult task.[4] Efforts must be made on a variety of fronts, and the choice among the mix of programs must be made quite carefully. It was with the express purpose of facilitating this choice that we have analyzed the economic potential of black capitalism.

FOOTNOTES

[1] This selection is an excerpt from Andrew Brimmer and Henry Terrell, "The Economic Potential of Black Capitalism" (Paper presented at the Eighty-second Annual Meeting of the American Economic Association, New Orleans, La., December 29, 1969).

[2] Brimmer and Terrell defined black capitalism as "black business ownership and location of these businesses in the ghetto."

[3] Bernard H. Booms and James E. Ward Jr., "The Cons of Black Capitalism," *Business Horizons*, Vol. XII, No. 5 (October 1969), p. 25.

[4] For an excellent discussion of these problems and alternative solutions, see Lester C. Thurow, *Poverty and Discrimination* (Washington, D.C.: The Brookings Institution, 1969). For a specific treatment of the question of bringing business to ghettos, see Sar A. Levitan and Robert Taggart III, "Developing Business and Entrepreneurs in the Ghettos," Background Paper Prepared for the Community Self-Determination Steering Committee (Washington, D.C.: April 17, 1969).

David K. Banner

MINORITY EMPLOYMENT—AN ASSESSMENT

The Nixon administration wants to encourage minorities to "jump into" the capitalist mainstream of our country and get a few of the profits that whites have monopolized for years. This article makes a case for effectively utilizing minority employment strategies either separately or in conjunction with "black capitalism" approaches to promote economic parity among the disadvantaged minorities in this country.

There are many reasons why employment should be considered a major strategy for minority economic development. In the first place, there no longer exists the great impetus for self-employment in the United States that once characterized our economy, particularly during the period from 1870 to 1920. The economy has become increasingly dominated by large corporations; this has made it increasingly difficult to enter the competitive marketplace. Compared with majority-operated businesses, Negro and other minority businesses are disproportionately located in ghettos. This fact, combined with the ghetto's high crime and low income make the picture bleak for the black entrepreneur. The mortality rate of small minority businesses is quite high and probably exceeds the nonminority-owned small business rate of failure, which has been estimated at 80 percent after five years.[1]

EMPLOYMENT AS AN ALTERNATIVE

Many factors seem to point to the use of increased minority employment as a vehicle, for economic development. More people are now working for larger manufacturing and service companies.[2] These kinds of jobs represent the quickest way to get money into the minority community, in contrast to the longer period required for the maturation of small businesses.

Employment may also be the quickest way of integrating society at all levels. One efficient way to accomplish integration through jobs is by transferring military skills to the civilian sector. Many blacks and other minorities have received valuable training as hospital corpsmen, mechanics, and other occupations; these skills can be transferred to civilian life.

Another reason for increasing employment is the legal/institutional framework that has been constructed to open employment at all levels. Legislation such as Title VII of the Civil Rights Act of 1965, various National Labor Relations Board (NLRB) rulings, some state statutes, and presidential executive orders now provide a fairly comprehensive framework for enforcing fair employment practices and, in some cases, may even require affirmative action to overcome past inequities. In addition, several efforts by the federal government and the private sector, for example, the National Alliance for

Businessmen (NAB-JOBS), have aided in expanding opportunities for minority representation in the work force. Finally, increased educational training opportunities have been made available within private enterprise. Different educational requirements are dictated by a national goal of developing minority entrepreneurs and/or managers (which can be stimulated by the attainment of business education degrees like the BBA, MBA, or the professional license of CPA, by minority members) as against a goal of developing minority workers (which can be promoted by minority hiring and training programs).

One final note on the advantage of an employment strategy: even if a minority member wishes to become ultimately self-employed, much valuable experience can be obtained from first acquiring the necessary technical skills as an employee of a larger firm. Then, after sufficient experience, the minority member can "spin off" and form his own firm.

REVIEW OF PAST AND PRESENT EMPLOYMENT SITUATIONS

General Employment Trends

Farm-to-city migration of minorities, beginning with World War I, has been a major demographic trend.[3] Another very important trend is that nonminorities are moving rapidly from the inner city to the suburbs. The exodus from the large cities to the outlying suburbs continues. Although there is some shifting of the black middle class to the suburbs, it is minuscule when compared with the massive white movement to the suburbs.

Another trend, that of increasing industrial decentralization and subsequent relocation in the suburbs, further reduces job opportunities in the inner city. The movement of industry to the suburbs may be motivated by a number of factors including better tax breaks on land, better environment (less congestion and pollution), ease with which a better educated (white) force can be obtained, and covert racism. Still another factor motivating the movement of industry to the suburbs is fear—fear of employees to travel into the inner city, and employers' fear of vandalism, arson, and so on. To overcome this trend, incentives must be offered by the federal government to encourage existing industries to remain in the inner city and to encourage others to return. At the same time educational/training opportunities for minorities must be increased.

Comparison of Minority/Nonminority Employment Patterns

In relatively high-status areas such as professional, technical, managerial, and proprietary ownership, minorities have made some gains in the past 10 years. Census data indicates that, from 1959 to 1971, the number of minority persons below the poverty level declined from 55 to 32 percent.[4] This should indicate an improved employment picture for the minorities, if one can assume that increased median income is directly attributable to increased employment and/or higher paying jobs for minorities.

The percentage of black males in the professional and technical categories has risen from 1.1 percent of all black males in 1910 to 13 percent in 1971; similarly, black females have improved their position in professional and technical categories from 1.4 percent to 13 percent in the same time period.[5] The rise in employment of blacks and other minorities continues. Employment gains for this group averaged about 200,000 a year since 1969, with gains concentrated in the upper half of the occupational pyramid, among white collar (notably clerical), craftsmen, and operative jobs.[6]

Despite advances, in 1960 proportionately fewer nonwhites than whites in 1970 were in the professional, managerial, and other white collar or skilled groups.[7] A group that reviewed the recommendations of the 1968 Kerner Commission found that, while gains have been greatest in the professional, technical, clerical, and craftsmen occupations, blacks are still seriously underrepresented in high-pay, high-status jobs. They still comprise only between 3 and 8 percent of total employment in the skilled craftsmen and white collar occupations.[8] In 1967, while 11.2 percent of all men were officials or managers, only 1.1 percent of the black and 2.5 percent of the Spanish-speaking Americans had that status.[9] Major improvements in minority representation in high-status jobs was occurring only in those industries where minority representation was already above average. While minorities are gaining both in absolute numbers of work force participants and in higher status jobs, relative gains are somewhat less impressive. A large credibility gap remains between what business claims it is doing and what it is actually accomplishing in opening up white collar jobs.[10]

Comparison of Minority/Nonminority Training and Education

Black males, beginning with 6.5 median years of school in 1940 (compared with the then white average of 10.5 years), have progressed to near parity with 12 median years of schooling as compared to 12.5 years for whites. As recently as 1958, two-thirds of young blacks dropped out of high school without finishing; as of 1971, 54 percent are sticking it out until twelfth grade.[11] However, while minorities are attaining higher *levels* of education, the *quality* of this education in some urban and rural settings is markedly inferior to that received by white students.

Since 1959 increasing numbers of blacks have entered institutions of higher learning. Proportionately fewer blacks than whites go to college, but from 1947 to 1961, the number of nonwhites in college rose at a faster rate than the number of whites.[12] The emphasis on advanced education is reflected in the fact that about 700,000 blacks were in college in 1972—two-thirds of them in predominantly white institutions. The percentage of blacks completing four years of college has risen from 4.3 percent in 1960 to 6.3 percent in 1971.[13]

A New York college professor has recently shown that white/nonwhite job differences are the least when comparing highly educated whites and nonwhites.[14] This would suggest that, to win job equality for blacks in this country, special continuing efforts should be made to improve college and university level opportunities for blacks. However, according to this source, the problem is still primarily one of racism, rather than lack of education. This remains our most intransigent problem. Nonwhites must obtain equal quality educational experiences and employment opportunities commensurate with educational attainment.

In the important area of management education, the inequities are pervasive. A voluntary survey undertaken by the Educational Testing Service indicates that in the 1972-73 academic year, out of almost 67,000 students enrolled in full and part time M.B.A. programs, 4,252 or almost 7 percent are minority students. An additional 9,000 would be required for parity now, but would, of course, provide no catch-up capability. From 1909 to 1968 fewer than 600 minority group members have received graduate business degrees (346 of these graduated from the predominately black Atlanta University School of Business). A survey in the *Journal of Accounting* (October, 1969) revealed that of 100,000 certified public accountants in the United States, 136 were black. The question remains: Can these serious inequities be corrected by encouraging minorities to participate in our graduate business educational system through increased programs of financial aid and by upgrading educational deficiencies needed for entry into graduate or undergraduate business programs? And, more importantly, will such participation materially improve the opportunities for minority members to participate in our free enterprise system?

GOVERNMENT PROGRAMS

Historic Development of Government Involvement in Antidiscrimination

The development of federal manpower programs presents an interesting pattern of development. Initially, individual states began implementing their own separate antidiscrimination legislation. Accordingly, the power of their agencies to act in cases of discriminatory practice varied widely, from "persuasion" to actual affirmative action or legal restraint. The first presidential order was executed by President Franklin D. Roosevelt in 1941 and has been followed by several presidential "affirmative action" orders. Roosevelt acquiesced to the demands of black labor leader A. Philip Randolph, who threatened to cut off minority manpower to the war effort if discriminatory policies were not stopped by executive action. In 1944, due in part to Randolph's increasing pressure, a landmark U.S. Supreme Court case (*Steele v. Louisville and Nashville Railroad*) ruled that a union must perform "its statutory duty to represent non-union or minority union members of the craft without hostile discriminations, fairly, impartially and in good faith." All of these efforts culminated in 1964 when the Civil Rights Act was enacted and, more specifically, by Titles VI and VII of this act. Finally, several NLRB rulings since the early 1940s have aided in the movement toward nondiscrimination.

Employment discrimination is an obvious handicap. Minorities are discriminated against by government—local, state, and national—as well as by private industry. The inferior education received by Negroes in many areas presently disqualifies many blacks from high-level employment; this provides a convenient "out" for white employers.

In 1941, the federal government began to move against employment discrimination. Executive Order No. 8802 stated that "there shall be no discrimination in the employment of workers in defense industries or government because of race, creed, color, or national origin. . . . " Although long on principle, this order was short on procedures for implementation. The Fair Employment Practices Committee (FEPC) was set up, but it had virtually no power.

The first five years of federal fair employment practices saw blacks make great gains in the labor market, but some of these gains were no doubt attributable to the wartime manpower shortage. Employers unable to find usable white manpower often turned to blacks as a last resort.

Shortly before the Federal Fair Employment Practices Committee expired in 1945, New York enacted a statute that was to become a model for statutes drawn up by other states. These statutes: (1) made discrimination a misdemeanor, (2) gave the injured party the right to recover damages from the discriminator, and (3) empowered a public agency making a contract with a contractor to deduct a penalty from the contractor's fee because of discrimination.

Why has racial discrimination remained common despite the presence of these statutes? One reason is that state commissions often lack the power of initiation; they cannot seek out the discriminator on their own but must wait for formal filing of a complaint by an aggrieved party. This is a real problem because many victims of racial discrimination are ignorant of their legal rights or are cynical about the prospect of minority rights being enforced by white authority.

Other problems which have hurt the commissions' effectiveness include: lack of intragovernmental cooperation, investigators' fear of adverse reaction by powerful corporate entities, inadequate budgets, and heavy responsibilities.

Federal Intervention—The Civil Rights Act (1964)

The Civil Rights Act (1964) includes a whole battery of substantive prohibitions found in the typical state antidiscrimination law. An important section of Title VII of this act was the creation of the Equal Employment Opportunity Commission (EEOC). This five-member commission was established to insure compliance with Title VII on the part of the employers, employment agencies and unions.

Restricted by many political compromises, the EEOC has proven to be weak in enforcement.[15] The EEOC is authorized under Title VII to use informal methods to resolve discrimination complaints; the act specifies "conference, conciliation, and persuasion" as methods to use to combat unfair employment practices. However, the EEOC, under a 1971 amendment to Title VII, has the power to go to court without recourse to the Attorney General. Private litigants can now bring suit under Section 706, but only after they have exhausted the relevant state and EEOC procedures.

Affirmative Actions—OFCC (Executive Order No. 11246)

In 1966, employers with federal contracts (primarily defense and aerospace) employed an estimated 24 million Americans, approximately one-third of the total labor force. Executive Order No. 11246, issued by President Lyndon B. Johnson on September 24, 1965, in addition to prohibiting discrimination, requires that federal contractors take "affirmative action to insure that applicants are employed, and that employes are treated during employment without regard to their race, color, or national origin" (Section 202-1). This order provides for separately administered compliance programs, coordinated and supervised by the secretary of labor through the Office of Federal Contract Compliance (OFCC). Every federal agency employing contracts in its operation comes under the OFCC. OFCC has been an effective motivator of fair employment practices among federal contractors. The major criticism of OFCC from civil rights leaders is that there has been a failure to apply sanctions and penalties against major contractors.

Various Manpower Training and Employment Services

Two basic causes of inequality in employment are discrimination, and disadvantages in terms of job preparation and training. Title VII of the Civil Rights Act and Executive Order No. 11246 both focus on discrimination. However, eliminating discrimination is not enough. Largely as a by-product of discrimination, minority members are not as well-prepared for jobs as are their white counterparts. Federal manpower programs are designed to help ameliorate this problem.

The United States Employment Service (USES), established in 1933 as a part of the Department of Labor, is the operational center of the government's manpower system; two thousand local offices of state employment services provide job referral, counseling, and testing services and administer the various manpower programs of the government. Also, the Concentrated Employment Program (CEP), a relatively new Labor Department program for the disadvantaged, operates independently of USES.

The Office of Economic Opportunity (OEO) in manpower programs, established by the Labor Department in 1965 to administer Title VI regulations (part of the Civil Rights Act of 1964), was formed to: (1) exercise civil rights surveillance, (2) investigate Title VI complaints for all manpower programs for the Department of Labor, and (3) conduct special equal opportunity reviews on request from departmental officials. Most inspection visits, while infrequent, are unannounced.

The Human Resources Development program (HRD) was initiated in 1966 by USES to "provide intensive services for the chronically unemployed." These services are conducted at youth opportunity centers run by state employment services. "Outreach" staff members help the chronically disadvantaged through counseling at HRD centers. Other manpower programs include Neighborhood Youth Corps, Job Corps, New Careers, and Special Impact. These programs grew out of black dissatisfaction with the status quo.

Private Sector Programs

The Manpower Development and Training Act (MDTA) of 1962 initially sought a mix of institutional and on-the-job training to upgrade minority competitiveness for jobs. Its goal was to retrain "mature, experienced, family heads who had been displaced by technological and economic change while providing them with income to make the training possible."

The most widely known program to result from federal pressures is the NAB-JOBS program.[16] A recent report shows that the latest phase of NAB-JOBS, the MA-5 program, has employee retention rates of 40 percent and below in most cities.[17] This report also concluded that the disadvantaged who were hired would probably have been hired anyway without the NAB-JOBS commitment. However, this conclusion must be weighed against the formidable measurement problems associated with determining the effectiveness of such a program. Some recent improvements in the JOBS program, such as the fuller use of contract funds by employers, upgraded assistance by the government, and eased financing arrangements, are designed to increase the program's efficiency. This program channeled resources into impoverished rural areas as a complement to the urban based JOBS program.

UNIONS AND NONDISCRIMINATION

Historical Perspective

The Industrial Revolution created intense rivalries between native-born whites and foreign-born whites competing for available jobs, but both of these groups joined in the exclusion of blacks. Initially, after the Civil War, blacks were encouraged to form their own unions by organizations like the National Labor Union (the first national federation of trade unions). This situation led to the formation of the Colored National Labor Union as an arm of the Republican Party. The union declined with the Panic of 1873.

The Noble Order of Knights of Labor, organized in 1869, attempted the first integrated union; by 1886, it could boast of 60,000 Negroes among its more than 700,000 members. However, the order's participation in the May Day demonstrations in Chicago and the Haymarket bombings caused unfavorable publicity from which it never recovered.

The AFL Model

At its inception in 1881, the American Federation of Labor (AFL) included as part of its working statement that "working people must unite and organize, irrespective of creed, color, sex, nationality, or politics." With all these good intentions, the AFL found it impossible to implement them because of prevailing attitudes, so it organized blacks into separate locals. The AFL was, and is, made up of many small craft unions whose view toward admitting blacks is rather narrow. For this reason, enforcement of civil rights guidelines presents a formidable task.

The CIO Model

Under pressure from rising black protest against AFL discrimination, a number of AFL leaders launched a series of organizing campaigns in the mass production industries, and ultimately formed the Congress of Industrial Organizations (CIO) in 1935. The resulting AFL-CIO rivalry caused a break in the ranks of labor—one which led the CIO to concern itself primarily with the organization of the steel, auto, mining, packinghouse, and rubber industries, all of which employed large numbers of Negroes. In coal mining unions, John L. Lewis, a major CIO leader, pioneered policies of nondiscrimination which were carried forth by such men as Philip Murray, president of the steel workers, and by Walter Reuther, head of the auto workers.

After the AFL-CIO merger in 1955, pressure continued for the combined union to live up to the pledge of nondiscrimination originally made by the AFL. Many gains have been made to date. Covered by labor-management contracts and two important pieces of labor legislation, the National Labor Relations Act and the Railway Labor Act, the black man has seen his earnings increase and his working conditions improve. He has also enjoyed a number of fringe benefits such as health services, insurance coverage, paid vacations, and pensions. Representation on governing councils of both local and national unions has given blacks a voice to air racially initiated grievances. As of 1956, two black leaders— A. Philip Randolph, president of the Brotherhood of Sleeping Car Porters, and Willard S. Townsend, president of the United Transport Service Employes—had won positions on the 79-man executive board of the AFL-CIO.

In the last decade, the AFL, through its constitution, has established a civil rights committee to help develop organizational guidelines on hiring and union membership, as well as for maintaining liaison with the proper agencies of the federal government and with civil rights groups. However, discrimination still persists. Under attack from critics, the AFL-CIO maintains that, despite its shortcomings, the labor movement has done more for the Negro than any other group, a defense which some observers regard as an explicit admission of guilt. The dominant trend, however, appears to be one of racial reconciliation in the unions; things are getting better for minority workers.

Trade Unions—The Construction Industry

The Philadelphia Plan, the first of a series of plans (which are special cases of "affirmative action" required by executive orders) to correct longstanding racial discrimination in the construction trades, is a program devised by the federal government to increase minority employment in various building and construction trades. It requires contractors to make "good faith" efforts to attain specific levels of minority hiring on federally assisted construction projects costing more than $500,000. It is important to note that no arbitrary quota system is used here; before standards are set, the availability of minority craftsmen is investigated. Builders are required to submit "affirmative action" plans for minority hiring when they submit project bids; acceptance of bids is therefore partially determined by acceptability of a contractor's hiring plan. An entire project can be shut down by the failure of one subcontractor to comply with the hiring specifications.

Blacks have not moved into better jobs and top union positions in proportion to their numbers in the labor force. Until equity is achieved in this area, blacks will continue to pressure unions and management to remove racial barriers, to increase opportunities, and to bring about the changes they seek.[18]

PROSPECTS FOR THE FUTURE

Short Term

Blacks in the 1970s have a larger but still lagging share of the American economy. Young blacks have made gains in the amount of formal schooling completed. The proportion of blacks graduating from high school each year has been rising rapidly and the educational gap between blacks and whites is narrowing. However, the unemployment gap between whites and blacks who leave high school each year has not closed. In 1960, the black unemployment rate was about twice the white rate and, in 1971, the rate continued to be about double (in 1960, 30 percent for blacks as opposed to 12 percent for whites).[19]

Black people have made occupational gains in the last decade. The proportion of black workers in white collar jobs and skilled occupations has gone up; however, they still hold a disproportionate share of the less skilled jobs. There is a distinct lack of upward mobility programs and plans for minority workers. It is one thing to hire a black; it is yet another to help him gain the expertise with which to move up in the company.

In spite of lagging employer commitment to minority employment, future trends point toward more white collar and service occupations in general because of the effects of increased technology and automation. White collar workers will outnumber blue collar workers by more than 50 percent by 1980.[20]

The shortcomings of the white society in rooting out racism are evident. More effort needs to be placed on changing white *attitudes* and *behavior* as well as the basic structure of such institutions as schools, labor unions, and political parties. One good technique for encouraging such changed behavior is through tax incentives for training hardcore unemployed. A test program under the Nixon administration was discussed with two variations: (1) offering a tax credit for a portion of the employer's payroll expenses for hiring hardcore unemployed and keeping them on the job, the percentage of reimbursement rising the longer the workers stay on the job, and (2) reimbursing employers for part of their payroll costs and for a percentage of training costs. However, there has been, to date, no action on these proposals.

Long Term

It is the distribution of opportunity that remains the doubtful accomplishment. The mid-1960s were years of frenetic legislation and administrative activity; these efforts were experiments in remedial action. The failure of the problems to go away after six or seven years of concentrated effort appears to have produced a mood of frustration among policymakers. Apparently, these policymakers did not realize the difficulty inherent in creating new institutions and reorienting established ones; there seems to be a tendency to abandon or de-emphasize existing programs just as they appear to be settling down to positive contribution. New programs are being put into effect without adequate research into potential problems or side effects. Our political system, as well as most other institutions in this society, are not designed to reward those who think beyond short term issues involved in elections and appropriations. Giving permanence to a system of employment preparation and remediation requires different insights than planning for emergency efforts. We must change our focus and our values about what is truly important in society if we hope to improve on our performance of the 1960s.

FOOTNOTES

[1] Addison Parris, *The Small Business Administration* (New York: Praeger, 1968), pp. 51-55; also Edward Roberts, "Entrepreneurship and Technology," in Donald Marquis and William Gruber, *Factors in Technology Transfer* (Cambridge: The MIT Press, 1961), pp. 224-225.

[2] U.S. Department of Labor, *U.S. Manpower in the Seventies* (Washington, D.C.: U.S. Government Printing Office, 1971), p. 17; also Thomas M. Stanback et al. *The Metropolitan Economy – The Process of Employment Expansion* (Springfield: National Technical Information Service, 1970), p. 27.

[3] Charles E. Silberman, *Crisis in Black and White* (New York: Vintage Books, Inc., 1964), Chapter 2.

[4] U.S. Bureau of the Census, "The Social and Economic Status of the Black Population in the United States, 1971," *Current Population Reports*, Series P 23, No. 42 (Washington, D.C., U.S. Government Printing Office, 1972), p. 40.

[5] *Ibid.*, pp. 66-69.

[6] Department of Labor, Bureau of Labor Statistics, "The Social and Economic Status of Negroes in the United States" (Washington, D.C.: U.S. Government Printing Office, 1969), p. VIII.

[7] Department of Labor, Bureau of Labor Statistics, "A Century of Change: Negroes in the U.S. Economy, 1860-1960" (Washington, D.C.: U.S. Government Printing Office, 1962), p. 1364.

[8] Philip Meranto, ed., *The Kerner Report Revisited* (Urbana, Illinois: Institute of Government and Public Affairs, June 1970), p. 15.

[9] Department of Labor, Bureau of Labor Statistics, *Job Patterns for Minorities and Women in Private Industry* (Washington, D.C.: U.S. Government Printing Office, 1967), p. XXXVI.

[10] Ulric Haynes, Jr., "Equal Job Opportunity: The Credibility Gap," *Harvard Business*

Review, Vol. 46, No. 3 (May-June 1968), p. 113.

[11] "The Negro and the City," (New York: Time-Life Books, 1968), p. 84 and "The Social and Economic Status of the Black Population. . . ," *op. cit.,* p. 83.

[12] Department of Labor, Bureau of Labor Statistics, "A Century of Change," p. 1362.

[13] U.S. Bureau of the Census, "The Social and Economic Status of the Black Population," p. 51.

[14] "White/Nonwhite Job Differences Least for Best and Worst Educated," *Urban Employment*, Vol. 2, No. 8, April 1971, p. 1.

[15] Richard Nathan, *Jobs and Civil Rights* (Washington, D.C.: U.S. Commission on Civil Rights, April 1969), p. 14.

[16] See Robert Yancy, Stewart Krawil, and John C. Rahiya, "The National Alliance of Businessmen; Its Purpose, Interactions and Results," this volume.

[17] "Jobs Program Gets Poor Marks," *Business and Society*, Vol. 3, No. 5, September 8, 1970.

[18] "Blacks Will Play Major Union Role in '70s," *Urban Employment*, Vol. 1, No. 21, November 30, 1970, p. 1.

[19] U.S. Bureau of the Census, *The Social and Economic Status of the Black Population*, p. 51.

[20] U.S. Department of Labor, *U.S. Manpower in the Seventies* (Washington, D.C.: U.S. Government Printing Office, 1971), p. 12.

THE CASE FOR MINORITY CAPITALISM

The indigenous ghetto resident is born and lives in a state of deprivation, yet he commutes everyday into American affluence to his neocolonial manufacturing or domestic service job. He moves back and forth daily from sophisticated metropolitan property to his slum. And in doing so, he exports the ghetto's only asset, labor, because unlike frontiers, colonies, or underdeveloped nations, the ghetto has no natural resources to attract foreign capital investment.

What the ghetto black lacks is an effective way into the system with more impact than job training or education. He needs a way to develop himself and his community based on competitive economic achievement. He must have a business stake in the American business culture. There is a great hope of this in the "black power" and "black capitalism" movements. . . .

It will be a test of actions and policies abroad as well as at home. If the American system can adapt to include minorities in its midst, it will be better able to cooperate with underdeveloped nations, where the population of "have nots" is even greater. In both cases we must establish an effective way for them to participate.*

*Howard Samuels, "Compensatory Capitalism," in *Black Economic Development*, William Haddad and Douglas Pugh, eds. (Englewood Cliffs, New Jersey: Prentice-Hall, 1969).

*Fred C. Allvine**

BLACK BUSINESS DEVELOPMENT[1]

BLACK POWER

One of the objectives of the black power movement is to turn the "colony" into a "domain." In a domain, as opposed to a colony, control resides inside rather than outside the territorial confines. Many who are trying to solve the business-economic problems of the black community put forward some version of the "colonial theory." These problemsolvers include Stokely Carmichael, former director of the Student Non-Violent Coordinating Committee (SNCC), and Charles Hamilton, political scientist, the co-authors of *Black Power*; Reverend Jesse Jackson, national director of People United to Save Humanity (PUSH); Roy Innis, director of the Congress of Racial Equality; and Elijah Muhammad, head of the Black Muslims.

"Colonialism" is a polite way of saying blacks live in a racist society whose decisions seek to subordinate and control them. The term derived from the colonial powers such as Athens, Rome, France, and England. Their colonies were largely controlled by the empire's rulers and used for development and exploitation. The blacks claim that their position is analogous to that of the colonial states. The primary difference is that the black colony is not a separate country —it exists within the larger state.

Those who advance the colonial hypothesis contend that control over blacks is maintained by institutional mechanisms, such as white political machines and police forces, by long-standing discriminatory practices, which have withheld from blacks the means and credentials to progress, and by a presumed cultural myth that blacks are inferior beings—a myth which helps to cleanse the conscience of the larger society. The blacks view their past role in the scheme of things as simply being exporters of cheap labor for menial tasks. They believe that whites have withheld opportunities that might have enabled them to become producers of goods for themselves or even for the larger society. As the blacks see the situation, the tentacles of the white man reach back into the community through ghetto businesses which have "sapped [it] senseless of what economic resources it does have."[2]

The concept of black power evolved as a result of black feelings of despair and frustration in relation to the progress they were making in the white society. While gains were substantial in the 1960s, expectations were rising faster than were concrete achievements. The new strategies and tactics that were needed gave rise to the black power movement.

*Fred C. Allvine is an associate professor of marketing, Graduate School of Business Administration, Georgia Tech.

Black power is an attempt by blacks to redefine themselves with the purpose of ultimately creating a meaningful position for blacks in American society. They want to begin by reclaiming their history and culture; this desire accounts for nationwide pressures for Afro-study programs in the public schools. As Afro-Americans, instead of Negroes, blacks are called upon to see themselves as energetic, intelligent, beautiful, and peace loving, instead of seeing themselves as society has tended to portray them, members of a race that is lazy, dumb, ugly, and militant.

Some people see black power as a sinister plot that is attempting to cultivate black racism. However, the black power movement is not designed merely to agitate the races and catalyze further confrontation. It is intended to unify the blacks and foster self-respect and pride.

The black power movement represents, for the present, a rejection of "integration." Those endorsing black power generally look upon integration in one of three ways:

(1) En route to integration the black community must first develop greater independence so that someday it can fully participate in society.

(2) There really is no such thing as integration and the "melting pot." The only integration that has ever taken place is work integration, between 7 a.m. and 6 p.m. After working hours the vast majority of Poles, Jews, Italians, and other ethnic groups move back to their own communities.

(3) Integration is a myth designed by whites to maintain the colonial status of the black community.

Regardless of the rationale, black power does not have integration as one of its objectives. Its objectives are political and economic self-determination.

Once there is a psychological redefinition—pride in being black, a development of self-respect, and an awareness of community—the black community will be in a position to make major advances.

THE BLACK BUSINESS VOID

The black community has been systematically deprived of the opportunity of developing substantial businesses. Blacks have been denied business opportunities not only in the white community, but in their own black community as well. The dearth of black businesses is related to white control of the capital base in the black community and to the virtual monopoly that whites have over the management and technical skills requisite for running businesses.

The business void has created several problems for the black community. Leadership is not broad based; it is left primarily in the hands of the church, the one organization in the black community relatively unhampered by white society. As a result, the church is the avenue through which leadership and power have developed in the black community. However, the black clergy generally has not been particularly skilled in providing the necessary guidance to reduce acute economic and business problems. Business leaders are needed to complement the efforts of religious spokesmen in the economic arena. Studies of community power structure reveal the difference in leadership in the white and black communities. In the white community, businessmen are typically the most influential and moving force. The business leaders are followed in varying ranks of importance by political leaders, spiritual leaders, union leaders, and directors of civic organizations.

Another problem associated with the dearth of substantial black businesses is that few black businesses are successful enough to serve as success models. The black businesses that do exist are typically small service establishments and marginal product retailing businesses that have little to offer the capable and ambitious black. As a result, the blacks with the drive and intelligence to run businesses are skirting business opportunities in the black community in favor of government service, teaching, or working for whites.

Social and political progress will be severely constrained unless blacks develop a large number of reasonably secure and independent businesses. A middle class black engaged in business may be more politically active and may develop and support independent political machinery. If this happens political power can be wrested from big city machine organizations that neither represent black people nor recognize the need to precipitate changes necessary for black social and economic progress.

THE EXTENT OF BLACK BUSINESSES

Blacks primarily operate those segregated businesses that would be difficult or unattractive for outsiders to operate. Typically, these businesses are the marginal ones that are either too small or involve too frequent or personal contact with blacks to be run by outsiders. Even in the case of marginal black businesses, the property and building usually are owned by outsiders.

The types of businesses operated by blacks are illustrated by a 1969 study of businesses in the predominantly black Kenwood-Oakland community on Chicago's South Side. Kenwood-Oakland comes close to representing a typical black community—it is neither among the poorest nor among the well-to-do. It is densely populated with 52,000 people crowded into 1.1 square miles. There are 244 businesses, 142 of which (58 percent) are black owned. These numbers fail to tell the whole story of those businesses. As shown in Table I, the vast majority of black-operated businesses are small service-oriented establishments which include barber shops and beauty parlors, repair services, service stations, lounges and eating establishments, and funeral homes.

By contrast, the white businesses generally are less service-oriented with lower labor to sales ratio. They are relatively big businesses engaged in high volume operations that tend to siphon black dollars out of the community. These are also the businesses requiring large capital investments and sophisticated business skills. In essence, whites control the mainstream businesses—supermarkets, automobile agencies, supply companies, financial institutions,

Table I

All Businesses in the Kenwood-Oakland Area in Chicago—1969*

	Black		Total Businesses		White	
	142		244		102	

Black Dominated Businesses			Black-White Shared Businesses			White Dominated Businesses		
Description	Black Owned	White Owned	Description	Black Owned	White Owned	Description	Black Owned	White Owned
Barber Shop & Beauty Parlor	30		Dry Cleaning & Laundry	15	11	Laundromat		9
Eating Establishments	19	2	Small Grocery	7	6	Liquor Stores	1	8
Lounges and Taverns	14	2				Currency Exchanges		8
Repair Shops	14					Drug Stores	3	6
Service Stations	6					Construction		6
Store Front Churches	4					Furniture	2	4
Funeral Homes	4					Real Estate	1	4
Clothing Stores	2	1				Supermarkets		4
Record Shops	2					Light Manufacturing		4
Pool Halls	2					New and Used Cars	3	
Miscellaneous	13					Supply Companies		3
						Hardware Stores		2
						Meat Markets	1	2
						Shoe Repairs	1	2
						Optometrists		2
						Insurance Agencies		2
						Storage Warehouses		2
						Medical Center		1
						Bank		1
						Wholesaler		1
						Miscellaneous		6
Total	110	5	Total	22	17	Total	10	80

*Data in this table was supplied by the Kenwood-Oakland Community Organization, 1969.

light manufacturing, contracting, warehousing, and so on. What is left for the blacks is pitifully small and insignificant.

BLACK CAPITALISM

"Black capitalism" is often advanced as a way to create black businessmen and to correct the existing imbalance between white and black entrepreneurship. This terminology appeals to blacks who recognize that without black capital there will be little black power. Similarly, black capitalism is acceptable to most white businessmen who live by the capitalist system and understand the orderly process by which capitalism produces economic development.

While there seems to be general support for black capitalism, some black and white leaders are concerned about the prospects for this new program. Some are afraid that it will lead to the initiation of more marginal businesses that will then be used to exaggerate the number of supposedly successful businesses in the black community. Others believe that black capitalism will be directed to developing small businesses that will be swept away in the movement toward giant businesses. There is also concern that it will discourage outside businesses from making needed investments in the community. Finally, there are those who believe that black capitalism will further reinforce the present pattern of apartheid.

Most militant blacks do not ask for apartheid; what they do demand is the same control over their own economic communities as that enjoyed by other ethnic groups. They want to become the shopkeepers in their own communities, and they want to engage in the light manufacturing and distributing that does not require massive capital investment.

ANALYSIS OF BUSINESS PLANNING

Black capitalism has received support from blacks and whites with diverse points of view because of their individual interpretations. However, there are differences of opinion as to how black capitalism should be implemented. Whites tend to think that the thrust of black capitalism lies in the building of new businesses by black entrepreneurs. These new businesses probably would include small retail and service businesses, distributing operations, and light manufacturers that would sell to the ghetto as well as some light manufacturers selling to nonsegregated markets.

Some black leaders are skeptical about black capitalism programs that primarily involve new businesses. First, they reason that only a small fraction of all new businesses succeed and that the rate of failure is bound to be even higher for black businesses. As a result, the cost of starting a few successful black businesses will be high in relation to what will be gained by the black community. Second, much seed money is being poured into small businesses such as restaurants, haberdasheries, service stations, painting and decorating services, which, even if they do succeed, will not amount to more than a small percentage of the ghetto business, and they will not employ many blacks. Third, they question whether there is such a thing as "white capitalism" or "entrepreneurship" today. In the early formation of our economic system, white capitalism and entrepreneurship played a major role. However, conditions have greatly changed since this was true; big business, large chain operations, and multi-billion dollar companies control the thrust of most industries today.

Transfer Ownership of Ghetto Businesses

Those blacks who are not enthusiastic about the prospects for starting a number of viable black businesses recommend another program. They would prefer that a large portion of the funds now being appropriated for black capitalism be channeled into financing purchases of existing businesses. This might include major corporations selling to nonsegregated markets or ghetto businesses run by outsiders. An example of the first situation is the proposal by Richard America, Jr., who suggests that a cross-section of major corporations be transferred gradually from white to black ownership and control.[3] While America's proposal might be workable, it is not consistent with political realities. However, the essence of his proposal could be applied in the gradual and smooth transfer to blacks of ghetto businesses owned by outsiders.

Most retail businesses run by blacks have been small, highly service-oriented types of businesses. This type of retailing will continue to present limited opportunities in entrepreneurship, and it may serve as a learning experience for black businessmen. However, blacks are increasingly interested in the more substantial types of retail and service businesses traditionally run by outsiders. Some of the more coveted businesses include automobile agencies, appliance stores, supermarkets, furniture stores, liquor stores, and loan companies.

Impetus for the transfer of ghetto businesses from nonblack to black ownership has been provided by the somewhat selective looting and burning of ghetto stores owned by outsiders. In addition, the growing hostility of blacks against nonblack merchants has convinced many white ghetto merchants that it is not worth staying in the black community. As a result, many nonblacks in the ghetto are looking for blacks to take over their ghetto operations, and they are willing to arrange favorable long-term payback programs. Purity-Supreme Stores in Boston decided to sell two of its ghetto stores to black-owned Freedom Foods, Inc. Since Purity wants to recover its investment, it is anxious to see Freedom Foods succeed. As a result, Purity makes available free management consultation and has agreed to remain a source of low-cost merchandise supply as long as Freedom Foods finds the arrangement advantageous. Similarly, the white owner of a successful men's clothing store on Chicago's South Side wants to sell his ghetto business to a black so he can concentrate his efforts on his two suburban stores in white communities where there are no racial problems.

Large Scale Manufacturing and Black Businesses

It is practically impossible for blacks to engage in a large number of manufacturing businesses that require large capital investment and a high level of sales because of a lack of available capital and a generally impoverished clientele. Nevertheless, because of the growing black awareness and consciousness and the desire to increase their control of their own community, blacks may have the opportunity to run marketing and distributing businesses. Instead of engaging directly in manufacturing, blacks can contract to purchase merchandise under their own brand from large-scale manufacturing businesses. Black businesses can associate with large-scale, capital-intensive manufacturing enterprises. Without the problems of production, a company could be relatively free to concentrate on a wide range of marketing activities, including variety and equality of product line, packaging and labeling, pricing, promotion, selling, and distributing. Such arrangements are not without precedent; several large consumer product companies purchase their merchandise from companies specializing in manufacturing.

In contrast to the private branding approach, a group of influential blacks are proposing a rather unorthodox arrangement with large-scale manufacturers. Their plans do not include a wide range of marketing activities. With one exception, they want manufacturers to market their products in the usual ways. The difference is that they intend to distribute the products of selected manufacturers to established retail outlets.

This business would be tied to a black distribution center that would control the flow of certain types of products into the ghetto. Of particular interest to the blacks are high-volume, frequently purchased products such as milk, bread, beer, soft drinks, and newspapers. Many of these products would arrive in trailer or boxcar loads; similar products could be combined for distribution to stores by black-owned delivery trucks. The blacks believe that what they are proposing is not unusual; they liken it to the general merchandise delivery operations existing in many cities. The primary difference is that retail operators, rather than the ultimate consumers, would receive shipment.

Small-Scale Manufacturing Businesses

The previous discussion touched on some businesses in which black manufacture of products would be particularly difficult because of capital requirements, complex technical skills, or large-scale production. However, there are light manufacturing and processing businesses for which these barriers do not represent too much of an obstacle. In industries such as industrial product firms which do aluminum and wood fabricating, electroplating, and chemical mixing, long hours, imagination, good business practices, and hard selling are the keys to business success. In the consumer products field, there are opportunities in food processing (sauces, bread, soft drinks, and sausages), blending of chemicals for household use (wax, bleach, and detergent), and cosmetic manufacturing (skin lotions, deodorants, and hair care products).

The plans of manufacturers in each of the three consumer products categories are illustrated by the cooperative effort of five black manufacturers with operations in Chicago.[4] The primary products of the five manufacturers were lemon juice, floor wax, drain opener, pine oil, and hand lotion. Three of the five products came into existence as a result of the door-opening efforts of black organizations, and the other two were materially helped by black agencies. Initially, these products were sold only through ghetto stores, but distribution was increased to include all stores in the chains which distribute such products.

DETERMINANTS OF BLACK BUSINESS DEVELOPMENT

Blacks generally are enthusiastic about the new opportunities for them to enter the capitalistic system. They have engaged in a great deal of planning, but the extent to which plans are converted into reality depends upon the response of the larger society in three areas:

(1) For blacks to become capitalists, large pools of equity funds must be made available under realistic conditions.

(2) The business and technical skills of blacks must be developed and strengthened.

(3) Larger numbers of white companies will have to "cut black companies in" and do business with them if blacks are ever to develop markets for their products.

Capital Needs

The low level of per capita income in the black community means that little discretionary income can be converted into savings. As a result, blacks do not have adequate funds to invest as risk capital in black businesses. This means that blacks are unable to obtain the debt financing they need because they do not have the equity cushions which act as insurance for loans. The situation is aggravated by the banking practice of "red lining" (means of calling to the attention of those appraising the loan application that the applicant is black) loan applications from blacks. This practice further reduces the financial leverage that blacks can obtain to run their businesses. This business capital trap will continue to seriously constrain black business development unless creative programs can be found to increase the capital flow into the ghetto.

Developing Business Skills

Directing capital flow into poverty areas to assist businesses is only a first step toward developing the black business potential in the ghetto. It must be supplemented by carefully thought-out programs for imparting technical and managerial skills to existing and prospective black businessmen. There seem to be two types of needs:

(1) direct problem-solving assistance for the individual businessman

(2) educational programs to increase general business skills in the black community

Black businessmen need the advice of consultants to help them overcome basic problems. Throughout the country, volunteers from businesses, consulting companies, and schools of business are giving free assistance in areas ranging from the incorporating of businesses through the development of marketing programs. In addition, paid consultants have been provided through programs financed by the Office of Economic Opportunity (OEO) and the Office of Minority Business Enterprise (OMBE). While the cost of such programs may be high (For instance, the Chicago Economic Development Corporation budget for 1970 was $597,000, and it helped its client businesses obtain $2.4 million in loans.), evidence has indicated that the paid consultants were able to work more closely with black businessmen than were the volunteers. Regardless of whether the consultants are volunteer or are paid, their efforts are invaluable in the building of black businesses.

While man-to-man or team consulting is important for dealing with the particular problems of individual businesses, a more formal approach to developing basic business knowledge is also needed. In Chicago one of the pioneering efforts in this area is the Free School of Business Management. The Cosmopolitan Chamber of Commerce of Chicago has primary responsibility for the program; its co-sponsor is the Small Business Administration. The program, which covers a wide range of subjects, consists of 16 two-hour class sessions taught by businessmen. More than 800 students have attended and completed the course. What is now needed are specially designed courses in the fundamentals of business, including accounting and finance, production, marketing, and personnel. It is hoped that the academic community will step forward with some creative programs.

Buy Black Products

The efforts put into financial assistance programs and the building of business skills will not bring maximum results unless white businesses help black businesses get started. Many black businesses will fail if they are frozen out of the opportunity of dealing with white businesses which control the mainstream of business in both the white and black community. To launch a large number of black businesses, white companies are going to have to buy black products. In essence, they will be holding an umbrella over these infant businesses until they are strong enough to stand on their own.

The efforts of some of the major supermarket chains in Chicago to help black companies producing grocery products are particularly noteworthy. For a variety of reasons, the supermarket chains found that black products were not being given a real chance to succeed. As a result, each chain named a black liaison man to help producers get their products moving in the chain stores.

Similarly, the Ford Motor Company worked with a black company to develop a new carwash product that Ford is now purchasing in thousand-case quantities. There is no doubt that Ford could have purchased a comparable product for the same price, or less, from an existing supplier with much less effort. More companies must show themselves willing to purchase black products and give assistance where they can to black businesses.

CONCLUSION

Blacks can either be shut out of the capitalistic system or they can be brought into it. Currently, the desire of blacks to participate in the free enterprise system is running high. If concrete and adequate steps are taken now, the black economic community can be launched and ultimately developed to strengthen the overall economy. However, if white America turns its back on the ghetto or tries to prescribe unacceptable programs, the black community may drag down the larger economic system.

FOOTNOTES

[1] This paper is excerpted from Fred Allvine's, "Black Business Development," *Journal of Marketing*, Vol. 34, No. 2 (April 1970), pp. 1-7. Published by the American Marketing Association. Some of the data has been updated.

[2] Stokely Carmichael and Charles V. Hamilton, *Black Power* (New York: Random House, 1967), pp. 18-20.

[3] Richard America, Jr., "What Do You People Want?" *Harvard Business Review*, Vol. 47, No. 2 (March-April 1969), pp. 103-107.

[4] For a detailed discussion of this cooperative venture see the article "United Distributors," a case study by Ann Huff included in this volume.

THE CASE FOR COMMUNITY ECONOMIC DEVELOPMENT

*Elliott D. Sclar**

THE COMMUNITY BASIS FOR ECONOMIC DEVELOPMENT

Since 1964, when President Johnson first declared "War on Poverty," a great many battle plans have been developed to attack the problem from many different angles. A dominant strain that has run through many of the early programs has been an attempt to treat the outward manifestation of the problem. One of the principal problems of the poor has been lack of employment opportunities. Consequently, a vast array of programs designed to increase employment possibilities has been assembled. There were programs designed to increase the lifetime opportunities of the poor by improving their chances to succeed in the educational system. There were programs to bring people to jobs and jobs to people.

The initial hopes that these programs would defeat poverty have given way to a more pragmatic belief that, while these programs may help, the problem of poverty has roots that go far deeper than was first thought. Thus, while the problem is still considered capable of solution, it is clear that far more resources will be required, and programs must be developed which address themselves to the more deep-seated causes of the problem.

*Elliott Sclar is an economist and active member of the Union for Radical Political Economics. At the time his article was written, he was a fellow at the Center for Community Economic Development, Cambridge, Massachusetts.

Recently, the "minority enterprise" approach has come into vogue. In its simplest terms, this program represents an attempt to establish minority group members, principally blacks, in their own businesses. This program is intended mainly for urban areas, in particular the urban ghettos. It differs from other approaches, which also attempt to address the deep-rooted nature of the problem, in its reliance upon the individual entrepreneur as the primary vehicle to bring about improvement in the lives of the poor. It must be distinguished from the use of cooperatives or community development corporations or any other program that places principal reliance upon community organization and development as the principal vehicle of social change.

THE THEORETICAL BASIS FOR MINORITY ENTERPRISE

While the literature on capitalist economic development goes back at least two hundred years to Adam Smith, the best theoretical discussion of the ways in which a competitive free enterprise grows and develops appeared about sixty years ago. It was Joseph Schumpeter's *The Theory of Economic Development.*[1] There are two essential parts to Schumpeter's view of the way capitalist change takes place. The first part concerns the entrepreneur, and the second concerns the ability of change to create the conditions for further change.

The entrepreneur was the driving force behind the engine of capitalist development. The term "capitalist" had a very precise meaning for Schumpeter. He distinguished between the managerial function and the entrepreneurial function. Although the word "entrepreneur" usually connotes a person who owns and runs his own business, Schumpeter felt it necessary to isolate exactly what he meant by the term. Owning and running a business was to Schumpeter a *managerial* function. It was a function which anyone with intelligence could be taught to perform. As necessary as it was to the functioning of the capitalist economy, it was not the vital element in making the capitalist economy a dynamic mechanism. This dynamic function fell upon those individuals whom Schumpeter called entrepreneurs. An individual was an entrepreneur only at the moment in time when he was "innovating," that is, when he was introducing a new product or process to the economic stream of goods and services.

The effects of the entrepreneur successfully working his new innovation into the economic flow are twofold. First, there is the profit he receives (the principal motive for entrepreneurial behavior). Then there is the benefit which redounds to the entire society. Innovations can be generally thought of as either reducing the costs of producing existing products or creating new products. In either case, society's resources are being used more efficiently; in the case of a new product which displaces an older one, the innovation is more in keeping with the desires of the individual members of society. Thus, the continual introduction of new products and production processes by a class of profit-seeking entrepreneurs is responsible for the continual material betterment of the whole society.

The other element of the modern view of the capitalist state is the relationship of the marketplace to democracy. Starting with Adam Smith's "invisible hand" and coming right down to the present, there has existed a strong belief that a market economy and a democratic state are highly complementary if not inseparable. In an economy dominated by competitive markets, all are price takers: no individual or firm is large enough to dominate the market. Consequently, all must react to the prices prevailing in the marketplace when making economic decisions. The observed changes in prices and output are not the workings of any one individual but rather the workings of the general social will. Thus, an individual can not get rich by exploiting his fellows; he can only become prosperous by providing them with the products that cover his costs but are not high enough to yield excessive profits. Any excess profits that do exist would ultimately be wiped out by the entrance into the market of competitors who would undersell the profiteer. Since no individual can impose his will on his fellows under such an arrangement, the chances of the competitive market are also an extension of the values of democracy.

Drawing heavily upon the work of Schumpeter, I have described the American "conventional wisdom" on the subject of capitalist development—a wisdom also enshrined in academic thought.[2] Most programs that advocate using the market as a focal point around which to build a policy for ending poverty (such as minority enterprise) have some version of this rationale underlying them.

The problem with this rationale is that it is grounded in many assumptions no longer applicable to the conditions prevailing in the American economy. In an economy where 64 percent of the total industrial sales are made by only 500 corporations (only 17 percent of the corporate entities in the nation), it is hard to conceive of great numbers of firms too small to effect market decisions carrying out the important economic decisions of the society.[3] Thus, competition, the great leveler of a bygone era, no longer operates as it did in Schumpeter's time. As Galbraith has pointed out, the emergence of the giant corporation as the dominant economic institution has greatly changed the ways in which economic decisions are made.[4] In particular, this new economic organization, according to John Kenneth Galbraith, has a great deal of control over innovation and the rate at which it is introduced. Thus, the entrepreneur, as the keystone of progress, is virtually extinct.

In the final analysis, minority enterprise is not grounded upon the Schumpeterian entrepreneur. Minority enterprise advocates visualize the black entrepreneur as one who owns a business in an already existing industry that can serve blacks. Therefore, we must view the policy of minority enterprise not in the context of a bygone day but in the context of present day pressures and problems.

THE HISTORICAL BASIS FOR MINORITY ENTERPRISE

It could be argued that, although a program of minority enterprise would only produce managerial businessmen in a Schumpeterian sense, it might be enough to provide a sound economic base in minority communities. If we look at the experience of earlier urban ghetto residents, that is, the immigrants of a bygone era, the types of businesses they engaged in were not, by and large, of an innovative nature. Yet they played a very vital role in allowing these groups to achieve the success they ultimately achieved. Nathan Glazer recently pointed out the ways in which small business helped to move the members of immigrant communities up the social scale.[5] Specifically, he detailed six ways in which small business aided the individual and his community.

First, the small businessmen provided knowledgeable voices within their communities. By the nature of their work, small businessmen had to be independent, and they needed more knowledge about the outside world than workers did. This knowledge was gained from having to know "about prices and markets, about credit and banking, about customers and buyers, about the cop on the beat and the local politician who could help them or ruin them, about their own community that provided their primary market, or even if it did not, provided advice, loans, and manpower." The knowledge developed as a response to economic needs meant that the community had in its small businessmen a corps of people who "could speak for the community, intercede for it, and even by their actions, educate it."

Second, the small businessman was of value to his community because, even if he did not become rich, he became relatively affluent. And as he became affluent, his money helped not only himself and his family but also his community. Put another way, the profits the small businessman realized were valuable to him and his family, but he made them available to the community as well. On the more obvious level, these contributions are generally thought of as "charity." Most important among these acts of charity were contributions to institutions that provided education, guidance, and material things like food and clothing to the less fortunate members of the community, in particular the young.

Third, the small businessman often provided a network of jobs and opportunities for other members of the community. Thus, he generally would take his own children or the children of relatives into the business. He would use lawyers and accountants from his own community. He would buy from friends and relatives. His own enterprise thus often helped support salesmen, clerks, lawyers, contractors, and other workers from his community.

Fourth, due to the structure of taxes, a businessman is often much better off than the scale of the enterprise might suggest because many expenses that contribute to the businessman's standard of living are also legitimate business expenses deductible from his taxes. In addition, because of the host of transactions in which even a small businessman is involved, much income completely escapes taxation.

Fifth, the ownership of a successful business means not only that the individual and his family will have an income, but also that as discrimination on the part of financial institutions dissolves, he will have a very valuable asset that can be used as leverage capital for the further betterment of himself and his community.

Sixth, business enterprise that comes into being to serve a unique specialty of some minority further acts to strengthen the mutual ties of the members of the community. These contributions toward the betterment of the whole community are hardly what we would expect from enterprises operating to maximize their own individual wealth. As will be seen in the next section, it was only because of the existence of a very special set of social institutions that the enterprises acted as Glazer described rather than in the more self-seeking manner we would expect from Schumpeter's analysis.

Max Weber has theorized that the rise of Protestantism led to the type of development which the West European nations and the United States underwent in the past two hundred years. According to Weber, the rise of Calvinism led to a drastically different attitude concerning work on the part of workers. Without evaluating the merits of Weber's theory, an important issue is raised: What is the relationship between social institutions and the rise of capitalism? This is the question we must explore in examining the Irish, Italian, and Jewish experiences. What social institutions within these immigrant communities led to their economic development? Do these institutions exist in black urban ghettos today?

In discussing the growth of small business in immigrant communities, Glazer has pointed out that this growth was accomplished in the face of a great deal of discrimination toward the immigrants by the wider community, in particular by the financial institutions.[6] In addition to a lack of access to capital markets, the predominant form of work available to these groups was low and semi-skilled work. This in turn meant that the income stream into the community, though steady, was quite small. The above two observations present us with a problem. If the income stream into the immigrant community was small and if the immigrants were denied effective access to the existing capital markets, then where did the capital necessary to the establishment of the small businesses that did emerge come from? The answer seems to lie in the ability of the social institutions of the immigrant community to act as accumulators and investors of capital. Because of the institutional arrangements in the community, the meager income of the community was not only conserved but also was partially converted into capital. While the ways in which this occurred were many and subtle, varying from community to community, a discussion of two major institutions that appear to have existed in all three communities should suffice to describe the ways in which social institutions affect economic development. These are family structure and religion.

Family structure in the immigrant communities was, by and large, extended. Regardless of cultural differences, an expanded family structure almost certainly leads to economy in day-to-day living arrangements because many items are not used as intensively as possible in nuclear families. For example, childrens' clothing often lasts longer than one child's use of it. An arrangement that allows for more intensive use of clothing can lead to considerable savings. Living space, too, becomes usable in a more intensive manner in an extended family. Generally kitchens, bathrooms, and other shared parts of living space within homes tend to be underutilized in nuclear families; without necessarily being cramped, extended families can use the same amount of living space as a nuclear family that has fewer members. Meals for 10 people can be prepared in the same size kitchen in which meals are prepared for 4. The purchase of food for larger numbers of people also is more economical. While hard data on these observations generally is lacking, the savings realized in a supermarket by purchasing a typical market basket in the largest available quantities can be substantial. In one survey, the overall savings amounted to 17 percent.[7]

Religion also served to organize the community into a unit so that individual members viewed their own advancement as being tied to that of the rest of the community.

While it is difficult, if not impossible, to detail all the ways in which extended families aided the development of small businesses in the ghetto communities, consider the following: In a study of a middle class section of Chicago during the last half of the nineteenth century, Richard Sennett found that the offspring of extended families tended to be more upwardly mobile than the offspring of nuclear families.[8] That is, the sons of extended families "followed the footsteps of their fathers into good white-collar positions, with almost total elimination of manual labor in their ranks as well."[9]

To insure that the gains from economic growth went to the community, the social institutions of the community helped to mold it into a cohesive unit by minimizing the leakage of gains out of the community—a natural result in the absence of these institutions. This in turn allowed the immigrant community to use its gains to launch another round of economic growth.

In addition to maintaining a fairly closed community, it was necessary to have a source of income from which the social institutions of the community could extract capital. This was provided by the low-skill, low-wage work in which members of the various communities were engaged. Not only did the immigrants engage in low-skill work, but they tended to specialize. In New York, the Irish worked around the port, the Italians worked in the construction trades, and the Jews were employed in the needle trades.[10]

In summary, we have seen that the question of who becomes the entrepreneur and how he behaves is matched in importance by the question of what encourages him to behave as he does. This is a function performed by the institutions that form the individual's values and perspectives, especially in the case of the immigrant groups. Whether or not the individual consciously sought to aid the community is not as important as the fact that the community and its values helped to create and channel entrepreneurial development to the needs of the entire community. In addition, the income from such things as low-skill work could be turned into capital for the further development of the community because the community's institutions were strong.

In the case of the immigrant community, the entrepreneur is a vehicle that the community uses to transport itself rahter than an individual who pulls his community up the social ladder. If minority enterprise is a viable means of community development, how similar are conditions for blacks today to those of the earlier immigrant groups?

THE BLACK EXPERIENCE AND THE SOCIAL INSTITUTIONS
OF IMMIGRANTS

The conditions that poor urban blacks face today differ substantially from those faced by the earlier immigrant groups. Furthermore, they differ substantially from those needed for entrepreneurial development. On the most obvious level, the character of the distribution and production systems is quite different today from that prevailing in the heyday of the small business system.

When the immigrant groups were arriving, retailing consisted almost exclusively of small stores as opposed to the massive chains and giant operations that exist today. Since few immigrants spoke English, their need for specialty businesses was far more acute than that of the black migrants from the South who spoke English and thus could be served by black entrepreneurs.

The export base provided by the immigrant community's ability to supply cheap labor to the larger economy is, at best, greatly curtailed today. As the report of the National Advisory Commission on Civil Disorders states:

> Since World War II, especially, America's urban-industrial society has matured; unskilled labor is far less essential than before, and blue-collar jobs of all kinds are decreasing in number and importance as a source of employment. The Negroes who migrated to the great urban centers lacked the skills essential to the new economy, and the schools of the ghetto have been unable to provide the education that can qualify them for decent jobs. The Negro migrant, unlike the immigrant, found little opportunity in the city; he had arrived too late, and the unskilled labor he had to offer was no longer needed.[11]

Although it exists to some extent, the steady stream of income into the ghetto that could provide the purchasing power needed to support an indigenous black retail community is not of a magnitude comparable to that of the earlier immigrant communities. This diminished income stream also means that even if the black community had the necessary capital-building social institutions, the income stream could not be expected to do the job.

In addition to the lack of export base and the competition from mass marketing, there is another more serious problem that must be faced. As outlined by Schumpeter, economic development is a cumulative process that benefits the whole community. If the goal of minority enterprise is this type of development, then the question of social institutions becomes vital. The two main institutions that acted to cause capital accumulation and the reinvestment of the gains within the immigrant communities do not exist within the black community. The extended family and a single religion, which served as the mainstay of the immigrant community, are not characteristics of the urban black community today. Thus, the gains to the community from any concerted program of minority enterprise will be marginal at best. While there may be some who will gain substantially, minority enterprise will do virtually nothing to alleviate a very severe social crisis unless and until there are institutions that cause the gains to be captured for use by the community.

The argument developed here is not the Moynihan-type argument that blacks are poor because they have matriarchal and disorderly families. Indeed, the black family structure that developed after the Civil War was a very rational response to the conditions in which black people found themselves. Although the end of the Civil War brought with it an end to slavery, it did not bring an end to the economic basis upon which slavery rested. The large plantations that were the backbone of the pre-War South were not broken up by a land reform program after the abolition of slavery. Thus although blacks were "free," they really had no option other than to remain on the plantations. They stayed on as sharecroppers. Given the heritage of America's "peculiar institution," blacks came out of slavery as nuclear families. Because agricultural work could be performed productively by young children, the black family structure after slavery developed into large nuclear families. Had blacks been allowed to remain as sharecroppers, they probably would have developed extended families and settled into their new roles. However, the last half of the nineteenth century was ripe with business cycle downturns. These downturns forced many people off the land and into the city. Thus, the black migrations to urban areas were underway almost as soon as slavery ended. While the substantial northward migrations did not begin until the twentieth century, there was nonetheless enough economic instability in the South of the last half of the nineteenth century to impede development of stable, black, extended families.

After one major and several less severe depressions and a declining demand for unskilled labor, twentieth-century cities certainly did not provide an atmosphere for the development of strong communal and familial ties for the arriving blacks. At least the immigrants arriving from Europe had a heritage of extended families, a separate language, and a single religion around which to rally and to build the necessary community institutions when they reached America's urban ghettos.

While the family structure that blacks developed may have been a rational response to the conditions America imposed upon them, it presents a number of problems for the application of policies of minority enterprise. The question is not how to foster a black family structure suited to the policies we would like to use. Rather, the question is: How do we formulate a policy that relates to the conditions of life today for black people? The types of institutions suited to the earlier entrepreneurial development are not only nonexistent in the black community, but available evidence indicates that they also are fast disappearing in the larger society. The pressures of modern capitalism are such that mobile family units are far more suited to the demands of the economy than extended families are. Since the end of World War II, more and more of the vital economic needs of American society are being satisfied by vast national and multi-national organizations. These include not only the large corporations but also a government complex that must administer and regulate the national economy.

What does this realignment of our capitalistic institutions indicate? Such organizations take a broad geographic view of their interests, and employment in these organizations consequently necessitates a great deal of moving. Since these organizations loom larger and larger in our lives, pressures for the establishment of nuclear families far outweigh the pressures for extended families.

In addition to the dissolution of extended families, the needs of giant firms for mass markets mean that ethnic and social differences are being systematically destroyed. People must learn to express their tastes and preferences for goods and services in standardized units for standardized products if mass production is to operate efficiently.[12]

The development of a large mass society with a high standard of living has been accomplished at a price. That price has been the destruction of workplaces and communities in which individuals, if not always in total control of the situation, could at least perceive their identity within the social order.

CONCLUSION

Let us now look at the implications of this paper for the development of a policy to overcome urban poverty. First, minority enterprise as an approach to this end rests upon a number of theoretical and empirical assumptions at variance with the experiences of blacks in urban ghettos today. Second, given today's strong search for community, a policy that is mutually supportive of this trend is desirable and would have a good chance of being successful. Because it relies upon the individual, abstracted from his community, minority enterprise is not this type of approach. This, in turn, leads to the conclusion that programs in the community development mold are better suited to the problems and needs of urban blacks and should be encouraged.[13]

A program built around the overall development of the community represents an attempt to suit the policy to the community. A program of minority enterprise would appear to be an attempt to suit the community to the policy.

FOOTNOTES

[1] Joseph Schumpeter, *The Theory of Economic Development*, English translation by Redvers Opie (New York: Oxford University Press, 1961); first published in English by Harvard University Press, 1934; original German version published in 1909.

[2] The term "conventional wisdom" was coined by John K. Galbraith in his book, *The Affluent Society* (Boston: Houghton Mifflin Company, 1958). Galbraith used the term to

describe ideas that people hold to be correct because they are part of the generally held wisdom rather than because they are carefully thought out positions. Most of the time the conventional wisdom is wrong.

[3] This point has been made many times by critics of the rationale for the social system it represents. For a recent critique, see Gar Alperovitz, "National Perspectives," *Occasional Bulletin No. 1*, (Cambridge: Cambridge Institute, October 1969).

[4] John Kenneth Galbraith, *The New Industrial State* (Boston: Houghton Mifflin Company, 1968).

[5] Nathan Glazer, "The Missing Bootstrap," *Saturday Review* (August 23, 1969).

[6] This is not to say that those people hired or goods and services bought from within the community were necessarily selling at a higher price than the immigrant businessman could have obtained from outsiders. Rather it is to argue that nonmarket considerations weighed at least as important as market ones.

[7] Elliott Sclar, "A Pilot Study on Food Price Discrimination" Master's Thesis, Tufts University, 1966.

[8] Richard Sennett, "Genteel Backlash: Chicago 1886," *Transaction*, Vol. 7, No. 3 (January 1970), pp. 44-50.

[9] *Ibid.*, p. 48.

[10] Glazer, *op. cit.*

[11] Report of the National Commission on Civil Disorders.

[12] For a good discussion of the ways in which mass production imposes constraints on social behavior, see Thorstein Veblen, *The Theory of Business Enterprise* (New York: Kelly, 1904).

[13] See Matthew Edel, *Community Development Corporations* (Cambridge: Center for Community Economic Development, January 1970) for more discussion of the CDC approach.

Stewart E. Perry [*]

THE GENESIS OF THE COMMUNITY DEVELOPMENT CORPORATION

The community development corporation (CDC) has its roots in early organized efforts against common economic problems, some of which go back as far as the earliest history of the American colonies.[1] Other origins of the CDC can be

*Stewart E. Perry is Director of the Center for Community Economic Development, Cambridge, Massachusetts.

traced to later economic development institutions, such as the city booster corporations of thirty or forty years ago. Whatever its derivations, the CDC represents a contemporary thrust against a very current and troubling problem— the drive of the poor and of minorities, especially blacks, to achieve a new, significant, and respected place in American society..

The CDC takes various forms, but it ordinarily has these features:

(1) It is an institution focused upon developing a specific territorial neighborhood or area.

(2) Its corporate structure offers shares or membership primarily to residents of that selected area. If shares or membership are offered to nonresidents, the offering allows the residents to keep control.

(3) Its goals are multiple, but they always include the creation of new economic institutions—fiscal, industrial, or business.

(4) The new economic institutions are designed to promote a multiplicity of goals. While the businesses need to be profit-making, they must serve such community priorities as substantial increased employment or convenience shopping.

(5) Its constituency is usually economically disadvantaged and concerned with changing those institutions that have contributed to its disadvantaged position.

What makes the CDC different from earlier attempts to improve the status of the poor in America? Is this just another name for the private and public antipoverty efforts of the past? Why should the CDC be considered so different from, for example, the community action agencies, the poor people's organizations sponsored under the programs of the Office of Economic Opportunity? Is it not true that many of today's CDCs are supported primarily by OEO funds, just as the community action agencies (CAAs)[2] have been? All these questions and others must be answered in order to recognize what the CDC may mean in the years to come.

First, it is not possible to understand what the organizations described in this paper really represent unless one considers the impoverishment of the neighborhoods and groups from which they arose. It can fairly be said that the poor and the blacks, the Spanish-Americans, and certain other minorities have suffered not only from a debased status within our society, but most excruciatingly from the absence of their own institutional resources—local, self-developed, and meaningful—to challenge the remainder of society to cede them their rightful place. This lack has been represented especially in economic institutions such as businesses, banks, credit facilities, and industries.

The people of the ghettos and barrios, the depressed rural counties, and forgotten mountain regions of this country have had to make do with organizations and resources that came to them from that very outside that never gave them a fair shake. It is no wonder then that the "underclasses" (as Michael Harrington has called them) have not managed to improve their position dynamically, because the energy was always from outside and was never mobilized from within. That is the new promise of the innovative institutions that have begun to emerge. The community development corporation, an innovation of the poor themselves, a self-developed instrument for their own mobilization, may be the means by which they will fundamentally change their relation to the rest of us.

A second significant orientation for understanding this new institution is that the CDCs are not inherently a part of the federally sponsored poverty program. In fact, the beginnings of CDCs were independent of any government activity. This fact is meaningful on two counts: first, it means that these new institutions are truly a creation of the people they are designed to serve; second, they are therefore likely to be more precisely directed to the needs of their constituencies and will be more clearly expressive of exactly what their constituencies consider important.

Historically, the CDCs probably developed out of activites generated by the civil rights movement and poverty programs. The community action agencies had offered assistance and hope to a growing and evolving leadership in the poor communities, but at the same time, they clearly frustrated many of the aspirations of those communities. Local poverty programs offered crucial jobs in community organizing to a considerable number of people who had informal influence within their neighborhoods (or who developed that influence through their new jobs).[3] It also provided the poor with a certain experience in dealing with the established power structure. These means included the CAAs themselves and the whole panoply of rules of the game in dealing with the federal government, with local city or county or state officials, and other local majority community leaders in such areas as business, welfare, and health.

In short, through the medium of the CAAs, a generation of poverty community leadership has been subsidized and taught to deal with the structures that had been closed to them in the past. Thus, help from the outside provided a means of mobilizing their own people. For example, it was no longer necessary for a woman to earn her living as a domestic and have only a small amount of energy and time to work for such community goals as the betterment of her neighborhood through such measures as organizing neighbors for better garbage collection from the city. Such a woman now has a chance to be *paid to do just that sort of organizing.*

So the poverty program did in fact offer certain resources. On the other hand, the experience of the emergent leadership from the poverty program activities was not very encouraging. For one thing, the CAA was not the instrument exclusively of the poor; it was, as its name clearly denoted, the instrument of the community—the *whole* community, including the rich and the middle class. It was, in fact, *intended* as a meeting place and common mobilization point for the entire community; it was to be an organization, of course, including the poor and for the benefit of the poor but certainly not exclusively *of* the poor. Sometimes, the CAA would encourage the initiation of subsidiary groups that were composed entirely of poor people, and occasionally these were effective groups, but they still operated within the context of the overall vehicle of the larger community—the CAA.

Thus, the interests of the poor were commonly compromised in the arena of negotiation, within the CAAs themselves, presumably as other interest groups compromised with the poor. That, indeed, was the name of the game—to get the rest of the community into contact with those who had been effectively ghetto-ized and isolated from significant relations with the majority world. By doing so, the groundwork could be laid for getting more resources and changes for the advantage of the poor. The poor learned, however, that the CAA was not their instrument, no matter what the rhetoric. They also learned that the business sector was involved in everything that happened.

Out of this experience came the new vehicle, the CDC, that would represent the poor neighborhood only, express its priorities only, advocate its goals with-out the immediate compromise that participation in the CAA requires. More-over, this new vehicle for self-determination would seize upon the means that meant real power and change in the neighborhoods—the economic muscle of business development.

If it were to do the ambitious job it was designed to do—to set priorities, plan, and execute plans for a whole neighborhood or sub-area of the city—then it would not be simply another community organization. It would represent the entire neighborhood, and it would bring the leadership from all of the com-munity groups together in the immediate poverty area to create a coalition that would make overall planning possible and provide a united front to the outside world in economic and political negotiations.

The community development corporation depends upon the basic strength and mobilization of the community and upon the strength of its leadership. The mere existence of a CDC is not an indication of community unity, energy, and strength of purpose—especially today, when the idea of the CDC may take on the aura of a panacea to be initiated without any prior community organizing.

The publicity that the CDC has received in low-income areas has led to the creation of many such corporations. Some of these newer organizations may go on to important work; others will disappear without accomplishing anything. Yet, coupled with increasing political energy and sophistication on the part of the disadvantaged, the CDC seems likely to provide a new and powerful means for the underrepresented poor of our society to begin to make themselves felt.

FOOTNOTES

[1] See, for example, John McClaughry and Patricia M. Lines, "Early American Community Development Corporations: The Trading Companies," Paper prepared for the Center for Community Economic Development 1969.

[2] CAAs are authorized by the Equal Opportunity Act of 1964 to maximize citizen partici-pation in local and economic development programs.

[3] It is instructive to note that so many of today's leaders of the minority communities, even if they no longer participate or even believe in the utility of the poverty programs, got support from CAAs, and similar organizations, at some early points in their careers.

SECTION TWO:
JOBS—
A PARTIAL ANSWER,
A MIXED RECORD

Employment has been, and should continue to be, a key strategy for minority economic development in the United States. Beginning in the 1930s, individual states began implementing their own antidiscrimination legislation (fair employment practices) to help minorities get into the economic mainstream through jobs. Several presidential orders, the most recent of which requires "affirmative action" to prevent discrimination, followed to further enhance minority members' legal rights. The landmark 1944 *Steele* v. *Louisville and Nashville Railroad* case ruled that unions must represent nonunion or minority union members of the craft "without hostile discrimination." The culmination of this antidiscrimination framework was the 1964 Civil Rights Act. All of these historical developments point to a policy commitment by the government, federal and state, to make equal employment opportunity a reality.

Why should employment be considered a viable economic development strategy? The case for employment made by Andrew Brimmer and Henry Terrell in "The Economic Potential for Black Capitalism," states that black capitalism is founded on the premise of self-employment, but they argue that opportunities for employment and upward community mobility are substantially greater in the nonminority business since self-employment is a rapidly declining factor in our economy. Thus, they argue that black capitalism is a strategy dependent on an economic way of life that can provide opportunities for only a fortunate few of the population, minority or nonminority. Brimmer also contends that black capitalism puts the burden of the high risk and failure rates of small businesses on those least capable of accepting such risks and that, in fact, black capitalism may discourage full participation in the national economy.

David Banner, in his case for employment in "Minority Employment—An Assessment" agrees with Brimmer that the trend is away from self-employment and that the economy is dominated by large corporations; this trend makes entry and successful competition difficult, particularly in the ghetto communities where the crime rate is high and income is low.

Minority employment is a viable vehicle for economic development. It is the quickest way to get money into minority communities, in contrast with the longer period required for maturation of a small business, even a successful one. Assuming equal employment opportunities will be increasingly available at all levels of the job market, minority employment also has the ability to integrate the society at all levels.

Also, with greater employment opportunities, more people bring money into the community; this will help to raise the income level of the community and to improve the chances of success for the small businesses that already exist or may develop in the community. In addition, by working for a large company, the potential self-employed person can acquire experience and learn valuable skills that will reduce his risks should he spin off to begin his own business.

One of the greatest fears about minority capitalism is that it implies continuing and perhaps institutionalized social as well as economic segregation.

While minority capitalism does have value as an economic development strategy, its target population may be quite small. Not everyone, minority or non-minority, has the ability or the desire to become an entrepreneur; therefore, a strategy with wider applicability, such as employment, must supplement a minority capitalism approach.

Another facilitating factor for employment is the legal/institutional framework designed to aid minority representation in the workforce. This framework includes affirmative action to overcome past inequities and increased educational/training opportunities through the private sector.

Although such a strategy has a number of positive features, many obstacles still exist for equal employment opportunities. Many jobs are no longer located in the inner city where minorities are concentrated, and there is a strong trend for industrial movement to the suburbs. Lower taxes, availability of "better quality" (meaning white) workers, and a more pleasant environment are among the reasons for this movement. This problem is particularly acute in some of the more innovative, high-growth industries such as electronics, data processing equipment, scientific instruments, and the like. The suburbs remain predominantly white so that the interplay between segregated housing and jobs produces a net loss for minorities in terms of job opportunities in geographical proximity to their communities.

Another barrier to minority employment is that its success is heavily dependent on business cycles. In a recession minority members are the first to be laid off. "Last in, first out" is an unwritten code of industry policy toward minority employment when times get sour and retrenching is required. Businessmen will argue that this is not discrimination but sound business practice, because the extra cost of hiring and training "hardcore unemployed" is a luxury during bad economic periods. There is a difference between firing a minority member who meets employment qualifications and firing a true "hardcore" problem during periods of economic contraction. It becomes difficult for managers to enforce antidiscriminatory practices in a poor economic environment. After all, much of the so-called "blue collar backlash" is nothing more than fear for jobs; minorities represent a threat to the jobholder's economic well-being, and, accordingly, white managers must be expected "to look after their own."

Discrimination in hiring, training, and promotion is a complex phenomenon. Part of this phenomenon is clearly the result of overt racism, that is, a visible, objectively verfiable intent to discriminate. However, some, and perhaps the major part of discrimination in employment today, results from a variety of institutional arrangements, no one of which specifically is intended to discriminate. Such requirements as a high school diploma or a college degree, or certain apprenticeship training or other professional credentials as a qualification for employment or upgrading are usually perceived as neutral as far as discrimination is concerned. However, in the past, minorities have had limited access to education or apprenticeship programs and are often effectively screened out of employment opportunities by such institutional requirements. Still, if employers can show that such requirements are directly related to success on the job, then most of us would find no discrimination in such requirements.

However, the employer could provide the training himself or work with local government or private educational institutions to provide the needed education or training for the educationally disadvantaged. Such affirmative action is not required by Title VII of the Civil Rights Act. Thus, the employer is left free to act in this area as his conscience dictates and corporate social responsibility budgets allow.

This section of the book presents different approaches to the task of equal employment and in each case questions the effectiveness of the existing approach. One of the efforts of the private sector to deal with the employment problem has been the National Alliance of Businessmen (NAB). The NAB has support from the president and funds available from the Department of Labor to encourage private enterprise involvement in the JOBS program. The article by Robert Yancy, Stewart Krawil, and John C. Rahiya is an attempt to analyze the goals and stated accomplishments of the NAB to determine if there has been adequate evaluation of the JOBS program, or if "proper implementation has been more a dream than a reality."

A specific company's attempt to meet the demands of increased social awareness is presented in the article by L. G. Lavengood, Martha Ottinger, and Steve L. Schlect. In 1968 fires broke out at four Chicago State Street stores; the fire at Carson Pirie Scott and Company was the worst (approximately $7 million damages)—Carson's, the first Chicago department store to fill a management position with a Negro in 1948, and which in 1957, broke the unwritten "color line" on State Street by hiring the first black salesperson.

Although the cause of the fires was never proven, the white community said "Negroes are burning up State Street;" however, there was much skepticism in the black community that a black had set the fires. Yet the situation was the impetus for Carson's to reevaluate their position and to try to develop new ways to do business in order to thrive in the new urban setting with which they were confronted. They conducted seminars and conferences for over 80 top level executives, 500 Chicago area supervisors, and 190 store managers and first line supervisors. Their goals were to establish training programs for current and future minority employees for supervisory entry level positions and to support black business. They established programs to analyze training needed for new supervisors; how to increase opportunities for those locked into lower level jobs; scholarships for full-time study at the Chicago campus of the University of Illinois for six "educationally disadvantaged and culturally distinct associates." Have the verbal commitment, the seminars, the committees, the programs produced significant changes? Follow-up progress is reported at the conclusion of the article.

The final article in this section looks at the Chicago labor market and presents some interesting statistics for white and nonwhite employment.

Concentrating on the air transport, steel, and banking industries, Director and Doctors describe some of the problems and experiences of minority workers in Chicago in relation to the type of employment and implications of regulations, unions, industry policies, and existing training programs.

They conclude that although some changes, mainly related to overt instances of discrimination, have occurred since the 1964 Civil Rights Act, covert institutional practices still effectively screen out minority access to these industries and severely limit the upward mobility potential of minorities, if they are hired. Even if all discriminatory personnel policies were eliminated, minority workers would still face major obstacles: residential segregation and unequal educational opportunities.

*Robert Yancy, Stewart Krawil, John C. Rahiya**

THE NATIONAL ALLIANCE OF BUSINESSMEN; ITS PURPOSE, INTERACTIONS, AND RESULTS

INTRODUCTION AND BACKGROUND

The National Alliance of Businessmen (NAB) is a private, independent, non-profit, voluntary agency composed of businessmen pledged to fight for amelioration of critical employment problems of the "hardcore" unemployed and veterans.

In January, 1968, President Lyndon B. Johnson called together some of the nation's top business leaders to discuss the problem of the inner cities' hardcore unemployed. He admitted the federal government's inability to solve the problem single-handedly. The President "pleaded" with business leaders to cooperate in a joint government-industry effort to attack the problem head on.[1] The governmental thrust was called JOBS. The result of business' cooperation led to the formation of the National Alliance of Businessmen. Its original goal was to find five hundred thousand jobs in the nation's fifty largest cities during its first three years.

Within six months the alliance had mobilized a team of 8,000 business and government employees, had secured 310,000 job commitments, and had placed 140,000 people in jobs.

The NAB/JOBS plan for hiring the disadvantaged appeared to be a promising one. Under this program, an individual was to become a breadwinner, earning full wages while he learned and acquired skills. Properly implemented, this program could make significant inroads into the problem of chronic unemployment in this country. However, economic conditions in the early 1970s wreaked havoc with NAB programs. It is impossible to measure what the cost to this nation would have been had there been no JOBS program. However, reports have shown that many millions of dollars were wasted in the government-supported JOBS program. Also under attack is the retention rate of those employed under the program. (NAB reports 1973 figures at 53 percent.) While dollar waste and percentage of retention can be submitted to empirical measurement, it is difficult, if not impossible, to compute the value this program would have had if it had fulfilled its early expectations of significant and rewarding job opportunities for all the disadvantaged wishing such opportunities.

*Robert Yancy is currently an assistant professor at Atlanta University's School of Business Administration. Stewart Krawil and John C. Rahiya did much of the research for this paper while they were M. B. A. students at Northwestern. This case study was written under the direction of Professor Samuel I. Doctors.

THE NAB/JOBS PROGRAM

The primary aim of the National Alliance and the local alliances is to encourage private enterprise to participate in the JOBS program. NAB offers participating businesses help in hiring and training persons, the rewards of extensive publicity and, for those who desire it, assistance in obtaining reimbursement through the Department of Labor (DOL) for costs of orienting, counseling, on-the-job training, and education.

The DOL specifies who is eligible to participate in a government-subsidized training program. Briefly, the criteria are: poor persons who do not have suitable employment, and who are either:

1 school dropouts
2 45 years of age or over
3 under 22 years of age
4 handicapped
5 subject to special obstacles to employment.

The criteria section defines as "poor" one who is a member of a family that receives welfare, or one whose annual net income does not exceed a certain specified level (for family size).

Membership in NAB is strictly voluntary, even though President Johnson and President Nixon have named NAB board chairmen who serve one-year terms. The original chairman of NAB was Henry Ford II, and the vice-chairman was J. Paul Austin, president of Coca-Cola. The executive board is composed of some of the top business leaders in the country. Each metropolitan area has a similar board composed of top local business leaders.

The chairman of NAB for 1972 was Gordon M. Metcalf, chairman of Sears, Roebuck and Company. Under the NAB system, corporations take one-year turns running the program, with the corporate chairman nominally heading the operation and a lower level executive actually stationed in Washington to direct operations. The 1972 NAB annual report states three achievements for the year:
(1) 246,000 disadvantaged people were hired, 9 percent above the goal set.
(2) 136,369 veterans found jobs.
(3) 151,000 disadvantaged youths obtained summer employment.

In February, 1973, President Nixon restated his support for NAB and asked that it set priorities in the following areas:
(1) develop jobs for minorities, especially those under 25 years old and veterans who are disadvantaged or handicapped
(2) locate summer and part-time year round jobs for needy youth
(3) carry out programs designed to break the poverty cycle by encouraging minority and disadvantaged youths to complete their education and prepare for meaningful careers in industry
(4) find jobs for ex-offenders
(5) promote the hiring of public assistance recipients in the private sector and the use of Work Incentive Program (WIN) tax credit.[2]

The major impact of the JOBS program has been that it provides full-time employment, full pay, and other benefits from the time of the first work day. The trainee can earn at least a minimal living while he learns a skill or occupation; usually the wage level is set somewhat above the federal minimum wage level. This aspect is touted as being greatly superior to programs that provide training at "trainee wages."

CONTRACT ADMINISTRATION

Although NAB functions in close cooperation with the DOL to solicit job pledges under the Manpower Assistance (MA) contract series, the majority of pledges are filled without the use of an MA contract. Many firms seem to feel that hiring the hardcore unemployed is inherently good, and they feel obligated to take on the responsibility. Nonparticipation in MA contracts also is due to a desire to avoid government red tape, control, rules, and regulations. For example, as of July 1, 1971, only $56 million had been claimed by NAB employers' contracts; $250,000,000 had been made available by the Department of Labor.[3]

The training contract presently being administered under the auspices of the Manpower Development Training Act (MDTA) is called the MA-7, or "JOBS '70." Its purpose is to hire and train a specified number of unemployed, or underemployed, persons in permanent employment, in jobs that provide an opportunity for advancement to jobs of higher responsibility.

The JOBS '70 contract is divided into two parts. The "Entry Program" is directed at hiring and training the hardcore disadvantaged. Under provisions of this section, a company must agree to hire all employees prior to training. The "Upgrading Program," recognizing that in industry there are many persons who lack the skills and training to advance without unusual assistance, provides funds for the upgrading of a limited number of present employees.

The elements of the training program itself are left to the employer. The actual on-the-job training must be provided by the employer; however, the other services may be subcontracted to other agencies. Some of the suggested elements of the program are:
(1) initial orientation and counseling
(2) job-related basic education
(3) on-the-job training
(4) special counseling and job coaching
(5) medical and dental services
(6) supervisory and human relations
(7) transportation
(8) child care assistance.
The list is not meant to be all-inclusive; it merely presents some of the key elements. However, on-the-job training, special counseling, and job coaching are mandatory. The overall length of the program is not less than 8 weeks or longer than 45 weeks.

Since the amount and type of training and services will vary with employers, the funds granted are based on the training and services actually provided. The employer submits receipts and vouchers to the government for reimbursement of actual expenses. This simplified approach was instituted to eliminate some of the previous administrative difficulties and complexities.

A second major function of NAB is the procurement of pledges for hiring the hardcore disadvantaged. A valuable service provided by NAB is the arrangement of support programs. Supervisors and management must be aware of the special problems that hardcore employees have. NAB offers a *first line supervisor workshop*, as well as a *middle managers workshop*, designed to train supervisors and middle managers to work and communicate effectively with the new employee.

A third support service introduces the employer to the *buddy system*. Here, an experienced worker assists the new employee in adjusting to his new environment.

METRO ORGANIZATIONS

The operations of NAB are conducted through local offices—Metros—located in standard metropolitan statistical areas of the country. Initially 50 in number, there are presently 168 Metros.

The Metro, like the national office, is staffed with volunteers from the business sector. The key executive, the chairman in each office, is appointed by the president of the United States. Another executive, selected from within his firm by the Metro office chairman, provides the active administration of office activities, and he and the office chairman serve as Metro directors. A manager of job procurement and placement is responsible for soliciting pledges. A manager of recruiting and government programs works with local public and private agencies that can refer unemployed persons to job openings. Additional staff for the Metro office is solicited by the chairman from other major companies in the Metro area. Most of the staff personnel and executives are on loan from such companies.

Some of the clerical personnel within the Metro organization are employed by the DOL, and they remain at their assignments indefinitely. Volunteer personnel serve for one year, after which a new chairman is appointed and a new staff is recruited by the chairman.

Members of each Metro organization call on area businessmen and encourage them to participate in the JOBS program. The nature of the solicitation program is left to the Metro chairman. These programs often involve at least one major affair, such as a dinner-banquet, followed by various solicitation schemes. Each Metro directs extensive recruiting efforts toward a target number of employees to be placed and/or companies to be sold.

ACHIEVEMENTS AND CRITICISMS OF THE NAB

In its first four years, NAB claimed to have provided more than 965,000 job opportunities through almost 56,000 participating companies. Seventy-five percent of those hired were trained at the expense of the participating businesses and without the help of the MA contracts. The program had the potential not only to relieve the welfare rolls of some of their burdens, but also to save tax money which could then be used to finance more MA contracts.

While the president of the United States, the National Alliance of Businessmen, and the local Metro offices have proclaimed the successes of their program, others have expressed doubt and skepticism. An article in the October 27, 1969 issue of the *New York Times*, under the headline "Dissidence in JOBS Aid Alliance," reports some of the questions skeptics are asking. The article alleges that more than half the people hired under the JOBS program have left their jobs. The quality of jobs was questioned, and many were said to be low-level "dead-end" jobs such as porters, maids, parking lot attendants, and dishwashers. The question of participation of black businessmen and professionals in NAB decision making and staff activities was raised, and some blacks were quoted as being displeased at not having been consulted or included. In the same article, Roy Durbin, speaking for the Chicago Metro, cites low-level jobs as a "way to get a foot in the door" of the business establishment.

Are the people being hired actually "hardcore" or would they find employment without the JOBS program? The criteria listed earlier (that participants are school dropouts, over 45 or under 22 years old, handicapped or subject to special obstacles to employment) allow considerable latitude in the selection of employees. These questions go to the heart of the federal government's actual commitment to the program and the effectiveness of private industry's efforts.

Senator Gaylord Nelson found that the NAB figures for employment were not verifiable.[4] Because 75 percent of the participating companies were not receiving DOL funds, the government could not require them to submit to employment audits. Moreover, it was revealed that on occasion NAB had intervened with DOL compliance officers on behalf of the 25 percent of firms holding MA contracts. The intervention was aimed at preventing what NAB considered harassment of these firms by government officers in requesting more detailed documentation of this MA contract work.

The hearings, held by Senator Nelson, also revealed that the NAB may report pledges received as being actual placements. Sometimes a firm may make a pledge but fail to follow through on it. Thus, reporting of pledges, as well as nonreporting of terminations, served to inflate statistics regarding the success of the NAB program.

The Committee also cited the following deficiencies in the program:

(1) It is vulnerable to economic recessions, and it may bring much frustration, especially to JOBS employees who were hired and then laid off.

(2) There are questions as to whether the on-the-job training, basic education,

medical services, and other benefits paid for by the DOL have, in fact, been supplied. In some instances, it is clear that they have not.

(3) The desire for quick results, both by the DOL contract negotiators and NAB personnel, and pressure from NAB sponsors preclude serious monitoring of the program.

(4) There is a high turnover among disadvantaged youth under 21 years of age.

(5) Frauds are perpetrated by "fly-by-night" consulting and education agencies. Some employers suspect even legitimate agencies of abbreviating their programs so that employees can be put to work rapidly. These employees sometimes are retained at the minimum wage until the government subsidy expires, and then they are dismissed.

(6) Dead-end jobs offer few prospects for long-run advancement.

NAB RESPONSE TO CRITICISM

NAB is aware of the criticisms leveled at the group. Their response has been to point to the record. They say the program is succeeding overall in doing what it was designed to do: provide meaningful employment at full pay and benefits to people otherwise considered unemployable. NAB adds that 75 percent of the firms participating in the JOBS program do not claim any DOL funds under the MA programs. Rather, these firms themselves absorb the full costs of training. As for the accuracy of the data, NAB agrees that evaluation and monitoring are not as rigorous as they might be. With a 75 percent rate of company-financed participation, they feel that there is little need to harass businesses about the accuracy of their data. NAB contends that these companies have nothing to gain or lose by inflating the information they give. Why should their integrity be impugned by headcounts and by peering over the shoulders of their volunteers?

As for the remaining 25 percent of the participating firms, NAB denies any attempt at circumventing DOL compliance reviews of companies. They recognize the necessity of auditing to insure that federal funds are being properly spent, but they request that the federal government recognize their volunteer status and not harass them with paperwork requirements and excessive on-site reviews.

Even NAB officials admit that there is no way to insure that noncontract people actually do what they say they are doing. Chicago, cited by DOL officials as one of the three or four most active Metro offices in terms of rendering follow-up service to volunteering companies, has been criticized with regard to noncontract people. In the previously cited senate subcommittee hearings, auditors of the Government Accounting Office revealed that a review of the files of 283 enrollees in Chicago indicated that one-third of the employees hired were ineligible to be called hardcore unemployed, and 62 files did not have sufficient data so that any determination could be made.

If this is any indication of the effectiveness of the NAB/JOBS program, especially taking into consideration that 75 percent of the enrollees are noncontract companies, then proper implementation has been more a dream than a reality.

FOOTNOTES

[1] Donald M. Graham, former chairman of Chicago Alliance of Businessmen, speech before Graduate Management Association, Northwestern University, November 4, 1969.

[2] President Nixon letter to Gordon M. Metcalf, chairman of NAB, February 5, 1973.

[3] "Getting NAB's Number," *Business and Society*, Vol. 2, No. 8, (October 14, 1971).

[4] Senator Gaylord Nelson, chairman of the Senate Subcommittee on Employment, Manpower and Poverty, of the Committee on Labor and Public Welfare, Ninety-first Congress, 2nd Session, held hearings on the NAB in April, 1970. These hearings tended to substantiate much of the adverse publicity which the NAB had received.

Lawrence G. Lavengood, Martha Ottinger, Stephen L. Schlecht *

CRISIS AT CARSON'S

Until about 10:40 AM on Friday, March 29, 1968, business was going on as usual in Carson, Pirie, Scott's State Street store. At 10:45 AM, fire alarms were sounded throughout the store. Four thousand customers and employees were swiftly evacuated. No one was hurt, but seventy pieces of fire department equipment raced to the scene. Four hundred firemen battled blazes discovered in six separate locations in the building. A public address system blared out to the people milling in the streets: "Carson's is closed until further notice. Please go home and listen to the news for information."

That evening the news media reported fires at four Chicago department stores, all within three blocks of each other. Goldblatt Brothers and Wieboldt's reported slight damage. Montgomery Ward and Company estimated its loss at $50,000. This figure paled into insignificance alongside the report from Carson, Pirie, Scott and Company. Carson's officials set the initial damage estimate at $20 million.

This material was prepared by Martha Ottinger, utilizing public sources, material furnished by Carson, Pirie, Scott & Company, and a student report by Stephen L. Schlecht. It was done under the supervision of Professor L. G. Lavengood of Northwestern University's Graduate School of Management.

"Who?" and "why?" were the questions uppermost in the minds of Chicagoans. A security guard at one of the stores reported that a Negro youth had been seen fleeing from an area where a fire was later discovered. A rumor started and spread as fast as the fires: "The Negroes are burning up State Street."

At 9 AM the following Saturday, Carson's executives, assisted by carpenters, sales people, stock clerks, and clerical people, began "Operation Cleanup." There was to be no "fire sale"; instead, all smoke-damaged goods were to be replaced with fresh, clean merchandise. The store was to reopen as soon as possible.

John T. Pirie, Jr., chairman of the board, told reporters, "It's definitely arson. We have evidence."[1] He offered a $25,000 reward for information leading to the conviction of the persons responsible for igniting the fires.

BACKGROUND

Those who scanned Carson's history and its present operations in search of clues to explain the fires were baffled.

After C. Virgil Martin joined Carson's in 1948, a Negro was hired to fill a management position at the downtown store. It was not only a first for Carson's; it was a first for any Chicago department store. Nine years later, Carson's broke the unwritten "color line" on State Street when they put a Negro into a "visible" sales position. Martin, who had been manager of a council of social agencies in Indianapolis before he entered the retailing business, saw to it that the store actively supported the Chicago Urban League and the Chicago Commission on Human Relations.

Under Carson's Double E program,[2] additional progress was made in the area of minority employment. The program began in 1961 when Carson's hired 59 high school dropouts aged 16 to 21. Each employee was assigned to a job in the store for three days a week and attended school two days a week; three teachers were furnished by the Chicago Board of Education. Two students were assigned to each paying job. While one worked in the store, the other attended school. Pay began at $1 per hour for every hour spent on the job. In the classroom, regular subjects were taught, but special emphasis was given to matters related to retailing. Of the 59 who entered in July, 1961, 39 successfully completed a year with the program. Most took permanent jobs with Carson's and indicated that they would complete their education at night. Some returned to high school full time. The pilot program was considered such a success that Carson's continued it. An average of 50 Double E students per year were hired by Carson's after they had completed the program. The entering classes are carefully balanced between male and female and black and white.

Between 1948, when the first black person was hired in management, and 1968, the year of the catastrophic fire, Carson's continued to hire blacks. A 1968 report submitted to the Department of Labor showed that 19.2 percent of Carson's State Street work force were from minority groups, with the largest proportion being black.

Recalling this record in minority employment, the Carson's associates asked, "Why us?" as they went about cleaning and restocking the store, which common opinion held had been damaged deliberately by a black person or persons.

EVENTS LEADING UP TO THE FIRE

In Chicago's black community, there was a strong skepticism that a black had set the fires. On April 2, 1968, Chicago's leading black newspaper, the *Chicago Daily Defender*, carried an article that read:

> Is a Negro arsonist responsible for the rash of fires that struck State Street stores last Friday? The Chicago Police Department seems to think so, and consequently has issued for circulation a pencil drawing of a Moorish-looking youth with slanted eyes and square jaws.
>
> But some black people think the police and white community in general is acting out of panic. Russ Meek, chairman of the militant Black Impeachment Committee, said: "I think they are doing this out of fear. This is merely a "bogeyman" conjured up because of the uprising in Memphis. People who are guilty of the genocidal exploitation of blacks, as white merchants are, would naturally feel from massive guilt complexes that any incident that inflcits damage upon their property or person results from a deliberately designed retribution by the object of their persecution.

The uprising in Memphis was a strike for higher wages by that city's garbage collectors. The Reverend Martin Luther King, Jr., was assassinated after he had lent his personal support to the garbage collectors. Part of the national reaction to this event of April 4 was violence in the cities; Chicago was one of the hardest hit.

In the time between the date of the fire and the death of Dr. King, the associates of Carson, Pirie, Scott and Company had made a magnificent effort, and much of the store was reopened for business on Wednesday, April 3, 1968. Many shoppers came in on Wednesday and Thursday. Then came Dr. King's assassination. Riots and fires in the ghetto areas of Chicago were followed by looting. The West Side of the city was aflame for two days. The Chicago Police Department proved unequal to the challenge and turned to the governor of Illinois for help. The Illinois National Guard and guardsmen from other states came to Chicago to help bring the city under control.

At Carson's there were few shoppers on Friday and Saturday. The long hours put into "Operation Cleanup" seemed almost futile. The massive fire, the assassination of Dr. King, and the subsequent rioting indicated to Carson's top management that a new understanding of the problem of operating a business in the inner city was necessary if Carson's were to remain in business in Chicago.

REORIENTATION TO THE "URBAN CRISIS"

Approximately two weeks after the fire, Norbert F. Armour, executive vice-president of Carson's, met with William Cohea, Jr., executive director of the Chicago Business Industrial Project. Established in 1963 with the help of the National Industrial Mission Association, the group was known as a dialogue center for competing groups inside and outside the city's power structure.

The meeting between Armour and Cohea sparked a full-day off-site, "off-the-record" conference for 21 top executives at Carson's. The topic was the "Urban Racial Crisis." John T. Pirie, Jr., chairman of the board, and C. Virgil Martin, president of Carson's, were deliberately excluded from this conference so that the other executives would talk more freely. Invited to attend were the executive vice-presidents of the retail division, the wholesale floor coverings division, the planning and development area of the real estate division, eleven vice-presidents of various areas in the retail division, the president of the international airports restaurants, and six of the company's corporate officers.

Excerpts from Armour's introductory speech give the purposes of the initial meeting held on May 29, 1968:

> The best comparison I know is as though we had decided to enter a foreign market. We would expect to analyze it, research it, learn all about how to do business in a new market. We would try to determine the costs and the possibilities of making a profit. Only if we were satisfied with all we could find out would we enter the market.
>
> In this situation, we are not going into a new market. The new market is coming to us. And we don't have a choice about whether or not we are going into it. If we are going to continue in the retail business in the metropolitan areas of Illinois, we are going to have to learn the facts about this situation, and learn them fast. . . .
>
> These consultants are here to tell us about the new setting for our business as they see it. We are here to do two things. First, to learn all we can from what the consultants have to tell us, and second, to talk together with complete frankness about what we think of what we hear and try to answer the question, "What does this mean for Carsons's?"
>
> It is not important whether we approve or disapprove of what our consultants have to tell us. "Good" or "bad," "right" or "wrong" doesn't matter. We think we have consultants who will tell us what *is*. And we're not here to say we "like" or "dislike" what we hear. I suspect most of us will not "like" it. But it is important that we *understand* what is happening, *hear* what is being said, and *see* the new circumstances in which we have to do business.
>
> We want our discussion to be frank and open. It has to be if ever top management at Carson's is going to handle our business in the future in this new setting. I promise there are going to be no notes taken about who said

what or what somebody felt about something. Personalities are not important. I want to know what you think and what you propose for the future because what we need is solutions. We need to find out the new ways we have to do business if Carson's is to thrive in the new urban setting with which we are confronted. Nobody knows all of the answers. But if we are frank and open, all of us have parts of some of the answers. And we can develop directions leading to solutions.

As most of you know, Carson's caught the attention of Chicago in the 1950s when we began to integrate our staff of associates. Whatever we may have thought of it then, I think we can all acknowledge now that the move was good—good for Carson's and good for the community. But what was good then may not any longer be sufficient. We may have to do something different if we are going to be the leaders in the 1970s that we were in the 1950s. That, I hope, is what we are here to learn, and what we are here to discuss together.

RESPONSE TO THE REORIENTATION PROGRAM

The reaction to the first session was positive. The participants felt that they had gained an awareness and sensitivity to the black condition.

Sixty more executives attended additional sessions in August, 1968. At these, the black panel members spoke freely and forcefully. They used shock techniques to acquaint participants with black ghetto life and with the concept of black power. Four-letter words were used frequently. Role playing and game simulation techniques were used to illustrate differing points of view about race perspectives.

When the August sessions were completed, it was agreed that every supervisor in every Chicago-area store should receive similar training on the urban racial crisis.

After the two August conferences, the seminars were expanded to two days. More than 500 people were divided into groups of 15 to 25. A great deal of planning was required so that the work areas would be covered while supervisors attended two-day conferences, which began in October, 1968 and were completed in July, 1969.

The seminars were considered most helpful because of the introductory talks by the black panelists and the role playing. One participant said that the role playing made him feel the frustration that blacks experience in so many areas of life. Another participant said that black people must be given more responsibility in order to be able to prove their ability. Most participants reported receiving new insights into black problems. The question, "What new insights have you gained into white problems?" puzzled many participants. One responded, "The white problem is that they have never realized that the black problem is their problem."

Questions such as "What was most helpful?", "What was least helpful?",

"What new insights have you gained into black problems?", and "How do you rate your leadership?" were asked of each participant. The composite of all answers was an indication of where to start acting on some of the ideas that had come in. The leadership of the sessions was rated on a scale of 1 to 10 with 10 being the highest award. By far the greatest percentage of the participants rated the leadership in the 8, 9, and 10 area.

A series of three-day workshops on human and race relations for branch store managers and assistant managers, personnel managers and first-line supervisors was held concurrently with the Chicago Business Industrial Project workshops for State Street supervisors. Their program was conducted by Applied Behavioral Science, Inc., under the direction of William DeVries, executive director. Sixteen workshops were held with a total of 190 participants. Confrontation and shock techniques were avoided with these people. Emphasis was placed on informative lectures, film documentaries, group introspection, and practical tools which supervisors could use in relating to their daily tasks. Course topics included a study of individual attitudes and preconceived notions about people from other social and ethnic groups, presentations on the attitudes and social conditions of various minority group people, and exercises in applying human relations principles and good management.

The outcome of the first three conferences was:

(1) There was immediate clarification and support of a personnel policy dealing with fair employment.

(2) A "Policy and Design" committee was established. Chaired by Executive Vice-President Armour, the committee was broken into four task forces covering the areas of personnel, economics, community, and sales promotions. Each task force was subdivided into relevant subcommittees. Fifteen executives comprised the "policy and design" committee and another 40 were assigned to the task force subcommittees.

A SEARCH FOR NEW POLICIES

After attending the urban crisis seminars or workshops, Carson employees were asked to help solve some of the problems by signing up with one of the task forces. In a report to the National Retail Merchants Association in August, 1969, Personnel Vice-President William G. Mitchell reported that 133 associates from all divisions of Carson's were actively examining past practices, assessing necessary changes, and developing new programs and techniques.

The 15-member Policy and Design Committee included 8 of the 21 executives who had attended the May seminar, 3 divisional merchandise managers from the retail division, 2 additional employees from the personnel department, and 1 from the operating division. The first two meetings of the whole committee were on October 14, 1968 and November 5, 1968. However, the associates were reluctant to attend meetings just as the heaviest sales period of the year was beginning. When some of the subcommittees met and came up with new ideas, no one was available to evaluate or implement these suggestions. As the need for a staff coordinator became obvious, Mary Dolan, previously on the executive staff of a Chicago race relations agency, Friendship House, was named to the post. Almost immediately after Miss Dolan joined Carson's staff, criticism arose because a white woman had been named to this position.

Discontent was also expressed because the Policy and Design committee had no black representation. The committee's original purposes had been:
(1) to reach out and define areas where Carson's was lacking the commitment to the total urban community which the 1970s require
(2) to make recommendations to bring about change.
But no Carson's minority group associates were on the committee that was composed of top management; no minority group people held positions in top management.

A December, 1968, memorandum from J. Gordon Gilkey, director of civic affairs, set priorities for the Policy and Design committee:
(1) establish a continuing training program for the current and future minority employees and continue training for supervisors, particularly supervisors of employees at "entry level" positions
(2) encourage black business; try to buy from black vendors, deposit some of the Carson's money in black-owned banks, and advertise in black newspapers.

The Policy and Design committee did not meet after December. Spring of 1969 brought the task force subcommittees out of hibernation. The employment subcommittee took seriously the statement from the United States Equal Employment Opportunity Commission that "at the foundation of any new policy is the company's firm and explicit commitment to visible progress in minority participation." A survey of Carson's established that the number of minority group associates was good but that weak spots existed. The employment subcommittee made a detailed analysis of patterns and planned to interview managers of areas with few minority employees to show them how to correct the situation.

The training subcommittee analyzed the type and range of training needed for job advancement. The first need was identified as training for new supervisors. The subcommittee members planned to work with experienced trainers to develop a pilot program.

The identification subcommittee attempted to determine how to increase opportunities for those associates who were "locked in" at lower level jobs. Two black associates were sent to a new management skills program at the University of Chicago.

Job posting was begun at the State Street store so that associates would know when better jobs were available. Forty-five associates were involved in "Project Upgrade"—an in-store program of part-time education that would give employees in entry level jobs the chance to obtain basic skills and increase their chances of promotion.

Carson's opportunity scholarships were made available to six "educationally disadvantaged and culturally distinct" associates for full-time study at the Chicago Circle Campus of the University of Illinois.

When C. Virgil Martin was asked about the cost of all these seminars and the administration costs of the "employee opinion survey," he replied that rough estimates were in the area of $250,000. He pointed out that there was no way to determine the benefits in relation to the amount spent. Top management was inclined to defer benefit analysis in this area, unless the store's reports should indicate that the company was losing money. The annual report for the fiscal year ended February 1, 1969, stated:

> We are, of course, pleased to report to you that, despite this major upheaval (the fire), Carson Pirie Scott & Company registered another year of growth. Again, we must express our most sincere appreciation to the loyal personnel and customers who made this possible.

The original estimate of $20 million in damage made on the day of the fire was reduced considerably. The insurance company reimbursement to Carson's was $7 million.

In May, 1969, 25 management people at Carson's were interviewed to determine if there had been any significant change in attitudes after a year's time and after so much money had been spent to help the associates learn to do business in a new setting. Some of their comments were:

> "We're so far out in front today, why should we do any more?"

> "The structure of the subcommittees on Policy and Design was bad—people were assigned to them instead of being allowed to choose. P & D really has no direction and doesn't know where to go."

> "Our shopper traffic at State Street is 60 percent black. We have a morale problem. There is significant shoplifting. The buyers are frustrated—too many demands are made on their time. The fire served to show us what we hadn't done."

> "We would like to arrange a joint venture in the black community and would put up $250,000. We recognize the need for a strong economically viable community in which to do business. We have no desire to work with other State Street merchants."

> "Carson's definition of its relation to the community has not changed over the last ten years; it has been a gradual implementation of ideas; the fire, if responsible for anything, created somewhat of a backlash among top management—a questioning of what they had been doing."

> "I was strongly offended by the vulgarity in our urban crisis sessions—and concerned for my female associates."

> "The design of the 'feedback training sessions' was haphazard."

> "The Policy and Design Committee has no direction and we haven't made any progress. Maybe the vendors sub-committee could really do some-

thing—my committee can't (Banking and Finance)."

From a female divisional merchandise manager: "Policy and Design is an extracurricular activity. My training subcommittee has only met once. There aren't any blacks ready to serve on the committee. My buyers and I resent having employees with jail records. We are scared."

"The objectives of top management are 'internal'—i.e., hire more blacks, assimilate and integrate them into the system."

"Our first black mannequin appeared in State Street windows three years ago. We have limited advertising in the *Daily Defender*. I don't think it has much significance. The fire provided the momentum for all this, but management hasn't really changed for the most part—they're just playing the game."

"There are too many meetings for us to get our jobs done. First they tell you to concentrate on your job because of the profit squeeze and then they require you to spend time away from the job at meetings."

What is the white salesperson's reaction to the changes at Carson's? Some indication of what still remains to be done can be gleaned from the following interview with a white salesperson who had been employed at Carson's for seven years:

Let me tell you 'they' are going out to get these people and they're getting the better jobs.

They go to school every day for two hours and get paid 25 cents an hour more when in school than when on the floor. That doesn't sound like much but it's $10 a week and $40 a month.

Fair's fair—certainly they should be hired but they should be treated equal—not better.

Changes are evident at Carson's. Black models are used in advertisements. There are black mannequins in various departments of the store. In February, 1970, a black cosmetician demonstrated makeup designed especially for black skins. Large crowds were attracted to her week-long demonstrations, and the store now stocks her full line of cosmetics.

An assessment of Carson's reorientation program is perhaps best summarized by the comments of two managers intimately connected with the program. They state:

While there were, for obvious reasons, a variety of reactions on the part of the many hundreds of individuals at Carson, Pirie, Scott and Co. who were involved in the program, on balance, it would be our conclusion that the final result was on the constructive and positive side.

Many individuals learned far more than they had known before about the frustrations and problems of being members of minority groups within the Chicago metropolitan area. A number of individuals, as a result of the program or stimulated by what they had experienced through the program, have become involved in constructive activities both inside and outside the store. The company as a whole was sensitized to the seriousness of the problem, and while no easy answers have been found, the search for solutions has continued. We would be the first to recognize that the search has not been as vigorous as many minority people might wish, but it is our conclusion that the search on the part of Carson's for constructive and viable solutions is both more informed and more energetic because of the program than it might otherwise have been.

It can be stated as a fact that we are not satisfied with the progress made, and we are continuing our efforts, recognizing the seriousness of the problem and that the future well-being of the community and the company rests upon our success in finding answers.

FOOTNOTES

1 *Chicago Daily News*, March 30, 1968, p. 1.

2 Employment and Education Program.

Steve M. Director, Samuel I. Doctors *

BLACK EMPLOYMENT IN THE CHICAGO LABOR MARKET: A CRITIQUE

THE BLACK IN THE CHICAGO LABOR MARKET

The 1970 population of the Chicago Standard Metropolitan Statistical Area was slightly more than 7 million persons. Approximately 1.3 million (about 20 percent) of these persons are nonwhite. (Since blacks constitute more than 95 percent of the area's nonwhite population, the terms black and nonwhite will be used interchangeably in this paper.) Despite the large growth in the black population (up almost 20 percent since 1960), Chicago remains one of the most residentially segregated cities in the nation, and the minority population is therefore distributed very unevenly throughout the metropolitan area. Several neigh-

*Steve Director is currently Assistant Professor, Wayne State University, Graduate School of Business Administration.

borhoods in the far northwest sections of the city had no black residents at the time of the 1970 census, while the residential area just south of Chicago's central business district contained two large neighborhoods (with combined population of almost 124,000) where more than 99 percent of the residents were black.

Of the slightly less than 1.3 million nonwhites in the metropolitan area, 59.5 percent were classified as labor force participants in 1970. During 1970, the Chicago unemployment rate for white males 20 years and older averaged just over 2 percent. The jobless rate for black males of the same age was approximately twice this figure.

The figures stated above are metropolitan area averages and do not accurately reflect the severity of the problem in many of Chicago's black neighborhoods. One Chicago neighborhood, which was among six poverty areas surveyed in 1969 by the Department of Labor, contained 79,300 nonwhite and 2,800 white labor force participants. Of the area's white males 20 years and older, 8.3 percent had experienced unemployment during the previous year. The proportion of the area's 35,400 blacks 20 years and older who had experienced unemployment was 18.6 percent; for blacks 16 and older, it was 24.3 percent. Forty percent of the black males over 20 who experienced unemployment had remained unemployed for more than a month, 20 percent for more than 3.5 months, and 7.5 percent for more than 6.5 months. These figures compare with overall metropolitan unemployment figures of one-third or less those found in this black neighborhood. Since many of the persons in the male/over 20 category are family breadwinners, the duration of unemployment becomes a critical factor. Similar conditions existed in the five other cities included in a survey conducted by the Bureau of Labor Statistics in 1970.[1]

The same survey recorded the occupational distribution of 33,000 of the area's employed black males over 20. Not surprisingly, the survey revealed that 75 percent were blue collar workers, 11.4 percent were service workers, 8.1 percent held clerical jobs, and only 4.3 percent could be classified as either professionals, technicians, or managers. The occupational distribution of the black workers in this neighborhood is not unusual; Equal Employment Opportunity Commission (EEOC) statewide data indicates an even greater concentration of black workers in blue collar and service categories. Obviously, this type of occupational distribution results in lower incomes for black families. In 1970, the average annual income for all black families was $6,279; for white families, it was $10,236. (The overall figure for nonwhite income, nationally, was $6,516 in 1970. See Table I in James Weaver's "Economic Causes of Social Unrest" in Section I of this volume.)

The white business establishment sometimes has tried to deny that such statistics as presented in this paper constitute proof of discriminatory hiring and promotion practices. These persons do not argue with the validity of the statistics, but they argue that the statistics simply reflect economically rational responses to racial differences in education and occupational experience. To a degree, this is true. However, as Barron and Hymer point out, "At every educational level and in every occupational category, Negroes have a considerably higher rate of unemployment than whites."[2]

This paper will attempt to describe some of the problems and experiences of the minority workers living in the Chicago area, with emphasis on three specific industries: air transport, steel, and banking. These industries were chosen because they each have a major impact on the Chicago economy and because they exhibit many of the types of problems faced by minority workers. Also, they represent quite different growth characteristics: banking is a high-growth industry, steel is a low-growth industry, and air transport is in the middle range of growth. If career opportunity is assumed to be related at least partially to the industrial growth rate, then one would assume that these industries would exhibit significantly different levels of opportunity. However, no claim is made that these three industries are representative of all industry in the United States or even of all industry in the Chicago area.

CHICAGO'S AIR TRANSPORT INDUSTRY

The 11 largest U.S. airlines account for more than 90 percent of the industry's annual revenues and employ more than a quarter of a million persons. Four companies dominate the industry. Department of Labor statistics indicate a steady growth in airline employment between 1947 and 1960, with a particularly rapid expansion during the 1960s after the jet-powered aircraft was introduced. The Chicago area has participated more than proportionally in this growth and is a major employment center for 8 of the 11 large airlines.[3]

Chicago's blacks have not been able to take advantage of these rapidly expanding employment opportunities. A 1969 EEOC survey revealed that blacks, as 15 percent of the area's population, held only 6.9 percent of the area's airline jobs.[4] At least part of this underrepresentation has been attributed to the fact that most of Chicago's blacks live in the inner city, while most of the airline jobs are located at Chicago's two major airports, a considerable distance away.

If distance to the work site were a major factor, one would expect that, as Albert Rees and George Schultz have demonstrated,[5] only those individuals who hold the most desirable jobs will be willing to tolerate the considerable time and expense involved in commuting. However, one finds that those blacks who *do* work at the airports are concentrated in the lowest paying and least desirable jobs. According to the 1969 EEOC data, of 1,254 airline officials and managers in the Chicago area, 10 were black males and 2 were black females. In 1969, Chicago area airlines employed 2,364 professional people, 5 of whom were black males, and 1 was a black female. Comprising 8.3 percent of the industry's Chicago area male work force, blacks held 32.3 percent of the airline jobs in the laborers' category and 35.6 percent of the jobs in the service worker categories.[6] Although comprising only 5.5 percent of females employed by Chicago airlines, black women constituted 87.8 percent of those female employees categorized as laborers! The EEOC study also pointed out that job discrimination in the air transport industry has been just as hard on Chicago's Spanish-surnamed (with 1.4 precent representation) and American Indian populations (with 0.0 percent representation).

Before further examining minority employment patterns in the Chicago area, it is necessary to describe certain industry characteristics that have a direct bearing on employment practices. Approximately 90 percent of the industry's revenue is derived from ticket sales to business and vacation travelers. In recent years airline sales and profits have been low. The direct impact of this situation on black employees becomes clear when one considers that personnel costs represent 38 percent of airline operating expenses. Special training or upgrading programs for minority employees, plus the higher costs of recruitment, absenteeism, turnover, and reduced efficiency that are often initially associated with "disadvantaged" workers become a corporate cost which the companies eliminate in lean times.

Few, if any, industries are more closely regulated than the air transport industry. This regulation influences all aspects of the industry's operation, including its personnel practices. The Civil Aeronautics Act of 1938 not only specified certain employment practices (primarily those relating to pilots), but it also required that carriers conduct their labor relations in accordance with the provisions of the Railway Labor Act. This prohibited industrial unionism and restricted collective bargaining units to a "craft or class."

Having a different union for each craft has worked as a serious impediment to the upgrading of minority employees. For example, if a semiskilled person in a ramp or aircraft service group wanted to be a mechanic, it is unlikely that he would be able to transfer from one union to the other, and retain his seniority in the old union. With most blacks currently concentrated in the least skilled jobs, the craft system is making it very difficult for them to advance.

The airlines also are subject to regulation specifically designed to enhance the opportunities open to minority employees. The two primary regulatory agencies in this area are the EEOC, which administers Title VII of the Civil Rights Act of 1964, and the Office of Federal Contract Compliance, which enforces Executive Order No. 11246 pertaining to the minority employment practices of contractors to the government. (The airlines are contract carriers of the U.S. mails.) Both of these agencies have no doubt been a prime force behind the airlines' efforts to increase the percentage of black employees in the industry's rapidly growing work force.

The paucity of black officials and managers is due to several factors. First, most of the airlines' top officials have been promoted from within the industry. Since blacks have only recently been allowed to enter the airlines' management hierarchy, they have not yet had time to progress along the corporate job ladder. Airlines also recruit managers from among former pilots, a group that historically has contained very few nonwhites. Like many industries, the airlines now are attempting to hire young black college graduates as management trainees, but these efforts have had no significant impact because few blacks possess the desired technical or business degrees.

There are more than 35,000 commercial pilots and co-pilots in the U.S., but less than 100 of them are black.[7] The airlines recruit 90 percent of these pilots from among former military fliers, so that it appears that any increase in the number of black commercial pilots will have to be preceded by a corresponding increase in black military pilots. This does not seem likely to occur in the near future: as of 1969, only 252 of 52,650 Navy and Air Force flight personnel were black.

Airlines also employ lawyers, meteorologists, engineers, economists, and accountants, but the number of blacks with such professional credentials is so small that even the most aggressive minority recruitment program is likely to have little effect in the near term.

The stewardess category is one for which there is probably no shortage of qualified black applicants, but this is an area from which blacks historically have been excluded. Not until the late 1950s did the airlines, at the insistance of state fair employment practices commissions, begin to hire black stewardesses. After an initial period of apprehension over customer reaction (during which the airlines made a special effort to hire light-skinned blacks and avoided placing them on Southern routes), the airlines became more aggressive in their attempts to recruit black stewardesses. Many airlines now recruit at predominately black schools and through other black organizations. Although the proportion of black stewardesses is still small (less than 3 percent in 1970), it is growing rapidly.

Because of the public contact aspects of the job, airlines were slow to employ blacks as ticket and reservation agents. However, in recent years, the airlines have significantly increased the proportion of blacks in these positions. This could be an important development, because these positions have the earliest potential for movement into the supervisory and management ranks. Because these positions do provide an opportunity for promotion, and because high turnover necessitates frequent hiring, the ticket agent category has often been suggested as the most logical area in which to initiate special minority-upgrading programs.

Since blacks in our society traditionally have been servants, it is not surprising that airlines followed the railroads' example of employing black porters. These "skycaps" were once considered an ideal internal source of black labor that could be upgraded through the airlines' affirmative action programs, but many skycaps refused entry into these programs. While some may have been reluctant to make a change, the decision against upgrading was economically rational for many: with gratuities, their incomes (in some cases allegedly up to $15,000 per year) not only exceeded the training wages, but they often exceeded the wages of those considerably higher in the job progression. Most skycap crews are still all black, but many young blacks no longer wish to accept such positions.

Four major Chicago-based airlines currently are conducting upgrading programs. Three of these airlines conduct federally-assisted training classes for about 150 persons each, while the fourth airline, which receives no outside funds, trains 22 people. While all four programs were designed for any disadvantaged person, regardless of race, blacks comprise the vast majority of trainees.

To be accepted into these programs, the prospective trainee must meet two basic criteria: (1) he must be socially disadvantaged with severe problems in securing employment because of race or educational limitations; and (2) he must possess the physical ability and mental attitude that will enable him to develop into a useful employee. One company requires its trainees to pass a physical examination and to receive a favorable recommendation on the basis of a personal interview. The one company not receiving federal assistance adds the following requirements:

> Criminal records must be on the mild side, education, although not completed, must indicate potential to complete, must be 18 years of age or more, and must have demonstrated sometime in the past the usual qualities we seek in employment, that is, the willingness to learn, to cooperate and improve his personal situation.

If interpreted strictly, this restriction would screen out many of these persons most in need of the opportunities the training program could provide.

The initial training ranges from 8 to 25 weeks, followed by a 3 to 6 month probationary period. The training period consists of an orientation to the airline's structure, practices and equipment, and includes instruction in basic reading and mathematics. During this period, the trainee receives daily counseling from his instructors and a full-time personnel counselor.

After the orientation period, the trainee either is transferred to an additional school or is placed in the work force to receive on-the-job training. While working alongside and competing with persons hired through normal channels, the trainee continues to receive individual counseling for up to 12 months if necessary.

At each airline studied, management attempted to persuade supervisors to give the trainee every possible chance to succeed in his new job. This "convincing" often took place at meetings between management and supervisory personnel held prior to placement of graduates. Supervisors were told the objectives of the program and the types of problems that might arise, and they were told that they *would* cooperate because the program was supported by the airlines' chief executives.

Many airline officials felt that while the trainees were physically and mentally capable of holding most of the jobs held by other employees, they often were psychologically unready to assume too great a degree of responsibility. One airline does start a small percentage of its trainees as reservation and ticket agents, but the other three start all their trainees in low-status positions (aircraft cleaners, janitors, kitchen workers, cargo handlers, and so on). Hopefully, advancement to higher status positions will follow.

Even if programs such as those just described do continue, it is unlikely that they will significantly change the racial composition of the airlines' work force either nationally or in the Chicago area. During the 1960s when the airlines made their greatest progress in employing blacks, total airline employment increased by one-third. Today, if one telephones the employment offices of almost any Chicago-based airline, a tape recording will explain that the company is not accepting any employment applications (other than for stewardesses) and will suggest that the caller try again in a few months. Until the situation improves, blacks will be unable to increase their numbers much, even at the lowest occupational levels. At the managerial and professional levels, the supply of qualified black applicants is not even sufficient to meet the low demand of the country's present economic situation.

THE NEGRO IN CHICAGO'S STEEL INDUSTRY

The steel industry is a major employer in the Midwest, employing roughly 59,100 persons in the Chicago area and an additional 63,800 persons in nearby Gary-Hammond-East Chicago. The steel industry differs from both the air transport and banking industries in that it has not experienced steady growth in recent years; in fact, total industry employment is declining steadily. The major factors influencing the job situation in the industry over the past decade have been:
(1) declining employment
(2) large advances in technology resulting in adjustments in the work force and major capital expenditures
(3) the poor profit position of almost all companies in the industry
(4) significant imports of foreign steel that have threatened the competitive position of U.S. firms.[9]
    The steel industry has had to contend with all four of these problems at the same time it was struggling with the problems of recruiting and upgrading Negro workers.
    Blacks are *not* underrepresented in the steel industry work force. In 1969, blacks accounted for 25.5 percent of the industry's Chicago area employment and 21.3 percent of the industry's Gary-Hammond-East Chicago area employment. These statistics, however, do not tell the whole story, especially in regard to discriminatory employment practices in terms of upgrading.
    In 1930, 12.8 percent of all workers in the steel industry were Negro. Wage surveys conducted by the Bureau of Labor Statistics in 1935 and 1938 clearly revealed that the Depression affected black labor more seriously than white labor. Nevertheless, in 1937, the bureau reported that:

> The iron and steel industry is of outstanding importance as a field of employment for Negroes, since it is one of the few manufacturing industries in which Negro employment equals approximately the proportion of Negroes in the total population.

It is interesting to note that the 1969 EEOC data also indicates a 13.6 percent nationwide participation rate for Negroes in the primary metals industry.

In spite of the high percentage of blacks employed in Chicago steel plants, the industry has been accused of discriminatory hiring. Blacks have charged that steel mills do not hire them as laborers because of their race. Steel companies have denied this, but they have admitted that almost all persons hired as laborers were recommended by relatives, friends, or labor union officials, most of them past or present employees. Since most black applicants were unable to obtain recommendations from employees already in the industry, they were denied jobs. Obviously this type of referral system, which is practiced in many manufacturing industries, tends to perpetuate existing racial employment patterns.

In spite of discriminatory practices, many blacks have found employment in the steel industry. A large proportion (roughly 75 percent) of jobs in this industry can be done satisfactorily by blacks with limited education and experience. Blacks were allowed early access to steel industry jobs because of the dirty, unpleasant, backbreaking, and sometimes dangerous nature of the work. The steel industry has more black craftsmen than do the automobile, aerospace, rubber tire, petroleum, or chemical industries. One reason for this may be the fact that the industry uses many bricklayers, a trade in which blacks traditionally have been very strong.

The steel industry nationally is a major employer of blacks, and steel mills in the Midwest employ greater percentages of minorities than do those of any other region. The Midwest region employs not only the greatest percentage of blacks, but also has the largest proportion of skilled black workers, and it ranks second in the proportion of semi-skilled workers.

In recent years the number of blacks at *all* occupational levels has been increasing rapidly. This is true throughout the industry and particularly in the Chicago area. However, while important gains have been made in the number of blacks employed as officials and managers, steel companies still are not sending black salesmen to call on white customers.

There has been some upgrading from the unskilled and semiskilled levels. Rowan and Northrup have shown that many of the skilled jobs in steel are in the maintenance (craft) departments from which blacks have been traditionally excluded. Blacks work mainly in production departments with heavy black concentrations. So, in spite of a job structure which relies on seniority as the primary criterion for promotion, one can see why blacks cannot move to the top in many areas of the steel industry.

Collective bargaining agreements have rigidly defined an interplant mobility system that allows for only slow upward movement along departmental seniority lines, with loss of seniority and pay if departmental barriers are crossed. Thus, as in the airline industry, many black steelworkers have found themselves in departments where, regardless of seniority, there is little chance of ever reaching the craftsman level, and transferring out of the department would mean considerable sacrifice. Although the Steelworkers Union welcomes Negro members, it helps perpetuate the results of past discrimination by refusing to modify the basic departmental seniority system.

The greater degree of upward mobility enjoyed by white steelworkers is not totally attributable to departmental placement and seniority systems. Most white steelworkers were hired with the expectation that they would be promoted as rapidly as seniority allows, while most blacks were not expected to progress up the promotional hierarchy. White applicants thus were screened more closely and needed considerably higher qualifications than blacks needed. This meant easier entry for many blacks, but greater opportunities for most whites.

The industry is attempting to aid its minority workers. In May 1967, seven major American steel producers and the United Steelworkers of America, with the aid of $1 million in Manpower Development Training Act (MDTA) funds, initiated a 14-month pilot program to upgrade the basic education of 1,600 underprivileged steelworkers in the Baltimore and Chicago areas.

The Chicago-area participants were Inland Steel, National Steel Corporation, Youngstown Sheet and Tube, and United States Steel Corporation. Students were recruited on a voluntary basis from the ranks of those already employed. More than 50 percent of the students graduated in September 1967, had raised their grade level in reading from 3.2 to 6.0 and in arithmetic from 3.3 to 5.9. While numerous blacks did benefit from this program, the majority of the participants were first- and second-generation European immigrants who were illiterate or semi-literate long-standing employees.

The federal government provided an additional $900,000 to improve employment opportunities for those who had been rejected for jobs because of their limited education. This MDTA project was designed to run through November, 1969. All persons recruited for this program were processed through state employment agencies for "hardcore certification," based on need alone; no one was rejected because of his prison record, lack of identification, or poor past work record. In fact, persons with such histories were screened in, rather than out.

Recruits became trainees and employees at the same time. Many potential recruits found it hard to believe that they would be paid while going to school. To overcome this skepticism, various combinations of work, training, and schooling were tried during the 50-week program. Some participating companies also provided training for the supervisors in order to better equip them to understand and deal with the special problems of the "hardcore."

It is still too early to evaluate the impact of the program on the career potential of the trainees, but it is encouraging that foremen at Inland Steel recently rated a sample group of graduates significantly higher than a control group of nonparticipants in attitude toward work, understanding of verbal orders, job performance, and promotability.

Although the steel industry continues to engage in similar federally assisted training programs, it is unclear whether or not the number of black workers in the industry will continue to rise. As its total employment declines, the steel industry, once a leader in both the number of and proportion of Negroes employed, has been surpassed by the automobile industry and others with rapidly expanding employment opportunities.

THE NEGRO IN CHICAGO'S BANKING INDUSTRY

In contrast to the steel industry, banking is one of the country's leading growth industries and is likely to continue to provide numerous job opportunities for blacks. Many of these jobs will be located in downtown areas, close to many black communities. Besides obtaining incomes and careers for themselves, those blacks who enter banking management ranks could potentially have a considerable impact on the industry's investment decisions. Since banks are the nation's largest source of investment capital, a favorable shift in their investment policy could facilitate minority economic development.

The banking industry in the United States has grown steadily since its stabilization by the Federal Deposit Insurance Corporation in 1934. Currently there are more than 14,000 banks in the United States with total deposits and assets in excess of $400 billion and $500 billion, respectively. The 10 largest of these 14,000 banks control 25 percent of the total assets.

The nation's 50 largest banks are concentrated primarily in three states: New York, California, and Illinois. In Illinois, where branch banking is prohibited, large numbers of banks have located in the major metropolitan areas. Chicago is by far the largest of these metropolitan centers, and approximately 43 percent of all Illinois bank deposits ($31 billion) are in Chicago-area banks. In June, 1970, the Chicago-area banks employed 44,172 people.

Historically, total bank employment has grown rapidly, while the percentage of black employees has remained constant and small. In 1940, blacks comprised only 1.5 percent of the industry's 475,660 employees. By 1960, total industry employment had more than doubled, reaching 1,018,046 persons; however, minority representation still was less than 2 percent.

Substantial changes in the racial composition of the banking workforce did not occur until the mid-1960s. The personnel director of one of Chicago's largest banks estimates that, from 1960 to 1970, minority representation reached 20 to 24 percent of the work force. Although the trend is clear, the above estimate seems somewhat high. The most recent EEOC data (1969) indicates that of all Chicago Standard Metropolitan Statistical Area banking industry employees, only 10.4 percent were black and 1.9 percent were Spanish-surnamed Americans.

The EEOC data shows that in 1969 less than 13 percent of all Chicago area bank employees were members of minority groups. A 1971 study by Northwestern doctoral student Gerald Grey found 29.3 percent of bank employees at 21 Chicago area banks to be minority group members. It is probably misleading to conclude from these two figures that minority participation has doubled since 1969. Several factors could have contributed to this seemingly large differential.

First, during this period there was a significant (but less than 20 percent) increase in minority representation. An important factor which may have contributed significantly to this differential is the difference in the samples utilized by the two studies. Grey investigated 21 Chicago banks employing about 19,000 persons, while the EEOC surveyed 86 banks employing about 28,000 persons. Thus it can be seen that the EEOCs sample included a greater percentage of small banks. It is quite possible that these small banks were responsible for lowering the average minority participation rate.

Bank size has been demonstrated to correlate directly with the percentage of blacks employed.[10] The fact that large banks tend to be located in the central city rather than the suburbs may be one explanation for this. Grey found that the Chicago banks with the greatest proportions of black employees were located in the south and southwest areas of the city; the ones with the lowest percentages were located in the northern and far western sections. Anyone familiar with Chicago will recognize that this pattern correlates exactly with the rigid system of residential segregation found in Chicago. Location affects minority employment in two ways. It allows blacks quicker and cheaper access to the workplace, and it also causes management to be less reluctant to hire them. In white neighborhoods, management has often feared adverse customer reaction to black employees, but this is not a problem in neighborhoods where a large percentage of the customers are black.

It also has been suggested that large banks employ blacks because these banks have more sophisticated personnel officers and have more formalized hiring procedures. Larger banks are also more likely to possess the organizational and budgetary flexibility necessary to engage in special minority training and recruitment programs.

The distribution of minority workers within banking's job structure reflects the same types of discrimination present in other sectors of our society: the minorities are concentrated at the bottom. This type of racial workforce composition continues to exist despite the industry's efforts to change it. Approximately 50 percent of the banks studied by Grey had made special efforts to hire minorities. Some personnel officers working for banks that had made no such efforts stated that they felt hiring on the basis of race rather than on qualifications would violate fair employment practices. Others explained that strained budgets did not permit special recruiting and hiring efforts.

In some banks, "attempting to hire black employees" meant merely compiling information on available jobs and providing this information to potential employees through the Urban League or through ads in minority-oriented media. Other banks, however, have initiated special programs to increase minority employment opportunities. The largest of these is the program developed by the Chicago Chapter of the American Institute of Banking (AIB). This program, which has been described in a case study by Robert Campbell and Gary L. Seiner, began in 1969 when 7 Chicago banks hired 20 trainees. It has since developed into a consortium of 11 banks and 91 trainees.[11]

The participating banks contribute $775 for each trainee they hire. This amount is then matched by federal funds. While receiving a full day's pay, the trainee is taught basic English and arithmetic in the mornings and given on-the-job training in the afternoons. Evaluations of the success of the program have been mixed, with most of its critics pointing out the high rate of turnover among the "disadvantaged."

Since most banks fill the majority of their positions through internal promotion, one would expect that, once hired, a reasonable number of blacks would be able to rise to the higher status, better-paying positions. This has not happened. One bank official told Grey that the attitude of other minorities was not favorable to minority members who were promoted, sometimes charging those not promoted as being "high-handed and arrogant." In some cases, blacks reportedly refused promotions because of their unwillingness to encounter such treatment from their peers. While this problem may have significant short-term implications for bank management, it should cease to be a problem once black supervisors cease to be a rarity.

Another banker told Grey that he believed minority employees felt a tremendous pressure to succeed when promoted; he hypothesized that this pressure results from the feeling that minority group members will be judged by the performances of those who are promoted. Many less self-confident blacks, preferring to remain in the security of their present positions, might therefore pass up promotion opportunities.

It is not fair, however, to attribute the major portion of the black workers' immobility to their own attitudes. First, promotability depends largely on the skills acquired through informal on-the-job training and experience. If his white co-workers choose not to share their skills with him, the black employee can not expect to compete successfully with others who have received this aid. Cultural and social differences will often prevent white supervisors from getting to know their black subordinates as well as their white ones. Thus, in addition to the tendency to recommend one's friends, the white supervisor may not actually know enough about black subordinates to evaluate their potential for a higher position. The factor of racial prejudice also cannot be ignored. In recent years as blacks have gradually increased in numbers in certain job categories, the prestige level of the jobs has decreased.

In the bank messenger position, originally an all-white position, a few blacks did manage to obtain jobs. In a pattern strikingly analogous to recent residential changes, as the proportion of blacks in the classification increased, those whites already there became increasingly eager to make a move, and the number of whites seeking these jobs declined rapidly.

Banks offer the same defense for the absence of blacks at the managerial level as do most other industries (in 1969 1.3 percent of officials and managers at Chicago banks were black): there simply are not enough qualified blacks. This statement is unquestionably valid, but it does not tell the whole story. Those few blacks who have entered middle management have not been placed in departments that provide eventual access to the top level positions. While it has not been documented, it is probable that black managers in many industries fall victim to this same form of discrimination. As one bank's top executive commented, "The most specialized and prestigious departments are about ready to hire Jews; it will be several years before they will be ready to hire Negroes."[12]

CONCLUSIONS

Considerable progress has been made since the Civil Rights Act of 1964 banned discrimination by employers or unions, but it remains difficult to argue with the conclusion of a 1968 Urban League study that "any criterion used to measure the positions of the Negro worker in the Chicago labor market testifies that he is systematically confined to a second-class status." Racial discrimination continues to exist in hiring standards, screening procedures, recruiting procedures, internal allocating rules, and the rules governing wage determination.

Although discrimination is present in almost every industry, the type and degree vary considerably. Blacks have been traditionally excluded from industries with high percentages of white-collar workers (Banking is 90 percent white-collar.), but they have been allowed to participate extensively in industries with a high proportion of blue-collar workers. (Steel is 75 percent blue-collar.) Blacks have been excluded from positions involving critical customer contact, such as bank tellers and airline ticket agents, but they have been allowed to work behind the scenes as laborers and sometimes as craftsmen. When blacks have been allowed to come into contact with the customer, it has always been in an appropriately subservient role, for example, the airline skycap. Blacks traditionally have been allowed to occupy only the least prestigious positions.

Although changes are occurring, employment discrimination is still a serious problem. Even if all discriminatory personnel policies were eliminated, black workers would still face major obstacles. As long as blacks are not free to live in the same neighborhoods and attend schools of the same quality as their white counterparts, they cannot successfully compete in the labor market. These problems do not seem to be nearing solution. School segregation in Chicago actually has increased since 1963. Chicago also continues to preserve its traditional system of strict housing segregation. With industry continuing to move to the suburbs, the concentration of blacks in the inner city is becoming an even greater obstacle to minority employment. It has been estimated that as many as 112,000 unskilled black workers might move from Chicago's ghettos to housing near suburban workplaces if they were free to choose locations similar to those available to low-income whites employed at the same workplace.

The black labor force is growing faster than the white labor force and is projected to total 12 million men and women by 1980.[13] Workers under 25 will account for a large portion of this increase, but the most spectacular growth will occur in the age group 25-34.[14] There is no reason to assume that in 1980 these 12 million persons will not still find their employment opportunities limited by the color of their skin. As Piori and Doeringer point out:

Racially discriminatory practices are customary in nature; and because of the ability of the majority of the labor force to enforce custom, their complete elimination may require changes in custom itself.[15]

FOOTNOTES

[1] U.S. Department of Labor, "Employment Situation in Poverty Areas of Six Cities," Bureau of Labor Statistics Report No. 370 (Washington, D.C.: U.S. Government Printing Office, October 1970), p. 17.

[2] Harold M. Baron and Bennett Hymer, "The Negro Worker in the Chicago Labor Market," in *The Negro and the American Labor Movement*, Julius Jacobson, ed. (Garden City, New Jersey: Doubleday and Company, 1968), p. 234.

[3] Herbert R. Northrup, Armand J. Thieboldt, and William N. Chernish, *The Negro in the Air Transport Industry* (Philadelphia: University of Pennsylvania, February 1971), p. 26.

[4] Equal Employment Opportunity Commission, "Job Patterns for Minorities and Women," Equal Opportunity Report No. 2 (Washington, D.C.: U.S. Government Printing Office, 1969), p. 157.

[5] Albert Rees and George Schultz, *Workers and Wages in an Urban Labor Market* (Chicago: University of Chicago Press, 1970).

[6] Most of those in the labor category were cargo handlers, janitors, and aircraft cleaners. Most service workers were porters and food service workers.

[7] "Air Lines Seek More Negroes," *Chicago Tribune*, May 18, 1969, p. 4.

[8] *Ibid.*, p. 4.

[9] William J. Howard, "The Negro and Equal Employment Opportunity in the American Steel Industry," Unpublished (Chicago: Northwestern University, Graduate School of Management, March 1970) p. 9 and EEOC, *op. cit.*, p. 149.

[10] Armand Thieboldt, *Negro in Banking Industry*, (Philadelphia: University of Pennsylvania Press, 1970), p. 90.

[11] Robert H. Campbell and Gary L. Seiner, "Role of Disadvantaged in the Chicago Banking Industry," Unpublished, (Chicago: Northwestern University, Graduate School of Management, 1970).

[12] R. David Corwin, *New Workers in the Banking Industry: A Minority Report* (New York: New York University, June, 1970), p. 88; and EEOC, *op. cit.*, p. 166.

[13] Bureau of Labor Statistics, "The U.S. Labor Force Projections to 1985," Special Labor Force Report No. 119, (Washington, D.C.: U.S. Government Printing Office, 1970), p. 5.

[14] Baron and Hymer, *op cit.*, p. 284.

[15] Michael J. Piori and Peter B. Doeringer, *Internal Labor Markets and Manpower Analysis*, (Lexington, Mass.: D.C. Heath and Co., 1970), p. 47.

SECTION THREE:
MINORITY CAPITALISM
AND THE
MINORITY ENTREPRENEUR

The previous section of this book has presented readings dealing with minority employment—jobs and training at various levels of the employment market. "The Case for Minority Capitalism" was presented in the articles by Fred Allvine and Theodore Cross. This section will present readings and cases focused on minority capitalism—some problems, some failures, and some successes.

Capitalism is an integral part of our nation's economy, and the need for capitalistic growth in the minority communities so that minority people can combat the economic conditions in their communities should be an important national goal "there is a growing realization that there should be an organized force to work for the inclusion of Black businesses in the American economic mainstream, and for the development of a viable economic base in the Black community to effect political, social and cultural change within the community."[1]

Much has been expected of black capitalism, but little has been delivered. Despite the plethora of government agencies and private organizations marching under the banner of black capitalism, capital assets acquired by new black owners and operators over the past two years amount to only 0.005 per cent of U. S. industry's capital expenditures for the same period.

Clearly, the rhetoric of black capitalism needs scaling down. Black capitalism is not going to bring an end to discrimination, poor education, underemployment—a 300-year legacy.

But what about the reality of black capitalism? There are successful black entrepreneurs; there are other blacks who desire to become entrepreneurs. There are opportunities available. And there are many organizations that stand ready to help. Why, then, have successful new ventures by black entrepreneurs been so few?[2]

The first article in this section sets the environment for minority enterprise. This background is desirable before discussing specific examples of minority capitalism because it provides a framework for understanding the problems and frustrations inherent in minority enterprise. Although the environment is national in scope, the succeeding examples are drawn from the Chicago experience. With its ghettos, large minority population, and traditional black/white business relationships, Chicago provides many examples of the inherent problems and opportunities for minority development.

Of particular interest is discrimination in the marketplace—whites buy from whites (racism?) and middle income blacks buy from whites (the social pressure to assimilate?). Thus, low-income ghetto dwellers comprise the major consumer population for the minority-owned business. Why is this the major marketplace for the minority entrepreneur in a society which traditionally encourages ownership and applauds business development? Why are minorities discouraged from entering business or management in nonminority businesses through scarcity of opportunities, lack of financial and managerial resources, and diminished capacity to find debt money, working capital, and trade credit; Historically, minorities have faced a hostile environment whenever they have sought to start their own businesses in nonminority communities or to obtain management positions in non-minority-owned businesses.

Doctors and Appel argue that the present federal program can not fill the very wide ownership disparity and that what is needed is a much more broadly based program. Such a program must allocate significant resources for business and technical education and provide for long-term, planned development. They also analyze in detail the nature of the existing disparities in business ownership and education which make the problem so complex.

Statements of concern and support have come from high government officials and from agencies which have programs for increasing minority enterprise. The government has established a variety of programs that do not have specific goals; these programs are intended to increase merely the *number* of minority business opportunities with little or no reference to their long-term impact on the overall economic status of the minority community. Some agencies grant contracts to minority businesses, while others provide direct financial assistance to small minority business development and community-based development corporations. The question, of course, is how effective are these programs and whether or not the federal concern and support is truly a commitment to significant change or merely a short-term infusion of dollars. One legitimately can ask whether the existing federal programs have any potential to effect significant long-term change in the economic base of minority communities nation wide, or whether it is primarily an attempt to reward middle class black and Spanish voters for their support of the present administration.

Doctors and Lockwood propose a broad-gauged new strategy for minority enterprise development based on encouraging entry into higher growth potential businesses in areas that provide an advantage for minority entrepreneurs. The authors feel that present federal minority enterprise programs may have the effect of widening further the economic gap between minorities and non-minorities since most government-guaranteed loans and technical assistance grants have been for businesses in low growth potential areas. This article suggests that future government efforts should support a number of minority businesses that can grow at a rate substantially greater than that of the GNP or that can accelerate minority community economic development in general. The article also discusses specific examples of higher growth potential such as outreach health care and environmental protection and discusses the importance of the federal government in creating market opportunities in these and other higher growth areas.

Black Pride, Inc., is an example of a Chicago-based corporation that was established to draw upon black consumers' consciousness.[3] Such black community consciousness translated into purchases could help retain dollars in the black community that would otherwise move directly out of the community. Such purchases on a larger scale would expand the traditional roles of blacks as consumers in the development of black proprietors and/or entrepreneurs. If enough dollars had been generated and kept in the black community through indigenous capital development and greater control of resources, then corresponding political and social power have been developed.

Director and Fenster contend that there is a growing pride and racial identity in the black community which could provide a significantly better environment for this type of enterprise development. The entrepreneurs who initiated Black Pride, Inc. believed that this change in the black community would provide a natural opportunity for their product to appeal directly to this growing racial pride. However their faith was not translated into enough sales dollars, and Black Pride closed its doors in 1971. The idea appears sound and may yet achieve its vindication in other enterprises.

In any discussion of minority enterprise, a major problem that always arises is lack of capital in the minority community.[4] Commercial banks are the major sources of capital for enterprise development in the nonminority community. Very few banks, minority or nonminority, have ever located in the ghettos or barrios of this nation. A great upsurge of interest in minority banks has been coupled with the growing interest in minority capitalism. Two divergent viewpoints have recently been expressed concerning the value of minority-owned and managed banks for economic development. Federal Reserve Board Governor Andrew Brimmer sees minority banks as ornaments, as inefficient, and as unlikely to make any significant contribution to minority economic development.[5] Dr. Edward Irons, on the other hand, contends that minority banks have made an important contribution to minority economic development. In regard to their future, Irons states that this group of banks has made dramatic progress in the last decade, almost quadrupling asset values and making an increasingly important contribution to their respective communities.[6] "Black Banking: Problems and Prospects" is an attempt to look at the questions raised regarding black banks and to analyze the banking situation from a study of 38 banks (18 black and 20 from the industry at large). What is the future of the black bank located in the ghettos, where the status of wealth is substantially lower than the general population, and where there are few trained or experienced black managers in banking? Banks can offer a leadership base to the community, and they are essential if blacks are to participate in the control of the finances of the nation because they provide the principal source of working capital for all businesses and are important sources of consumer credit and mortgage money.

A case study of Independence Bank, Chicago's first black bank illustrates many of the problems of a minority-owned bank. Independence opened its doors in 1964, with the support of a white correspondent bank which holds deposits with Independence, serves as its agent in various types of transactions, and has assisted in training personnel. Alvin J. Boutte of Independence says that "success depends on the corporations and institutions which do business in the community, to deposit funds in Independence. Corporate social responsibility is necessary, or the government may have to do the job."

In addition to the difficulty due to the scarcity of trained and experienced personnel, minority manufacturers suffer from one generic problem of small manufacturers: the high costs of promotion, of sales, and of shipping outside the manufacturer's immediate metropolitan area. The case study of United Distributors presents an example of a cooperative effort of seven Chicago-based black companies to develop and supply their products within a 500-mile radius of Chicago. United hoped to be a model of cooperation for black manufacturers to become competitive with white manufacturers. United experienced problems both as a group and within the individual companies. In the opinion of the Northwestern University professor, who worked with United as a marketing advisor, many of the problems were related to the lack of response from the retail chain stores. Finally, United was forced out of existence; however the concept seems worth pursuing, when the opportunity for such a cooperative program arises in the future, if adequate resources and technical assistance can be provided to give the concept a fair test.

An additional problem facing the minority entrepreneur is the community demand that he be socially conscious, that he hire the disadvantaged, train them, and in general gear his business to maximize community development rather than simply to make a profit.

Given all the problems of lack of capital, higher crime rates, lack of trained personnel, community pressures, and racism that confront the minority entrepreneur, one wonders whether, in the eyes of the nonminority community, any minority enterprise can be expected to succeed.[7] While it is true that only a few minority entrepreneurs have established and run sizable enterprises, with none even approaching the size of the smallest of the country's 1,000 largest corporations, there are nevertheless notable examples of very successful minority entrepreneurs including John Johnson of Johnson Publications, Henry Parks, Jr. of Parks Sausage, and George Johnson of Johnson Products. The largest black enterprise, as measured by sales, is Motown Industries, which had sales of $40 million in 1972. The next largest nonfinancial business is Johnson Publishing with sales of $23 million in 1972, followed by Johnson Products with sales of almost $18 million in 1972.

To provide one example of an eminently successful minority business, a brief case study of Johnson Products is provided as the final article in this section. Johnson Products was started with an initial capital of $500 in 1954 and in 1972 showed a capital structure of more than $12 million—a truly phenomenal example of small business success.

Johnson Products illustrates one business strategy for developing successful minority businesses discussed in the "New Directions" article, that of developing a market area which relies uniquely on a sensitivity to growing market demands by minority consumers. Johnson was able to develop a market which interested non-minority cosmetic manufacturers very little despite a fairly rapid growth in minority discretionary income and thus a growing demand for quality luxury products.

FOOTNOTES

[1] This is Operation PUSH (People United to Save Humanity), 1972 pamphlet of PUSH background, philosophy, and programs.

[2] Laird Durham, *Black Capitalism* (Washington, D.C.: Arthur D. Little, Inc., 1970), p. 1.

[3] Fred Allvine, "Black Business Development," in this volume; and Elliott Sclar, "The Community Basis for Economic Development," in this volume.

[4] Henry Terrell in a recent article "Wealth Accumulation of Black and White Families: The Empirical Evidence," a paper presented to a joint meeting of the American Finance Association and the American Economic Association, Detroit, Michigan (December 28, 1970), documents this relative lack of capital accumulation in the minority community.

[5] See Andrew Brimmer, "The Black Banks: An Assessment of Performance and Prospects," Paper presented before a joint session of the 1960 Annual Meetings of the American Finance Association and the American Economic Association, Detroit, Michigan (December 28, 1970).

[6] Theodore Cross, *Black Capitalism* (New York: Atheneum, 1969), pp. 50-55; for a detailed discussion of the inherent problems of ghetto-area banks and see also the discussion in Brimmer, *op. cit.*

[7] See generally Cross, *Op. cit.*

*Samuel I. Doctors, Veta T. Appel** *

NIXON'S MINORITY CAPITALISM PROGRAM:
FULL STEAM TO WHERE?*

During the fiscal year (FY) 1973, the federal government will have provided almost $1.5 billion to minority businesses by way of loans, loan and bond guarantees, management and technical assistance, direct development grants, and procurement of goods and services.[1] The total program budget for the five-year period, FY 1968 through FY 1973, will exceed $3 billion. The $1.5 billion figure is projected to increase to $1.8 billion in FY 1974, representing a 20 percent increase from the FY 1973 budget and more than a 1000 percent increase from the FY 1968 budget.[2]

Of course, only about $250 million of the $1.5 billion FY 1973 total represents out-of-pocket cost because much of the $1.5 billion is by way of guarantee reserves in the U.S. Treasury or payment for goods and services that are needed by the government.

This minority capitalism program has become, next to law enforcement, the fastest growing domestic initiative of the Nexon administration[3] and the only major initiative in minority development by this administration.

This very large increase comes at the same time that other socioeconomic programs designed to assist minority development are being cut back or cut off.[4] Funds have been cut back or cut off in minority communities for health care, education, housing, and manpower development. Why, then, has there been this dramatic increase in one relatively narrow area of minority development, that of enterprise development? Also, why have no clearly articulated goals been established for this program? Only vague or ambiguous administration pronouncements have been made concerning the desired impact of this billion dollar plus development program on minority socioeconomic development. Nor has any evaluation been made of the impact of the program specifically on minority enterprise development for either the short or long term. Nor has data been gathered which would allow a retrospective evaluation of program impact. The Small Business Administration (SBA) has in fact cut back its data gathering and evaluation over the past five years. More generally, we do not know whether the $3-billion-plus which has been spent on loans, loan and bond guarantees, procurement, technical assistance, and other miscellaneous purposes during the past five years, has had or will have any impact on the socioeconomic status of the various minority communities. We are not even sure that the overall impact will provide any positive long lasting benefits for minority businessmen, because most of the support is being provided to businesses with a low potential for

*Portions of this article have appeared in the Fall 1973 issue of *Business and Society Innovation Review*.
**Veta Appel is a research assistant, Northwestern University, Graduate School of Management.

substantial growth in profits and asset accumulation. It appears that not only is the approach to minority development a limited one, but it also may not even be sound within its limitations.

The program has gone forward on the general assumption that small minority enterprise development is necessarily a good and beneficial program for minority development in general; and that such enterprise development could go forward quite independent of other areas of development such as health care, education, housing, and employment; and further that such enterprise development could be fostered largely by making a number of small loans and procurement contracts.

We know that most of the nation's recent economic development is clustered in businesses employing a very highly educated work force with strong management capability.[5] We also know that the very high failure rates among all small businesses is highly correlated with a lack of business/management education and training and related technical education and training. Yet, virtually no federal funds have been provided for minority business/management training and education and related technical education and training. The failure of the minority enterprise program to come to grips with this fundamental deficiency is just one indication of a general lack of strategic planning or general understanding of the prerequisites of economic development so necessary for any program that is expected to have significant long-term impact. One has the impression that the minority enterprise program has just grown and grown and grown with no one really concerned about the whether and why—except that a given amount of money is disbursed to minority businessmen each year.

What may be even more discouraging is raising the hopes of the minority community for substantial economic gains to be derived from this program when the impact is so uncertain and planning for substantial impact so deficient. We know that, in terms of direct impact on numbers of people, this enterprise program will have an immediate and direct impact on far fewer persons than many of the now defunct poverty development programs such as the community assistance projects, the development projects of the Economic Development Administration, or Housing and Urban Development's Model Cities program.

In order to understand the very rapid growth of this program and to explore alternative explanations, it is important to know something of the status of minority enterprise and something of the substance of the federal program. We will also examine the available evidence as to the effects of this federal program on minority enterprise development. We will then analyze the reality of the present program for an ultimate goal of parity ownership of business assets by minorities within a reasonable period of time. Finally we will explore alternative explanations as to the rationale behind the very rapid growth of the program.

NATURE AND STATUS OF MINORITY BUSINESS ENTERPRISE

The 17 percent of the population who are native American, Negro, Asian, or of

Spanish-speaking ancestry control only a tiny fraction of the productive resources of the nation. The most recent census of minority business ownership (1969) showed that about 322,000 business enterprises in this country were owned by minority group members. This represents about 4.3 percent of total U.S. enterprises (7,489,000).[6] Gross sales for these 322,000 businesses totaled $10.6 billion, or about 0.7 percent of the total $1,498 billion receipts figure for all U.S. business.[7] Thus the average minority business had sales of just under $33,000 while the average nonminority firm had sales of just under $182,000. This $10.6 billion sales figure was equal to the sales of *one* nonminority firm in 1972, General Electric.

Contributing to the picture is the nature of many of these minority-owned enterprises. Sixty-one percent of all minority businesses are either small retail or service establishments, largely lacking in capital assets. The businesses in these two categories account for 62 percent of all sales of minority businesses.[8] No minority business is included in the *Fortune* listing of the 500 largest American corporations, and the sales of the largest minority firm, Motown Industries, were about one-fifth those of the smallest of the 500 largest domestic corporations (Varian Associates, $204 million sales).[9] As such, minority control of capital is only a fractional amount of their 4 percent of business ownership. It has been estimated that minority businesses account for only about 0.3 percent of all business assets or about $2.6 billion out of the total U.S. business nonfinancial (corporate) assets of $859 billion in 1971.[10]

The statistics for financial institutions, the backbone of economic development, are similarly unequally distributed. The combined assets of all minority banks and the combined assets of all minority-owned insurance companies are about $2.6 billion, or less than 0.2 percent of the industry total of $1,607 billion.[11]

The continuing disparity of personal capital accumulation has significantly hampered the development of the economy of the minority community as well as the opportunities for enterprise development by individuals. The average minority family has assets of $3,398 as opposed to $19,612 for the nonminority family.[12] In 1970, the average minority family income was about 66 percent that of white family income, or about $6,650. While this represents a substantial relative income gain during the decade of the sixties, this gain was unevenly distributed so that the lowest 20 percent of the minority population actually fell further behind during the sixties.[13] There was little gain in relative unemployment rates, which stood close to the historic level of 2.0 times those of nonminority unemployment in 1970. Also, we know that minorities are undercounted substantially, perhaps by as much as 10 to 15 percent, by the census takers. Thus, gains are unlikely to be as large as the government income and employment figures would indicate.

Studies show that technical and business education is highly correlated with most successful small business development, yet minorities have been even more disadvantaged in the pursuit of educational opportunities than in the income and employment areas. In the area of formal business training, consider the following statistics. In the years since the inception of graduate business education in this country (1908), less than 600 minority group members received graduate business degrees through 1969. Of these, about 350 were graduates of the Atlanta University School of Business Administration. In 1969-70, there were approximately two thousand, Ph.D. and D.B.A. candidates enrolled in U.S. schools of business, but less than fifty of these were minority group members. There are today less than 150 minority persons holding doctorates in business or economics.[14] In 1969, of approximately 100,000 certified public accountants in the U.S. only about 150 were black.[15] The data for Mexican-Americans and native Americans is even more discouraging.[16] Other statistics show that, while 21.7 percent of all white males ages 25-34 years have completed four or more years of college, only 6.5 percent of black males in the same age bracket have done the same.[17] At the same time, 58.7 percent of blacks over 20 have not completed high school, compared with 36.4 percent of whites.[18] Another voluntary survey undertaken by Educational Testing Services indicates that, in 1972-73, out of almost 67,000 students enrolled in full and part time M.B.A. programs, 4,252 or almost 7 percent are minority students. Certainly this is an improvement, but it still is not the kind of improvement that will provide parity of opportunity in business and management within the near future. Given present enrollment, about 12,000 would be required to reach parity, and untold additional thousands would be required to reach parity among graduate MBAs.

Minorities comprise approximately 17 percent of the U.S. population, yet they are represented by 11 percent of the undergraduate enrollment and only 8 percent of the graduate population. Persons of Spanish-speaking ancestry are least represented, with 2 percent college enrollment and 4.5 percent of the population. The only minority group above average in educational attainment is the Asian-American group, with .7 percent of the population and 1.9 percent of the graduate school enrollment. Thus, there is a general trend for minority members to complete less formal education than their nonminority counterparts, and this trend becomes further accentuated when dealing with formal business education.

FEDERAL EXPENDITURES FOR MINORITY ENTERPRISE

The federal government has involved itself directly in promoting minority enterprise development through technical assistance, direct grant programs, loans, loan and bond guarantees, and purchasing of goods and services since 1964 under the Johnson administration. However, expenditures were nominal until Richard Nixon took office in 1969. Shortly after he took office, in March, 1969, he issued Executive Order 11458 establishing a new agency, the Office of Minority Business Enterprise (OMBE), to coordinate a minority enterprise program that was to become the most important minority enterprise development program of his first five years in office. Except for some minor changes to the

SBA act specifically aimed at minority enterprise development, there has been no new legislation legitimatizing this program. No tax incentives or direct subsidies have been provided for private sector involvement and no new agency has been legislatively established; not even an assistant secretary level job has been established, despite the specific recommendations of the President's Advisory Council on Minority Business Enterprise.[19] Still the program has grown larger than some agencies headed by a cabinet level administrator.

The government has attempted to stimulate nonminority business investment and technical assistance for minority enterprise development through a variety of exhortations to civic duty and appeals by various members of the administration. However, other than guarantees for bank loans to minority entrepreneurs, very little by way of direct federal dollars has been made available to private sector firms as a stimulus for the investment of monetary or technical resources in minority enterprise. Nor are there any real incentives, when loans are guaranteed to 90 percent, for banks to be concerned with the business problems experienced by minority clients.

The only articulated goal of the present federal program is the one enunciated by former Secretary of Commerce Maurice Stans of doubling the number of minority businesses between 1970 and 1990. Merely doubling the number of businesses is hardly a useful guideline. No goals as to increases in asset ownership, sales or growth potential, employment opportunities, skill development, or overall impact on minority economic development have been articulated by the Nixon administration.

This lack of goal formulation or evaluation of effectiveness has not slowed down the growth of the government's program for minority enterprise development. In fact, as we have seen, the projections for 1974 show a substantial increase of approximately 20 percent.

The federal program for minority enterprise development is generally divided into three categories: loans, loan guarantees (including bond guarantees for construction), grants which include technical and management assistance, and procurement. The loan program went from a total of $107 million in FY 1969 to a projected $750 million for FY 1974. The grant program went from $25 million in 1969 to an estimated $200 million for FY 1974. The procurement program, which channels government purchases of supplies and services to minority firms that might otherwise not be able to compete with nonminority firms, totaled $13 million in FY 1968 and is scheduled to increase to over $700 million in FY 1974.[20]

The greatest portion of this money comes from the two agencies with the biggest involvement in government minority business development—the SBA, which claims that FY 1974 total spending for minority enterprise will exceed $1 billion, an increase of 265 percent since 1970 and about 1500 percent since FY 1968; and OMBE, which had a budget of $3 million at its inception in 1969 and is projected to have $91 million for FY 1974. (This $91 million includes $17 million of impounded 1973 funds and $39 million from the now defunct Office of Economic Opportunity for community development corporations.)

THE FEDERAL PROGRAM:
ITS IMPACT ON MINORITY BUSINESS DEVELOPMENT

Although there has not been any comprehensive evaluation of the impact of the federal minority enterprise program, a few recent studies provide some idea of impact.

One of these studies compared black business development in Atlanta among recipients and nonrecipients of SBA loans. The study found little or no difference between the two groups and concluded that SBA lending seemed to be having no appreciable effect on black business development in Atlanta.[21]

Another study analyzed 400 black businesses that were recipients of SBA loans in Boston and New York. This study found that over 50 percent of these businesses were not meeting their repayment obligations and over 33 percent were being liquidated.[22]

A third study which analyzed all SBA lending nationally (between FY 1968 and 1971) found that minority firms experienced financial problems with their loans five to six times as often as nonminority borrowers. Also, most of the loans were made to minority businesses in low-growth, low-profit areas such as retail stores, commercial printing, and automobile car washes.[23]

OMBE indicates that it has initiated some sort of evaluation function, but thus far published reports are not available. Thus we must rely on such studies as those cited here. Clearly from the available evidence, the present federal program appears to be having a marginal impact on minority business development.

The only exception may be minority banking, where federal efforts to increase deposits have resulted in at least several hundred million dollars being deposited by both the public and private sectors. However, even here there has been no attempt to measure the effects of these new deposits on the economic viability of the minority banks, and some of the new deposits are short term and require, relatively speaking, very large collateralization. Thus little of these new deposits may be available for loans in the minority community and the banks' limited equity capital may be drained further.

Parity versus Reality

Although the administration has never clearly articulated any definite and meaningful goals for the minority enterprise program, let us assume that parity of asset ownership, within a reasonable period of time, should be a major ultimate goal of any program. The current estimate of 0.3 percent asset ownership would thus have to be increased about 56 times (5600 percent), representing a dollar increase of almost $243 billion over the present $2.6 billion.

Presumably, the number of businesses would have to be increased more than fourfold to achieve parity in terms of numbers of businesses; in other words about 1.1 million businesses would have to be added to the present 322,000. Also, parity in ownership of financial institutions would require an increase of about 100 times (10,000 percent) the present level, or about $270 billion in terms of 1971 financial asset ownership.

The present minority enterprise program including procurement, loans, loan and bond guarantees, and technical and management assistance amounts to almost $1.1 billion. With this amount of money, approximately 11,000 business loans were made in FY 1973, and approximately 3,000 minority businesses received contracts from the federal government. OMBE affiliates and SBA helped initiate approximately 2,000 new businesses in FY 1973. Of course, documented failure rate of minority businesses receiving SBA loans appear to be running about 25 to 40 percent within two years after receipt of the loan, and this figure may run much higher if loan recipients are analyzed several years hence. Can we expect the businesses that do remain in operation to achieve the 5600 percent growth rate in assets which would be needed to achieve parity? From available SBA figures, we know that most of the loans and contracts are being made to minority businesses in lower growth areas such as retailing, restaurants, barber shops, or gasoline stations. Thus it is not even clear that the SBA loan program will help minorities keep up with present average annual growth rate of the economy of slightly over 4 percent a year. In terms of numbers of new businesses, present government programs will provide a total net increase of about 1400 new minority businesses in FY 1973. At that rate if one had to depend only on the government, it would take about *800 years* to reach parity in the numbers of businesses. Aside from the government-sponsored minority bank deposit program, there are no direct aid programs to minority financial institutions. Still, there has been a very substantial rise in minority bank assets of about 300 percent over the last four years. At this rate it will only take about *100 years* to reach parity in bank asset ownership.

There is, of course, also private sector investment in minority enterprise development. But exact figures for these investments are not available. Some fragmentary statistics indicate that over 100 new automobile dealerships have been added during the past five years, as have almost 4,000 new gasoline and service stations and approximately 1,300 goods and service franchises. But there is no data as to whether these businesses will be operating in five years or whether they will contribute anything to the economies of their communities.

Private industry has invested a significant, though untabulated, amount of volunteer time in counseling minority businessmen. Almost 75 percent of all the loan money provided to minority businesses in FY 1973 is private sector bank money, usually guaranteed at 90 percent by the SBA. Also, the private sector has invested over $25 million in Minority Enterprise Small Business Investment Companies (MESBICs).

In addition, there is the possibility that the present public and private investment will be substantially enhanced by the growth of the minority small businesses that are being or will be assisted from the various public and private sector programs. However, there is no indication that this is likely to occur, because there has been little or no attempt to assist existing minority businesses or to motivate new business development in areas of potentially higher growth. Nor is there any strategic planning that would allow shaping the present program to provide for higher growth opportunities (including the use of government purchasing and market creation power to stimulate minority business development) in such areas as pollution control, health care, or leisure time activities. Nor are any significant amounts of money being spent to encourage minority education in business/management and related technical areas so vital to any longer term attempt to build a significant minority business development program.

Nonminority business development has always taken place in an environment which had an abundance of public and private sector programs in education, health care, housing, research and development, capital base development, and other related areas. All successful, higher growth business development has been built on a strong supportive base of programs and existing development in all of these areas, and nonminority small business development still has significant risk attached to it, failure rates are as high as 80 percent after the first five years.

How then can the Nixon administration hope to establish a strong minority business community while it cuts back or entirely cuts off support in all these other areas? How can the administration hope to significantly increase minority asset ownership if, in addition to cutting back or cutting off all related community development programs, it also fails to help minority businessmen enter areas with higher growth business potential through a carefully planned and articulated long-term economic development program, or to provide adequate business/management education and training opportunities?

The present short-term business development program is inappropriate where the disparities are so great and the socioeconomic base is so poor. All that is likely to happen to the present rapidly growing minority enterprise program is that some financial support will be provided to some middle class minority businessmen and women; this support may raise community expectations, but it will result in marginal gains, if any, to the community as a whole unless a variety of presently cancelled or curtailed programs are also dramatically expanded to provide a viable base for enterprise development.

Thus the question still remains: Why this dramatic increase in funding for this one narrow program of minority development?

Speculations on the Unanswered Question—Why the Rapid Growth?

Thus far we have presented a discussion of the economic status of minorities in the United States, particularly in the area of minority enterprise; the government expenditures directed toward minority enterprise development; the relative effectiveness of those programs; and an analysis of the implications of parity of asset ownership as a major ultimate goal of the program. If, in fact, no demonstrated correlation exists between government efforts and the improvement of minority economic status, why then is the funding being continued and even being increased? Why are the increased amounts of money being spent without adequate, if any, long-term planning, research and evaluation?

It is essential to emphasize that it *is not the intention of this paper to minimize the importance of minority enterprise development*; rather the purpose of this paper is to pinpoint the serious deficiencies of the program, particularly those deficiencies related to cutbacks in other socioeconomic programs. The major issue remains: Will this one limited approach enable the 17 percent minority population to achieve socioeconomic equality with the nonminority population? It is the contention of this paper that the only course to this end is a comprehensive program capable of building a sound economic and social base in the total minority communty.

While the federal budgets for law enforcement and defense continue to increase, minority development programs have been hard hit by the new budget policy. Programs to improve the housing, health, educational and manpower development of the disadvantaged are the most negatively affected. Improvement of these socioeconomic conditions would lead to long range improved economic status of minorities and have a significant impact on the environment for minority enterprise development.

It would be presumptuous to make any definite statements as to why the Nixon administration focuses such a large percentage of its minority development efforts in only one area; however, there are a number of possible explanations.

(1) This type of program fits more closely with the "self-help," "free market" ideology of the Republican party, notwithstanding the many increased federal subsidies to nonminority business from the Nixon administration. The importance of this ideological commitment to minority development through business development was first enunciated in President Nixon's "Bridges to Human Dignity" address of the 1968 campaign. "What we need is to get private enterprise into the ghetto, and put the people of the ghetto into private enterprise—not only as workers, but as managers and owners. Then they will have the freedom of choice they do not have today; then the economic iron curtain which surrounds the black ghettos of the country will be breached."[24]

(2) The President also needed some minority development program that would provide some social program for liberal Republicans but would not alienate the other elements of the party.

(3) Just as the poverty programs tended to reward the minority poor who, in the main, supported the Kennedy/Johnson candidacies, so the minority enterprise program tends to reward the minority upper and middle classes who would be the most likely supporters of the Nixon candidacy among minority groups.

(4) Almost 40,000 business loans have been made to minority entrepreneurs since President Nixon took office and an additional 14,00 loans are projected for FY 1974. This program is likely to have some effect in building a larger minority middle class constituency for the Republican party.

(5) Finally, minority enterprise is a politically "safe" approach to minority development in that it does not help to develop a broadly based infrastructure in the way that the now defunct OEO Community Action Program (CAP) did. The CAP program provided employment for thousands of community organizers and

tended to develop new political power centers—not under the control of established political parties—in the communities. Similarly the Model Cities program was intended to place primary control for neighborhood development in the community.

These five explanations are of course only speculations, but they do provide a reasonable rationale for the rapid growth of this one area of minority development almost to the exclusion of other areas. Minority enterprise development is not an unimportant program. It is crucial for the economic, social, and psychological well being of minorities that assistance be given in the development of economic power consistent with the 17 percent minority population. Only with economic power will minorities be able to deal from a position of strength and dignity. However, to attain economic power minority development must include increased, not decreased, spending in such areas as housing, health care, education, and manpower development, since it is only by the interaction of all these areas that the position of minorities as a whole can improve. Also, any development program must be planned with longer term goals in mind because the existing disparities will not be alleviated by short term, politically motivated programs. And program results must be carefully measured against goals to insure effective use of available resources. Finally, far larger resources must be provided for minority enterprise development itself if there is to be any hope of changing the extreme disparities between minority and nonminority enterprises within a reasonable period of time.

FOOTNOTES

[1] Data supplied by the Office of Minority Business Enterprise (OMBE) and the Small Business Administration (SBA) during 1972 and 1973. For the purposes of this paper we recognize three major minority groupings: *Non-whites* (blacks and Asian-Americans); *native Americans* (Aleuts, Eskimos, Hawaiians, and Indians); and *persons of Spanish-speaking ancestry* (Cubans, Mexicans, Puerto Ricans, and other persons of Latin American extraction). Asian-American is broken down into four categories—Chinese, Filipino, Japanese, others. In total these minority groups comprise slightly over seventeen percent of the American population or about 36 million people.

[2] While SBA minority loans and loan guarantees have been increasing tenfold, overall SBA lending has increased more than fivefold during this same six year period. Estimated minority business loans in FY 1974 will be almost as large as all SBA lending in FY 1968. However SBA staff has hardly increased at all during this six year period which probably means there is inadequate staff to monitor this increased loan program.

[3] National League of Cities, *Federal Budget and the Cities: A Review of the President's 1974 Budget in the Light of Urban Needs and National Priorities* (Washington, D.C.: National League of Cities, Feb. 1973) and *Budget of the United States, 1973 and 1974.* Sponsorship of law enforcement grants has gone from $59 million in FY 1969 to a projected $891 million in FY 1974 or an increase of almost 1500 percent in 5 years.

[4] See Report of the National League of Cities, *op. cit.*

[5] A number of economists and business scholars have reached this conclusion, including Edward Denison, *The Sources of Economic Growth in the United States and the Alterna-*

tives Before Us (New York: Committee for Economic Development, 1962); Robert Solow, "Technical Change and the Aggregate Productions Function", *Review of Economics and Statistics* 39, No. 3 (August 1957), pp. 312-20; Edward Roberts, "Technical Entrepreneurship" in Donald Marquis and William Gruber,, eds. *Factors in Technology Transfer* (Cambridge, Mass.: the M.I.T. Press, 1969), pp. 219-237. See also Samuel Doctors and Anthony Ahel, "Federal R & D Expenditures and Industrial Productivity," *Business Perspectives* (Summer, 1973).

[6] U.S. Department of Commerce, Bureau of the Census, *Minority Owned Businesses: 1969* (Washington, D.C.: U.S. Government Printing Office, November 1971, pp. 1-2.

[7] *Ibid.*

[8] *Ibid.*

[9] The sales figure for Motown Industries is from "The Nation's 100 Top Black Businesses," *Black Enterprise* (June 1973), p 37; the sales figure for Varian Associates is from *Fortune 500* (May 1973), p. 240.

[10] The 0.3 percent figure was supplied by OMBE in 1972 and the $859 billion is from *Statistical Abstract of the U.S. 1972*, 93rd ed. (Washington, D.C.: U.S. Government Printing Office, 1972), pp. 438,477.

[11] *Ibid.*

[12] James H. Weaver, "Economic Causes of Social Unrest," unpublished paper, American University, Economics Department, 1972.

[13] *Ibid.*; also various Census Bureau special studies on minority social and economic status.

[14] HEW Task Force on Minority Business Education and Training Preliminary Report, January 1973.

[15] Bert Mitchell, "The Black Minority in the C.P.A. Profession," *The Journal of Accountancy* (October 1969), pp. 41-48.

[16] United States Senate Committee on Labor and Public Welfare, *Indian Education: A National Tragedy—A National Challenge* (Washington D.C.: U.S. Government Printing Office, 1969), p. 80; and Leo Grebler *et al.*, *The Mexican-American People* (New York: The Free Press, 1970), p. 216.

[17] Department of Commerce, Current Population Reports, *The Social and Economic Status of the Black Population in the United States* (Washington, D.C.: U.S. Government Printing Office July 1972), p. 84.

[18] Department of Commerce, Current Population Reports, *Educational Attainment, March 1972* (Washington: U.S. Government Printing Office, 1973), p. 7.

[19] The President's Advisory Council on Minority Business Enterprise, *Minority Enterprise and Expanded Ownership: Blueprint for the Seventies* (Washington, D.C.: U.S. Government Printing Office, June 1971).

[20] Figures taken from a variety of OMBE reports 1971 to the present.

[21] Robert Yancy, *Federal Government Policy and Black Business Development*, doctoral dissertation, Northwestern University, Graduate School of Management, June 1973.

[22] Timothy Bates, "An Econometric Analysis of Lending to Black Businessmen," Paper presented at the 1971 meeting of the Econometric Society.

[23] Samuel Doctors and Sharon Lockwood, *SBA Data Study for the President's Advisory Council on Minority Business Enterprise*. Unpublished, (January 1972.)

[24] Address on CBS network, April 25, 1968.

Samuel I. Doctors, Sharon Lockwood

NEW DIRECTIONS FOR MINORITY ENTERPRISE*

Minority enterprise historically has been limited to small retail establishments, personal service business, and small construction contractors. Despite the fact that minority groups constitute about 17 percent of our population,[1] they own less than 3 percent of the nation's businesses.[2] Perhaps even more significant is the fact that these businesses control less than 0.5 percent of the nation's business assets.[3]

Present programs for minority business development have emphasized loans, grants, and/or subsidies to small businesses primarily in retail services and construction areas. Almost all of these businesses are in crowded business sectors, small margin, low growth-potential areas such as gasoline service stations, barber shops, or small retail food markets, and they often serve an impoverished clientele. The historic failure rate for these types of business is quite high.[4] Although data are scarce in this area, it appears that less than 20 percent of all new small businesses survive their first five years.[5] New minority businesses are even more vulnerable due to a lack of access to financial and technical resources.[6] However, even those that do achieve a modest degree of success are unlikely to achieve growth rates that would create high-leverage business opportunities for very many members of the minority community. Moreover, these businesses often lock their owners into a life of long hours and hard, unstimulating work with little or no opportunity to break out of the pattern of marginal growth opportunity.

Surveys of existing minority businesses indicate that there are very few whose gross sales are even as large as $1 million a year and none whose sales approach those of the 500 largest white-owned and white-controlled corporations.[7] Nor do we find minority group members in positions of control or decision making in the large American corporations where they might gain the managerial experience to start companies that might grow to a place among the largest American businesses.

Other data indicates that minority business development, although receiving some stimulus from present public and private efforts, still shows no signs of the exponential growth rate needed to catch up with white business development, and relatively speaking, may in fact be falling farther behind. We have raised the expectations of our minority groups for examples of such exponential growth but have neither formed nor created models capable of achieving these catch-up growth rates.

As may be seen from the sample of minority businesses presented in Tables

Reprinted with permission, from a symposium Community Economic Development, appearing in *Law and Contemporary Problems* (Volume 36, No. 1, p. 51, 1971), published by the Duke University School of Law, Durham, North Carolina. Copyright, 1971, by Duke University.

As may be seen from the sample of minority businesses presented in Tables I and II, the minority entrepreneur tends to enter the more marginal types of businesses. Table I indicates that a disproportionate number of minority entrepreneurs are in the personal service area. While some facets of the service industries are higher growth areas, the more disaggregated data in Table II reveals that the minority entrepreneurs are not in these higher growth areas.

Little attention has been directed toward guiding the minority entrepreneur to more lucrative business opportunities. Most government and nongovernment programs are grounded in the concept that simply establishing a minority member in a business is sufficient. This reasoning requires serious consideration. If minority businessmen are not guided to the higher growth areas, their businesses will not help the minority economy approach the national economy.

To lift minority enterprise from ghetto and the barrio, a strategic thrust must now aim at providing opportunities for higher growth-potential models of minority enterprise. These model businesses should be capable of growing at the rate of 10 to 20 percent or more per year over the next 5 to 10 year period.[8] Such new enterprises will help meet rapidly rising expectations provide true upward mobility, stimulate capital formation, and furnish attractive alternative routes for minority employment and success models for future programs.[9]

Many new opportunities for minority entrepreneurs to obtain financial assistance have become available not only in the Small Business Administration, but also in the Department of Commerce, the Office of Economic Opportunity, and the private sector. New and expanded business opportunities capable of leveraging this expanding source of capital funds must be provided to stimulate the creation of enterprises that can multiply their intitial investments many times over.

Much of this development should occur in higher growth industries, although medium and low profit-, low growth-potential industries should not be completely excluded. They may provide needed goods and services for the community and may serve to keep a larger amount of capital within the minority

Table I
Distribution of Minority and Non-minority Business Enterprises[1]

Category	Minority Owned	Non-minority Owned
Personal Service	26.9	7.3
Other Service	15.1	20.3
Construction	10.8	9.0
Manufacturing	2.2	7.9
Retail Trade	34.0	34.9
Other Industries	11.0	21.6
Total	100.0	101.0

Source: U.S. Small Business Administration, Office of Planning, Research and Analysis. *Distribution of Minority-Owned Businesses.* Unpublished report (Washington, D.C.: Small Business Administration, June 1969), p. 7, Table I.

Table II

Categories and Types of Black Business Enterprises

Category	Number	Percentage
Food and beverages	173	30.7
Public Services	101	17.9
Merchandise Sales	37	6.5
Professional Services	35	6.2
Contracting Services	31	5.5
General Sales and Service	169	30.0
Other	18	3.2
Total	564	100.0

Source: Flournoy A. Close, Jr., *An Analysis of Black Entrepreneurship in Seven Urban Areas* (Washington, D.C.: National Business League, 1969), Appendix I, p. i-ii.

community. A medium or lower growth-potential business may also provide some training opportunities for a number of potential minority entrepreneurs and managers. Thus, this latter type of business may also play some role in long-term economic development of minority communities.

Today's minority entrepreneur is finally ready to gain a more advantageous position in the economy. Higher minority educational levels, increased minority incomes, a wider range of business opportunities, the changing attitude of public and private institutions toward minority entrepreneurs, and an attitudinal change in the minority community toward business as a career have combined to bring about an environment which can fit the minority entrepreneur for entering higher growth industries.

The educational level of minorities is now improving more rapidly than that of the population as a whole. As enterpreneurs are usually drawn from the middle classes rather than from the most disadvantaged groups,[10] this increase in educational level will undoubtedly be reflected in a growing pool of potential and actual entrepreneurs (Table III).

Increasing family income of minority groups (Table IV) is reflected in the growing purchasing power in the minority community. This increased purchasing power can support a larger number of minority businesses and a wider range of products and services. Thus, an increased range of business opportunities should be available within the minority community. The increased educational level and the extensive needs of the general public in the areas of goods and services should increase the range of business opportunities for the minority entrepreneur in the national economy.

There has been an increasing concentration of the minority community in urban areas during the decades of the 1950s and 1960s (Table V). This increasing concentration in the urban areas may, on the one hand, help consolidate purchasing power to the advantage of the minority entrepreneur. On the other

Table III
Percent Distribution by Years of School for Persons
20 Years Old and Over, by Age, 1970

Black	Less than 4 years high school	4 years of high school	College, one year or more	Median years of school completed
20-21 years old	33	44	24	12.4
22-24 years old	37	42	21	12.3
25-29 years old	44	39	17	12.2
30-34 years old	50	38	12	12
35-44 years old	59	29	12	11.2
45-54 years old	71	20	9	9.3
55-64 years old	83	11	6	7.9
65-74 years old	90	5	5	6.1
75 years old or over	93	4	3	4.6
White				
20-21 years old	18	40	43	12.8
22-24 years old	17	46	37	12.7
25-29 years old	22	45	33	12.6
30-34 years old	26	45	29	12.5
35-44 years old	33	42	25	12.4
45-54 years old	39	40	21	12.3
55-64 years old	54	28	18	11.2
65-74 years old	67	18	15	8.9
75 years old or over	75	14	11	8.6

Source: U.S. Department of Labor, Bureau of Labor Statistics, *The Social and Economic Status of Negroes in the United States, 1970* (Washington, D.C.: U.S. Government Printing Office, 1971), p. 79.

Table IV
Median Family Income in 1971, and Negro Family Income, 1959-1971,
as a Percentage of White, by Region

	Median family income, 1971		Negro income as a percentage of white			
	Negro	White	1959	1966	1970	1971
United States	$6,440	$10,672	51	58	61	60
Northeast	7,601	11,291	69	67	71	67
North Central	7,603	11,019	74	74	73	69
South	5,414	9,706	46	51	57	56
West	7,623	10,803	67	72	77	71

Source: U.S. Department of Commerce, Bureau of the Census
Cited in: U.S. Department of Labor, Bureau of Labor Statistics, *The Social and Economic Status of Negroes in the United States, 1971*, p. 32.

hand, with the move to the suburbs by the nonminority middle class, much of the capital and markets needed for economic development is no longer available.

One of the most interesting elements in today's minority enterprise climate is the changing attitude in the minority community toward the status of the entrepreneur. Heretofore, the ambitious black perceived the obstacles to a business or would not provide these services to the black population.[11] Highly motivated blacks, unlike the highly motivated in other racial groups, were discouraged from entering business and were diverted to the professions. The black population valued the contribution of the black professional and tended to diminish the contribution of the black businessman. In fact, until recently it was considered prestigious in the black community to purchase name brands from nonminority enterprises. The goods of the black merchant were thought to be inferior, apparently for no other reason than because the proprietor was black.[12]

This paper will suggest that there are a number of important principles which must be considered in a program to establish viable minority businesses. Minority enterprise opportunities should be developed which:

(1) contribute to the capacity of the various minorities to take advantage of business opportunities beyond particular ethnic or racial markets.[13]

(2) have a capacity for growth and capital creation

(3) capitalize upon the skills and knowledge of all elements of the minority population

(4) promote areas of comparative advantage such as health care, job training, day care, and communications in the minority community

(5) promote short and long-run community development objectives

Table V
Negroes as a Percentage of Total Population by Location,
Inside and Outside Metropolitan Areas, and by Size of
Metropolitan Area, 1950, 1960 and 1970

	Percentage Negro		
	1950	*1960*	*1970*
United States	10	11	11
Metropolitan areas*	9	11	12
Central cities	12	17	21
Central cities in metropolitan areas of:			
1,000,000 or more	13	19	27
250,000 to 1,000,000	12	15	18
Under 250,000	12	12	11
Suburbs	5	5	5
Outside metropolitan areas	11	10	9

*Population of the 212 Standard Metropolitan Statistical Areas as defined in 1970
Source: U.S. Department of Commerce, Bureau of the Census, *op. cit.*

(6) make effective use of government-created and -protected markets, particularly in new, higher growth areas.

Economic indicators show where the potential for minority business lies. Real economic growth of the United States is expected to average over 4 percent per year, so that the Gross National Product (GNP) will increase from the third quarter 1970 level of $1 trillion to $2.4 trillion by 1990.[14] With this increase, the consumption rate of nondurable goods is expected to decline from 62 percent to 60 percent during the period from 1967 to 1980.[15] At the same time, increases in family formation, rising incomes, and replacement of old and substandard housing is projected to push demand for new housing to 2.4 million units per year in the late 1970s. This factor will account for the rise in private domestic investment growth from the 1967 level of 15 percent to over 16 percent of the 1980 GNP.[16]

Expenditures on consumer durable goods will show the highest rate of growth largely because of rising affluence between 1967 and 1980: real disposable income per capita is projected to increase at an annual average of 3.1 percent, doubling the proportion of families with real incomes of $10,000 or more from around 25 percent of all consumer units to around 50 percent. Higher incomes, along with increased leisure time, will influence demands for recreation equipment such as boats, motors, automobiles, televisions, pleasure aircraft, and sporting goods. There will also be large demands for household furnishings because of the large increase in the 25 to 34 age group.[17]

Consumer spending for nondurable goods will continue to grow at a slower rate than total spending. By 1980, Americans are expected to spend only 38 percent of total expenditures on consumer nondurables, compared to 44 percent in 1967 and 55 percent in 1968. A large share of the consumer nondurables will be for clothes, household supplies, gasoline and oil, drugs, personal grooming aids, and reading materials. Spending for food and beverages will decrease as a proportion of total nondurable expenditures.[18]

Statistical data from the Department of Commerce indicates that consumers will, for the first time in American history, spend more money on services (air travel, car rentals, beauty parlors, advertising and management consulting, life insurance, and so forth) than for nondurable goods. Even though the prices for services have risen at a faster than average rate, services have proliferated and their coming preeminence will present a whole new set of opportunities and challenges. Major components within the services field will be housing, business expenditures, medical services, and education and research.[19] These are prime areas for minority enterprise to enter.

Using projections from the Bureau of Labor Statistics, an examination of output demand can be used to show the national trend in higher businesses. The data reveals obvious business opportunities in those industries with projected substantial increases in growth rate. These include the following industries: optical, ophthalmic, and photographic equipment; electric, gas, and sanitary services; business services; and office supplies.[20]

Industries for which the projected demand for output is expected to grow at moderately high and increasing rates include nonferrous metal ores, new construction, household furniture manufacture, manufacture of other furniture and fixtures, manufacture of paper and allied products except containers, printing and publishing, manufacture of stone and clay products, wholesale and retail trade, medical and educational services, nonprofit organizations, primary nonferrous metals manufacture, manufacture of electrical industrial equipment and apparatus, manufacture of miscellaneous electrical machinery and equipment and supplies, scientific and controlling instruments, miscellaneous manufacturing, hotels, and personal and repair services except automobile repair services. Some discretion must be used in evaluating those industries for which high rates of growth are projected for the 1965 to 1980 period, but for which the relative growth rate has decreased during the 1957 to 1965 period. Whether or not opportunities exist for minority entrepreneurs depends on such factors as:

(1) the production capacity of existing firms
(2) the number of new firms to be developed during the coming decade
(3) product developments
(4) the ability of minority firms to reduce production costs
(5) the sales promotion success of minority and rival firms
(6) other factors such as the availability of capital and of trained minority managers and technicians.

TECHNOLOGY-INTENSIVE INDUSTRIES

A large number of higher growth opportunities exists in technology-intensive industries.[21] In the past, entry into these industries has been eased in many cases by government contract support, both in terms of direct support for research and development (R & D) expenses and through creation of a market for at least a limited number of new products. The importance of government market creation has been dramatically demonstrated by the hundreds of new firms initiated in the Boston, Palo Alto, and Los Angeles areas since World War II.

Research and development is a potentially profitable area, but it presents many problems such as the substantial investments which are needed. In addition, these areas require technological expertise, managerial and entrepreneurial expertise, and sales promotion expertise.

Given these requirements, how can a minority enterprise launch itself into a high growth-potential industry? The answer may lie in nonminority corporate support of minority spin-off (subsidiary) firms, perhaps in conjunction with direct government grants or tax incentives. For example, a large manufacturing firm could set up a minority-run supplier to manufacture components for the manufacturer, or to provide a specialized service. One example of such a high technology spin-off is that established by the Bendix Corporation's Communications Division—Baltimore Electronic Associates, Inc., in Baltimore, Maryland.[22]

In a study of more than 200 new technology-based firms founded by former employes of the Massachusetts Institute of Technology R & D Laboratories, the total proportion of failures found during the first five years of these spin-off firms was only 20 percent, as compared with 80 percent failure during the same period for all firms.[23] In addition, the spin-off firms showed an exponential growth in sales during this same five-year period. During their preliminary stages, these firms were mainly preoccupied with government research and development, but they tended to diversify rapidly into consumer markets.[24]

Potential minority businessmen seeking out areas of high growth might also look to the industries in which significant technological advances are expected, as there appears to be a correlation between research and development or technological research expenditures and long-run profits.[25] Minority businessmen must not only enter fields in which subsidized research and development will occur, but they must also enter fields which are already technology-intensive and in which expenditures on innovation will translate themselves into substantial profits during the coming decade.[26]

One can not predict with absolute certainty precisely which industries will experience significant technological changes, nor can one predict with absolute certainty where an innovative thought will occur. But the growth of investments in, and profits from, research and development expenditures appears to be closely correlated with government expenditures in any given area.[27] While government expenditures for the 1960s were concentrated in the areas of aerospace, electronics, and atomic energy, increased emphasis will be placed on R & D in such areas as medical research and ecology.[28] If minorities are seeking high-return investments, they must look toward these new areas of increasing government investment.

America has typically accepted technological advances with insufficient consideration for problems of physical health, sanity, and aesthetics—for example, the noisiness of airplanes and air pollution from automobiles. Thus, one higher growth business opportunity (in terms of government R & D expenditures) will be in technologically intensive areas dealing with the problems of advanced technology.

DISCRETIONARY PURCHASE INDUSTRIES

Another source of high growth opportunities is the discretionary purchase industry. Business opportunities may be said to lie in the areas of fad industries and intermediaries for labor-intensive production.

The fad industry is one area of business opportunity that can show high growth but that does not necessarily involve a high level of technology. Increasing income and increasing leisure time will stimulate a tremendous increase in goods and services that will soon outgrow their stylishness. Despite the fact that employment for minorities may be cyclical or unpredictable and sporadic in these industries, the fad industries give unusual returns on capital. The toy industry is one example of business opportunity requiring little capital outlay (as compared to returns), much innovation, market appraisal, and extremely good sales promotion.

An additional source of business opportunity is the area of businesses that provide special services as well as social services. The following areas of comparative strength may contribute to rewarding business opportunities by drawing on the strengths and knowledge of an ethnic or racial group: developing minority resources, capitalizing on ethnic or racial identities, experiences and attitudes, and providing research social services to minorities.

In the first area—resource development—minorities could act as developers and agents for talented minorities. For example, black recording stars, actresses, athletes, artists, and writers might also have black agents—provided adequate training, financing, and necessary contacts were available. The entrepreneurial part requires an aggressive sales promoter. Not only might this minority talent-public intermediary operate a highly successful business, but this business venture also would be one means of stopping the flow of minority talent to nonminority capitalists. For Indians and Mexican-Americans (many of whom are engaged in the making of handicraft, pottery, dolls, and carved items), an intermediary might exploit the rising market for custom goods by acting as a go-between for labor-intensive producers and retailers. Where possible, both types of intermediaries might also function in the final stages of trade or production.

Minorities operating in minority-identity fields might have a better understanding of minority needs than other business firms would. A chain of soul food kitchens might be highly successful, especially if it combined good food with pleasant surroundings and serviced both minorities and nonminorities. Clothes, cosmetics, and hair products catering to minorities have, on the whole, met with widespread acceptance; however, they are often so expensive that they are beyond the means of many potential customers. In an allied area, Latin minorities could investigate the development of import-export linkages with the increasingly important Latin American market; blacks could likewise involve themselves in African trade exchange.

An important minority advantage includes the administration of social services in minority communities, since a minority individual, capitalizing on shared experiences, can better communicate with others of the same minority group.[29] In the areas of mental health programs, drug and crime rehabilitation, and social welfare, a minority enterprise to administer social services, staffed by professionals in their respective social fields and with paraprofessional minority community residents, might have considerably more success and prove to be much less expensive than a similar governmental agency.[30] Formal education and professional experience can not overcome a lack of communication, distrust, and lack of common experience. Among groups with language problems, language training by bilingual minority members may capitalize upon a strategic weakness from a point of strength. In addition, minority firms could do urban research into the quality of public services, and might well have an advantage over a similar nonminority firm.

GOVERNMENT CREATION AND ENCOURAGEMENT OF MARKET DEVELOPMENT

Since World War II, the federal government has become a very important force in the creation of new markets in both the public and private sectors of the economy.[31] Everyone is familiar with the very visible market, which has amounted to several hundred billion dollars over the last ten years,[32] created by the federal government in the aerospace area, but the government also creates market demand in many other ways, such as licensing, grants of insurance, and protection of monopoly status. Perhaps most important for minority enterprise development is that the government can use its market creation power to provide numerous protected market areas that are so necessary for the development of most new enterprises; the government also can assume the role of the primary risk taker.

Of course, there are numerous other ways in which the government may create a protected market, such as by the granting of a radio, television, or interstate commission carrier license. As previously noted, the government may also create substantial incentives such as financial guarantees, subsidies, and grants for nonminority business to assist minority business. There is a variety of ways in which the federal government may use its powers to promote the development of minority enterprise. The following list is a brief survey of federal government market creation and development powers:

(1) *Risk Taker*. The government has become the primary risk taker in many new technical areas such as radar, computer development, micro-electronics, and, more recently, in supersonic air transport and artificial organs.

(2) *Direct Purchaser of Goods and Services*. Many hundreds of new companies including almost the entire aerospace industry, have been initiated and sustained through government contracts.

(3) *Tax Incentives*.[33] The use of tax incentives has stimulated many different types of industrial development. The most widely publicized have been the various mineral depletion allowances and the investment tax credit. However, a large variety of taxes is commonly used by government at all levels for selective stimulation of business development.

(4) *Allocation of Scarce Resources*. The issuance of licenses in regulated industries, such as air transport, communications, and interstate transport, has provided substantial opportunities for business development. The grant of grazing, mineral, or timber rights on federal lands has also been quite important.

(5) *Insurance*. The guarantee of investments by agencies, such as the Agency for International Development (AID), or the guarantee of loans by SBA or EDA, has been quite important in business development. New areas of proposed govern-

ment insurance include surety bonding for minority contractors and guarantee of equity investments in minority enterprise.[34]

(6) *Direct Loans*. The government makes a significant amount of direct loan money available, particularly through SBA and EDA programs.

(7) *Tariffs and Quotas*. The selective use of trade barriers has provided substantial opportunity for industrial development in a number of industries.

(8) *Supply of Capital Equipment*. The government has often stimulated industrial development by allowing private firms to use and/or buy at reduced rates government-purchased equipment.

(9) *Subsidized Markets*. The use of agricultural subsidies has provided a substantial impetus toward the creation of a highly efficient agriculture industry in this country.

This list indicates ways that the federal government can use its powers to stimulate business development. However, minority businessmen have been almost totally excluded from such government programs. They have participated, if at all, only recently and then primarily through the direct business loan.[35]

At present, government spending is approximately one-fifth of GNP, and spending by the government (federal, state, and local) will increase during the period from 1970 to 1980 by an average annual rate of seven percent.[36] The greatest increase in government spending will be for housing and community development, both of which are immediately concerned with fulfilling social needs. In general, government expenditures will focus increasingly upon housing, urban renewal, and other social benefits. Large increases in government expenditures for health and hospitals, conservation, and recreation will occur, while spending on national defense is expected to show the slowest growth rate of government spending. Thus, much government spending for the decade (1973-1983) will complement high-growth industry in such areas as housing, education, and health care. All of these areas will promote community development; also the community should be able to exercise some control in the letting of contracts and grants in these areas. Thus, minority enterprise could be given a substantial portion of this new, higher growth business.

DEMOGRAPHIC/ECONOMIC TRENDS AND BUSINESS OPPORTUNITY

Population changes in geographic areas, changes in the work force, and changes in the number of people employed in specific occupations indicate that there will be an increase in manpower resources to take advantage of emerging business opportunities and to provide increased purchasing power. Such population changes constitute significant changes in business opportunties.

Four sets of interacting population movements which affect business opportunities and markets can be identified: (1) regional population trends; (2) the movement from rural to urban setting; (3) the movement of city population to the suburbs; (4) an exchange of population according to race.

In general, the greatest rate of job growth and population has occurred along the rim of the country—moving along the West Coast, through the Southwest, and over to Florida. Higher-than-average growth increases also took place in the South and the Far West. The Far West will show the fastest gains in population and income, and the Southwest will show the fastest gains in employment. Florida (Southeast), Arizona (Southwest), Colorado (Mountains), California and Nevada (Far West) will be the states spearheading the growth of their respective regions.

Within even those states that lost population, there has been a substantial decline of rural populations and an increase in metropolitan areas. Rural population decreased from 54.4 million to 53.9 million in the 20 years from 1950 to 1970. At the same time, metropolitan population increased from 96.8 million to 149.3 million people.[37]

There is also a kind of geographic concentration present among the states experiencing the fastest growth in services. Of the six states experiencing the greatest increase in service dollars spent (Maryland, South Carolina, Georgia, Florida, Alabama, and Hawaii, in that order), the five that are growing fastest are in the Southeast.

Moreover, the service field, compared to retail trade, is, geographically, a highly concentrated market. The two leading states in spending for services are New York and California. These two states do in excess of one-third of the service business, although they contain only one-fifth of the nation's population. Illinois, Pennsylvania, Texas, and Ohio are the other national leaders in service dollars spent. All of these states contain substantial minority populations that could benefit from the growth of these service industries if an appropriate national strategy were developed now to channel substantial amounts of this new business to minority enterprise.

Given the above facts, it is obvious that business and job opportunities do not necessarily lie either in the northern United States or in the large cities. Business opportunity is growing more rapidly in the Deep South (where the black minority population is concentrated) than the national average. Medium-sized cities may have better business growth opportunities than the inner city areas of the large cities. Thus, opportunity for entrepreneurial advancement may lie closer to home than one might think—if one knew the rate and direction of population and investment growth by geographical location.

Finally, there have been surprising increases in the population of small nonmetropolitan cities. In other words, the movement from the farms is not necessarily to the big city. This suggests that there are important areas of business opportunity in smaller sized cities, even in predominantly rural states.

It is important to realize that these population trends are not merely population movements; they are *opportunity* movements—opportunities for jobs and business—because they reflect an underlying growth of business and government in the fast-growing areas. This data gains importance when it is realized that the movement of the minority population is apparently going in almost the opposite direction. (Some of this impression comes from observation, as data according to race is scarce.)

An example is New England. Its average annual employment growth rate during the 1960s was next to the lowest of the regions, 2.3 percent[38], but its increase in nonwhite male workers was the fastest in the nation; and this increase is expected to continue to grow at a rapid rate.

During the past twenty-five years, the proportion of nonwhites in the central city population has doubled, but *it has declined in suburbia*. In fact, between 1960 and 1970, the black population in American central cities went up by 33 percent. It remained constant for whites.[39] Meanwhile, industry and manufacturing have abandoned their old quarters and followed or even preceded the general movement of the more affluent population and business to the suburbs. (The contrast is: blacks go into the city while the jobs and businesses are moving away.)[40]

The South of the United States has increased in population, but the net growth is accounted for by the white population; the blacks have moved to the North and to the big cities. In 1950 blacks comprised 68 percent of the total Southern population. By 1970 only 53 percent was black. Migration of blacks from the South has taken place at a rate of 145,000 to 150,000 persons per year during this 20 year period.[41]

When total population movements are related to the population trends of minorities, that is, increasing immigration from higher growth areas), they suggest the need for a network to inform minorities of business opportunities based on demographic changes. At the very least, such information is needed to enable the minority entrepreneur to make realistic calculations about risks and opportunities. Rather than proposing a mass migration of minorities to higher growth areas, it is proposed that some business opportunities for minorities be matched to specific areas of comparative advantage. Fortunately, there will exist in the 1970s not only rapidly growing horizons for business growth in rapidly developing geographic districts, but also the opportunity in the inner city and the large metropolitan areas. These are often considered *passé* by majority group entrepreneurs thinking in terms of economic and business growth opportunities.

CONCLUSION

It is clear that greater opportunities for business development must be made available to minority entrepreneurs to provide one important component of total community development. It has not been suggested that business development, without other facets of development such as greater education, health care opportunities, and greatly expanded job opportunities in nonminority business, is a panacea. However, business development is necessary to provide success models and opportunities for self-development in minority communities.

Present programs for minority enterprise development are largely focused on short-term goals, such as providing quantities of equity and debt capital to numbers of minority enterprises, almost without regard to the growth potential of these enterprises. If the vast bulk of the minority businesses has a low growth, low profit potential (less than 4.4 percent), then present programs may have the long-term impact of widening the gap between minority and nonminority businesses. It is, therefore, important that we attempt to make available to minority entrepreneurs the full range of business opportunities, with particular emphasis on higher growth-potential opportunities.

It is possible to identify a number of areas of higher growth potential through a variety of indicators, such as projections of government spending, consumer demand, and socioeconomic patterns and demographic projections. All these changes represent new and often important higher growth potential opportunities. It is important to identify these areas, make this information available to minority entrepreneurs, and provide necessary financing, management assistance, and technical assistance.

Such a program of business development requires comprehensive planning that includes a broadly based strategy designed to meet the many development deficiencies in the minority community. Such a comprehensive program has recently been proposed by the National Advisory Council on Minority Business Enterprise (NACMBE), which includes more than 75 recommendations for new and expanded programs in business opportunities, education, community development, and finance.[42] Only this type of comprehensive program will provide the human and technical resources needed to implement the business development strategy discussed in this paper.

The role of the federal government is crucial in the implementation of the proposed strategy. It may be desirable to delegate much of the actual implementation of the proposed strategy to the private sector, but only the government can provide the financial incentives and create the markets needed to provide numbers of higher growth-potential minority enterprise. The government can fill this latter role by:

(1) the direct purchasing of goods and services
(2) acting as a guarantor and subsidiser
(3) providing licenses
(4) acting as a risk taker
(5) providing tax incentives or direct grants to motivate nonminority business involvement.

To summarize the proposed business opportunities analyzed, a comprehensive business opportunity strategy should concern itself with moving on all possible fronts. It must match community and individual resources with business opportunities. It must focus on higher growth areas while performing a variety of community development functions, including employment, capital creation, and the production of needed goods and services. This mix of functions, will permit a "staging" for entrepreneurial development that can make a meaningful contribution to overall minority economic development.

FOOTNOTES

[1] "Minority group" is defined for this paper to include only blacks, persons of Spanish-speaking ancestry, and American Indians.

[2] U.S. Small Business Administration, Office of Planning, Research and Analysis. *Distribution of Minority-Owned Businesses.* Unpublished report (Washington, D.C.: Small Business Administration, June 1969), p. 1; Theodore Cross has estimated that in Manhattan there are only a dozen black businesses that employ 10 or more people. See *Black Capitalism* (New York: Atheneum, 1969), p. 60.

[3] SBA study, *op. cit.*

[4] See generally, *The President's Task Force Report on Improving the Prospects of Small Business* (Washington, D.C.: U.S. Government Printing Office, March 1970), pp. 21-27.

[5] *Ibid.*, and see Edward Roberts, "Entrepreneurship and Technology," in Donald Marquis and Will Gruber, *Factors in Technology Transfer* (Cambridge: The M.I.T. Press, 1961), pp. 224-225; and Addison Parris, *The Small Business Administration* (New York: Praeger, 1968), pp. 51-55. Of course most business failures are not outright bankruptcies; still, for every five new businesses started, another 3.5 go out of business each year.

[6] One estimate of minority business failure may be obtained by examining the relative default rates on SBA loans between nonminority and minority borrowers. Parris estimates that minority defaults were running 10 to 20 times the rate of non-minority defaults (3 percent). See Parris, *op. cit.*, p. 116. However, this estimate is based solely on the Economic Opportunity Loan (EOL) Program through 1968 and a more recent analysis of the SBA minority loan program indicates that overall default rates are likely to be lower than was previously true for the EOL program. See unpublished report, *Evaluation of the Minority Enterprise Program* (Washington, D.C.: SBA, 1971). See also Cross, *op. cit.*, pp. 21-30, for a discussion of the difficulties of running a ghetto-based small business.

[7] See SBA study, *op. cit.*, and a recent Office of Economic Opportunity (OEO) survey of larger minority businesses. This study attempted to identify minority businesses with annual sales in excess of $500,000, and which showed a profit for the last two years. The largest business so identified in 1969 was about $33 million, and this was three times the size of the next largest minority business, Johnson Products, Inc. About 100 companies were included in this study; of these, 24 met the sales and profitability criteria. See OEO memo, Paul London and Susan Davis to Theodore Cross, "Minority Business Successes," May 19, 1970. The smallest company listed among the *Fortune* 500 had sales of $162 million in 1969. *The Fortune Directory* (May 1970), p. 23.

[8] The 216 Boston "route 128" spin-off companies studied by Edward Roberts and his colleagues had an annual five-year growth rate of over 20 percent per year. Roberts, *op. cit.*, pp. 225-227. The same type of growth rate was exhibited by a sample of 13 companies used in a technology transfer study by the author. See Samuel I. Doctors, *The NASA Transfer Program: An Analysis* (New York: Praeger, 1971). Much of the growth achieved by these companies has been made possible through the creation of a protected market by the federal government. Clearly this same federal government power could be used in the development of minority enterprise as it has been used to develop an aerospace industry.

[9] It is assumed, contrary to Andrew Brimmer, that the promotion of minority enterprise does not have the sole objective of providing employment for larger numbers of blacks. It is assumed that the creation of numbers of viable minority-owned enterprises may serve a number of other socioeconomic objectives. It is also assumed that minority economic development requires a holistic approach to such development, including the parallel provision of improved employment, business, educational, and health care opportunities. Just as in the nonminority community, the synergistic interaction of a variety of factors will result in significant development. See Andrew Brimmer and Henry Terrell, "The Economic Potential

of Black Capitalism," Paper presented before the 82nd Annual Meeting of the American Economic Association (December 29, 1969).

[10] Idea suggested by the work of Frazier, McClelland, and Roberts. E. Franklin Frazier, *Black Bourgeoisie* (New York: Collier Books, 1968); David McClelland and David Winter, *Motivating Economic Achievement* (New York: The Free Press, 1969); Edward Roberts, "Entrepreneurship and Technology," in *The Transfer of Technology* (Cambridge: The M.I.T. Press, 1969, pp. 219-237).

[11] A recent survey of the graduates (346–1946 to 1969) of the School of Busines, Atlanta University's (AU) School of Business Administration, indicated that most of their graduates, prior to 1968, had entered nonbusiness occupations. AU has produced over half of all the black M.B.A.'s in the period 1908 to 1969.

[12] Especially true for the black middle class. See Frazier, *op. cit.*

[13] The core recommendations of the National Advisory Council on Minority Business Enterprise (NACMBE) placed great stress on the need for greatly expanded training and educational opportunities, and has recommended the allocation of $160 million over the next three years to assist materially in this area.

[14] Labor Department forecast, November 1970, and The Conference Board for the White House Conference on the Industrial World Ahead: A Look at Business in 1990, *The U.S. Economy In 1990*, (New York: The Conference Board Inc., 1972), pp. 4-5.

[15] Predicasts, Inc., *Predicasts*, Issue 39 (April 20, 1970), p. 3.

[16] *Ibid.*

[17] Predicasts, *op. cit.*, p. 3.

[18] National Consumer Finance Association, *Finance Facts Yearbook* (1970).

[19] *Sales Management–1970 Survey of Buying Power*, Vol. 104, No. 13 (June 10, 1970), p. A-21.

[20] It should be noted that the SIC code groupings may, in general, bring together different kinds of growth areas within one industrial code. Thus, further breakdowns of a given area may be necessary to find particularly desirable opportunities.

[21] Technology-intensive industries may be defined as those industries which have characteristically spent a much larger than average amount of their funds on R & D, which employ a significantly higher than average percentage of technologists; and which depend on the production of new technology-based products for their retention and expansion markets. Such industries would include: aircraft, scientific instruments, chemicals, and electronics. See *Research and Development in Industry, 1968* (Washington, D.C.: Government Printing Office, 1970).

[22] Bendix helped several of its minority employees establish a business to manufacture electrical components needed by Bendix. Originally the components were manufactured by the company, but it was thought that they could be produced less expensively by an outside source. Bendix has supplied management and technical assistance as well as help in purchasing for the new corporation, Baltimore Electronics Associates.

[23] Edward Roberts, *op. cit.*, pp. 224-229.

[24] *Ibid.*, p. 228.

[25] See for example U.S. Department of Commerce, *Technological Innovation: Its Environment and Management*, prepared for the Secretary of Commerce (Washington, D.C.: U.S. Government Printing Office, January 1967); Edwin Mansfield, *The Economics of Technological Change* (New York: Norton, 1968), pp. 43-98; and Christopher Freeman, "Research and Development in Electronic Capital Goods," *National Institute Review* (November 1965), pp. 40-91.

[26] Samuel Doctors, "Federal R & D Funding and Its Effects on Industrial Productivity," unpublished paper prepared for the New England Research Application Center, University of Connecticut, January 1968.

[27] *Ibid.,*

[28] National Planning Association, *Looking Ahead*, Vol. 17, No. 4 (May 196), p. 11.

[29] See the discussion of new career opportunities in Arthur Pearl and Frank Riessman, *New Careers for the Poor* (New York: The Free Press, 1965), particularly Chapters 3, 4, 5, and 7.

[30] Business and Defense Services Administration, Department of Commerce, prepared for the Small Business Administration. *Selected Industry Profiles: Detailed Analysis of Minority Business Opportunities*, pt. I-V, October 11, 1968-April 4, 1969.

[31] State and local governments also purchase large quantities of goods and services, and create markets in many other ways, but this article will concentrate on the role of the federal government, leaving for future works the exposition of the importance of the non-federal public sector for minority enterprise development. The ratio is about two to one in terms of present tax collection expenditures in favor of the federal government. *Survey of Current Business*, 1970.

[32] Aerospace R & D expenditures, alone, have totaled over $100 billion during the last decade. See National Science Foundation, *Federal Funds for Research, Development, and Other Scientific Activities: Fiscal Years 1968, 1969, and 1970* (Washington, D.C.: U.S. Government Printing Office, 1969).

[33] PACMBE has recommended the use of tax incentives both for direct nonminority business assistance to minority businesses and for training minority managers.

[34] OEO's newly initiated Opportunity Funding Corporation (OFC) will attempt to determine the efficacy of using federal government guarantees in a wide variety of applications to stimulate minority business and capital base development. See OEO *Opportunity Funding: An Economic Development Demonstration Program* (Washington, D.C.: OEO, 1970).

[35] A recent survey (by PACMBE) of SBA lending practices revealed that most loans to minority entrepreneurs were direct Equal Opportunity Loans (EOL) of $25,000 each, while those to non-minority entrepreneurs were considerably larger, averaging $56,000, and were guaranteed loans. The findings of the PACMBE indicate that minority businessmen have been almost totally excluded from most government business development programs.

[36] National Planning Association, *Looking Ahead*, Volume 17, No. 4, (May 1969), p. 11 and The Conference Board, *op. cit.*, pp. 4-5

[37] The Bureau of the Census in *Characteristics of the Population*, Volume 1, Part A, Section 1, (Washington, D.C.: U.S. Department of Commerce, 1972), p. 42.

[38] *1969 Manpower Report of the President*, U.S. Government Printing Office, Washington, D.C. April 1968, p. 35.

[39] *Current Population Reports*, Department of Commerce, Bureau of the Census, Series p-23, No. 42, 1971, p. 18.

[40] *1968 Manpower Report of the President*, U.S. Government Printing Office, Washington, D.C., January 1969, p. 132.

[41] Department of Commerce Series 23, No. 42, *op. cit.*, p. 15.

[42] See PACMBE, *Minority Enterprise and Expanded Ownership: Blueprint for the 70's* (Washington, D.C.: U.S. Government Printing Office, February 1971).

*Steve Director, Ross Fenster**

BLACK PRIDE, INC.

Although blacks comprise approximately 11 percent of America's population, they own only 2.2 percent of all businesses in the United States.[1] Therefore, black consumer dollars flow mainly *out* of black communities and *into* the white business community, where they are recirculated, thus generating further capital development in the white community. In the black community, where the money flow is outward, dollars are not circulated within, and resources are not capitalized.

How can the money flow generated within the black community be kept and recirculated in that community? An obvious answer is black ownership of business. In Chicago, a corporation known as Black Pride, Inc., was formed in June, 1969 to address itself to this end.

Black Pride, Inc., sought to set up businesses that would be patronized by blacks in their own communities. In this manner the organization sought to expand blacks' historical role as consumers by turning them into proprietors and/or entrepreneurs.

The corporation's founders related the concept of black pride to the community at large by stating that black economic power is the vehicle for black liberation. If enough dollars are generated and kept in the black community through the capitalization and control of its resources, corresponding political and social power will develop.

The officers of BPI stressed that BPI's stockholders were "plain folk, marginal income people," who invested BPI because of the concept of black pride and its meaning to the long-run revitalization of the black community. They also pointed out that, although obtaining initial capitalization required a real selling job, not all interested investors were accommodated because of philosophical differences. Dividends were not assured and members of the board of directors, who were very active in management, were unsalaried. Of the two or more work days per week that each director contributed, a portion of this time was usually devoted to nonmanagerial tasks such as loading and unloading trucks, warehouse arrangement and cleaning, and routine clerical matters. It was not uncommon for Edward McClellan, BPI's president, to make deliveries himself if regular truck drivers were not available.

INITIAL VEHICLE OF CAPITALIZATION— THE BEER INDUSTRY

In order to implement the concepts of BPI, it was necessary to find a product

*Steve Director is an Assistant Professor at Wayne State University, Graduate School of Business Administration and Ross Fenster was an M. B. A. student at Northwestern University at the time he worked on this paper.

that would provide a profit potential adequate enough to allow for capitalization of future businesses.

Market studies indicated that upwards of $51 million was spent annually on beer by blacks living on the south and west sides of Chicago. The Chicago beer market was dominated by three large brewers. No established black distributorships of beer existed, and no black-owned, private label distributorships existed in Chicago or elsewhere. Obtaining only five percent of the black market in Chicago would translate into revenues approaching $3 million.

A private label beer distributorship was an attractive initial product vehicle for other reasons. First of all, in Illinois, beer is sold to the retailer on a cash basis, allowing for fluid inventory and cash flow.[1] Second, a strictly cash basis business would adapt itself to relatively low initial capitalization. Third, the relatively close shipping point of the product supplier requires less cash to maintain an inventory. Finally, the beer industry is comprised of many complementary businesses in addition to distributing, none of which is black-owned or operated to any significant degree. One single bottle of beer is the product of brewing, distribution, farming (of hops, barley, rice, corn, and malt), labeling, bottling (glass and metal), and trucking. Success as a private label distributor could lead to future profitable endeavors.

OBTAINING THE PRODUCT VEHICLE— BLACK PRIDE BEER

The first project of BPI was the marketing of Black Pride Beer. As was expected, the originators of BPI were not met with open arms when they began approaching brewers concerning a black-owned private label distributorship.

From a competitive standpoint, the larger brewers saw a private label beer catering to the black community as an economic threat which they had to ward off. A representative of one large producer expressed doubt as to the community-based financial support that would be forthcoming, and brewers had nothing significant to gain from producing and packaging Black Pride Beer. However, if someone else produced the beer, it might pose a future economic threat to the larger brewers.

After lengthy negotiations extending over six months, a contractual agreement was reached with the West Bend Lithia Brewing Company of West Bend, Wisconsin. Lithia's own financial difficulties and excess production capacity may have in part explained its willingness to gamble on a company such as BPI.

Black Pride, Inc. agreed to buy, and Lithia agreed to sell, a minimum of 5,000 barrels of beer a year (one barrel is slightly more than 11 cases) and up to a maximum of 20,000 barrels a year. Lithia also agreed to train a black brewmaster and to furnish Black Pride Beer to any future franchised distributors of BPI.

Located 120 miles north of Chicago, Lithia is a relatively small family-owned regional brewer. In business for more than 120 years, the company sells two local brands (Old Timer and Lithia) in the West Bend area. With an annual

capacity of 75,000 barrels, a contract the size of BPI's is economically important. If BPI were to buy the minimum number of barrels contracted for, namely
25,000 barrels over a five-year period, this would represent about seven percent
of Lithia's annual output. Fulfillment of the 20,000 per year barrelage would
represent between 26 and 27 percent of Lithia's annual output. BPI guaranteed
the contractual obligation by putting $40,000 of the initial $65,000 raised
through the sale of stock in an escrow account with the West Bend Bank. The
West Bend Bank allowed Lithia to order supplies and inventory under the "Black
Pride" name, borrowing against the escrow account.

Lithia's shipping contracts were made available to Black Pride Beer at the
rate of 35 cents per hundredweight. If a black were qualified to obtain a hauling
permit, a significant cost savings could be realized. However, BPI felt present
union politics would preclude this possibility for the immediate future.

The remaining $25,000 raised through the sale of stock was used to obtain
the necessary licenses, bonds, warehouse facilities, delivery trucks, and service
personnel. The beer division of BPI began its commercial existence on November 24, 1969.

Marketing

The market which BPI was attempting to penetrate was difficult to enter. Although consumer loyalty for beer does not equal that of liquor, factors such as
high volume production and extensive use of advertising have been causing a
trend toward concentration of the beer industry. In fact, the number of breweries in operation in the United States decreased from 329 to 211 between 1953
and 1963, and the percentage of sales by the largest brewing companies increased during the same period. Seventy percent of the premium beer market is
held by the three largest brewers.

BPI's management realized that they could not compete with the larger
breweries in terms of mass media advertising, and even if they could, they felt
such advertising would not effectively reach their initial target market.

BPI's management expected that the successful introduction of Black Pride
Beer would require both time and confidence; consumers would need time to try
Black Pride Beer several times in order to decide whether to buy on a continuing
basis, and time to develop their confidence in the product, both as to taste and
the psychological benefits which consumers think they could obtain from drink
ing Black Pride Beer. BPI found it more difficult to gain consumer acceptance
than to get the product on the retailers' shelves. Retail sales effort were concentrated initially on the high volume carry-out outlets—supermarket chains, package stores, and chain drug operations. Because of the lack of product advertising,
there seemed to be no "image" conjured up by Black Pride Beer—for instance,
the Schlitz outdoorsman who grabs all the gusto he can is a product of such
image building. Since lager beer is basically undifferentiated by taste, beer manufacturers must create differences through their advertising.

BPI used many low-cost marketing vehicles, such as bumper stickers announcing the coming of Black Pride Beer, matchbooks carrying similar announcements, Black Pride Beer story parades through the South and West Sides of Chicago, and publicity handouts. BPI President McClellan pointed out that one of the major problems for BPI was to convince the black community that there was no white money behind Black Pride, Inc., and that Black Pride beer was owned and financed exclusively by blacks. He explained:

> It is perhaps fortunate that our lack of great capital resources has not enabled us to be tempted to become involved in extensive advertising. The brewing companies through their own brand advertising promote beer generically and, of course, we'll benefit from that. But slick, professionally produced advertising appearing extensively on TV and billboards on behalf of Black Pride beer at this time would only reinforce any suspicion that we might be fronting for white money.

Word-of-mouth advertising was heavily relied upon. The stockholders of BPI also were used effectively. Shareholders spent two to three hours nightly soliciting orders in their own neighborhoods and spreading the word about Black Pride Beer. This was not to suggest, said Mr. McClellan, that any pressure tactics, threats of boycotts, and the like were used on retailers: "A 'no thanks' or 'I'm not interested' would be graciously accepted, but that hasn't yet been the response our people have received."

Market Research

A class in marketing communications at the Graduate School of Business of the University of Chicago cooperated with Black Pride, Inc. in the development of its promotional efforts.

Only a very limited amount of marketing research was undertaken. Informal taste tests were conducted in two or three taverns and one liquor store on the South Side of Chicago. In one case, customers were given beer to drink from a glass and then were asked to name the brand. Practically all (69 out of 70) identified the beer as either Budweiser, Schlitz, or Miller High Life. The brand used in the test was actually Old Timer—the same beer later sold as Black Pride. This result seems to agree with some marketing research studies showing that beer drinkers can not distinguish among brands of beer when the bottles are unlabeled.[2]

Some limited research also was carried out on the label. A proposed label was rejected because the colors used were not sufficiently eye-catching when viewed side-by-side with other major brands. Modification resulted in a label which used stronger colors of gold, copper, yellow, and black, and the slogan "A beer as proud as its people." Included, too, was the Black Pride, Inc. trademark: the letters "BPI" within the flame of a torch—indicative of the "look to a brighter future" for all blacks that the Black Pride concept represented—and a lion, a reminder of the African heritage that blacks have in common.

The company also was aware of strong emotional buying motives associated with beer. It seemed, therefore, that beer was an appropriate product to associate with appeals to "buy black." (It should be noted that companies such as Soul Brothers Scotch have tried this appeal unsuccessfully.)

Personnel

Black Pride, Inc. (BPI) was headed by a board of directors composed of nine prominent members of the black community. Several were businessmen; one was an attorney and all were active in such organizations as Operation Breadbasket and the NAACP. Although they were strongly committed to the goals of BPI, their involvement was on a part-time basis.

When BPI was founded, President Edward J. McClellan was the Urban Program Director of the South Side branch of the NAACP. This followed 17 years with the Chicago Police Department and 6 years of counterintelligence work in the Army. McClellan was the prime mover behind BPI and took responsibility for many of the decisions regarding Black Pride Beer.

From November 24, 1969 through February, 1970, most accounts were signed up through word-of-mouth solicitation. In this time period, five people were employed by BPI—a secretary, office manager (cashier), two drivers, and one warehouseman. No full-time salesman or operating manager was employed.

The beer business requires constant professional solicitation of new accounts and follow-ups of established accounts. Shareholder solicitation was adequate as an initial impetus, but it was inadequate to the task of ongoing market merchandising. The lack of full-time salesmen caused follow-up problems and offended some initial accounts.

During this same period, BPI was searching for a fulltime operating manager to manage the beer division. Finding a person who was familiar with the beer business and was willing to leave his present employment and accept the inherent risks involved in the management of a newly formed, private label distributorship was difficult at best, and no qualified person was found outside the organization.

Because a full-time operating manager was needed to establish and promote efficient and effective operating procedures, Earl Vivian, vice-president of BPI, retired from the National Guard during this period and assumed management of the beer division.

Additional Personnel Perspectives

The only major personnel problem was the hiring of qualified salesmen and driver salesmen. Qualified salesmen and driver salesmen employed by established distributors were at first unwilling to leave their high-paying and secure positions to take lower paying and insecure positions with BPI.

The board of directors was very active in the management of BPI. Although no board member, including Vivian, had had any previous experience in the beer industry, the business expertise they did possess was appropriate to the task.

Insurance, real estate, and union management are representative of this base of experience.

Sales

Vivian projected first-year sales of Black Pride Beer to be approximately 120 barrels per week. This represents approximately 1350 cases per week, 6200 barrels per month, or 71,000 cases per year.

At an average gross margin of $1.28 per case, first-year gross sales of Black Pride Beer approached $91,000. The prospectus accurately estimated a profit margin of 25 cents per case, and a first-year profit of approximately $18,000. In accordance with the original agreement, no profits were distributed for at least three years. If the sales curve had remained constant for five years, BPI would have exceeded its minimum obligations to Lithia by more than 11,000 barrels. Vivian estimated that there are 2,200 accounts on the South and West Sides of Chicago. Of these, BPI was servicing approximately 1,200. BPI signed a two-year contract with the Procurement Officer of the Fifth Army (Midwest). This contract placed Black Pride Beer in all Fifth Army Officer's Clubs, N. C. O. Clubs, and Post Exchanges.

Vivian did not expect the sales curve to level off. He projected the annual market for Black Pride Beer to be 150,000 barrels within five years. This projection broke down to 50,000 barrels per year for the Chicago market, with 100,000 barrels sold through franchised distributorships in other market areas. Franchised distributorships would be charged a minimum fee of $5,000 per year (negotiated in terms of market potential) plus 20 cents per case. All franchises were subject to annual renewal, and Black Pride, Inc. reserved the right to designate product producers and suppliers, display and marketing techniques, employee training, and administrative procedures.

Old Style Distributorship

In August, 1970, Black Pride, Inc. acquired an exclusive distributorship, within certain territorial constraints, for Heileman's Old Style Beer. Earl Vivian felt that a conservative estimate of the sales potential of this territory was $3,000 per week and added that the acquisition of this distributorship reflected both the soundness of the Black Pride concept and the sound financial management of BPI.

Initially unable to elicit any support from major brewers, BPI was approached by Heileman's concerning the distributorship. After initial investigation of BPI, Heileman's decided to look elsewhere. Unable to find a qualified distributor, they returned to negotiate with BPI. This time BPI was negotiating from a position of strength.

Before BPI, there was no black-owned-and-run distributorship for established brands in Chicago. Shortly after BPI's beer division opened, the three major brewers negotiated such distributorships. These three firms, however, were only distributors, not private labels, and therefore not black companies. McClellan explained that

> as far as competition from black-owned companies within the black community is concerned, nothing would please us more than seeing this develop for it would be the best kind of proof that our concept had taken hold. And by competition in the beer business, I mean something more than a few small and relatively unprofitable distributorships.

Pricing

The company decided to sell Black Pride as a premium beer priced a little below (4 or 5 cents) that charged per bottle for Budweiser or Schlitz. The price of cans would be the same as that charged by these leading brands. The decision to charge the premium price was based on McClellan's assessment of the black consumer as a quality-conscious buyer.

The price for Black Pride Beer was the same as that of Old Style. The average gross margin on Old Style was approximately $1.75 per case, as compared to Black Pride Beer's $1.28. This difference was partially explained by differences in shipping costs. Old Style, which ships to numerous distributors in the area, can achieve lower per case shipping costs than can Lithia, who, of course, supplied Black Pride Beer only to BPI. BPI paid the freight costs on all incoming merchandise.

SUMMARY AND PERSPECTIVE

This case study of BPI is an analysis of two distinct things. Narrowly viewed, this study is the story of the frustrations and risks a small business takes in its struggle for success. What differentiates this business from most other businesses is the long-term objectives and goals of BPI.

Narrowly conceived, the Black Pride Beer division simply went through all the nitty-gritty motions necessary to build a successful enterprise. On the other hand, Black Pride Beer represents the means to an end—the capitalization of the black community. The meaning of Black Pride, which is not adaptable to short-run analytical measurement, lies somewhere between these two points. The immediate and short-run profit picture of BPI was not particularly relevant. The long-term growth and uses of profit were possibly the only measurement of the success of BPI and similar businesses.

McClellan stated that, "In the months to come, as our success has an effect upon the community, as well as the shareholders, we must not be short-circuited in our long-range planning. Beyond Black Pride Beer is Black Pride Surety, Black Pride Investors, Black Pride Printers, Black Pride Maintenance, Black Pride Food Co-ops, and Black Pride Home Improvement."

POSTSCRIPT

Black Pride closed its doors in 1971 because of insufficient sales. Beer is a product which is differentiated by substantial advertising expense. Thus, insufficient sales indicate that either Black Pride was unable to mount a sufficient appeal to black identity or that black identity and consciousness does not play a significant role in influencing black consumer choice, or perhaps some of both.

However, the concept seems to be a good one, and further tests of this concept would seem to be a worthwhile experiment as a part of the over-all national minority enterprise development program. If such future tests are evaluated effectively, it may be possible to determine the validity of the concept of appealing to ethnic consciousness.

FOOTNOTES

[1] Bureau of the Census, *Census of Minority Owned Businesses, 1969* (Washington, D. C.: U. S. Government Printing Office, 1971), pp. i to v.

[2] Learned, Christensen, Andres, Guth, "Heublein, Inc., Case (B)," *Business Policy and Cases* (Homewooood, Ill.: Irwin, 1969), p. 315.

Edward D. Irons*

BLACK BANKING: PROBLEMS AND PROSPECTS

INTRODUCTION

After 30 virtually dormant years, more black banks were organized during the last two-thirds of the 1960s than at any time since the early 1900s. The advent of these new banks, and black banks in general, has been the subject of intense debate among bankers, businessmen, government regulatory agencies, educators, and private individuals.

The focal point of this debate has centered around a number of questions, the most significant of which are the following:

(1) Are these banks sound economic units?

*Edward Irons is Mills Bee Lane Professor of Banking and Finance, Atlanta University, School of Business.

(2) What is the nature of their operating experience?

(3) Do they serve a useful role?

(4) What are the prospects of these banks?

It would be the height of naiveté to suggest that even the most comprehensive and objective analysis would provide a definitive answer to all the above questions. It is hoped, however, that this paper will shed some light on these questions and provide a basis for further research.

A BRIEF HISTORY

In 1963 there were 10 black-controlled banks in the United States, mainly in the Deep South (Appendix B). By the end of December, 1970, this number had grown to 26 (Appendix A) to more than 40 in 1973. This number does not sound impressive in relation to the more than 13,000 banks in operation nationwide on June 30, 1970. However, when viewed within the perspective of the history of black banks, the advent of this increased number of banks suggests a mini-revolution.

By the end of the 1960s, the 10 banks had aggregate assets of approximately $115 million. Four of these banks had been organized after 1933—one in 1937, one in 1946, and two in 1947. Prior to 1963, all 10 black banks then in existence were organized under state charters. Of the 16 new black banks, 10 were organized as national banks. The remaining 6 were organized as state banks.

The first black bank in the United States was the Savings Bank of Grand Fountain United Order, True Reformers founded in 1888. During the 45-year period from 1888 to 1933, 134 financial institutions were organized by blacks, 40 of which could be considered commercial banks.[1] Most of these banks failed during the 1920s and early 1930s, as did approximately 14,000 other banks during this period.[2] During this era, the laws and regulations governing the banking industry were so loosely drawn that many banks opened for business without regard to adequate capital, management experience, or economic need.[3] Thus when a series of severe economic crises descended upon the country during the 1920s and 1930s, the banking system cracked at the seams, and all of its basic weaknesses were revealed. The result was an avalanche of bank failures that swept away not only the weak banks but also many sound banks. Wholesale withdrawal of funds from the banking system by the public caused the number of banks to drop from 29,415 in 1921 to 12,817 by April 12, 1933.[4] Had not President Franklin D. Roosevelt closed all the nation's banks for a three-day period, it is likely that many more banks would have failed.

Eight black banks survived the moratorium of 1933 (Appendix C). Of the 3,488 new banks that opened for business in the United States from 1933 to 1963, only 4 were black-controlled. In 1963, the first of a new group of black-controlled banks opened in Houston, Texas. The opening of this bank set a pattern in motion, the result of which is a larger number of black banks currently operating than in any prior period, with the notable exception of the "free banking" era.

Deposit Growth

The 8 black banks that survived the moratorium in 1933 held a total of $3.2 million in deposits at that time. By June 30, 1963, when the first of the new banks came into existence, the deposits had increased to $50.7 million, with a total of 11 black banks. From June 30, 1963 to June 30, 1970, there was a 428 percent growth in total deposits of black banks in the U. S. to a total of $267 million. Of the $303 million in assets that these banks had accumulated by that time, 57 percent was accounted for by the 16 new banks whose average age was 3.9 years (Appendix A). Forty-three percent of this growth was accounted for by the 10 banks that were in existence prior to 1963, the average age of which was 43.7 years.[5] By June, 1970, the largest black bank had $41.9 million in assets (Appendix A). It is clear that the emergence of the new banks had a synergistic effect upon the older banks. While the older banks have increased their growth rate since 1963, the bulk of the deposit growth has come from the new banks.

THE SAMPLE

In an effort to put the experience of these black banks into proper perspective, a sample of similar-sized banks ($10 million to $25 million) was selected from the industry at large. Where possible, banks were selected within the same cities as the black banks. The year selected for analysis was 1969, the latest year for which data was available.

Specifically, all black banks that were at least 5 years old, a total of 18 banks, were selected. While there is nothing sacrosanct in the selection of banks with a minimum of 5 years of age, an attempt was made to compare banks of similar maturity.

The sample of 18 black banks breaks down into 10 banks that were organized before 1963 with an average age of 43.7 years, aggregate deposits of $115.7 million, and average deposits per bank of $11.6 million. The 8 remaining banks held aggregate deposits of $120.5 million with an average of 5.8 years of age and had average deposits per bank of $15.0 million.

The 8 black banks not studied here that are less than five years old have aggregate deposits of $69 million, with an average of $8.6 million per bank. Their average age is 2.9 years. Their break-even time typically ranges from 1 to 4 years. Of the 8 banks in this category, 5 have broken even and become profitable, while 3 have yet to reach the break-even point. The return on capital of the group ranges from a negative 9.6 percent to a positive 13.1 percent.

For this study, 20 banks were selected from the industry at large using the following criteria:

(1) They would have assets ranging from $10 million to $25 million.

(2) Ten of these banks would be high-earning banks, and 10 would be low-earning banks with 6 percent return on capital being the cut-off point between low and high earning banks.

(3) They would be situated in the same cities as the black banks, where possible. (4) National averages of the same bank size category were used to provide additional perspective. In 1969 there were 3,180 banks of this size in the United States.

The sample has two obvious weaknesses: it is small in size and includes only one year's activity. It is conceivable that the smallness of the sample size may not be representative of the true universe of banks with $10 million to $25 million in deposits, or that one year could conceivably be an aberration rather than a norm. In spite of these weaknesses, the evidence appears to suggest that the conclusions derived from the analysis may be generalized.

Emphasis will be focused upon the operating results derived from the asset management techniques and the attendant earnings and expenses associated with these techniques. And, finally, the net result of these operations on return on capital—the principal long-term purpose of any private business—will be measured.

Following this aspect of the analysis, an attempt will be made to place the experience of the black banks into further perspective by analyzing briefly certain other variables that affect the operating techniques and results of these banks. Finally, a brief assessment of prospects of these banks will be set forth.

Asset Management

Beginning with the cash and securities which, taken together, constitute a significant indication of the liquidity position of the bank and which also constitute a combination of nonearning and low-earning assets, Table I illustrates that, of four groups of banks, the black banks have the highest percentage of their assets invested in this class of assets (36 percent). On a relative basis, this is 35 percent higher than the 27.5 percent which the high-earning banks hold, and 15 percent higher than that held by the low-earning banks. Thus, whether the black banks consciously or circumstantially keep this percentage of their assets in this class of assets, the downward pressure on earnings is the same.

Table I
Percent of Cash and Government Securities to Total Assets, 1969

| | Banks by Earnings Rank | | | |
	High	*Low*	*Black*	*National**
Number of Banks	10	10	18	3,180
Cash and Due from Banks	10.5	12.2	11.7	11.9
U.S. Treasury Securities	12.5	12.1	13.7	15.7
Securities of other U.S. Government Agencies	4.5	7.3	10.9	3.7
Totals	27.5	31.6	36.3	31.3

Source: FDIC Records
*All banks, the samples included, fall within the $10 million to $25 million in deposits, except two black-controlled banks.

Since the highest relative earnings rate typically stems from the loan portfolio, any significant difference between the groups in the relative amounts of assets invested in this class of asset should have a corresponding affect upon the earnings differences of the respective groups, all other factors being equal. From Table II it can be seen that, while black banks held the lowest percentage of their assets in loans, the difference was not significant. With 51.7 percent of their assets in loans, this was approximately six points below the group with the highest loan/asset ratio, which, ironically, in this case, is the low-earnings group

Table II
Percent Loans to Total Assets, 1969

| | Banks by Earnings Rank | | | |
	High	Low	Black	National*
Number of Banks	10	10	18	3,180
Loan and Discounts	54.7	57.9	51.7	52.9
Commercial	8.2	17.0	7.3	10.5
Agriculture	2.1	0.01	0.1	4.8
Real Estate	20.2	11.9	22.0	16.8
Individuals	19.9	18.8	13.3	15.8
Other	5.2	8.8	8.9	4.9

Source: FDIC Records
*All banks, the samples included, fall within the $10 million to $25 million range in deposits, except two black-controlled banks.

of banks. The amount was three points lower than the high-earning banks. The breakdown of the loan portfolio into its component parts does not shed additional light on the subject. Significantly, with the exception of the low-earning banks, it can be seen from Table II that small banks generally invest their loans in the following order: real estate, individuals, commercial, and all others. Black banks fit this pattern with little variation.

The manner in which a bank invests its assets is contingent on the mix of its deposits. For example, if a bank's deposits are dominated heavily by time and savings deposits, it may be appropriate to invest heavily in real estate loans; conversely, if the deposits are heavily demand oriented, the bank must look with caution before investing significantly in real estate.

It can be seen that, in the management of the bank's most significant assets, *black banks maintain a higher percentage of their assets in cash and securities, and consequently a lower percentage of their assets is invested in loans.* This does not suggest conclusively that these banks are wrong in maintaining a higher liquidity base than other small banks.

Table III illustrates that *there is almost no difference between the bank groups and the distribution of their deposits between demand and time.* For example, the black banks with a ratio of 54.8 percent time to total deposits

Table III
Selected Balance Sheet Items as a Percent
to Total Deposits, 1969

| | Banks by Earnings Rank | | | |
	High	Low	Black	National
Number of Banks	10	10	18	3,180
Demand	46.0	47.6	45.1	45.8
Time	53.9	52.4	54.8	54.1
Cash Accounts	11.8	14.5	13.1	13.3
Cash, U.S. Treasury & U.S. Government Agency Securities	28.0	37.7	41.2	35.1
Total Loans	61.6	69.5	58.2	59.3

Source: FDIC Records

constitute the highest of the groups, but this is only 2.4 percentage points higher than the lowest group. It can be said, therefore, that *the aggregate deposit structure of black banks is essentially the same as other small banks in the nation.* Equally important as the aggregate structure of the deposit accounts is the average size of the deposit accounts of the banks. Smaller accounts, typically, are more active and thus more costly for the bank to handle.

In this regard, Table IV reveals that the size of the deposit accounts of black banks is substantially smaller than both the high- and low-earning banks. Paradoxically, the average account size of the low-earning banks is $1,816, slightly more than twice the $832, which is the average account size of the black banks. The average account size of the high earners is approximately 50 percent larger than that of the black banks. *The average account size is thus what distinguishes black banks from other small banks.* While the evidence is insufficient in this study to verify it conclusively, it can reasonably be assumed that the small, higher activity accounts exert a downward effect on the profitability of black banks.

Table IV
Average Size of Deposit Accounts, 1969

| | Banks by Earnings Rank | | |
	High	Low	Black
Number of Banks	10	10	18
Mean Average Accounts Size			
All Deposits	$1,288	$1,816	$832
Demand	918	1,981	864
Time	1,793	1,771	762

Source: FDIC Records

Income Generation

Having explored the manner in which each of the groups invests its assets, we will look at the income-producing results of their asset management efforts, examining both the gross revenue produced by the assets and the rate of return received on each asset type. In Table V, it can be seen that the *black banks ranked favorably with each of the other groups in both rates of return on the several asset types and gross operating revenue as a percentage of assets*. In fact, the black banks earned 7.4 percent return on investment or a slightly higher amount of revenue as a percentage of their assets than was earned by the other groups. This phenomenon reflects the highly structured nature of the banking industry—the price policy, or interest rates on both the loan portfolio and the investment portfolio are set largely by the market and rarely is there any major difference in rates for similar types of loans or investments, irrespective of the size of the bank. This, then, accounts for the similarity of revenue generated by each of the separate groups.

There is one significant difference in the above pattern between bank groups in the area of revenue producing, namely service charge earnings related to demand deposits: while each of the other groups earn within a range of 0.7 percent to 0.8 percent to assets, the black banks earned at slightly more than double this rate, or 1.9 percent. This could be due to one or a combination of two causes:

(1) higher service charge rates
(2) higher account activity

While we do not have sufficient data on the rates charged by the several groups to be conclusive, a limited check revealed that there is very little variation in the service charge rates among the groups. It is, thus, reasonable to conclude that the difference stems essentially from the degree of activity among accounts in the respective groups. The *black banks obviously had a higher account activity than the other banks*, since the black banks' accounts are only half as large on the

Table V
Total Operating Revenue and Rates of Return on Assets, 1969

| | Banks by Earnings Rank | | | |
	High	Low	Black	National
Number of Banks	10	10	10	3,180
Rates of Return on:				
Loans	7.7	8.3	8.2	7.5
U.S. Treasuries	5.3	5.5	6.2	5.2
Securities of other U.S. Government Agencies	3.3	7.0	4.7	4.1
Service Charges/Demand Deposits	0.75	0.8	1.9	0.8
Total Operating Revenue to Total Assets	6.3	6.7	7.4	6.1

Source: FDIC Records

average as those of the other banks. For example, the cost of opening a $1,000 account would be nearly the same as the cost of opening a $100,000 account. Similarly, the cost of making and collecting a loan of $5,000 would be nearly the same as that of a $100,000 loan. Thus, the smaller loans and accounts require greater activity and create a larger service charge for a given volume than larger accounts do.

The relative sources of income associated with the management of bank assets as a percentage of total income corroborate the conclusions set forth in the above section regarding gross revenue as a percentage of assets. In Table VI, it can be seen that *black banks generate less income from loans as a* percentage

Table VI
Income by Asset Component as a Percentage of Total Income, 1969

| | *Banks by Earnings Rank* | | | |
	High	*Low*	*Black*	*National*
Total	100.0	100.0	100.0	100.0
Income on Loans	64.7	67.0	58.6	64.2
Interest on U.S. Treasuries	11.9	11.5	14.1	15.0
Interest on U.S. Government Agency Securities	2.9	9.0	8.7	3.7
Service Charges on Deposits	4.6	5.2	10.7	5.2
Other	15.9	7.3	7.9	11.9
Net Current Operating Earnings	28.6	10.4	8.9	21.8
Net Income	23.5	8.3	7.5	15.5

Source: FDIC Records

of total income than either of the other three groups generate. This follows logically from the fact that black banks held a relatively smaller amount of their assets in loans than did the other groups. With 51.7 percent of their assets invested in loans, the black banks received 58.6 percent of their income from loans. Both of these percentages were the lowest for the groups studied. Predictably, these banks earned relatively more of their income from securities than did the other sample groups. Thus, with 24.6 percent of their assets invested in securities, the highest of the sample groups, the black banks earned 22.8 percent of their total income from securities, also the highest among the sample groups (Table I & VI).

Relative income from service charges on demand deposits corroborates the small-account, high-activity nature of the black banks. It may be recalled that the black banks held accounts that were approximately one-half the size of the other sample banks. The attendant high activity associated with these small accounts generates twice as much income as a percentage of total income as is true of the other sample groups. From Table VI it can be seen that *10.7 percent of the earnings of black banks derived from service charges on demand accounts, or about twice as much as other banks earned from this source.* This compared to 4.6 percent for the high-earning banks and 5.2 percent for the other two groups respectively. Thus while the relative sources of income of black banks differ from the other sample banks as a percentage of total income, it is significant that black banks compare favorably with total operating revenue as a percentage of total assets (Table V).

Operating Expense

Having examined asset management and the income generation related to management of those assets, we will now examine the expense associated with asset management. While black banks compare favorably with the other sample groups in regard to income-generating ability, they compare unfavorably with these groups in relationship to the expense associated with the management of their assets. From Table VII, it can be seen that *black banks have the highest operating expense associated with the management of their assets of any sample groups*. With an operating expense of 85.6 percent as a percentage of total revenue, it costs the black banks 18.2 percent more to manage their assets than it costs the high-earning banks, which require only 67.4 percent. Relatively speaking this is a 27 percent greater cost for black banks than for the high-earning banks.

There are three significantly different expense items that have the greatest impact on the cost of operating the black banks:

(1) salaries
(2) provisions for loan losses
(3) other expenses.

Since banking requires a large labor force, it is predictable that salaries would be one of the most significant expense items. Until 1963, when the competition for time deposits became such an important factor among banks, salaries had always been the number one expense item.[6] Salary expense is currently the number two

Table VII
Operating Expense as a Percentage of Total Revenue, 1969

| | Banks by Earnings Rank | | | |
	High	Low	Black	National
Number of Banks	10	10	20	3,180
Ratio to Total Revenue:				
Total Operating Expense	67.4	81.3	85.6	77.4
Salaries	17.0	22.6	27.3	19.4
Pension & Employee Benefits	2.9	2.4	2.5	2.4
Interest on Deposits	33.6	31.8	29.1	34.9
Net Occupancy Expense	.0	.0	.04	3.4
Provision for Loan Losses	1.4	3.0	5.7	2.3
Other Expense	12.5	22.5	21.0	15.0

Source: FDIC Records

Table VIII
Selected Employee and Salary Ratios, 1968

| | Banks by Earnings Rank | | |
	High	Low	Black
Average Number of Employees	32	29	45
Average Salary per Employee*	$6,475	$7,151	$5,611
Average Total Assets ($ Mil.)	17.3	14.8	
Average Number of Employees per $ Mil.	1.8	2.4	3.5
Ratio of Salary Expense/Total Assets	1.2	1.7	1.9

Source: FDIC Records and individual bank records
*Includes all full-time personnel, inclusive of officers

expense for most banks; interest expense ranks number one, with only a slight variation between the groups (Table VII). As for salary expense, it can be seen that the *black banks have the highest salary costs of any of the sample groups*, with 27.3 percent of the total revenue. This is 10 percent higher, or on a relative basis, 59 percent higher than the high-earning banks, which, at 17 percent, constitute the lowest of the sample groups. Similarly, from Table VIII, it can be seen that black banks have the highest salary cost as a percentage of total assets, or 1.9 percent. This is also 59 percent higher than the 0.7 percent represented by the high-earning banks. Predictably, the difference between the relationship of salary to assets and salary to earnings between these two groups is the same. In the same vein, black banks have almost twice as many employees as the high-earning banks, or 3.5 employees per million in assets. However, they pay an average of 15 percent less than the average salary paid per employee in the high-earning banks, or $5,611 to $6,475 for the high-earning banks. All of the above factors involving salary costs tend to corroborate the small-account, high-activity nature of the black banks.

The second important expense item that distinguishes the black banks from the other sample groups is provision for loan losses. From Table VII, it can be seen that *black banks have the highest rate of loan loss provision of all the groups*. Black banks set aside 5.7 percent of their revenue for loan losses, or 4 times as much as the 1.4 percent which the high-earning banks set aside, and almost 2.5 times as much as the national average. This suggests one or a combination of two causes:

(1) higher loan risks
(2) less experienced management on the part of the black banks.

The final expense item that distinguishes the black banks from the other sample groups is "other expense." From Table VII, it can be seen that *black banks rank with the low-earning banks in having the highest "other expense" category*. Black banks allocate 21 percent of their revenue to this catchall category, more than twice the high-earning banks. While information was insufficient to determine the specific reason for the significant difference in this category, it can be said that this account is a residual account containing all expense items not otherwise delineated on the income and expense statement.[7] Perhaps the most significant item in this account is computer costs for revising bank records. While most small banks do not have their own installations, they typically will have their records processed for a fee by computer service companies. It is conceivable, therefore, that with higher activity associated with the smaller accounts, the black banks incur a higher service cost. This, however, will require additional research before definitive conclusions can be drawn.

Return on Capital

Thus far, it is clear that black banks invest a smaller percentage of their assets in loans than other banks do. They generate approximately the same amount of revenue on their assets as the other banks, and it costs substantially more, primarily in salary costs, to service the assets of black banks. From the viewpoint of the stockholders, the question is: How do these banks fare regarding return on capital?

From Table IX, it becomes clear that relative performance of the several bank groups is significantly different from the gross earnings performance.[8] It will be recalled (from Table V) that blacks led all of the sample groups in total operating earnings as a percentage of assets by a small margin, the highest being 7.4 percent, the lowest being 6.1 percent.

After considering the impact of expenses upon that income, it can be seen from Table IX that *black banks rank last when comparing net income to total assets*. In this regard, black banks earned 0.56 percent on their assets while the high-earning banks earned 2.0 percent, or slightly more than 3.5 times the black bank rate. When we move to net income as a percentage of capital, the rankings change slightly, with black banks moving to third place and the low-earning banks taking last place. The high-earning banks again come in first with 21.9 percent, or slightly less than three times the 7.7 percent earned by the black banks.

As for the sample groups, it may be revealing that the high-earning banks

Table IX
Earning and Selected Capital Ratios

| | *Banks by Earnings Rank* | | | |
	High	*Low*	*Black*	*National*
Number of Banks	10	10	18	3,180
Net Income/Assets	1.0	.7	.56	.9
Total Capital/Assets	6.8	11.4	7.7	7.5
Net Income/Capital	21.9	4.4	7.5	12.7
Dividends/Capital	4.1	1.3	1.9	3.2

Source: FDIC Records

held a capital/asset ratio (6.8 percent) that was in the twentieth percentile in the U. S. among banks at $10 million to $25 million in assets. Thus, 80 percent of the nation's banks maintain a higher capital/asset ratio than this group does. On the other hand, the low-earning banks with a capital/asset ratio of 11.4 percent fell above the ninetieth percentile. These two groups, therefore, fall at the high and low extremes of the nation's banks within their size category. On the surface, it would appear that the low-earning banks are overcapitalized while the high-earning banks are undercapitalized. While this may be true, such a conclusion can not be drawn definitively without full knowledge of the market they serve, the quality of loans, and the stability of their deposits.

One might reasonably conclude that some of this high operating cost may be attributable to operational inefficiency due to inexperienced personnel. It would appear, however, that most of this cost results from the nature of the accounts serviced by black banks. Thus the small operating accounts, typically about half the size of the other sample banks, required twice as much personnel to service. The losses on loans were also larger, suggesting a higher risk market.

As a consequence of this cost structure, the return on capital of black banks was below the national average in 1969. During the past 10 years, black banks have earned on the average two percentage points less on their capital than the national average. At this time, it is not certain whether the larger earnings gap as reflected in 1969 is merely an aberration or an emerging trend. It is clear, however, that black banks operate under a wholly different cost structure than banks generally operate.

BLACK BANKS IN PERSPECTIVE

With the above background, let us consider the future of black banks. What is the nature of the market they serve? What role does size play? What about management? Do black banks serve a need? Can't big banks meet this need more effectively? Don't black banks contribute to a separatist philosophy? This section will attempt to shed some light on these questions.

The Market

With rare exception, black banks are located in the nation's ghettos. Since the growth and development of the bank is a function of the income and wealth of the market it serves, it may be enlightening to analyze the relative status of wealth of the markets served by the black banks in relation to the general population of the U. S.

The mean income of black families in 1970 was $6,576, or approximately 63 percent as much as their white counterparts. On an aggregate basis, black families earn 7.4 percent of total earned family income in the United States.

Black families have almost no capital income (income derived from assets other than labor). Only 10.4 percent of black families have capital income, and it amounts to only 1.1 percent of the total U. S. family capital income. Black mean annual capital income is $571, approximately 40 percent that of white families, which is $1,402.

Only 45 percent of black families have any liquid assets at all; this is about half the number of white families (88.3 percent) with liquid assets. Black families have a mean average of $953 in total liquid assets, or approximately one-fifth as much as white families at $4,900. Collectively, black families have only 1.1 percent of the liquid assets held by U. S. families.

Only one-third as many black as white families have checking accounts with a mean average balance of $374, which is approximately 49 percent as much as the white family average of $766. Almost twice as many white as black families have savings accounts. Slightly more than one-third of black families have savings accounts with a mean average of $824, about one-fifth as much as white families, which have $4,368.[9]

This environment, in large measure created by larger society, is the one in which black banks operate. This accounts for the small high-acitivity accounts with which black banks must operate, and the concomitant high cost.

What About Management?

Since blacks have only recently acquired bank management expertise, a number of black banks have begun to draw on management wherever it can be found, regardless of skin color.

Within the last two or three years, there has been a change in industry practice regarding black managers. As a result, a number of blacks are enrolled in nationwide management-training courses. If this pattern continues, within the next ten years there should be a pool of trained and experienced black managers at all levels.

Do They Meet a Need?

It is unlikely that one black bank in each major metropolitan city of the United States will ever meet the total financial need of the area, nor is it necessarily desirable that such a condition should obtain. If one accepts the premise that the general population needs a commercial bank that is convenient and empathetic to its financial and economic needs, should the black population aspire to any less? The black populations of the United States are being increasingly relegated to highly concentrated black areas. Will these areas be able to provide their black inhabitants with convenient and empathetic service?

Some observers maintain that black-controlled banks cannot survive because there is very little commercial activity in their markets. This argument has some merit; however, it is a known fact that commercial activity will never emerge until it has adequate banking assistance. Whether to organize a bank in an area or wait until commercial activity emerges becomes a question of which comes first, the chicken or the egg. Anyone who understands the economic development process knows that irrespective of which emerges first, neither can develop without the other.

Many observers have asked the question, "Can't the big banks meet this need better than the neighborhood bank?" The answer to that question is *yes*. However, the next question becomes, "Have they done it?" Perhaps to some degree they have, but the preponderance of the evidence suggests that big banks, by nature or by policy, devote a relatively small amount of their loan portfolio to small business, regardless of race.[10] Moreover, the increasing deterioration of black areas suggests that these areas can not possibly be adequately banked. The nation's banks obviously can not unilaterally affect the total economic development process of the nation's ghettos. The question arises, "Who is better qualified to lead the process than the nation's banks, large or small?"

By virtue of his strategic position in the community the banker automatically becomes a leader, but not all bankers are leaders. However, no other institution provides a better base from which to exert a strong positive leadership in that area, irrespective of its geographic boundaries. What areas within the United States are in greater need of this type of leadership than the nation's ghettos?

Black Banks as Separatists

Some observers believe that the development of black banks creates a separatist philosophy. Perhaps. But does a bank controlled by Irishmen create a separatist philosophy? Or by Germans? Italians, Poles? If it does, should we not dismantle all those institutions in the United States that are controlled by a particular ethnic group? The annals of banking are replete with these ethnic controls. For the first time in history, blacks are beginning to move in a meaningful way in that direction. Must we change direction at this time?

"But blacks should get management jobs in big banks," many people contend. True, but unless blacks also own some banks, they will never influence what happens to the banking assets. And if history is any teacher, those who control the finances of a nation control the direction of that nation. Up to this point in our history, blacks have been left out of this control process. What blacks are saying now is, "We want in."

PROSPECTS

Today's black bankers, in the same manner as black doctors, black lawyers, black businessmen, or black economists, are a mirror of contemporary American society. They reflect all the past constraints imposed by society. Potentially, black banks can be as sound as any group in the United States. However, if they are to become truly sound, a whole series of fundamental actions must take place.

In the first place, a public policy must never revert to the pre-1963 period, when blacks were systematically discouraged from seeking charters. Second, the black family must ultimately be given the opportunity to earn the same income as its white counterpart, thereby eliminating the 40 percent earnings gap between these two groups. Third, the federal, state, and local governments must begin to utilize these institutions as depositories in the same manner as other banks are used. Fourth, the major corporations, which sell their products in black communities, should consider using black banks as depositories. This would serve as a counterforce to the continual wealth outflow from these areas, a phenomenon which the author sees as a *chronic balance of payments drain*. Fifth, a supply of venture capital must be made available to the markets served by black banks as a means of stimulating significant commercial activity. Sixth, the fledgling start toward the training and upgrading of blacks to all levels of bank management must accelerate significantly and must continue unabated. And finally, when these banks and the bankers who manage them become accepted as integral parts of our total economic system, they will be capable of rendering competitive service to every sector of our society. In fact, wouldn't it be a boon to our system of free enterprise if we could look forward to the day when the top quality executives of these fledgling banks would be sought after as bank presidents in any market, when these banks would have evolved to the point at which they were no longer referred to as black banks, and the markets they serve would be little different from other American bank markets? These conditions are possible, but they will happen only if our total society wills it. And our society will not allow it unless significant voices, such as the American Economics Association and similar national opinion molders, are raised in support of black banking.

FOOTNOTES

[1] Abram L. Harris, *The Negro as Capitalist: A Study of Banking and Business Among American Negroes* (Gloucester, Mass.: Peter Smith, 1968), pp. 191-2.

[2] Ross. M. Robertson, *The Comptroller and Bank Supervision: A Historical Appraisal* (Washington, D. C.: The Office of the Comptroller of the Currency, 1968), p. 125.

[3] *Ibid.*, p. 61.

[4] *Ibid.*, pp. 98-123.

[5] One bank failed in 1965. This bank was one of a number of bank victims that had to close in the 1960s as a result of a widely practiced system used by money brokers to secure both deposits and loan businesses. The practice involves a borrower who agrees to get a money broker to deposit funds in the bank at least equal to the amount of and duration of his loan request. Theoretically, there is nothing wrong with the practice, as long as the loan is repaid as agreed and the money stays in the bank until the loan is repaid. The difficulty stems from the default in the loan and the subsequent outflow of the funds, which in the industry are referred to as "hot money." This practice caused a number of bank failures in the late 1960s and sparked an investigation currently being conducted by the U. S. Comptroller of the Currency.

[6] Federal Deposit Insurance Corporation, *Annual Report of the Corporation* (Washington, D.C.: FDIC, 1968), p. 200, Table 113.

[7] Federal Deposit Insurance Corporation, *Bank Operation Statistics* (Washington, D.C.: FDIC, 1969), Table E. Category "other expense" consists of all expense items, not otherwise delineated on the Statement of Income and Dividends.

[8] Jack M. Guttentag and Edward S. Herman, *Bank Structure and Performance* (New York: The Institute of Finance of the Schools of Business of New York University), pp. 181-196. Summarized studies of Alhadeff, Schweiger, and McGee, Gramley, Horvitz, Greenbaum, and Benston on the economics of scale.

[9] U.S. Bureau of the Census, *Selected Financial and Economic Indications* 1969 (Washington, D.C.: U.S. Government Printing Office, 1970).

[10] Guttentag and Herman, *op. cit.*, p. 145.

Appendix A
Minority Banks in Existence in the United States
June 30, 1970

Name of Bank	Location	Date Organized	Assets as of June 30, 1970 ($Millions)
Bank of Finance	Los Angeles, Calif.	1964 a	$ 17.5
Carver State Bank	Savannah, Georgia	1947 a	3.8
Citizens Savings & Trust Company	Nashville, Tenn.	1904 a	6.3
Citizens Trust Company	Atlanta, Georgia	1921 a	29.2
Consolidated Bank & Trust Company	Richmond, Virginia	1903 a	13.1
Douglass State Bank	Kansas City, Kansas	1947 a	14.2
First Independence National Bank of Detroit	Detroit, Michigan	1970 b	3.3
First Plymouth National Bank	Minneapolis, Minn.	1969 b	5.2
First State Bank	Danville, Virginia	1919 a	5.0
Freedom Bank of Finance	Portland, Oregon	1969 a	2.5
Freedom National Bank	New York, New York	1964 b	41.9
Gateway National Bank	St. Louis, Missouri	1965 b	10.1
Industrial Bank of Washington	Washington, D.C.	1934 a	22.8
Independence Bank of Chicago	Chicago, Illinois	1964 a	13.3
Liberty Bank of Seattle	Seattle, Washington	1968 a	3.9
Mechanics & Farmers Bank	Durham, North Carolina	1908 a	22.9
Pan American National Bank	Los Angeles, Calif.	1965 b	13.6
Peoples National Bank	Springfield, Illinois	1970 b	–
Riverside National Bank	Houston, Texas	1963 b	7.2
Seaway National Bank	Chicago, Illinois	1965 b	23.4
Swope Parkway National Bank	Kansas City, Missouri	1968 b	8.2
Tri-State Bank	Memphis, Tennessee	1946 a	10.8
United Community National Bank	Washington, D.C.	1964 b	8.5
Unity Bank & Trust Company	Roxbury, Mass.	1968 a	12.3
Unity State Bank	Dayton, Ohio	1970 a	–
Victory Savings Bank	Columbia, South Carolina	1921 a	3.4

State Charter   - a
National Charter - b

Appendix B
Black Banks in Existence in the United States
December 31, 1960

Name of Bank	Location	Date Organized	Assets as of Dec. 31, 1960 ($Millions)
Carver State Bank	Savannah, Georgia	1947	$ 1.1
Citizens Trust Company	Atlanta, Georgia	1921	10.1
Citizens Savings Bank & Trust Company	Nashville, Tennessee	1904	2.7
Consolidated Bank & Trust Company	Richmond, Virginia	1903	5.6
Crown Savings Bank	Newport News, Virginia	1908	4.0
Douglass State Bank	Kansas City, Kansas	1947	3.2
First State Bank (formerly Danville Savings Bank & Trust Co)	Danville, Virginia	1919	2.5
Industrial Bank of Washington	Washington, D.C.	1934	9.4
Mechanics & Farmers Bank	Durham, North Carolina	1908	8.7
Tri-State Bank	Memphis, Tennessee	1946	3.9
Victory Savings Bank	Columbia, South Carolina	1921	1.1

Source: Polk's *World Bank Directory*, 1961

Appendix C
Black Banks in Existence in the United States
December 31, 1933

Name of Bank	Location	Date Organized	Assets as of Dec. 31, 1933 ($Thousands)
Citizens Trust Company	Atlanta, Georgia	1921	$ 191
Mechanics & Farmers Bank	Durham, North Carolina	1908	648
Citizens & Southern Bank and Trust Company	Philadelphia, Pennsylvania	1925	498
Victory Savings Bank	Columbus, South Carolina	1921	71
Citizens Savings Bank & Trust Company	Nashville, Tennessee	1904	232
Consolidated Bank & Trust Company	Richmond, Virginia	1903	682
Crown Savings Bank	Newport News, Virginia	1908	315
Danville Savings Bank & Trust Company (name changed to First State Bank)	Danville, Virginia	1919	162

Source: Polk's *World Bank Directory*, 1934

Gerald M. Laures, James W. Laures*

INDEPENDENCE BANK OF CHICAGO

BACKGROUND

"I've read Andrew Brimmer's comments on black banks;[1] he couldn't be further from the truth," says Alvin J. Boutte, president of Independence Bank of Chicago, one of the city's two black-owned banks. "Brimmer made the claim that black banks were merely ornaments undeserving of any support; this statement gives everybody a way to cop out and turn their backs on the needs of a quarter of this country's population. Independence is more than just an ornament, It's a way up for blacks."

The Independence Bank of Chicago was first conceived in the fall of 1963 when Edward Aldworth, currently vice-president of the Commercial Department of National Boulevard Bank of Chicago, and Henry P. Hervey, presently a consultant for the National Bankers' Association and several insurance companies, recognized the need for a bank to serve the predominately black Chatham area located on Chicago's South Side. At that time, Aldworth, a white, was employed in the Commercial Banking division of the Harris Trust and Savings Bank of Chicago; Hervey, a black, managed the black-owned Service Federal Savings and Loan Association. The relationship between these men dates back to World War II when both served in the United States Air Force.

Aldworth approached Hervey with the idea of starting a black-owned and operated bank in the Chatham community. Recognizing the scarcity of black banks and anxious to establish more, federal banking authorities strongly encouraged groups in the Chatham community and other predominantly black areas to make a concerted effort to obtain bank charters.

With this impetus from the federal government, Aldworth and Hervey went to the Chatham community and recruited a group of influential business and civic leaders to organize and open Chicago's first black bank. This original group hoped to sell all the stock to members of the Chatham community. Unfortunately, all funds required for capitalization could not be raised inside the community, so the group was forced to seek the remainder from outside sources. At the time of the bank's opening on December 14, 1964, there were 40,000 shares of stock outstanding at $20 per share distributed among 400 stockholders. The ownership at this time was 50 percent black and 50 percent white. In 1971 there were 260 stockholders; more than 50 percent of the total shares outstanding was

---

*This case was prepared by Gerald Laures and James Laures, who were M. B. A. students at Northwestern University's Graduate School of Management at the time this case study was written. This case was written under the direction of Professor Samuel I. Doctors.

owned by two stockholders, President Alvin Boutte and George Johnson, owner of Johnson Products. Ownership is 90 percent black and 10 percent white.

The Independence Bank, located at 7936 South Cottage Grove, serves the Chatham community, a residential area with a population of 51,500 and a median income between $8,500 and $10,900. The area is 97.1 percent black and has experienced very little racial tension.

During its period of organization, the founders of Independence encountered some opposition from members of the Chatham community, who had begun organizing another bank in the same area. The two groups attempted to reach an agreement calling for the opening of a single bank in the area instead of two, but their meetings were unsuccessful: Independence Bank and Seaway National Bank of Chicago, the city's second black bank, opened their doors within a month of each other. The banks are located two miles apart. According to Arthur S. Littlefield, Jr., vice-president of the Commercial Banking department of Continental Illinois Bank of Chicago, the growth of both banks was slowed since they competed for essentially the same funds.

TRAINING EMPLOYEES

The Independence Bank is a correspondent bank of the Harris Trust and Savings Bank of Chicago—an arrangement under which the Harris Bank holds deposits with Independence and acts as an agent for Independence in various types of transactions. The Harris Bank became involved with the South Side bank largely because of George E. Johnson, chairman of Independence's board of directors. Johnson did much of his own banking at the Harris and consequently solicited the bank's help in organizing Independence.

Based upon economic feasibility studies, the Harris Bank had doubts as to Independence's success in the Chatham area. In spite of those doubts, the bank proceeded to help Independence because of government pressure for a black-owned bank in the area and because of Johnson and Boutte's reputations as successful businessmen.

In late 1964, the Director of Financial Institutions for the State of Illinois approved the Independence Bank's application at a capitalization of $800,000, $200,000 less than the normal capitalization usually required by the state. This was attributed to the work done by the Harris Bank. In the meantime, the FDIC approved Independence's application for federal deposit insurance.

To help Independence, the Harris sent people to organize and help train personnel in banking, a service that continues to a lesser extent today. Personnel were not brought to the Harris Bank for training; most training took place at Independence.

In 1971 Independence had 37 full- and part-time employees, excluding Boutte and his five officers. Most of these employees are hired by Lydia English, the assistant vice-president. Mrs. English expects a prospective employee to have the following general characteristics:

(1) some prior banking experience, although this is not an absolute necessity;

(2) adequate intelligence;

(3) willingness to learn

(4) at least a high school education.

There is no requirement that a prospective employee must be black. The present employee turnover rate is low, most having been employed for a year or more.

In 1970, employee salaries averaged about $6,860, a salary level which Boutte says is competitive with other banks of similar size. Employee benefits consist of hospital insurance, which provides full medical coverage, a life insurance program, and 10 days of sick leave.

According to Miller, some employees have been difficult to train, and supervisory personnel have not always been able to gain the respect of those directly under them. Many have not been able to relate to customers; many employees assume that the customers know as much about the bank's services as they do.

BOARD OF DIRECTORS

The original board of directors consisted of 11 men. The present board has 13 members of whom only 4, George Johnson, Alvin Boutte, Robert Bacon, and Edward Boshell, were original directors.

Six of the original eleven board members were black; the present board has ten black directors. Boutte wants to always have some white people on the board, and Bacon, one of the white directors, feels that as long as the bank is black-owned and black-controlled, some white involvement is advisable "to keep the communications channels open between the white community and the black community."

According to Boutte, the duties of Independence's board do not differ from the duties of any white-owned bank boards. The board essentially sounds out new ideas, reviews and makes policy decisions, makes sure that the president is doing his job, and gives the bank its direction. Director Cirilo McSween thinks that the board's primary responsibility is "to direct the bank's policy towards greater community involvement." "The board," he says, "should treat the bank as property of the community."

Johnson and Boutte now hold majority ownership in the bank. Boutte says that since he and Johnson now have such a large personal stake in Independence, they are much more motivated to make the bank succeed. Originally, the stock was widely held by more than 400 stockholders, with none of the owners holding any significant number of shares. According to Boutte, this spread of ownership made no one feel compelled to make the bank succeed. One black director feels that there was no commitment by the board; the directors would not send business to the bank because the bank was poorly managed. He accused the board of giving no support to the bank other than putting money into it.

Boutte agrees that the original board did little to bring business to the bank. "Why send business to a poorly managed bank?" he asked. "This continued," he said, "until the board acquired majority interest in the bank." Boutte feels the present board is the best one Independence has had.

PRESIDENT BOUTTE

Independence's fifth and present president, Alvin Boutte, came out of the Army in 1954, holding a degree in pharmacy which he had earned at Xavier University in New Orleans. After opening his first drug store, Boutte quickly built a chain of four stores under the name Independent Drugs, Inc.

In 1963, Boutte was asked to join a group of community leaders who were interested in opening the first black bank in Chicago. When Independence Bank opened in December, 1964, Boutte was elected vice-chairman of the board, a position he still holds. In mid-1970, he became executive vice-president of the bank. After a few months of training, Boutte was elected Independence's fifth president.

Bank Director Robert Bacon describes Boutte as the "best thing that ever happened to Independence."

The naming of Boutte as president was the major turning point in the bank's history. He's taken the bank from talking about growth to actually growing. He's the guy who went out and got money for the bank; he knows the market. To do a good job in this bank, you have to be black, aggressive, and know the market. Boutte has all of these qualifications.

Boutte feels the key to the success of Independence lies in convincing corporations and institutions doing a considerable amount of business in the community that they should deposit funds in Independence.

Bank Vice-President Thomas Lewis points out that most help has come from public sources. In 1970, federal, state, and local governments held 29.7 percent of the bank's total demand deposits; 18.7 percent of time and savings deposits came from these sources.

Boutte is convinced that many corporations are not doing their fair share to help solve the many problems faced by the minority community. If corporations continue to avoid their social responsibility, says Boutte, the government may have to do the job for them.

The City of Chicago, says Boutte, keeps all of its money in the downtown banks, a situation that he feels should be corrected. On the other hand, the State of Illinois has given Independence some deposits which are very small in comparison to what some other banks have received. "Evanston," he said, "has received over $9,000,000; they've just given us a carrot."

Anderson Schweich, a member of Independence's board of directors, would like to see Independence get part of the Chicago teacher's pension fund. "After all," he says, "there are 26,000 Chicago teachers, and 7,000 of them are black."

Independence now handles demand dsposit accounts for General Motors,

Control Data Corporation, City Colleges of Chicago, and the Atomic Energy Commission. Boutte intends to obtain more corporate, institutional, and public funds. Because Independence is a black bank, Boutte feels it has an advantage over white-owned community banks, the advantage being access to a national market that is unavailable to most small white-owned banks.

The basic strategy is to tap this national market; this is an individual program although other black banks and Capital Formation are carrying out similar programs.[2] Boutte feels that Independence can do a better job securing funds than Capital Formation can. To achieve this end, Boutte and Lewis have scheduled meetings in Chicago and throughout the country to sell the idea of black entrepreneurship and black capitalism. Boutte is confident of success.

Even now there are signs of success. The bank is currently making a monthly profit of approximately $15,000 and, for the first time in its history, will pay a dividend.[3] Another sign is the bank's recapitalization. Independence will be recapitalized at $1,350,000—a $550,000 increase over its original capitalization. This increase will give the bank greater loaning ability and will be financed by the sale of an additional 27,500 shares of stock at $20 per share. Johnson and Boutte probably will purchase most of these additional shares.

BANK OFFICERS

Independence's management has undergone continuous change since the bank's founding in 1964. None of the original officers are still employed at the bank. Three present officers, Assistant Vice-President Lydia L. English, Controller Betty H. Vance, and Assistant Cashier Phyllis Kellum, have been with Independence for several years. All of the officers are black, although this was not true in the past. Three of the five officers (excluding the president) are women. Boutte meets with his officers every Monday morning to discuss expenses and policies and to determine what programs will be emphasized during the coming week. In addition to this weekly meeting, Boutte meets monthly with his officers to review the previous month's operating results and to examine and discuss board reports.

Boutte says the bank will train its own future officers—individuals will not be sent to larger banks for training. Boutte feels, "We can't depend on others."

LOAN POLICY

Independence's assets have increased from $1,393,786 at the end of 1964 to $16,240,685 at the end of 1970. This is a yearly compounded growth rate of 32.2 per cent. During this same period, loans outstanding increased from $328,300 to $6,577,156. Of total loans outstanding in 1970, approximately $790,000 were installment loans, $1,800,000 were mortgages, and $3,910,000 were commercial loans. In 1971, the largest loan that Independence had outstanding is a $625,000 90 percent-guaranteed FHA rehabilitation loan.

The present loan portfolio is 80 percent black and 20 percent white. The 20 percent consists of:
(1) loans to referrals made by board members
(2) loans to finance companies
(3) participation loans with Hyde Park Bank of Chicago and American National Bank of Chicago
(4) two mortgages.

Chief Loan Officer Nelson says that although he wouldn't turn a person away just because he was white, he would "ask these people why they don't borrow from a white bank." Boutte says that he wouldn't turn away a white borrower because of the color of his skin, but Independence's responsibility is to the black community.

Independence's 1970 loan loss ratio last year was 2.5 percent. In Nelson's opinion this is below average for banks of comparable size.

The bank's biggest problem lies in finding qualified black borrowers. According to Boutte, "One problem of loaning to black businesses is that many cannot supply the usual collateral; the bank must take this into consideration." One man who approached the bank for a loan owned a drug store. Says Boutte, "This man did not have any liquid assets, but we considered the situation and gave the man the loan, using his fixtures and inventory as collateral."

SBA LOANS

Independence also makes Small Business Administration guaranteed loans. At the end of 1970, 10.4 percent of Independence's total loans outstanding were SBA-guaranteed loans. Two of these loans were inactive. The total amount of these loans was $802,000, which is approximately $50,000 per loan.[4] All of Independence's SBA-guaranteed loans are 90 percent guaranteed. The rates of interest on these loans are approximately 2 percent above the prime rate in effect when the particular loan was made.

For its size, Independence has been very active in the SBA-guaranteed loan area. Boutte says that Independence was one of the first banks to get and utilize SBA loans while white banks were not using them at all.

Independence processes and services SBA-type loans and provides any advice requested. Nelson says that if Independence lacks the expertise to help the borrower, it can request help from the Harris or the First National Bank of Chicago. "We want the borrower to be successful," says Nelson.

When asked who usually gets SBA guaranteed loans, Nelson replied, "Any large business that banks at Independence can probably get a regular bank loan, but any new business, especially one that does not have the usual collateral, will usually get an SBA-guaranteed loan. Such a loan is still dependent upon the borrower's idea, his character, his credit rating, and his standing in the community."

In reference to processing costs for SBA-type loans, Nelson says that they were higher than processing costs for regular loans because of the extra paper-work involved. "If someone comes in," he said, "and asks for an SBA loan, we would rather give him a regular loan if possible, because of the lower processing costs." But he cautions, "We need these types of loans in the community even though there is a higher cost involved."

The SBA's Lloyd Kaldor, chief of the financing division of the Midwest area, agrees with Nelson, "Processing costs are higher especially in the minority area where the bank has to do most of the paperwork for the applicant. The big banks feel it is cheaper for them to lend to the applicant without going through the SBA, and in this reasoning, they are right."

SPECIAL PROBLEMS

Boutte admits that black banking is not without its special problems. "The real problem of black banks," he says, "is the attacks against them." These attacks center upon the ability of black banks to succeed and to help the community. "We must convince people that we are for real," said Boutte.

Personnel Problems

One problem inherent in black banking is the shortage of trained personnel. This has constantly plagued Independence during its almost seven years of existence. High employee turnover has also been a problem for Independence.

During six years of operations, Independence Bank has had five presidents, of whom all except two have been white. Independence's first president, who served for 18 months, was William E. Scanlan, a former trust officer with Ex-change National Bank of Chicago. Scanlan was elected president after Harris Trust and Savings Bank recommended him for that position.

Scanlan was inexperienced in running a bank and Boutte felt that he lacked an understanding of the problems of the black community and that this made him unsuited for work at Independence.

Independence's second president, William Franke, was an elderly retired bank official whose background was in lending; he had served as executive vice-president of, and commercial lending officer of, Glenview State Bank. Franke, like Scanlan, had been recommended by the Harris Bank. Franke's temperment proved unsuited to the problems connected with Independence's personnel.

Henry P. Hervey became Independence's first black president in December, 1967. One of the original founders of Independence and the man thought to have been picked at the beginning to become Independence's first black presi-dent, Hervey had been vice-president and cashier, and had served on the board of directors. In Boutte's eyes, Hervey's lack of experience caused him to discourage many potential customers from banking at Independence. However, Boutte did say Hervey's election as president had a good effect on both the employees of the bank and the members of the community.

Hervey was succeeded by David F. DeVries, a cashier at Lakeside Bank of

Chicago. Boutte described DeVries and the job which he did at Independence in these words:

> He was an operations man who was more than conservative. In terms of operations, he did a fine job. In terms of profit and growth, he did a poor job. Unfortunately, he didn't have the right kind of personality to run this bank.

DeVries served as president until "he resigned to seek a better opportunity." His replacement, Alvin Boutte, was Independence's second black president.

Problems of Site Selection

Late in 1963, the failing Chatham Bank of Chicago was liquidated. The Independence Bank moved into the premises vacated by the Chatham Bank, although many persons, including the Harris' Miller, advised against such a move. Miller said that he advised Independence to move into another building because "things were going to be tough enough without adding one more problem." According to Miller, some area residents had been hurt by Chatham's insolvency, and "Independence would have to overcome that bad taste left in the mouths of many who had banked at the old Chatham Bank. Any new bank should not go into the shadow of a bank that failed."

Miller says the two major reasons why Independence moved into that particular building were that the board of directors wanted Independence open for business before Seaway National Bank and that the FDIC gave Independence a very favorable lease on the Chatham building.

Boutte agrees that Independence's choice of buildings did affect the growth of the bank, and he says that if he had it to do over again, he would not have moved into the Chatham Bank building.

Problems of Profitability

Profitability is another major problem area for black banking. According to Boutte, higher than normal servicing costs and loan losses reduce a black bank's profits. Boutte explains that the size of black deposits, whether they be time, savings, or demand, are one-third the size of white deposits.[5] "This," Boutte said, "requires more servicing because to get an amount equal to one white deposit, you must service three black accounts—this increases the servicing costs." The fact that these smaller accounts are also more active than larger accounts likewise results in additional servicing costs.

The average loan size is another item that increases a black bank's servicing expenses. Loans made by black banks are, on the average, smaller than loans made by white banks; these smaller loans also tend to be more active.[6] This means more servicing costs for the bank.

According to Boutte, the increase in servicing costs is reflected in a black bank's "salaries and wages" account and its "other current operating expenses" account.

CONCLUSION

Boutte stresses the fact that Independence Bank must be actively involved in the community. When he speaks of the community, he means the city itself: "What happens in Chicago affects me. We have a responsibility to the community—the total community. It's too bad all blacks do not realize this." (Independence assets went over the $50 million level in 1973).

FOOTNOTES

[1] Andrew F. Brimmer, "The Black Banks: An Assessment of Performance and Prospects," Paper presented to the American Economic Association, December 28, 1970.

[2] Capital Formation, Inc. is a nonprofit corporation created to raise $65 million in deposits from corporations, educational institutions, foundations, labor unions, churches, and others for deposit in minority-owned banks. To this amount will be added $35,000,000 from federal agencies. This new program includes no deposits provision for additional capital for the depository banks.

[3] A dividend of $0.25 per share was declared on June 30, 1971.

[4] As of April 30, 1971, the SBA had 499 minority guaranteed loans outstanding in the Chicago area and the Northern Illinois counties—most of them in the Chicago area. The average size of these loans is approximately $55,000. This information was obtained from SBA records in Chicago.

[5] There are three basic differences between demand deposits and time or savings deposits. With demand deposits, withdrawals may be made on demand. In the case of withdrawals from time or savings deposits, the depositor is required to give the bank at least 30 days' notice, although banks seldom enforce this requirement with savings accounts. A second basic difference is that demand deposits can be used directly as money: a demand depositor can pay for goods and services by writing a check for the amount due. Funds held in savings or time deposits must first be converted into currency or into a demand deposit before they can be used for making payments. A third distinguishing factor is that banks are allowed to pay interest on time and savings deposits but not on demand deposits.

The above information was obtained from Eli Sharpiro, Ezra Solomon and William L. White, *Money and Banking* (New York: Holt, Rinehart and Winston, Inc., 1968), p. 84.

[6] Edward Irons, "Black Banking: Problems and Prospects," in this volume.

*Anne S. Huff**

UNITED DISTRIBUTORS

United Distributors** was organized informally early in 1969 as a cooperative effort of seven black Chicago-based companies that manufactured products sold through supermarkets. Along with other producers, each company previously had gained a foothold in the Chicago market through Operation Breadbasket covenant agreements. However, the producers claimed that some of the Chicago supermarket chains that had ordered their products left black-manufactured merchandise in the warehouse or stockroom. Even when products were placed on the shelves, they usually were displayed ineffectively.

Because of the chains' slow reordering, Chicago-based sales of these black manufacturers' products had begun to level off by the end of 1968. The seven merchandisers would need additional income from outside markets if they were to operate at or near-profitable levels. Prior attempts to sell some of their products to supermarket chains outside Chicago had met with little success. Several members of the group had tried using white brokers in outside markets, but they had found them generally unable to sell black products competitively.

The goal of the group, which banded together as United Distributors, Inc., was to develop and supply materials within a 500-mile radius of Chicago. Through cooperation, they hoped to cut costs, improve effectiveness in delivery maintenance of stock, and change the attitudes of chain buyers toward black products. United had four objectives:

(1) act as a selling agency with responsibility for contacting chains, securing initial orders, and following up for reorders

(2) schedule pool shipments

(3) handle billing and receipts

(4) arrange for store" detailing" by an individual in the market area hired to straighten and clean merchandise, see that shelf space was sufficient and properly placed, check on rotation, price and periodic promotion of products, and attempt to get reorders for goods sold.

The group agreed that United was to deduct 10 percent from incoming receipts to finance these operations before payments were passed on to the individual companies.

The group which founded United hoped that this organization would become a model for the cooperation of black manufacturers by becoming self-sufficient in an environment dominated by whites. Each manufacturer in the

*This case was prepared by Anne Huff using materials supplied by Dr. Fred Allvine and part of a student report by Charles H. Curry. Prof. Huff is currently a Visiting Assistant Professor at UCLA's Graduate School of Management and Dr. Allvine is Associate Professor of Marketing at Georgia Tech University.
**The brand names of the products have been changed along with the names of the individuals associated with United Distributors.

group selected his leading product, based on performance in the Chicago area. Using these products to open markets outside Chicago, United became the sponsor of three chemical products, Van Winkle Floor Wax, Easy Way Drain Opener, and Green Pine Disinfectant; two cosmetic products, Keep Cool Anti-perspirant and Nefertiti Hand Lotion; and two food products, Sun Products Lemon Juice and Best Barbecue Sauce.

Shortly after United's initial marketing efforts, the president of Best Barbeque Products withdrew from the group due to disagreements over the organization, distribution of ownership interest, advertising strategy, and legal representation.

OBTAINING MARKETS

In May, 1969, United Distributors, Inc., made contact with the four largest supermarket chains in Cleveland and Detroit. These cities are the largest within a 350-mile radius of Chicago, and both have large black populations. United wished to reverse the history of chain insensitivity to black manufacturing problems by contacting the top executive in each chain for an educational and promotional meeting in which no sales were to be solicited. A registered letter, outlining United's goals and asking for a meeting, was sent to the chief executive officer of each of the eight chains. The author of the contact letter, an assistant marketing professor at Northwestern University working with United, assured the executive of product quality and manufacturer reliability.

Executives of each of the chains agreed to meet with a representative group. The initial presentation was made by the presidents of Easy Way and Sun Products. The Northwestern professor attended the meeting as the group's marketing advisor. A Breadbasket preacher also attended. United's representatives explained some of the problems that the group had encountered as black manufacturers. They outlined United's marketing strategy and asked for questions about their products and proposed campaign. The emphasis of their approach was on information and persuasion, an approach which differed from the initially successful leverage techniques used in Chicago by Operation Breadbasket. Each executive was given a promotional portfolio and was asked to help economic development of the black community by supporting United's products and by communicating that support to the rest of his organization.

United's strategy had been worked out in consultation with several advisors. The group was trying to enter an extremely competitive market with nationally known brands already established in the areas where they wanted to introduce their product lines. They based their strategy on:

(1) obtaining an endorsement from the chains' executives to support black products

(2) providing detailing support[1]

(3) pooling shipment for more economic freight rates[2] and more efficient handling of products by chains

(4) providing quality products that could be sold at prices considerably lower than those of advertised brands

Most of the companies involved in United Distributors had chosen their products carefully and were manufacturing items which the chains did not carry as a "house brand," or "private label." The only competition in most product lines came from one or more nationally advertised "name brands," which United felt it could underprice.

The manufacturers in United Distributors had decided they could not initially afford the promotional campaigns necessary to create a name brand that would be "pulled" into the stores by consumer demand. As explained by their marketing advisor, United's alternative was to establish a "value brand," with available promotional funds used to price goods competitively on the store shelf. Value brands, such as those of United's manufacturers, have to depend upon price, in-store promotion, and competitive placement of products for their success. (Value brands can only succeed if "pushed" by the store, and they have the best chance of this support when the store does not have a competing house brand, since house brands are promoted by essentially the same strategy.) United felt it could ask for this promotional support by the chain as partial compensation for lack of previous opportunities.

Executive commitment to the United Distributors' program was considered crucial. Prior problems with buyers and store-level management had convinced the group members of the necessity for pressure from the top. In the past, buyers had treated black products the same way as those produced by white manufacturers and had been interested primarily in the companies' abilities to provide advertising to create consumer demand. Such buyer requests were contrary to the program United had mapped out. Through compensatory justice, United Distributors hoped their products would be given the treatment of a house brand, while they maintained the independence of private manufacturers' labels.

A week after United contacted chain presidents in Detroit and Cleveland, secondary meetings were arranged with store buyers. Within 60 days, each of the chains placed orders for two to six of the items represented, far exceeding orders that the individual manufacturers previously had been able to obtain. The companies were generally pleased with their first efforts as "United Distributors."

EXPANSION OF UNITED DISTRIBUTORS

As United expanded, it hired an executive director, a former employee of Sun Products who maintained an office in the main office of Easy Way Corporation. One woman was hired in Cleveland and one in Detroit to cover the detailing functions promised the stores. Each woman was paid $100 plus expenses weekly, and she was expected to cover approximately 15 stores daily. A secretary was hired to keep the books and maintain correspondence. However, after several secretaries proved unsatisfactory, the director used the services of his host company's secretary when needed.

Within a year after its initial experience in Cleveland and Detroit, United Distributors had established additional outlets for its products in Pittsburgh, St. Louis, Champaign, Louisville, Cincinnati, Columbus, Toledo, Youngstown, Milwaukee, and Indianapolis. The group also was considering moving into New York City and other large metropolitan areas beyond a 500-mile radius of Chicago.

United continued to use the introductory strategy developed in Detroit and Cleveland. However, the cordial reception that was almost invariably accorded United's representatives by company officials was not necessarily translated into continuing substantial reorders. Most members of the group felt that they were not being given adequate time or support by the individual stores to establish the reputation of their products among consumers. They complained of a continuing lack of sympathy for black manufacturing problems.

UNITED'S PROBLEMS

United experienced several internal crises in its first year of operation. The principals met weekly to work on recurring developmental problems which were complicated by limited revenues. They also attempted to iron out the difficulties of allocating responsibilities and expenses among member companies. Not all the companies shared equally in incoming orders from United's contracts; initial bookkeeping problems led to resistance on the part of some companies to allow this function to be centralized, and the salaries and expenses of the detailing women were too expensive in relation to turnover of goods. Incorporation was

Figure I
Sales and Expense Statement for
United Distributors, Inc.
May 1, 1969-October 31, 1969[1]

Gross Revenue		$135,000	
Net Receipts (10% sales commission)			$13,500
Recent Monthly Expenditures[2]			
Executive director and secretary		$1,000	
Travel		500	
Detailing		1,200	
Office:			
Rent	150		
Telephone	100		
Supplies	50	300	
		$3,000	
Estimated profit (loss)			($1,000)

[1] This is a tentative estimate.
[2] Expenses have been made at a variable monthly rate as new phases of operations have started and some have been discontinued. As a result, current monthly expenditures can not simply be multiplied by number of months of operations to establish costs.

discussed with a lawyer brought in by one of the group members, but initial discussions resulted in little progress. It was agreed that a more forceful legal representative was needed. A second lawyer, approached through Operation Breadbasket contacts, came to one or two meetings and explained the Illinois law regarding incorporation, including the requirement that $1,000 in assets be maintained in the name of a profit-making corporation. The financially weaker companies had difficulty in contributing one-fifth the required money, and although several other members were willing to contribute the sum immediately, they felt that their greater investment should be matched by greater control of the organization. While the problems of allocating control were being discussed, the lawyer left the country for several months, during which time the group had no legal counsel.

United Distributors never was formally incorporated. The second lawyer drew up the initial incorporation papers, but his fee was not paid and the papers were not filed with the Secretary of State. A third lawyer attended several meetings and indicated his willingness to become involved with the group, but arrangements were not made and the legal arrangements of the group remained unclear. The issue continued to be brought up periodically at the weekly meetings, but no additional progress was made.

PROBLEMS OF INDIVIDUAL COMPANIES

In the meantime, the internal problems of several member conpanies threatened the continued existence of United Distributors. The president of Nefertiti Hand Lotion ended his association with United after an unsuccessful attempt to work out production, financial, and marketing problems in the Chicago market.

Keep Cool Spray Deodorant, the other cosmetic product handled by the group, continued to be represented by United, and the president of the company maintained an active interest in the group. However, undercapitalization and problems with the subcontractor who manufactured Keep Cool became acute. The company was unable to fill substantial back orders, and did not have revenue for United's support.

As for the other companies, the Green Pine Company benefitted by having their pine disinfectant exposed to markets outside the Chicago Metropolitan area, but the company was not always able to meet shipping commitments. The manufacturer of Van Winkle Floor Wax found little volume response among United's buyers. As a result, the floor wax company's product underwent its fourth package change in several years, during which time little revenue was available for United's support.[3] The two remaining companies, Easy Way and Sun Products, shared most of the cost and benefits of United Distributors during this period, and for both, the new markets led to internal expansion (Table II).

EVALUATION AFTER A YEAR'S OPERATION

A year after its first organizational meetings, United was unable to provide all the

Table I
Orders (cases) Received from July to October 1969*

	Sun Products	Green Pine	Nefertiti	Easy Way	Van Winkle	Keep Cool
Cleveland (2 chains)	240		50	120		
Columbus	60			60	60	
St. Louis (3 chains)	250	225	70	250	250	70
Detroit (4 chains)	700	1345	720	423	140	140
Waukesha, Wis.	60		60	60		
Milwaukee (2 chains)	200			770		
Hazelwood, Mo.	250			250	200	
Indianapolis	200			200		
Louisville, Ky.	175	75		175	175	
Yorktown, Ind.	200			200		

*Gross receipts recorded = $35,834 (does not include all receipts recorded for Green Pine and Sun Products).

services for which its members had joined together. The group's original hopes for United to act as a selling agency, post shipments, handle billing and receipts, and arrange detailing were now seen in the more realistic light of a year's experience.

First, the group's selling strategy had produced significant results for most of the companies. However, the time (and money) required for these visits was a drain on the small manufacturer with pressing concerns within his own business. Experience had shown that not all the companies represented by United could supply new markets at the same rate, and the variability in timing and amount of reorders further complicated individual members' selling needs.

Second, pooled shipments were similarly difficult to coordinate. Some members had to wait for cash on hand before they could ship new orders. In addition, the volume of orders from a specific area varied among the companies. In general, the anticipated lower freight rates did not materialize, and it even became necessary to ship goods in one of the member company's trucks to reduce out-of-pocket costs.

Third, the group never developed a successful bookkeeping system. Record keeping proved to be much more complicated than anticipated, and this unpopular task was attempted successively by several members. The smaller companies operated on very tight time margins, and delays in payments due to United's late billing made them fall behind in payroll and production expenses. These problems, coupled with the refusal of several companies to let United do their billing, meant that United's 10 percent margin was not always forthcoming from incoming revenue.

Fourth, the volume of United's business in any one city could not support the expenses of detailing. The director, whose former experience was primarily in detailing, occasionally would check on the display of products within individual stores on his visits to promote sales, but in general no detailing services could be provided. Figures on the break-even point in volume of sales, which would have supported this service, are not available.

In the opinion of the group's marketing advisor, many of the problems that United faced were related to the lack of sales response from the chains. For example, if United's products had been pushed by the supermarket chains, as initial meetings with executives and initial buyer responses had seemed to indicate, the individual companies undoubtedly would have had much more financial leeway, enabling them to move beyond some of the basic organizational problems that continually faced them. It might be argued that the pattern of United's development, with the inherent weaknesses of rapid and far-reaching expansion, was necessitated by the lack of chain support, particularly the lack of substantial reorders. A regional development strategy (which is generally adopted by even the largest manufacturers) would have helped to iron out problems of product distribution and promotion within one manageable area before new markets were developed.

In March, 1970, the executive director of United toured several cities to discuss United's impact on retailers. Most of the buyers felt that the only way United could adequately serve the stores' needs was to contract for the services of brokers. On the basis of this report, the group began to consider the feasibility of hiring professionals as market representatives.

OPERATION BREADBASKET BECOMES MORE ACTIVE

In April, 1970, events in Chicago significantly changed the outcome of United Distributor's last efforts. Noah Robinson, half-brother of Operation Breadbasket leader Jesse Jackson, came to Chicago to organize the commercial division of Operation Breadbasket. After several years of industrial experience, Robinson had received an M. B. A. from the University of Pennsylvania in 1968 and had started a nonprofit consulting corporation for black businessmen in Philadelphia. Most of United's activities gradually became submerged into the efforts of Breadbasket's commercial division, directed by Robinson. Several perishable products also were brought into the division, increasing the division's operating budget. Companies paid weekly contributions, which ranged from $25 to $150 per week, based on ability to pay, to the Breadbasket Commercial Association (BCA).

Robinson soon found it desirable to go outside Chicago in the same manner as United. He also selected Detroit as the first market to develop because of its size, proximity, and black population. In June, Robinson notified the Detroit supermarket chains that he would like to discuss marketing plans with them. Sizable orders were received from these chains.[4]

The president of Van Winkle Floor Wax became president of the group of manufacturers formed to advise Robinson.[5] Of the other manufacturers formerly in United Distributors, Sun Products Lemon Juice has relied least on the new efforts of the Breadbasket Commercial Association and has managed independently to promote large orders in markets first contacted by the United group (Case B).[6] The president of Easy Way, the other company to expand while a member of United Distributors, also has taken a less active role in BCA. Orders for Easy Way reportedly continued to increase, partly because of an informal agreement made in June, 1970, between Sun Products and Easy Way to attempt to open additional markets cooperatively in Washington, D. C., and Baltimore, Philadelphia, and New York City. The continuing cooperation and growth of these two manufacturers is seen by some observers as one of the major positive outcomes of United Distributor's experience. It is too early to compare their strategy to the alternative marketing route pursued by those manufacturers active in the BCA.

INTERVIEW WITH JEFF CARTER—JANUARY 18, 1971

Sun Products recently moved into newly constructed quarters in Evanston, Illinois. The office building includes a secretarial area and offices for the two partners of the company.

Jeff Carter agreed to discuss his company's past association with United Distributors and to update his company's activities since the organization was disbanded. Carter gave the following informal account of some of his experiences in United Distributors:

United Distributors was formed by about seven companies who were then attending the Wednesday afternoon meetings of Breadbasket's Commercial division. We each felt that we had pretty much penetrated the Chicago market by this time: as a group we went on to develop new outlets in Indianapolis, Louisville, Cincinnati, Cleveland, Detroit, Buffalo, Pittsburgh, Milwaukee, St. Louis, Toledo, and a couple more I can't think of right now, but that gives you an idea of the size of our operation.

Our approach was to take two or three white advisors when we went into a new city. We felt it lent credibility to our presentation if we could show we had support from the whites. Several guys traveled with us at various times, but the guy who went with most was an N. U. professor who also met with us fairly regularly and gave us advice about marketing strategy. When we contacted the various company presidents we always said that this wasn't a sales visit, we'd just like to discuss our ideas, and then come back later to talk with the buyers. Our idea was that the top man would then have time to funnel the information down to the buyers that these are some black guys the company wants to help. From our experience that's the kind of support we knew we needed if we were going to succeed.

We always got an answer, and although I could name one or two chains that weren't truly cooperative, in general we got fantastic results from that strategy. Of course, we learned a few things after our first few visits, like not to take in too big a gang. It got back to us once that one guy felt that he was intimidated by demands, when all we'd done was given him our regular presentation. One other time a guy seemed to be really insulted that white men would come with us, but in general I think integration was an important part of our approach. After the first four trips or so we started to save time by seeing the sales people the same day we made our initial visit, because the executive would usually just pick up the phone while we were in his office to talk with the buyers. We once went to see an executive who said to 'Skip the presentation, we know what you're trying to do, just leave your order blanks and we'll support you,' but we told him 'Nothing doing, we're ready to give our pitch.' We got a good laugh, and we've had great business ever since with that executive's stores.

We got good orders working together as United Distributors. In general, things worked out fine for all of us for about a year to fifteen months. As we expanded, we set up an office in Easy Way, hired an executive director who had been working for me, and a secretary to help with the bookkeeping. The director's job was to maintain our accounts by visiting the stores, to find out how we were doing, and if there were any problems. In many cases one of us would go with him on trips, but it's difficult to give too much outside time when you have a small business that needs more or less constant supervision. In general we all met together on Sunday, and during the week we kept in touch by phone. I don't think this arrangement could have been changed profitably. We might have kicked up volume a little with more attention to the stores, but our biggest problems weren't in this area.

To go back a little—we knew when we got together that United was primarily a door opener to new markets. Some of us had always known we would outgrow United, and we also felt it was quite possible that some of the other companies might not succeed. Several were part-time local ventures, without enough capital backing. They didn't even always have enough of their product to ship if they did make orders through United. But we thought we should give them a chance to make it if they could. After about two years, the bigger companies had really grown, but we weren't just going to leave the smaller guys without any support. What the president of Easy Way and I did do was go into additional markets that we were ready for. Still using the name "United," we went together to Washington, Baltimore, Philadelphia, and New York City. Today we're both shipping thousands of cases to those places.

A little after we made those trips, Robinson came to Chicago and set up 'Action Incorporated,' which was basically similar to United only it involved more companies and offered more services. There really wasn't any reason to continue our efforts as United, and we've pretty much each gone his own way. One of the reasons even the larger companies with the most to lose didn't push incorporation for United Distributors was that we could see this kind of thing happening and didn't want to be stuck with a formal organization that had outlived its usefulness. Even now Easy Way and I get bills that go back to United. We try to get help paying them off, but in general, we do it ourselves. They're not too big and it isn't worth the bad name to let bills hang on. I don't know if many of the stores we ship to realize there isn't a United anymore, though if they asked, we'd tell them what has happened. I don't usually see too many of the other products on the shelves. It would be interesting to see whether many of the smaller companies still sell outside Chicago.

The sales figures for Sun Products have doubled in the last year. I attribute that to two things. We don't demand and we put people on detailing. Noah has a group out detailing the stores too. But while you can get all the prime shelf facing you want, you can't necessarily force the customer to pick up the product. The smaller company that feels it has a potentially successful product has to price it competitively and has to create an image with the customer. We have a product that we feel is better product on the shelf, we've worked hard in an integrated company to service that product carefully, and we've had enough success to get the other guy worried.

Sun Products was founded by a white chemist and myself. We had heard a few complaints about the taste of commercial lemon juice, and it seemed like this might be a good area for a new product, especially since there was only one nationally known brand name. We did some analysis and found that the juice on the market used sulphur as a preservative. Then we found a better preservative without the side taste. That's not just our opinion, we had a comparison taste test done by independent laboratories. Once we formed Sun Products and were in production, we tried offering free lemonade on Saturday at some Chicago area stores so that shoppers could taste the difference, but couldn't see that it had much impact, and we've dropped that idea for now.

As the white guy who started this business with me got interested in other areas, he sold his interest in the company back to me. About a year later, I sold that interest to Paul, another white man. It may be difficult to picture a black man and a white man working together smoothly, but I've always worked to keep this an integrated company. We have whites and blacks throughout the company. At one time we were committed to hiring the hard-core unemployed, but as we've gotten more and more automated equipment, we're hiring both skilled and unskilled workers. We're still committed to putting something back into the black community. Part of our 'pitch' is that we put part of our profits into building plants and offer employment in low-income areas.

In Chicago and other cities, we have found stores that aren't too receptive to blacks. Not that they say anything to the black guys, but they hint at things to our white employees and brokers. Paul gets some of the same kind of thing occasionally too, but we feel comfortable with what we're trying to do. The country has become polarized; the power play is not the way to get business anymore.

Paul and I often go together to promote our product. We've found that the stores are so sophisticated they don't want to talk to you unless you can presell your product through the media, and we're gradually building up a nationally-advertised product. We use the radio and we have a policy of constantly pushing for in-store promotion. We just introduced Sun Products Prune Juice, and we've gotten free publicity on it from the Chicago *Tribune*. We also started advertising on TV in some areas, not regularly, but every three months or so. As we've grown, we've spent more money on promotion and offered more promotional allowances to the store. Our salesmen try to get so many front and interaisle placements from each store, but you've got to give the manager some incentive to give those places to you over the other guy. Only one chain we deal with has a policy of "must displays" in which each store is required to do so many pro-motions of a product during the year. They're a more aggressive company than most of the others, and the top brass has passed down the word and made it stick. In most of the other chains our treatment depends on the city. In one city we'll be very pleased with the response of a particular chain; in another we'll get only 'token' orders.

We use an ad agency to help plan our promotions—you're crazy not to in this business. For example, when we first started out we thought we had the prettiest label you could pick up in the store. But the ad people said it was all wrong, that it was too hot, the colors weren't food colors. They finally talked us into our present label, and you know, they were right, sales went up significantly after we changed.

We haven't always followed the advice we've gotten. Our advisors didn't think brokers were good for United Distributors, but brokers made this com-pany. We absolutely court our brokers, Paul taught me that. They have to be motivated just like any employee. We call them up and ask them how it's going, and tell them to give Jack a dozen roses for his wife for doing such a good job last week. We now have brokers representing us in thirty cities. Although we haven't felt the need for them in Chicago, in most cities they've been essential as we went out for more volume.

When we were in United we had our order sheets printed up with price quotations for 100 or 200 cases. Now we've gotten smart, we offer 200 to 1,000 cases, that's the only way we're going to come out ahead on shipping costs. Sun Products leases its own trailers now, and we're getting orders to ship by the trailerload. We're talking with larger chains, with maybe 200 or more stores in a fair-sized city. United was getting orders of maybe just 50 cases of one product from some of those chains, which just wasn't a sincere effort to push our products. We'd push and pull in United for at least a case a store and a case for reorder, so that we would break even on costs.

Looking back, there's also no doubt that the rate of expansion was a struggle for most of United's companies. Sun Products had to back up and tighten up some. We've got an investment in these markets now that we've got to protect. We've made sure that we're equipped saleswise (with three salesmen other than ourselves) to cover our territory. Now we've gone back to those same cities we opened up in United and picked up the next largest chains to extend our market in the same geographical location.

POSTSCRIPT

United Distributors disbanded in 1972 due to organizational problems and lack of support. The individual companies who participated derived varying degrees of benefits from the cooperative effort, but the concept of providing economies of scale in sales and distribution for small minority manufacturers seems worth pursuing in the future when opportunity appears. Of course, greater resources and technical assistance may be needed if the concept is to be given a fair test.

FOOTNOTES

[1] Leading brand name products offer detailing services as part of their salesmen's regular visits. Even when actual selling is done by a broker, a detailing man usually is hired by major companies to maintain their competitive position and promotion.

[2] Freight rates drop from 40 to 60 percent when carload shipments are made.

[3] The final package, which won an industrial award for design, began to reach the market in mid-1970, and sales have begun to respond more favorably.

[4] An additional development from this meeting has been a coalition of black producers from Chicago and Detroit. Presently, some of the Detroit companies are being aided by the commercial division to sell their products in the Chicago market.

[5] According to the first report of BCA, sales of Van Winkle have jumped from $20,000 to the $150,000 level in the last three years, with distribution in thirteen states.

[6] See interview with Jeff Carter, president of Sun Products, in this article.

Peter W. Berg, Robert A. Rist*

JOHNSON PRODUCTS, INC.

HISTORICAL BACKGROUND

Johnson Products, a Chicago-based, black-owned cosmetics and hair products manufacturer, was founded by George Ellis Johnson, who had been employed as a laboratory assistant by Fuller Products, a Chicago cosmetics manufacturer from 1945 to 1948, and then was promoted to the position of production chemist.

Johnson explains that Johnson Products, Co. was begun as a result of trying to help a barber friend solve a problem he was having with a hair straightener: "With the help of a well-known chemist, I was able to develop a product that solved the barber's problem, and with his help we perfected the product in his barber shop and decided to market it. I estimated that I could launch the business on $500 worth of capital—$250 from the barber and $250 from myself. He had his $250, but I had to borrow mine. Having once borrowed from a loan company, and my account being paid up and in good standing, I felt all I had to do was tell my story to the manager and I would get the money. However, when I finished with my story, he looked at me and said, "I am going to do you a favor, friend. This sounds like a ridiculous risk, and I am not going to give you the money." At this point I had a real problem, but after thinking about it a couple of days, I decided to go to another branch of the same company and ask for $250 to take a vacation to California. I got the money right away. From that $500, Johnson Products was started."

Johnson Products has grown from a husband and wife team with $500 in assets in 1954, to a corporation with assets of more than $12 million in 1972 employing more than 150 people. (A 1972 balance sheet is presented in Exhibit I.)

Operations began in 1954 in a storefront building where Ultra-Wave Hair straightener was manufactured. In 1956, after Ultra Wave had begun to sell profitably to the professional beauticians' market, Johnson Products moved to the second floor of a manufacturing building in Chicago. When the company was incorporated in 1957, Ultra Wave was introduced into the retail market. Rapid growth continued, and in 1960 Johnson took over the remaining three floors f the building. The corporation remained in these premises until October, 1964, when a fire destroyed the leased building. The fire provided Johnson with the impetus for construction of a building which is approximately 79,000 square feet in area, located on a three-acre tract on Chicago's south side. The original

---

*This case was prepared under the direction of Professor Samuel I. Doctors while the authors were M. B. A. students at the Graduate School of Management, Northwestern University. Material for the case was gathered from some interviews at the company and from generally available publications such as annual reports and newspaper accounts.

portion of the present building, completed in August, 1966, contains 32,000 square feet, 5,000 of which are utilized for office facilities. The remainder is used for manufacturing, docking, and warehousing of raw materials and inventory. The manufacturing facilities include seven fully automated production lines.

In 1968, the company began a three phase expansion and plant reorganization program. The total cost of the program was estimated at $615,000. The first phase of the program was completed in February, 1969, resulting in the addition of 42,000 square feet to the company's docking and warehousing facilities. In June, 1969, the company completed the reorganization of its manufacturing facilities that permitted the company to add the seven fully automated production lines. In May, 1969, the company began the third phase of its building and reorganization program which resulted in the addition of 5,000 square feet in office space.

ORGANIZATION AND PERSONNEL

Johnson Products is controlled by a board of six directors, three of whom also serve as corporate officers. George E. Johnson serves as president and chairman and is reported to directly by three vice-presidents in charge of operations, marketing and finance. Johnson also serves as chairman of the board for the Independence Bank of Chicago, as director of the Lincoln National Bank of Miami, and as vice-president of the Chicago Urban League. He is a member of the United States Chamber of Commerce, the Chicago Association of Commerce and Industry, and the Cosmopolitan Chamber of Commerce. Johnson is the second black man ever to be named a board member of Commonwealth Edison Co.

Johnson Products employed seven technical personnel in research, development, and quality control programs in 1970. Three of these employees were chemists and spent most of their time in the development of new products and the improvement of existing products. Not all those in high-echelon management jobs at Johnson are black; the plant manager, marketing manager, two of the chemists, and controller are white. Johnson wishes to provide more managerial opportunities for blacks. Since the company manufactures products made largely by black workers working in a black neighborhood for black consumers, it makes good business sense for Johnson to hire more black managers. However, he has had difficulty in locating and hiring blacks with adequate managerial experience and educational background.

Among Johnson Products' 150 employees, blacks comprise a majority of the personnel. While Johnson Products say they have made no concerted effort to hire only blacks, a natural attraction does exist between the black company and prospective black employees.

Employee relations are good. The company has initiated an employee's profit-sharing trust open to all salaried employees 21 years old and over who have completed one full year of service with the company. This is a noncontributory trust under the discretion of the company's directors.

There is currently no union activity at the company. An earlier attempt at unionization was defeated by a three-to-one margin.

DESCRIPTION OF THE ENVIRONMENT

The company operates in the toiletries and cosmetics industry. Total retail sales for the toiletries and cosmetics industry for 1969 was $4 billion. This market is dominated by approximately 25 manufacturers who account for nearly 90 percent of all domestic sales. Six of these manufacturers, Proctor and Gamble, Avon, Bristol-Myers, Revlon, Colgate-Palmolive, and Gillette, control nearly 50 percent of the domestic volume.

Within the cosmetic toiletries industry, Johnson Products is part of the hair products segment. This segment of the industry accounted for $1.1 billion in sales or 29 percent of the total industry output in 1970. The industry is characterized by extensive advertising efforts and other forms of product promotion. A notable lack of consumer brand loyalty seems to affect this industry, thus necessitating extensive advertising to maintain individual product position. Various toilet and cosmetic items lend themselves to mass marketing techniques. Thus, many of these items, including hair products, have been marketed increasingly through food and variety stores.

In addition to the product innovation of new cosmetic materials, package and design study and slight alterations to existing products play an important role in product marketing. The extensive use of aerosol containers is just one example. More aerosol containers are filled with cosmetics and toiletries than with all other products combined. Also, because of a high degree of point-of-purchase advertising and relative lack of brand loyalty, the package design is very critical.

Of course, within the industry segment of hair products, the Johnson Products market is further segmented into the black consumer market. The U. S. Department of Commerce has estimated that the black population reached 23.0 million in 1971 with a median family income approximately 60 percent that of whites with total black family income of almost $31 billion. Johnson Products appeals to a market of great potential, because the black population is growing at a faster rate than the white population and blacks purchase a higher percentage of cosmetic products (Table I).

The well-established prestige cosmetic houses and the industry newcomers have largely ignored the black market while competing intensively for the favor of white women. The black competitive environment is thus made up of smaller firms specializing in beauty products oriented specifically toward the black consumer. Many private label black cosmetics have appeared during the past decade. However, most of these, due to either lack of capital necessary for research and

Table I

Annual Expenditures per Household for Health and Beauty Aids

	Black	*White*
Cosmetics and Toiletries	$88.40	$51.00
Hair Preparations	74.88	46.00
Drugs and Remedies	94.48	53.00

*Source: The Market, "Magnificent Natural Products Co.," (Los Angeles, California: Undated), p. 12.

development (including market research) or a shortage of skilled development personnel, have made little progress since their inception.

MARKETING

Johnson Products' product line consists of hair preparations aimed primarily at black consumers. The competitively priced products are packaged in various sizes with larger sizes intended for professional use by barbers and beauticians and small sizes for direct consumer retail purchase. According to recent surveys, Johnson's line of hair preparations, is perceived by the black consumer as a high quality "prestige" product. Table II shows how Johnson Products' market share among Ebony magazine readers compares with market shares of its major competitors. Commenting on this survey, Johnson explains, "When you consider that in shampoos and setting lotion we are up against such big names as Toni, Clairol, Alberto-Culver, Breck and Prell—companies spending several times our earnings in just advertising—our ranking is most meaningful."

In its advertising, Johnson has been stressing the "Ultra-Natural look"; Ultra Wave, a hair straightener, is no longer advertised and is declining in sales. The Ultra-Natural is achieved with the assistance of Johnson's Ultra-Sheen Permanent Relaxer.

Johnson has found that many men and women thought it was unnecessary to treat their hair on any regular basis while wearing the natural. As a result, their hair dried out, broke off and lost some of its vitality, and Johnson Products sales suffered proportionately. Through clinics and advertising, Johnson has successfully conveyed the message that continual grooming with Afro-Sheen products is essential for healthy hair, and sales are again increasing strongly.

Advertising costs represented a significant portion of 1972's total expenses of $12.5 million. Major advertising expenditures went for spot commercials on local radio stations that attract black listeners, advertisements in magazines directed at black readers (such as Ebony, Tan, and Jet), and for billboards located in black neighborhoods.

In September, 1969, Johnson Products sponsored its first television

Table II
Consumer Preference* for Johnson Products

Brands of Hair Dressing Used		Brands of Hair Relaxer Used		Brands of Setting Lotion Used		Brands of Pressing Cream Used		Brands of Shampoo Used	
Product	Percent	Product	Percent	Product	Percent	Product	Percent	Product	Percent
Ultra Sheen/ Johnson	26.4	Curl Free	44.8	Dippity Do	30.8	*Ultra Sheen*	29.8	Press	23.8
Clairol	22.9	*Ultra Sheen*	19.2	Clairol	14.5	Posener's	20.1	Breck	19.9
Alberto VO-5	18.4	Posner's	14.5	Alberto VO-5/ Get Set	11.4	Apex	11.6	Head and Shoulders	16.7
Posner's/ Hi-Sheen	12.8	Curl Out	5.8	Breck Set	7.5	My Knight	3.4	VO-5	12.9
Dixie Peach	5.5	Epic	4.1	Posner's Wet Set Styling Gel	6.7	Dixie Peach	2.5	Halo	8.7
Apex	4.3	Vigorol	4.1	*Ultra Sheen*	6.0	Hair Rep	2.5	*Ultra Sheen*	7.8
Royal Crown	3.5	Perma Straight	2.9	Dr. Ellis - Lady Ellis	4.7	Royal Crown	1.9	Lustre Cream	7.3
Vaseline	3.5	Lustra Silk	2.9	Pre-Con Gel	3.4	VO-5	1.9	Clairol	5.3
Sulfur-8	3.2	Hair Straight		Lustra Silk	3.1	Lustra Silk	1.9	Avon	3.1
Lustra-Silk	3.1			Dep Set	3.1			Johnson's Baby Shampoo	2.5

"special," at prime time in selected major markets. Entitled *Black & Beautiful*, this investment marked the first time a black products manufacturer has assumed total sponsorship of a television program. The show featured an all-black cast as well as black directors and writers.

A high percentage of Johnson Products' sales occur in urban areas with large black populations; New York ranks first in terms of sales and Chicago second. The full product line is also sold in London and in the Caribbean. In addition to the black market, Johnson points out that "The Latin segment of our population also has potential for us. Some of our advertising dollars are being used in Spanish print and radio media."

Johnson Products has developed a district sales structure. New salesmen receive six weeks of intensive training from two sales training managers in class-rooms located at the home office in Chicago. The initial training period is followed by two weeks of field training supervised by district sales managers and experienced salesmen.

During the company's first nine years, most sales were made in the professional market. However, during the six year period, 1964-1969, retail sales grew to 75 percent of total sales. But from 1970 to 1972 there had been a somewhat lower percentage of sales in the consumer market and for the year ended August 31, 1972, 40 percent of sales were to the professional market. In general, the margin on retail sales is about 10 percent higher than professional sales. No single customer accounts for more than approximately 3 percent of net sales.

While pleased with this record, Johnson feels that the company has not yet come anywhere near its potential market penetration. Johnson states, "Our major opportunity lies in getting into high-traffic, high-volume retail outlets (food stores) where our line is not presently stocked. We have developed the kind of promotional programs which appeal to these aggressive merchandisers, and we also intend to apply the same techniques in obtaining greater depth of distribution through more shelf space, mass displays, additional items and sizes in those key outlets presently carrying Johnson Products. And remember, the name of the game is shelf space."

FINANCE

Johnson originally financed his operation through $250 of borrowed money. Since then most of the funds needed for expansion have been generated internally. The only debts incurred have been those of keeping company cars and of construction on the current site. In the early years of operation, Johnson ran his business on a "cash and carry" basis. This was possible since low inventory and production costs, combined with a consistently high demand for his products, enabled Johnson to avoid tying up large amounts of capital for extended periods of time. This very conservative method of financing still prevails in the Johnson organization. The $615,000 plant expansion program was financed entirely by cash. In fact, Johnson Products desired to accelerate the payments on the mortgage of the original building but was kept from doing so because of high penalty costs. Johnson Products, while highly profitable, exhibits the fiscal conservatism which Theodore Cross, author of *Black Capitalism*, identifies as typical of the ghetto economy. The company maintains high liquidity, with roughly $2 million in cash and U. S. Treasury bills, no preferred stock, and no long-term debt other than a small mortgage. Its ratio of current assets to current liabilities is extremely high: 4.4-to-1.

Johnson Products had sales of $17.6 million in fiscal year ended August 31, 1972, up 150 percent from $7 million in fiscal 1968 and nearly twelve times its $1.5 million volume of four years earlier in fiscal year 1965. Hair dressings accounted for about half of net sales of $9 million. The entire Afro-Sheen line, introduced in June, 1968, produced sales of $4.6 million in fiscal year 1972, 26 percent of total volume.

Johnson's profits were $2.6 million in 1972, up from $1.7 million in 1971 and more than ten times fiscal year 1965's $159,973. Earnings per share went from $0.08 in 1965 to $1.30 in 1972. Net profit-to-sales ratio improved from 10.7 percent in 1965 to 14.2 percent in 1972. (See Exhibit II for concise 5 year profit and loss figures.)

On December 10, 1969, a 300,000 share ($8.4 million) initial public offering of Johnson Products Co. common stock was snapped up by investors after reaching the market at $28 per share. Johnson and his family retained about 85 percent of the company's stock.

None of the proceeds accrued to Johnson Products. This offering resulted in income to Johnson and was undertaken by him for two reasons. First, the company becomes more attractive for future acquisitions if the stock is publicly traded. This way Johnson Products can offer cash and stock in acquiring merger candidates. Second, this offer will enhance Johnson's estate position in that he will now be slightly more liquid. The stock in 1973 was selling for about $30 a share and was listed on the American Stock Exchange.

The company is not presently engaged in an active acquisition policy. The supply and demand requirements of current operations is more than enough to keep management and production working at full capacity. However, as Johnson explains, "We are very interested in expanding through acquisition. We would be interested in one of several opportunities, either direct competitors or related products. There are about six privately owned companies in this category and numerous public firms. Our main problem is finding a company which has something to offer."

THE JOHNSON FOUNDATION

At the beginning of 1970, the Johnson Products Co. established the Johnson Foundation. The Foundation has an annual budget of $120,000 per year.

Of this sum approximately 50 percent goes to educational scholarships, while the remainder is donated to nonprofit organizations dealing with the problems of the black ghettos.

Shortly after its inception, Johnson asked Edwin C. Berry to direct the foundation. After Berry retired from his post as executive director of the Chicago Urban League, he accepted the position as executive director of the Johnson Foundation.

Although initially funded at $120,000 per year, the foundation is expected to grow proportionately to the growth in the Johnson Products Co. Berry proudly asserts that only $400 of the budgeted $120,000 is spent on administrative expenses. The balance is applied directly to the foundation's two-fold objectives.

The importance of the foundation to the community is obvious. The importance to the company is a bit more subtle. The foundation, although not publicized at the insistence of Johnson, adds a not easily measured amount of good will to the company. It also serves as a meaningful indicator of the "social consciousness" of the company. In the words of Berry, "I am here to serve as the official corporate 'conscience' of Johnson Products Company."

Much of Section III has presented examples of minority business projects that have not fared well, such as Black Pride and United Distributors. With the black banks it is still too early to tell the degree of success they will ultimately achieve. But George Johnson is without any doubt *now, today* a clear example of a highly successful minority entrepreneur—a man who started with few financial resources, but with a good business background and the drive to succeed in a relatively hostile business environment. He developed a new market area, one that nonminority businesses were unwilling or unable to develop. He had the good sense to enter a business which depends on the availability of discretionary income at a time when minority income was rising with the overall rise in national prosperity. He met a desire for grooming products by a growing black middle class that was demanding more and better products tailored to their needs.

It is quite easy, in retrospect, to analyze the success of George Johnson, but for the man himself the struggle was hard and the hours long. We often forget the 80 and 90 hour, seven day weeks that all successful small businessmen put in before they achieve a modicum of success. For George Johnson the struggle to succeed also required him to overcome the initial prejudice of the small loan company officer, and similar prejudice from suppliers, marketing agents and even from his customers. Still George Johnson has made it and his life is a model that young minority entrepreneurs and potential entrepreneurs can look to as a visible inspiration for their future endeavors. His business strategy is illustrative of one of the strategies advocated in the article by Samuel Doctors and Sharon Lockwood, "New Directions for Minority Business Entrepreneurs," in this volume.

Exhibit I
Johnson Products Co. Inc. and Subsidiaries
Consolidated Balance Sheet, August 31, 1972

Assets	*1972*
Current Assets:	
Cash (including certificates of deposit of $1,614,313)	$1,834,207
Commercial paper at cost which approximates market	802,766
Receivables:	
Trade, less allowances for doubtful accounts of $90,000	3,069,119
Other (Note 4)	111,289
Inventories (Note 2)	1,858,653
Prepaid expenses	407,512
Total Current assets	8,083,546
Long-Term Assets:	
Property, plant and equipment, at cost (Notes 3 and 6)	4,380,460
Less Accumulate depreciation and amortization	518,237
Total Long-Term Assets	3,862,223
Other assets:	
Cash value, officers' life insurance	272,698
Notes receivable and sundry items (Note 4)	48,085
Total other assets	320,783
Total Assets	$12,266,552

Liabilities and Shareholders' Equity	*1972*
Current Liabilities:	
Accounts payable	$ 651,820
Due to profit-sharing trust (Note 5)	150,000
Dividends payable	62,895
Accrued expenses	164,962
Federal and state income taxes	817,751
Total Current Liabilities	1,847,428
Other Liabilities:	
Deferred federal and state income taxes (Note 3)	119,391
Commitments (Note 6)	
Shareholders' Equity (Notes 4 and 7):	
Capital stock:	
Preferred stock, no par; authorized 300,000 shares, none issued.	
Common stock, $1 par; authorized 6,500,000 shares;	
issued 839,400 shares	839,400
Class B common stock, $1 par; authorized, issued and	
outstanding 1,171,800	1,171,800
Additional paid-in capital	10,273
Retained earnings	8,282,660
Treasury stock, 800 common shares at cost	(4,400)
Total Shareholders' Equity	10,299,733
Total Liabilities and Shareholders' Equity	$12,266,552

Exhibit II

Johnson Products Co. Inc. and Subsidiaries Five-year Financial Review

For the fiscal years ended August 31,	1972	1971	1970	1969	1968
From Operations:					
Sales	$17,567,507	$14,456,403	$12,637,161	$10,198,342	$7,005,824
Income before income taxes	$ 5,176,012	$ 3,512,817	$ 4,256,601	$ 3,900,723	$2,616,263
Percent of sales	29.5	24.3	33.7	38.2	37.3
Income taxes	$ 2,566,000	$ 1,711,992	$ 2,253,473	$ 2,068,850	$1,333,023
Net income	$ 2,610,012	$ 1,800,825	$ 2,003,128	$ 1,831,873	$1,283,240
Percent of sales	14.9	12.5	15.9	18.0	18.3
Advertising and promotion	$ 3,097,171	$ 2,830,063	$ 2,316,422	$ 1,539,827	$ 936,774
Percent of sales	17.6	19.6	18.3	15.1	13.4
At Fiscal Year-End:					
Working capital	$ 6,236,118	$ 5,843,318	$ 4,501,315	$ 3,966,361	$2,060,213
Current ratio	4.38	9.25	4.46	3.25	2.98
Capital expenditures	$ 1,867,449	$ 321,877	$ 356,585	$ 898,758	$ 164,724
Cash dividends	$ 251,636	$ 201,594	$ 150,251	$ 100,000	—
Long-term debt	—	$ 202,023	$ 211,208	$ 219,881	$ 228,070
Shareholders' equity	$10,299,733	$ 7,951,393	$ 6,362,589	$ 4,546,609	$2,750,943
Shares outstanding—both classes	2,010,400	2,011,200	2,011,200	2,011,200	2,000,000
Number of employees	240	200	170	140	100
Per Common Share:					
Earnings per share	$ 1.30	$ .90	$ 1.00	$ .92	$ .64
Cash dividends per share (common stock)	$ .30	$ .30	$ .30	$ .30	$ —
Shareholders' equity per share	$ 5.12	$ 3.95	$ 3.16	$ 2.26	$ 1.38

SECTION FOUR:
THE ROLE OF THE
PRIVATE SECTOR IN
MINORITY ECONOMIC
DEVELOPMENT

Peter Drucker in his *Age of Discontinuity* states that government is a particularly bad institution to effect social change. Government, he contends, is best suited to establish policy and provide incentives for the private sector to do the work. He labels this "new" approach to accomplishing social ends "reprivatization." He feels business is uniquely qualified to work at social change.

Drucker argues that what makes business particularly appropriate for reprivatization is that it is predominantly an organ of innovation; of all social institutions, it is the only one created for the express purpose of making and managing change.[1] All other institutions were originally created to prevent or, at least to slow down, change. They become innovators most reluctantly and only by necessity.

Business has two specific advantages where government has major weaknesses. Business can abandon an activity. Indeed, it is forced to do so if it operates in a market—and even more, if it depends on a market for its supply of capital. There is a point beyond which even the most stubborn businessman cannot argue with the market test, no matter how rich he may be; Henry Ford had to abandon the Model T when it no longer could be sold. Even his grandson had to abandon the Edsel.

What is more: of all our institutions, business is the only one that society will allow to disappear.

Reprivatization is still a heretical doctrine, but it is no longer a heretical practice. Reprivatization is hardly a creed of "fat cat millionaires" when black power advocates seriously propose making education in the slums competitive by turning it over to private enterprise, competing for the tax dollar on the basis of proven performance in teaching ghetto children. It may be argued that the problems of the black ghetto in the American city are very peculiar problems—and so they are. They are extreme malfunctions of modern government. But if reprivatization works in the extreme case, it is likely to work even better in less desperate ones.

Of course, the private sector, and more specifically the business community, is uniquely qualified to assist in minority enterprise development. The President's Advisory Council on Minority Business Enterprise was guided in its deliberations by a number of basic considerations:

> The Advisory Council feels that a policy of reprivatization of efforts in this area (minority enterprise) is essential, that is, the local communities and private enterprise assume a large share of the responsibility for the doing, leaving the overall strategy formulation to the government section.
>
> Private-sector initiative and leadership is a crucial element in establishing a viable system of minority enterprise; every effort should be made to encourage and strengthen private-sector involvement, with government providing incentives to encourage this involvement.

The private sector, particularly American business, has become quite deeply involved in a variety of programs aimed at developing the minority economy. Section II of this volume detailed some aspects of business involvement in hiring and training minorities. Business involvement in minority enterprise development is more recent, receiving its primary impetus from President Nixon's minority enterprise program initiated in March of 1969. Many prominent businessmen such as James Roche (General Motors), Arthur Wood (Sears), Lester Burcham (Woolworth), Thomas Watson, Jr. (IBM), and Sam Wyly (University Computing) have been actively involved in minority enterprise development. Businessmen see minority capitalism as a social program they can understand, identify with, and participate in effectively.

This section explores three different roles for the nonminority business community for assisting in minority economic development. The first role is that of providing technical assistance. The minority community both in its community organizations and individually owned businesses has been characterized by a lack of technical and professional skills. The white businesses can provide many of these skills through funding a resource center such as the Black Strategy Center in Chicago.

Stephen Schlecht, in his article on the birth and demise of the Black Strategy Center, analyzes the tactics used by black community leaders to force the hands of corporate executives. This Chicago case study shows how the black leadership was able to exert strong influence over the large white-owned businesses to establish a black resource center. The center solicited the money from large white-owned businesses and created a forum for the transfer of skills to the poor community. The article is noteworthy because it demonstrates both a new form of social institution, the Black Strategy Center, and changing power relations between the black community and the white business establishment in Chicago.

Another role for the private sector is that of providing capital for minority enterprises. Several government programs are directed at adapting existing federal agency programs to provide inducements for private sector investment such as those of the Small Business Administration (SBA) in providing virtually automatic 90 percent guarantees for bank loans to minority businessmen and the more widely publicized set of inducements provided to nonminority businesses that invest in minority enterprise small business investment companies (MESBICs). The adaptations consist of modifying existing SBA loans and small business investment company (SBIC) programs to meet the need for larger inducements for private sector investment in minority enterprise development. The MESBIC inducements include two or three to one matching of the invested funds with long-term government loans (up to 15 years) at favorable interest rates, a charitable income tax deduction for the investment, and often government technical assistance funding to help support the management expense of the MESBIC.

Traditionally, the private sector has avoided investments in the minority community because of the feeling that these were high risk investments. As banks generally are prohibited by law from making equity investments, they primarily provide loan capital for enterprises. Even the SBA direct loan or guarantee programs require that the minority entrepreneur provide about 15 percent of the financing for a venture in equity capital. Equity capital typically is provided from personal savings or other capital accumulation, but members of the minority community have accumulated little in the way of capital for such equity investments. To meet this essential need for equity capital, President Nixon initiated the MESBIC program early in his first year in office. The essay by Richard Chandler and Bruce Miller details the problem of establishing one such MESBIC, the Chicago Community Ventures Incorporated (CCVI). Most of the more than 45 MESBICs that have thus far been established by American industry in response to President Nixon's program have been capitalized at $150,000, the legal minimum equity investment, which really is an inadequate amount of equity capital. Also most MESBICs have been sponsored by a single company. On the other hand, CCVI is capitalized at more than $1 million and is sponsored by 20 leading Chicago corporations.

The MESBIC program has been beset by a number of problems, not the least of which has been a failure to recognize the need to provide significant amounts of management assistance to client companies of the MESBICs and the need to provide additional equity capital. Initially, it was assumed by the administration that the corporate sponsors would underwrite the operating costs of their respective MESBICs, but in some cases, the yearly costs of technical assistance have almost equalled the total capital investment.

The desperate need for loan and debt capital is only symptomatic of the very tiny capital base in the minority community. Theodore Cross sees the lack of an adequate capital base as the primary deterrent to significant improvement in the ghettos and barrios. Cross was invited to Washington by Donald Rumsfeld, the administrator of the Office of Economic Opportunity (OEO), to develop an experimental capital base building program. Out of this grew the Opportunity Funding Corporation (OFC), established in mid-1970 as a nonprofit quasi-private corporation. OFC is designed as an experimental demonstration program to test various combinations of incentives to motivate more of the business community to be actively involved in poverty area economic development. OFC programs include: (1) the banking programs—to help combat a major impediment to minority business development, which is the ghetto's inability to attract and maintain institutional credit; (2) surety bonding program—to improve the competitive position of minority contractors by furnishing surety bonds; (3) SBA/LDC local injection program—to act as a catalyst and leveraging agent, using existing government programs and resources of different organizations to put loan packages together. Two other programs are a flexible guarantee program and a real estate program.

OFC presents alternatives to the traditional welfare-style social action programs and to the present inflexible federal agency programs using an adaptable and businesslike approach to poverty area economic development. Through rigorous evaluation of OFC pilot programs, OFC demonstrations should be able to recommend appropriate administrative and legislative action. It is planned that successful OFC experiments will result in recommendations for changing existing agency inducements or for the creation of totally new methods of inducing private sector investment. These recommendations will require either changes in existing federal agency administrative operating procedures or new legislation.

The third role for nonminority businesses involves a more immediate problem for both the involved nonminority businesses and the minority community since it focuses on the role that nonminority businesses presently located in a ghetto area can play in developing their communities. Of course, many white-owned businesses have simply chosen to flee inner city neighborhoods that have become increasingly minority and often dilapidated. But, for those businesses that must remain because of the nature of their businesses (such as hotels, banks in nonbranch banking states, utilities and the like), or those that wish to remain to assist the community in rebuilding itself, there are a number of ways in which such businesses can assist. The two remaining articles in this section, those by Barsness and by Allvine and Star explore some of the ways in which such businesses can provide tangible help to their communities.

Professor Richard Barsness, in his case study of a major meat-packing firm, analyzes the problems which a socially conscious company may face in meeting its perceived responsibilities to the minority community. The company, located in the midst of a deteriorating neighborhood in a major urban center, must decide whether to expand its present plant to meet immediate needs or to build a new plant in the less hostile confines of a suburban community.

Professors Allvine and Star assess the overall role that white-owned businesses can or would play in providing and distributing goods and services to the minority community in the inner city. They conclude that the very rapid change in the inner city has, and will continue to have, a very substantial impact on white-owned business activity. White businessmen must either adapt to these changes or cease to do business in the minority community.

FOOTNOTE

[1] Peter Drucker, *The Age of Discontinuity* (New York: Harper & Row, 1968).

Stephen L. Schlecht*

A BLACK CENTER FOR STRATEGY
AND COMMUNITY DEVELOPMENT

INTRODUCTION**

On September 20, 1969, Chicago newspapers carried the announcement that a black strategy center was to be funded by the "top stratum" of Chicago's business and financial communities. As reported, the center would have three primary objectives:

(1) It would serve as a "think tank" for nationally known scholars who would be called together to look at black conditions in Chicago and establish priorities for improvements.

(2) It would train blacks who belong to community organizations to carry out action programs of their groups or of the center.

(3) It would develop projects in the fields of economics, education, health, religion, and culture.

The chief executives of eight large Chicago-based business organizations were listed as the principal supporters for the center. The eight firms they represented were The First National Bank of Chicago, Continental Illinois National Bank & Trust Co. of Chicago, Carson, Pirie, Scott & Co., Sears, Roebuck, & Co., Commonwealth Edison Co., Illinois Bell Telephone Co., Northwest Industries, and Inland Steel Co. Dr. J. Archie Hargraves, associate professor of Urban Mission at the Chicago Theological Seminary, became the chairman and chief executive of the organization, known as the Black Center for Strategy, Training and Community Development. According to Dr. Hargraves, the center would "provide black people with greater dignity and control of their own destiny than any other program in the country. . . . We emphasize that this is essentially a program of black self-development and self-determination."

The Black Strategy Center was to be a new experience in the relationships between the city's business community and black community. Traditionally, the business community had responded to the needs of the black community in Chicago through such well-established organizations as the Urban League. But the climate and the condition of the late 1960s produced an urgency that required nontraditional channels. Newer and much more militant spokesmen seemingly represented the black community. They confronted and threatened, at least perceptually, the power base of a well-established group of home-based industrial and commercial firms in Chicago.

*Steve Schlecht is in management at Jewel Companies, Inc. This paper was written while he was a M. B. A. student at Northwestern University, under the direction of Professor Lawrence G. Lavengood.
**This paper has been written from extensive interviews with many of the individuals instrumental in the formation of the Black Strategy Center.

To meet this challenge, business leaders bought a concept—one that had never been tested before—and they paid for it. The center was funded for one year, organized and staffed at a cost of approximately $600,000. As a concept, it never really had a chance to prove successful under the standards it had imposed upon itself. A review was made by an outside business consulting group less than one year after full-scale activities had begun. The review pointed out major internal administrative problems and the lack of program planning. It became the basis for the refusal of business sponsorship for a second year of operation. No immediate sequel to the center has been attempted.

The intent of this paper is to describe and analyze the motivations and dynamics involved in the sponsorship of the Black Strategy Center by principal executives in the business community. In order to view these dynamics, particularly the perceptions of a nucleus of white business executives, it will be helpful to understand some of the changing forces in the city—thus the discussion of the social climate in Chicago in the late 1960s. During its existence, the Black Strategy Center was viewed as a prototype for other urban centers. Its value, in retrospect, may be in understanding its failure.

BACKGROUND

The Black Condition in Chicago: A Capsule History

Chicago's black inner city areas had become a ghetto, both institutionally and physically, long before the 1967 and 1968 race riots. Racial conflict in the city dates back to the 1890s, when Negro migration from the South to Chicago reached conspicuous proportions. After the turn of the century, Negroes were actively recruited in the South by representatives of the Illinois Central Railroad and by professional Northern strikebreakers.[1] Negroes who came to the city were used as scabs in the stockyard strikes and the teamsters' strikes. It was during the latter strike, in 1905, that the first racial outbursts took place, culminating in the disastrous race riots of 1919. Hostility toward Negro scabs was easily translated into general antipathy toward Negroes. Racial tensions increased during the early 1900s, particularly in the boundary areas between black and white neighborhoods. From 1917 until the riots of the summer of 1919, the two neighborhoods were in continual conflict. White "athletic clubs" assaulted Negroes on the streets; one of the most notorious clubs was Ragen's Colts, a band of Irish youths. At the same time, "neighborhood improvement societies" bombed the homes of Negroes who dared to move into the fringe areas of a white neighborhood. Conflict finally erupted into racial violence in 1919. The spark was the drowning of a Negro youth who swam into the white section of Lake Michigan along a public beach. Four days of rioting and killing followed.

The race riots of 1967 and 1968 in Chicago indicated that remarkably little had changed since 1919. Although the black community had grown enormously —from 4 percent of the population in 1920 to about 32 percent in 1970—the black in Chicago was still unable to obtain housing beyond the confines of the ghetto. In his history on the black community in Chicago, Allan H. Spear found that the complex of separate institutions and organizations that had first developed between 1890 and 1920 had continued to serve an isolated black populace in the 1960s. Describing white hostility toward blacks in Chicago, he concluded:

> Negroes—forever marked by their color—could only hope for success within a rigidly delineated and severely restricted ghetto society. No physical wall has encircled the black belt. But an almost equally impervious wall of hostility and discrimination has isolated Negroes from the mainstream of Chicago life. Under such conditions, Negroes have tried, often against impossible odds, to make the best of their circumstances by creating a meaningful life of their own. But they have done so, not out of choice, but because white society has left them no alternative.[2]

The extent of isolation from the "mainstream of Chicago life" was realized by blacks in the 1960s as they became conscious of their own experience. Blacks held few management positions in Chicago's home-based business and financial corporations. They were denied entry into many trade unions.

A number of activist and militant black groups emerged in Chicago from the civil rights and black power movements of the 1960s. As these groups mobilized, they began to challenge many of the institutional configurations that excluded blacks from the mainstream. In so doing, they threatened the influence and interests of the white business community, particularly those large business corporations which were headquartered in the central business district of Chicago.

The Central Business District (CBD) of Chicago

While manufacturing industries in the central city had relocated to suburban areas, Chicago's central business district continued to grow and prosper in the 1960s. This growth is evidenced partially by the enormous financial commitment sunk into the construction of new office buildings in the CBD. Despite the dispersion of retail outlets into suburban areas, the State Street retail merchants continued to have a heavy financial stake in the CBD and took an active role in community affairs.

To protect their huge financial investment in the CBD, business executives of the major home-based business and financial corporations created a number of formal and *ad hoc* organizations, including the Central Area Committee, Commercial Club, State Street Council, and the Chicago Association of Commerce and Industry. In an effort to protect their interests in the city, these groups often have worked closely with City Hall.

The principal participants in these civic organizations traditionally have been business executives from firms most directly affected by the actions of the city government. These include the chief executives of department stores, utilities, banks, and newspapers. Because of the nature of their businesses, these companies have a strong interest in the city's economic condition. The ones more visible and accessible to community frustrations make easy targets for mobilized groups determined to challenge and change the established economic institutions of the city.

White and Black Perspectives on the Chicago Urban Scene

White View   The public interface of the banks, department stores, and utilities, along with the new urgency placed on solving the "urban crisis," provided strong motivations for the heads of these corporations in Chicago to take a greater interest in the relationship between the white business community and the predominantly black-populated neighborhoods in the city. Population calculations at the time indicated that the black community would be able to wrest political control of the city government from the white community by 1980.[3] Centrally located businesses would be drawing a greater proportion of their work force from the growing black community. As a result, a much greater responsiveness to the needs of the black community would be required of the white-controlled CBD-headquartered corporations.

It was economically essential to the success of these companies that the city remain healthy. Great financial commitments had been made to the future of the CBD in Chicago.

The principal supporters of the Black Strategy Center had a sizable investment in the future of the city. The First National Bank, a 60-story skyscraper, is the principal building in a 10-year, $200 million design for progress that will bring new life to the center of Chicago's Loop. Sears, Roebuck and Company is currently constructing the world's tallest building near Chicago's Loop. Commonwealth Edison projects an increase in service usage of 80 percent over the next 5 years in one large section of Chicago.

These business organizations, although enjoying considerable prosperity and success, have found themselves confronted with startling facts. One of the principal business executives supporting the Strategy Center had this to say about the Chicago he envisions over the next decade:

> The population of the city of Chicago is 3,304,000 or so. Of these, 1,101,000 are black—that is, 31.3 percent—a significant proportion. In 1950 it was 14 percent. In 1960, it was 22.9 percent.
>
> Blacks have larger families. By 1963, 50 percent of the children in the grammar schools of the Chicago Public School System were black. In 1964, the figure was 52 percent. The current figure, according to the Board of Education, is 54.7 percent.
>
> It doesn't take a statistician to see that in a few years the majority of the citizens of Chicago will be black. By 1980, the majority of voters in the city will be black.

The executive goes on to detail the poverty, unemployment, and the poor education of Chicago's blacks. He acknowledges the discontent in the black community, the frustration and the hostility that pervade this 40 percent of the city—this soon-to-be-voting majority. He told the audience:

> A proportion . . . thank goodness, a small proportion . . . of these blacks, unable to obtain by political, social, economic or other means what they consider to be fair and equal treatment, are attempting to attract attention to their plight by demonstrations and occasionally by riots and looting.
>
> You, the leaders of Chicago business, have a very large corporate stake in the City of Chicago. You have offices, plants, stores, investments and customers here. Therefore, you are and will be affected by the condition and the future attitudes of the blacks in Chicago.

Consequently, white business executives were deeply troubled by the destruction and violence of the 1967 and 1968 riots in Chicago. The fear of individual attacks loomed large after fires on March 29, 1968, did $7 million worth of damage to the Carson, Pirie, Scott and Co. building at the corner of State and Madison Streets. Carson's management, which had long prided itself on its pioneering efforts in community relations and in employment of minority groups, was convinced that the six separate internal fires had been ignited by black militants.[4] The Carson experience provided CBD business executives with a vivid demonstration of the vulnerability of their businesses.

As corporate planners looked to the future, they recognized the necessity of a healthy relationship with the black community. The problem, as viewed by the white business executives, was what form the achievement of this relationship should take.

Black View   The militant black activists who were to push for the Strategy Center viewed their community's condition as the result of institutional racism, a historic phenomenon that has made the American black man a second class citizen. The "problem" that they felt needed urgent consideration was the unresponsive white institutions that dominated economic, political, and social life in Chicago.

The black experience, as they perceived it, had shown that white institutions—whether schools, sanitation services, police protection, or businesses—did not serve the black community as well as they served their white constituents. In their eyes, the black community was an underdeveloped country: it had been exploited. Efforts by white institutions to develop it had failed. It was time for the black community to become self-supporting, strong enough to share in the affairs and decision making of the larger community. To reach this goal of self-support, new strategies would be required of the black community. The Strategy Center concept was the brainchild of the black community. It would be the agency that would think through new strategies that would remove the black community from its powerless condition.

THE INTERFACE

Origins

The origins of the Black Strategy Center can be traced back to a series of meetings held in early 1968 by a group of black activists. From January until March, this group met at the Urban Training Center for the Christian Mission, located in the annex of a century-old sandstone church on the Near West Side.

As a result of three months of study, the group organized itself under the name "Black Consortium." The Consortium was developed, according to one of its papers, "to unify and mobilize a broad variety of black organizations, institutions and resources in the Chicago Metropolitan area to make a significant impact on racism and change the Black Condition." The Consortium claimed representation of a cross-section of the black community, including civil rights groups, neighborhood organizations, youth gangs, black professional associations, and black clergymen.

Later in the year, the first white initiatives were made toward a black-white interface through nontraditional channels. The assassination of Dr. Martin Luther King, Jr., and the riots on Chicago's West Side following his death in April, 1968, made it vividly clear to some members of the white community that action and dialogue with the black community must be forthcoming from them or violence would continue for a third consecutive year. That fall, under the initiative of an executive of the YMCA, a small group of concerned whites gathered to determine how the gap between the two communities might be bridged. The Chicago YMCA had been under considerable pressure from black militants to make the "Y" more "responsive" to the needs of black youth. This group, comprised mostly of public affairs specialists from business-related organizations, met intermittently during a four-month period. After its third meeting, the group approached Dr. J. Archie Hargraves for suggestions. As a result, arrangements were made for a meeting on December 20, 1968, with 40 representatives of the Black Consortium and members of the white group.

At this meeting, it was readily apparent to the whites that the blacks had come well prepared. In fact, since September the Consortium group had been studying the form that an urban coalition in Chicago might take. Hargraves, the ideologist of the Consortium group, delivered a paper entitled "A New Kind of Partnership." Speaking for the black group, he stated "emphatically' that, at the next meeting between blacks and whites, the whites should be represented by their top business leaders in the city. The white group agreed to try to arrange such a meeting.

Dr. Hargraves' paper outlined six recommendations, based on the assumption that the condition of blacks in Chicago was the result of a white problem, in other words, institutional racism. He called for the transfer of "authentic power to the authentic leadership of the Black Community" by white men and their institutions. His six points were:

(1) Establish an Urban Coalition, with a unified group of black organizations participating, composed of decision makers drawn from the various corporate business and industrial systems, the industry of education, and the health and welfare industry.

(2) Reach an understanding with the unified group of black organizations that no attempt will be made to broker the black community. The privilege of brokering the black community is one that is reserved to the black unity group.

(3) The priority of emphasis in the black community is upon building operational unity. To make this unity a highly functional one, a black strategy center is needed to provide:

(a) a think-tank function for the benefit of the many organizations in the black community;

(b) a means of training organizers for the many organizations that want to move from rhetoric to more constructive action and programming;

(c) a means of developing skill and expertise in needed areas of economic, social, political, youth, religious, and housing development.

(4) For unity to persist, every segment of the black community needs to be organized to make for maximum participation in the uses of power. What is needed is at least three million dollars for an organizing effort in 15 primarily black wards of this city.

(5) Build a development bank which will handle loans and grants to specific projects. Eight million dollars would be required to begin operations.

(6) The role of whites in the urban coalition shall be to:

(a) provide funding of the strategy center

(b) provide skills, expertise, and counsel for development projects in the black community *when asked for*

(c) transfer expertise and skills by training blacks so that they may train other blacks

(d) set up an adjunct to the Community Fund Appeal for black organizations

(e) raise at least $12 million as earnest money to get a "process" started in the black community.

Of the six proposals, the fourth greatly troubled the white group. The request for $3 million to politicize the black community seemed unrealistic and likely to anger many whites. The white group assured the blacks that they would try to arrange a meeting with the top business executives in the city to discuss the six proposals. However, six months passed before the two sides met again.

An Urban Coalition Is Explored in Chicago

An urban coalition was being discussed by other Chicagoans while Dr. Hargraves was preparing his paper. In the wake of nationwide racial riots in cities during the summer of 1967, an emergency convocation of two thousand national leaders from minority groups, big business, labor, religion, and local government was held in Washington, D.C. A statement suggesting the establishment of a national coalition of those elements of society represented at the meeting was adopted. National offices soon were established to provide consultative support and technical assistance for local coalitions formed through local initiative. Each local coalition was to act as an alliance of a city's power structure to press for needed changes in both the public and private sectors. The essential element that would make this concept effective was to be business leadership working actively with and for the black community.

Attending the Washington conference was Mayor Richard Daley of Chicago. In January 1969, the Mayor was discussing the Urban Coalition with John W. Gardner, the head of the National Urban Coalition and former secretary of Health, Education, and Welfare. On January 29, Gardner came to Chicago to discuss with political and business leaders the idea of a local urban coalition in the city. Prior to a speech he delivered to the Commercial Club, Gardner met separately with black community leaders and with members of the white business community. Gardner received a cold reception from the black group. The more militant members of the group wanted complete control over any projects in the black community.

Shortly after Gardner's visit to Chicago, the mayor invited eight business leaders to discuss the coalition concept with him. Within the circles of business leadership, it was widely believed that the mayor opposed a local coalition. These eight business executives, however, were later to go on public record as advocating sponsorship of the Black Strategy Center. The mayor wanted advice from them on whether he should initiate a local urban coalition. The eight businessmen (hereafter to be referred to as the "Support Group") met on three subsequent occasions to study the applicability of an urban coalition in Chicago. Their recommendation to the mayor was that he should not initiate an urban coalition at that time since the attendant publicity might raise unrealistic expectations.

During its evaluation of the urban coalition proposal, the Support Group was not aware of Dr. Hargraves' paper. Their recommendations were based on the inactivity and lack of success of the 40 or more local urban coalitions throughout the country. One of the major failures discovered by the Support Group was that no follow-throughs had resulted from the issues and problems raised at coalition meetings. Implementation seemed to be the major stumbling block for the coalitions. From the Support Group's point of view, little ground had been covered toward effective dialogue with the blacks in Chicago, even considering their study of the coalition concept.

The Support Group did, however, conclude that it was of the utmost urgency to initiate some form of dialogue with the black militant leaders immediately. To implement this dialogue, three members of the group were selected. Their mission was to seek out channels for dialogue with the more militant leaders of the black community. The leaders of the Chicago Urban League and of the Chicago-based Operation Breadbasket were considered too establishment-bound.

Dialogue and Commitment

Dialogue was made possible on April 17, when Earl Doty and Dr. Hargraves approached Norman Ross, vice-president of Public Affairs for the First National Bank of Chicago and former Chicago CBS news commentator. Doty and Hargraves were concerned that an urban coalition might be established without the blacks having a chance to participate in its formulation. The blacks did not know that the Support Group had already evaluated the coalition concept and had rejected it. They told Ross that the Black Consortium group had been waiting since December 20, 1968, for a reply to their position paper. Ross suggested a meeting of the two groups, each group initially being represented by three persons. The two blacks felt that any group of three blacks could not be representative of the black community in Chicago. Ross then suggested an 8 to 8 ratio; the blacks agreed and a secret meeting was set with the two groups for June 3, 1969, at the Palmer House in Chicago.

Caucusing late into the night on June 2, the Black Consortium group was unable to reach agreement on the 8 representatives to the approaching meeting. The next day, still undecided, the blacks appeared at the Palmer House with 15 members, telling the white Support Group that they could agree to no less. The Support Group was apprehensive about the 15 to 8 ratio, but, reasoning that no agreement could be reached unless both sides assented, they agreed to it.

The Support Group attempted to follow its own agenda during the meeting. They assured the blacks that the white group was not at the meeting "to talk the blacks through a long, hot, summer." With this declaration, the Support Group wanted the blacks to agree to "no rhetoric" at the meetings, and the blacks agreed. The Support Group also requested that no publicity be given to the negotiations between the two groups; the blacks agreed, with the understanding that by entering into discussions with the Support Group, they were in no way restricted from actions or demonstrations essential to their cause.

Midway in the meeting, the blacks changed the agenda and worked from their own. They set forth four proposals—in their view "demands"—that they considered essential:

(1) funding of the Black Strategy Center

(2) release of one-half of the annual revenues from the Crusade of Mercy (that is, the Community Fund) for use in the black community

(3) funding of $8 million for a black-managed development bank

(4) establishment of an on-going instrument for dialogue between the black community and the white business community.

Consideration of these four proposals was tabled until the next meeting to be held a week later at a South Side black-owned restaurant.

At the June 10 meeting, task forces were set up to evaluate each of the three major objectives outlined a week earlier by the blacks. The Strategy Center was considered the number one priority of the blacks but other proposals were also discussed.

The third meeting, held in the board room of the First National Bank of Chicago, was a critical juncture in the discussions between the two groups. The blacks pushed for immediate funding of the center. When the Support Group asked for more time to study the proposal, one of the black spokesmen, Calvin Lockridge, produced a plan for raising the necessary funds for the center. The Support Group, under considerable pressure from the blacks, consented to gather funding support for the Strategy Center as a non-profit corporation.

Concurrent with meetings of the two principal groups, staff meetings were held with second-echelon members of the two groups. Studies were made of the two other major proposals. The blacks had hoped during the negotiations that their demand for one-half of the revenues of the Community Fund would be a point upon which they could bargain. They thought that industry was the major contributor to the fund and, consequently, should be sensitive to any unfavorable publicity about the fund's monies being turned over to the black community. It became apparent from the task force's evaluation that the Community Fund was less vulnerable than earlier anticipated by the blacks. Although the blacks had thought industry was the fund's largest contributor, only 40 percent of the fund's contributions actually came from industry; the other 60 percent came from private individuals. The white staff members pointed out that many corporations might be willing to see a portion of their contributions earmarked for black control, but resistance among white blue collar workers and white collar workers would most likely result in a drying up of individual contributions. Agreement was reached between the two groups that ways should be found for blacks to exercise more influence over the fund.

The other major proposal considered by the two groups was for the white business community to provide $8 million of start-up capital for the formation of a development bank, more properly a fund, that would make loans that were viable yet were sometimes considered too risky for commercial banks. Representatives of the two Chicago banks in the Support Group argued that there was no possibility of raising $8 million because banks simply would not turn lending money over to inexperienced people while money was tight. In addition, an organization called Urban Ventures, Inc., was being formed to serve the developmental capital need.

Funding

The Support Group arranged for two fund-raising luncheons, one scheduled for August 25 and the other for September 17. Principal foundation directors and corporate executives in the city were invited. They heard Gaylord A. Freeman, Jr., Rev. C. T. Vivian, Dr. Hargraves, and Arthur M. Wood explain the Strategy Center project, its need, background, and objectives. Freeman articulated the Support Group's concern for the urgent improvement of the black condition in Chicago. He also outlined the background that led to discussions between the black and white groups. Dr. Hargraves followed Freeman; he set forth the center's objectives, and suggested how the center would assist the black community.

Rev. Vivian, who would later become president of the center, presented a proposed operating budget for the center and described the responsibilities of the major positions on the center's full-time staff. Arthur M. Wood, president of Sears, Roebuck, & Company, addressed himself to concerns that the prospective sponsors might have had about the representation of the center's officers, their management capabilities, and the disinterested evaluation of their work.

The two luncheons and subsequent canvassing of Chicago area business firms netted commitments of $615,000, or almost 75 percent of the center's first-year proposed operating budget. Most of the monies, however, were given to the center pending determination of its tax-exempt status by the Internal Revenue Service. At the time of the fund-raising luncheons, the Support Group was enlarged to 15 members; new members included representatives from International Harvester Co., Marcor, Inc., Arthur Anderson and Co., Field Enterprises, the Tribune Corporation, CNA Financial, and Borg-Warner Corporation. The Support Group was now comprised of the principal utilities, home-based industrial firms, newspapers, department stores, and financial institutions in the city. One principal home-based retailing firm, Jewel Companies, Inc., remained skeptical of the Strategy Center project and withheld its support until a later date.

Tax-Exempt Status

The appropriate papers for tax-exempt status were filed with the Internal Revenue Service on October 3, 1969. According to the attorneys involved in the filing, the center would have to wait about two months for a response. However, seven months passed before the IRS exemption was acted upon. As a result, the interim period produced strain and anxiety between the Support Group and the principals of the Black Strategy Center.

Doubts and suspicion were raised on both sides. The tax exemption was considered critical to the success of the center. After two months of waiting, the leaders of the center agitated for pressure on Washington by the Support Group. Although this was perhaps a naive assumption, the black militants felt that, with former Chicago banker David M. Kennedy as head of the U.S. Treasury Department, the Support Group would have no problem in effecting the tax-exempt status. Citing his publicized disfavor of community action programs, some felt that President Nixon was thwarting the tax exemption. Support Group members saw the delay as part of the IRSs new policy of critical examination of tax-exempt organizations.

Events in the black community did little to improve the situation. A coalition of black organizations had been formed in the summer of 1969 to press the Building Trades Council for greater opportunities for blacks in the construction industry. The Coalition for United Community Action, headed by Rev. C. T. Vivian, closed down construction sites throughout the city; demonstrations by blacks and counterdemonstrations by white construction workers resulted. Members of the Support Group believed that Vivian's role in the coalition would be hard to separate from the Black Strategy Center, since most of the organizations that the center claimed to represent were also listed on the roster of the coalition. Members of the Support Group were not sure that the center could remain non-action-oriented, as tax-exemption rules required.

The Support Group's doubts were triggered by a series of events in December, 1969. A confrontation between Illinois State's Attorney police and members of the Black Panther party on December 4, 1969, resulted in the death of two party leaders, Fred Hampton and Mark Clark. Tension and suspicion of whites ran high in the black community during the period following the deaths of the two Panthers. Many whites were held suspect in what appeared to some to be a government plot to liquidate the Panther party.

On December 15, 11 days after the killings, Rev. C. T. Vivian called a press conference at which he read a statement prepared by Earl Doty and Mrs. Jorja English, who represented the United Front for Black Community Organizations, an umbrella group claiming to represent more than 100 black community organizations. Speaking for the United Front, Vivian read a nine-point plan that was designed to counter what the United Front called "a conspiracy by the forces of power in this city to crush the black drive toward liberation." The ninth point was a real psychological shock to the white community; it read: "Effective immediately, a 6PM to 6AM curfew is established for all whites in the black community." No plans were given to enforce the curfew. Vivian stated, "I want you to be very clear that we have not given orders to anyone."

The "curfew statement" hit the leaders of the white business community like a bombshell. Moreover, Vivian was repudiated by fellow blacks, despite attempts by prominent black activists to "clarify" what Vivian had announced. Members of the Support Group were bewildered by Vivian's remarks. His credibility was being questioned in his own community. Dissonance rather than unity seemed to characterize the black community.

The black community's major newspaper, the *Chicago Daily Defender*, had this to say about the black power movement in Chicago following the "curfew statement" controversy:

> The Black Power Movement is shook up because it has sold black people a pretty good line on unity while the black leaders themselves can't get together. The chief architects of Black Power are pounding nails in their own caskets because they're fighting each other instead of doing battle with the real enemy.[5]

Strong reservations were raised in the minds of members of the Support Group. Their primary concern was that the proposed leaders of the center were not representative of the black community in Chicago, and the chief claim the Black Consortium could offer the Support Group in return for its sponsorship was that it was a representative body. Despite these concerns, the Support Group held firm in its commitment to sponsor the Strategy Center.

The seven-month delay in receiving the IRS tax-exempt status played a crucial role in defining the objectives of the center and in assuring financial and program accountability. After Vivian's "curfew statement," many nonparticipating members of the Chicago business community voiced their skepticism of the Strategy Center project. Business leaders expressed concern that the Support Group "had been hustled by a group of black extremists." To some, the funding of the center had been a "no strings attached" proposition designed to "buy off" an emerging political threat to the business leaders' influence in the city.

In order to receive the IRS tax-exempt status, the principals of the center were required to define and articulate program objectives that would be confined to tax-exempt purposes as defined in Section 501(c)(3) of the Internal Revenue Code. The principles and procedures negotiated between the Support Group and the Strategy Center Group to adhere to the Internal Revenue Code made the criticisms of those skeptical of the center appear less valid.

Program Review and Accountability

The Support Group had been working since October, 1969, at the task of establishing mutually acceptable procedures and agents to ensure program accountability. The Program Review Committee of the Support Group had negotiated a written Statement of General Principles and Procedures with the principals of the center. This statement was accepted by the corporate officers and board of directors of the center on November 3, 1969. As designed, it set forth the basic understandings of the objectives of the center, the limitations on activities of the center, a procedure for start-up, and a method of on-going program review and evaluation.

General agreement was reached between the Support Group and the Strategy Center board of directors on the following nine "key principles":

(1) The Strategy Center board will have complete responsibility for establishing policy (defined as the setting of objectives and ordering of resources to accomplish the projected missions of the Center).

(2) The functions to be undertaken by the Strategy Center are generally as follows:

(a) Strategy and Program Planning. This will be based, first, on an assessment of the potential strengths and peculiarities of the black community and, second, establishment of projects and strategies designed to create needed change.

(b) Training. Stress will be placed on developing leaders and personnel who can carry out specific projects by working primarily with existing organizations.

(c) Community Development. This will consist primarily of working with existing community organizations, of assisting them to develop specific projects in the economic, housing, cultural and health and welfare areas, but may also include overall projects involving the total black community.

(3) The Support Group will not establish priorities, identify problems, or define

the programs of the Strategy Center. It will not endeavor to stop the Strategy Center from becoming involved in knotty or controversial issues just because they are knotty or controversial.

(4) The Strategy Center will do its utmost to insure that proposed programs are effective, soundly conceived, consistent with the best interests of the black community, as defined by that community, and that programs are aimed at strengthening black participation in the total metropolitan community.

(5) The Strategy Center will operate with fiscal integrity and will utilize sound management techniques. There will be strict accounting to the Support Group for all expenditures. No monies will be used for either partisan political purposes or illegal activities.

(6) Accountability of the Strategy Center board is to the total black community through the medium of the Coalition for United Community Action. There is report, review, and accounting responsibility to the Support Group with respect to the areas described in paragraphs (4) and (5) above.

(7) A continuing relationship between the Support Group and the Strategy Center board is essential and must be constructed in such a way as to build mutual trust and respect while each group respects the organizational integrity of the other.

(8) Financing by the Support Group of the Strategy Center's second year of operation will, as a practical matter, depend to a considerable degree on the nature of the projects and on the degree of cooperation and results obtained by the Strategy Center during its first year of operation.

(9) The Support Group wishes to give the Strategy Center whatever assistance it can, based on the years of experience of individual members of the Support Group. By this it is not meant that the Support Group has any expertise in the area of black problems or the types of programs needed to search for or achieve solutions. If this project is to be successful, it is recognized that black people must develop their own programs for grappling with the black community's problems and they also must oversee the implementation of those programs. However, in the areas of organization and management techniques, the Support Group does have considerable expertise to offer. The business community supporting this project will be vastly reassured if that expertise is utilized by the Strategy Center board.

Four limitations on Strategy Center activities were written into these key principles. The Strategy Center had committed itself to programs that were not only consistent with the best interests of the black community but also were aimed at strengthening black participation in the total community. The second constraint was that the center would operate with fiscal integrity and that there would be strict accounting to the Support Group for all expenditures. Third, no monies would be used for partisan political purposes or illegal expenditures. The fourth limitation would, in time, prove to be the greatest: the center's second year of financing would depend "on the nature of the projects, degree of cooperation, and results obtained" by the center during its first year of operation.

To insure that the limitations described above were not violated, the Support Group negotiated three procedures that served as control mechanisms with the center's officers. The Support Group was concerned that plans be made in stages rather than an attempt to implement the center's total plan all at once. Funds were made available to the center on a "block grant basis," with the first step consisting of $40,000 for start-up funds after the center had submitted a two months' budget. Once the start-up phase was completed, the center was to develop specific project plans. Funds were not made available to the center for implementation of these plans until they were reviewed by the Program Review Committee. The committee required that the center's plans include not only a description of specific projects but also a delineation of the organization and manpower needed to implement the plans. Any time the programs presented or action taken by the center fell outside the agreed-upon key principles, the Program Review Committee had the power to cut off funding of the center.

The third procedure allowed for detached evaluation of the center's programs and results. An evaluation agent, satisfactory to both the Strategy Center and the Support Group, was sought out. The agent would consult with the center in the development of its plans, would keep the Support Group informed about the center's projects, and would be able to evaluate the results of the center's efforts.

Financial Accountability

In addition to program review, the Support Group developed a set of guidelines for accounting and cash handling by the Strategy Center. The Support Group required the center to develop procedures and internal controls that were to be "no more strict or permissive than what is expected" of a business enterprise. Semi-annual audits were to be performed by an independent C.P.A. firm chosen by the center and agreed to by the Support Group.

Arrangements were made with the center for the transfer of funds from a depository account to an account upon which the center could draw periodically. Transfers were to be supported by a listing of expenditures so that the fixed balance could be restored by the Support Group. It was expected that some degree of explanation would accompany the listing so that the expenditures made could be related to approved activities.

The introduction of the fiscal and program controls persuaded the one major hold-out home-based company to join the Support Group. In February, 1970, Jewel Companies, Inc., the operator of more than 250 food retail stores in the Chicago metropolitan area, pledged funds to the Strategy Center. The entry of Jewel as an active member of the Support Group left no major Chicago home-based business or financial organization out of the Strategy Center project. The Strategy Center was an experiment in which a major portion of the business community had a stake.

Reflections

Funding of a Black Center for Strategy and Community Development, Inc., by white-controlled business and financial corporations stemmed from a number of economic and political considerations. Only after the white business leaders clearly saw the economic implications of the rising black militancy and growing size of the black community in Chicago did they seriously consider continued dialogue with and funding of a black organized "think tank." Some of the most influential members of the Support Group perceived the need for a vehicle to share power with the black community and realized that, by being directly involved, they could design some of the constraints under which the vehicle would function.

Others in the Support Group, however, were more concerned with safeguarding their investment in the city and were thinking about the business climate of Chicago under a black administration. The Chicago business community had no intention of abandoning its home base, and there was new construction activity in the Central Business District to prove it. The Support Group was seeking a stable political scene so that there would be no vindictiveness in such areas as taxation against business and business people when the political climate changed in Chicago.

Although motivations and the degree of sensitivity for the condition of black people in the city varied among members of the Support Group, this group of business leaders organized in *ad hoc* fashion to move directly against the critical racial situation as they perceived it in 1969. The direct involvement of the Support Group in establishing an instrument for change in the city was a new experience. The Strategy Center concept violated an established fact in Chicago: when you want something done, you go to the mayor.

The mayor had maintained a "hands-off" policy with respect to the Strategy Center. Under normal circumstances, the mayor's lack of interest could signal death to a newly emerging group. But the Strategy Center experience was different: the mayor, apparently, had faith in the sponsoring businessmen with whom he had had long and satisfying relationships. Yet, the mayor was highly conscious of the political threat posed by the center's leaders.

It was well known that the mayor opposed a local urban coalition for Chicago. In most other major American cities, local urban coalitions had been organized following the pattern prescribed by the Washington conference of two thousand national leaders from various public and private sectors. Chicago, in effect, already is served by an urban coalition. City Hall is the nexus for all established vested interests in the city. The mayor's office, with its control over a highly centralized political organization, permits the mayor to broker between the various vested interests in the city—whoever they may be.

The vehicle developed to formalize the direct interface between the loosely structured black activist group and the *ad hoc* group of Chicago business executives was a new model in city and community relationships. The Strategy Center was the first of its kind and carried with its development was the expectation that it would be a prototype for other urban centers. If the Chicago Strategy Center experience had been successful after the center's first year of operations, similar centers might have been attempted in other cities.

In reality, the Support Group had made a one-year commitment to the Strategy Center. Funding for a second year was contingent upon a thorough evaluation of the center's performance as a going concern for one year and also on its promise for accomplishing its stated objectives in the second year. The evaluation made by a Chicago consulting firm was approached in a very traditional way, the question being whether the center should be financed and operated for a second year, given its past performance. Little thought was given to ways the entire concept of the center might be changed.

The center's operations during 1970 were the subject of rumor and skepticism. A highly volatile political situation within the center became apparent. Frequent fights over leadership developed between the three black principals. Staff members were hired to bring some expertise to the center, but they too became involved in internal factional disputes, which resulted in the release of many of them. Few program accomplishments could be pointed to. A number of projects were started—some major in design and others quite small—but there was no program planning or setting of priorities.

The consultant's evaluation, completed in November, 1970, detailed quite explicitly the administrative problems of the center's operations. Without substantial changes in the center's organization and leadership, the evaluation recommended that the center should not be re-funded. A subsequent meeting of the Support Group finalized the report's recommendation. Although the Support Group gave some thought to an immediate sequel, the mood of the business community in Chicago had changed. The urgency (or threat) was not as great; the militant rhetoric of the three black principals of the center had been quieted.

FOOTNOTES

[1] Allan H. Spear, *Black Chicago* (Chicago: University of Chicago Press, 1967) p. 40.

[2] *Ibid.*

[3] Anthony Downs, Chicago Real Estate Corporation, did the primary research.

[4] See Steve L. Schlecht, "Carson Pirie Scott & Co.: A Case Study in Managerial Reorientation," in this volume.

[5] *Chicago Daily Defender*, February 7-13, 1970, p. 13.

Richard H. Chandler, Bruce L. Miller*

MOBILIZING CORPORATE SUPPORT FOR MINORITY ENTERPRISE

A PROGRAM FOR CHICAGO—BEGINNINGS

In May, 1970, a group of eight men met in a park on Chicago's near North Side and agreed on an objective. The group included two young corporate executives, a business school professor, two M.B.A. students, the director of a community organization, and two independent minority entrepreneurs. The group was divided evenly between whites and blacks. Their objective was to begin a minority enterprise small business investment company (MESBIC) in Chicago, financed by a consortium of Chicago corporations, capitalized at $2 million, and dedicated to earning a profit.[1] They called themselves the Chicago MESBIC Planning Committee which later became Chicago Community Ventures Incorporated (CCVI).

This article will describe two aspects of this committee's work: (1) the development of the CCVI plan, which Commerce Department officials have called the "best conceived MESBIC plan" they have seen, and (2) the implementation of that plan by the committee. The committee's efforts represent an attempt by young businessmen to mobilize the resources of Chicago's major corporations for a social cause.

The Nixon Administration Program

The idea that corporations have a social responsibility to use some portion of their resources in support of charitable goals gained momentum throughout the 1960s. This attitude was given a new outlet with Richard Nixon's 1968 campaign promise to stimulate "black capitalism." By late 1969, the administration was actively seeking corporate support for Project Enterprise, its program to develop minority business ownership through the vehicle of the MESBIC. The MESBIC is a special kind of venture capital company, privately owned but publicly licensed, designed to provide venture seed capital and management experience to minority-owned businesses.

A MESBIC operates in a similar fashion and has the legal status of the traditional small business investment company (SBIC).[2] To start a MESBIC (or a SBIC), the investor must supply a minimum capital base of $150,000. These

*At the time of this article (1970-71), Chandler was assistant to the chairman of the board. Bell & Howell; Miller was a consultant at McKinsey & Co. (Chicago) and they were co-chairmen of the CCVI fund-raising program.

funds are invested in small businesses in the form of straight loans, loans with stock warrants, convertible debentures, preferred stock, or common stock. Unlike a SBIC, the MESBIC is committed to financing only *minority-owned* small business concerns, and it also gives special emphasis to the provision of management assistance by the sponsors. To qualify for an investment, the minority business must be at least 50 percent owned and managed by individuals from minority groups that are underrepresented economically. The major eligible groups are blacks, Indians, Eskimos, Aleuts, and Americans of Mexican, Puerto Rican, Cuban, Filipino, or Oriental extraction. A "small business concern" is defined as one with assets under $5 million, net worth under $2.5 million, and annual net income of less than $250,000.[3]

The MESBIC must adhere to a number of operating requirements in order to maintain its license. It can not own a controlling interest in any portfolio companies. It can not invest more than 20 percent of its total equity in a single venture. Investments must be for a minimum of five years duration. Not more than one-third of total MESBIC equity can be invested in a single industry group. The MESBIC also must comply with certain SBA regulatory features, such as undergoing an annual examination and filing semiannual financial reports.

In compensation for these restrictions, the SBA license qualifies the MESBIC for two major financial benefits. First, it is accorded special tax treatment: (1) dividends received by a MESBIC may be excluded from taxable income; (2) MESBIC loan losses may be deducted from ordinary income; and (3) for the MESBIC shareholders, loss upon the sale or liquidation of MESBIC stock is treated as an ordinary loss rather than a capital loss.

The second advantage of a MESBIC derives from the government financing that enables it to leverage its privately invested capital. The SBA will purchase $2 in MESBIC debentures for every $1 in MESBIC equity below $1 million and $3 in debentures for every $1 in MESBIC equity above $1 million.* Thus, a $150,000 MESBIC will have total assets of $450,000 to invest, consisting of the original $150,000 equity plus an additional $300,000 in loans from the SBA. A $2 million MESBIC will have $7 million in total assets available, consisting of $2 million in equity, $2 million in debt matching the first $1 million in equity, and $3 million in debt matching the second $1 million.

Government leveraging goes even further to the extent that MESBIC capital (equity and debt) is combined with bank loans in a single financing package, with the MESBIC investment taking a subordinate position. Every $1 of MESBIC funds invested in a minority business can be combined with as much as $4 in SBA 90-percent-guaranteed bank loans to that same business, since MESBIC investments qualify as part of the 20 percent equity or subordinated debt required by the banks. When the bank leverage of 4:1 is applied to the MESBIC

---

*Under the amendments to the SBA Act of 1972, the break point on 3:1 matching has now been lowered to $500,000. Thus, a $2 million MESBIC could now have a total of $7.5 million in assets.

funds already leveraged at 2:1 or 3:1, the maximum potential leverage on each dollar of MESBIC equity totals 15:1 on amounts under $1 million and 20:1 on amounts over $1 million. Of course the ability of the minority business to service debt will place an effective limit on the extent to which bank loans are used to leverage MESBIC investments. It is likely that, in actual practice, the combined leverage will be closer to 6:1 or 8:1, with bank funds being combined in a 2:1 or 3:1 ratio to MESBIC funds.

Based on these tax and leveraging incentives, the federal government expected to generate 100 MESBICs by June 30, 1970; 114 MESBICs were pledged, and 16 were operational as of that date. By May 31, 1971, the number pledged had remained constant while those in operation had increased to 31.* It was apparent by then to most observers that the MESBIC program as originally designed was not sufficiently attractive to enlist as much private support as the Nixon administration originally had anticipated.

The Chronology of Events

About one year's time was spent from conception to realization of the CCVI plan, beginning in May, 1970. The first two months were occupied with building and organizing the committee membership. The third and fourth months were spent drafting and redrafting two basic documents, the offering prospectus and the sales presentation. The prospectus was a 102-page document outlining the proposal in complete detail, including more than 60 pages of recent background material on MESBICs and minority economic development. The sales presentation used projected slides to summarize the program for prospective investors.

During the fifth and sixth months, an advisory board was recruited, and the presentation was test-marketed. The advisory board was composed of 13 well-known Chicago business and professional leaders who agreed to help sell the program to the community. From December, 1970 through June, 1971, the final seven months, the committee devoted itself almost exclusively to marketing the proposal—in other words, fund-raising. Toward the end of that period, as the goal became more attainable, attention was shifted to operating details, such as management search, selection of board members, incorporation, and SBA license application.

THE PROSPECTUS FOR CHICAGO COMMUNITY VENTURES CORPORATION

The first job of the Chicago MESBIC Planning Committee was to develop a viable business plan for the new venture capital company. A basic document describing the plan and projecting financial results was needed as a basis for discussions with prospective investors. This prospectus was designed to answer all investor questions and at the same time communicate a high degree of professionalism. It was the joint effort of six committee members from various disci-

---

*By the end of 1973 over 45 MESBICs were operational.

plines. Frequent compliments on the thoroughness and professionalism of this document underscore the importance of beginning with a well-researched business plan.

The Issues

In developing the business plan for CCVI, the Chicago MESBIC Planning Committee debated at length several issues that represented key strategic decisions for CCVI.

Minority Control   Minority members of the committee felt strongly that CCVI should not be a white-dominated paternalistic effort that would probably ignore minority sensibilities. The committee agreed from the start that minority members should comprise the full-time management staff, despite the lack of experienced venture capital managers from minority groups. This was necessary for the minority community to identify CCVI with their own interests. It also promised to yield a better management team, as understanding the minority needs and culture was probably more essential to success than was familiarity with venture capital techniques. The latter could more easily be learned, the committee felt.

The composition of the board of directors presented a much thornier issue. It raised the question of whether or not corporations would be willing to make sizable investments in a high-risk venture capital company that was to be governed by minority members who probably would not be employees of the shareholding companies. The risk was that these directors would be too "soft" in favoring minority interests over safeguarding the shareholders' investment whenever these two interests conflicted. The committee finally compromised by agreeing that CCVI's bylaws should contain an ironclad provision that the board have a majority of nonwhites at all times, but that the entire board should be nominated and elected for one-year terms by the shareholders. Furthermore, any or all of the directors could be employees of the shareholding companies. In this way, the investing companies would be obliged to find minority group members who represented their interests—either employees, minority businessmen, or others. Throughout the planning, the committee agreed that the board should be composed of qualified businessmen or minority economic development experts rather than ministers, athletes, entertainers, or social workers.

In selling the program to the Chicago business community, the committee found acceptance for the idea that CCVI should be controlled by minority group members, provided that the board was elected by and accountable to the shareholders in the traditional manner.

CCVI's Target and Minimum Size   The decision concerning CCVI's target and minimum capitalization was influenced by two considerations. On the one hand was the knowledge that the financial results of small business investment companies over the past decade indicated that, in general, the larger the capitalization, the higher the average level of profitability. Below $1 million, SBICs have had great difficulty in earning a satisfactory rate of return (see Exhibit I). On the other hand, there was a practical limit to how much money could be raised in Chicago, especially since several large companies were committted to forming MESBICs of their own. Considering only the larger public corporations and several well-endowed universities, the committee figured the total market to be approximately 85 institutions. Judging from past fund-raising efforts, a 25 percent penetration level was considered realistic, yielding 21 participating firms. At an average investment level of $50,000 each, this would provide equity of $1,050,000; at $100,000 each, it would produce $2,100,000.

The committee concluded that $2 million was a practical upper limit and should be adopted as its capitalization target. At the low end, $1 million was chosen as the minimum equity, below which CCVI would be unable to achieve its profitability objectives. The committee agreed that all investor pledges should be contingent upon the achievement of that minimum level. As the financial projections indicate (see Exhibits 2 and 3), even at that level CCVI will have a declining book value until the eighth year. The committee could scarcely ask the shareholders for more forbearance than this if they were to treat their participation as an investment rather than a contribution. At $1 million, CCVI still would be one of the largest MESBICs in the nation, with significant economies of scale in relation to the minimum size MESBIC (see Exhibit 4).

Profit Objective   A third major issue concerned whether CCVI's primary objective should be profitability and its secondary objective social impact, or vice versa. Considerable minority sentiment within the committee argued in favor of leaving profitability as a by-product that hopefully—but not necessarily—would be achieved. In the end, the committee concluded that the success of the program hinged unavoidably on a strict profit-maximization philosophy. CCVI planned to take economic development out of the welfare category and turn it into a bootstrap, self-help process. Moreover had corporate "contributions" rather than investments been sought, $200,000 would have been a more realistic

Exhibit I
Comparative SBIC Rates of Return on Invested Capital, 1969-1970

	Percent of All SBICs		Percent of Top Quartile SBICs	
SBIC Capitalization	*1969*	*1970*	*1969*	*1970*
$300,000 or less	0.4	1.4	15.3	13.8
$300,000 to $1,000,000	6.0	3.1	24.2	18.0
$1,000,001 to $5,000,001	11.1	5.0	38.8	29.0
$5,000,001 and more	12.4	2.0	31.3	12.6
All SBICs	9.5	3.1	30.0	18.5

Source: SBIC Industry Review, Investment Division, Small Business Administration, Washington, D.C., December 1, 1969, and December 1, 1970.

Exhibit 2

Financial Projections, $1 Million Capitalization, 1971-80

	1971*	1972	1973	1974	1975	1976	1977	1978	1979	1980
Cumulative Investments (000)	$275	$675	$1,075	$1,475	$1,875	$2,275	$2,675	$3,075	$3,475	$3,875
Revenues (000)	80	67	173	198	176	199	268	332	357	360
Expenses, Including Losses (000)	127	128	243	285	291	297	303	309	315	321
Net Income (000)	(47)	(61)	(70)	(89)	(115)	(98)	(35)	23	42	39
Retained Earnings (000)	(47)	(108)	(178)	(268)	(383)	(481)	(515)	(493)	(451)	(412)
Asset Value/Share (year-end)**	96.28	93.63	93.14	94.22	96.73	98.80	103.02	107.43	111.60	115.48
Book Value/Share (year-end)	95.33	89.20	82.18	73.24	61.72	51.92	48.46	50.74	54.91	58.79

* Fiscal year ending 3/31/72
** Reflects estimated fair appreciated value of equity and convertible debt investments after allowance for losses

Exhibit 3

Financial Projections, $2 Million Capitalization, 1971-80

	1971*	1972	1973	1974	1975	1976	1977	1978	1979	1980
Cumulative Investments (000)	$550	$1,350	$2,150	$2,950	$3,750	$4,550	$5,350	$6,150	$6,950	$7,750
Revenues (000)	165	142	360	413	381	465	583	720	781	796
Expenses, Including Losses (000)	179	192	417	498	506	514	522	530	581	631
Net Income (000)	(14)	(50)	(57)	(85)	(125)	(49)	61	190	200	165
Retained Earnings (000)	(14)	(64)	(121)	(206)	(331)	(380)	(319)	(129)	71	236
Asset Value/Share (year-end)**	100.24	101.25	104.92	110.68	118.44	127.86	138.60	150.24	160.22	168.50
Book Value/Share (year-end)	99.66	99.29	96.82	93.96	89.70	83.43	80.98	84.04	93.55	103.53

* Fiscal year ending 3/31/72
** Reflects estimated fair appreciated value of equity and convertible debt investments after allowance for losses

Exhibit 4
Illustrations of MESBIC Leveraging
at Various Capitalization Rates

	Minimum Size MESBIC	CCVI Minimum Size	CCVI Target Size
MESBIC private capital (equity)	$ 150,000	$ 1,000,000	$ 2,000,000
SBA matching funds (debt)	300,000	2,000,000	5,000,000
Total MESBIC capital	$ 450,000	$ 3,000,000	$ 7,000,000
SBA-backed bank loans	1,800,000	12,000,000	28,000,000
Maximum funds available for minority community	$2,250,000	$15,000,000	$35,000,000
Estimated annual operating expenses	$ 80,000	$ 100,000	$ 110,000
Operating expenses as percent of MESBIC equity	53%	10%	6%

goal than $2 million. If by CCVI's equivocating in the pursuit of profit, each company's investment would have to be written off 5 or 8 years hence, it would have belied the committee's claim that CCVI shares deserved to be treated as an asset. On the other hand, if CCVI succeeded, the model could unleash much larger sums of money currently in the form of corporate marketable securities, university endowments, pension funds, and other traditional institutional sources of capital. There are many programs that claim to *give away* money wisely! CCVI planned to demonstrate that it could *invest* money wisely enough to achieve a fair return.

Investment Strategy   A fourth debate centered on the development of CCVI's investment strategy. Should CCVI turn its back on the so-called "mom and pop," small-scale business? Didn't many successful businesses start with only a few hundred dollars in capital? The committee finally decided to consider only opportunities in the larger, $50,000-and-up category for a number of reasons.

First, the smaller businesses' requirements were already being supplied by banks through the SBA 90-percent-guarantee program, which annually provides several hundred loans averaging $30,000 each to Chicago minority business-men.[4] In addition, there were other existing sources for meeting the equity requirement of the SBA loan program, including direct government funding and foundation grants. Large ventures had fewer options than small ones in trying to raise seed capital.

Second, CCVI's management staff would necessarily be so small that it could only handle six to eight transactions per year. The same basic operations would be required whether making a $10,000 or $100,000 investment. In order to maximize the impact of the program and cover management costs, it would be essential to concentrate on larger opportunities.

Third, it would be impossible for CCVI to achieve its profit objectives if it were to engage in small-scale loans. These kinds of investments are notoriously unprofitable, whether to white or minority entrepreneurs. In 1969, there was a 15 percent loss rate on SBA-guaranteed loans in Chicago.[5] Moreover, such businesses had little or no upside potential of ever selling out or going public. The committee concluded that, if CCVI were to maximize profits, it would have to concentrate on larger investments with more sophisticated minority managers and with upside equity potential. Exhibit 5 illustrates the types of business opportunities identified as potential investment opportunities.

Management Assistance   A final major point of discussion centered on whether CCVI should insist on its investors providing management assistance, in addition to their financial participation. Although the committee risked alienating some investors who viewed management time as their scarcest resource, it was concluded that this commitment was essential to the overall program. In the end, the management assistance program became a strong selling feature of CCVI rather than a liability. What better way for a company to recruit young MBAs, lawyers, and accountants than to give them the opportunity to become consultants to minority businesses and protect their company's investment in CCVI? Most prospective investors felt that management assistance was a critical ingredient to the success of CCVI and thus could hardly complain when this responsibility was passed back to the shareholders.

IMPLEMENTING THE PLAN FOR CHICAGO COMMUNITY VENTURES CORPORATION

The experience of the Chicago MESBIC Planning Committee demonstrated that it was easier to develop a business plan for CCVI than it was to raise the necessary funds. The committee members were experienced in preparing new venture proposals for the consideration of top management; several of them did this regularly as part of their jobs. In contrast, none of them had had any experience in raising $2 million from the chief executive officers of 85 major institutions.

The remainder of this article will describe the implementation of the plan for CCVI, with emphasis on marketing the idea to the community and on how this experience might provide a model for similar future efforts.

Building the Chicago MESBIC Planning Committee

The first task for the core group that established its identity and purpose that Sunday in May was to build an organization capable of implementing such a proposal. In recruiting the committee membership, the core group faced several important issues: size, representation, racial composition, and structure.

Exhibit 5
Examples of MESBIC Investment Opportunities in Chicago

Candidate	Financing Required (000)	Reasons for Lack of Financing Sources	Location	Years in Operation	Outlook for Company
Metal Manufacturing Company	$400	Lack of equity	South Side	1 year	Growth and profits are relatively assured due to commitments by a major auto manufacturer
Retail Drug Chain	$250	---	South Side	Buy out	Chain is attractively profitable and new management team expects to accomplish growth by: • Significantly increasing sales of existing chain • Ultimately expanding via national black franchise
Retail Center Development Company	$150	Low equity participation	Near West	New venture	Growth is envisioned via development of shopping center and subsequent equity participation in tenant businesses
Metal Stamping Company	$150	Too little equity Large proportion of intangible assets	West Side	30 years prior to proposed buy-out	Historically profitable and established customer base is expected to provide a platform for growth and expansion
Grocery Company	$150	Total requirements are over SBA maximum	South Side	Buy out	Good growth expectations • Prospective owners have 17 years' experience and are growth oriented • Plans for expansion via chain in inner city
Manufacturing and Distribution Company	$125	Debt covenants available are restrictive to growth	North Side	2 years	Good growth and profit potential • Proprietary, test marketed new product • Established and dispersed distribution channels
Specialty Manufacturing Company	$120	Lack of equity Large proportion of intangible assets (R & D)	Near North	2 years	Firm is expected to double sales in 3 years; has 2 new products ready for manufacture and substantial R & D invested in a third
Electronics Designer and Manufacturer	$100	Too little equity Large proportion of assets in intangibles (R & D)	South Side	4 years	Excellent growth prospects • Proprietary products • Exemplary technical competence
Public Contracted Transportation Company	$100	Lack of equity	South Side	4 years	Attractive profit outlook • Projected revenue increase of 40 percent by 1971 • Projected net after-tax profit at 13 percent of revenues in 1971
Industrial Laundry Company	$100	Low equity participation	South Side	5 years	Owner has profitably operated a wholesale laundry and dry cleaning establishment. His industrial consumer franchise has provided an opportunity to grow via expansion into the industrial linen supply area. Ultimate expansion into other metropolitan areas is foreseen.

Source: Small Business Administration, Talent Assistance Program, and commercial bank records

Size   Despite the attendant problems of communication and coordination, it was decided that a group of 50 or more members would be needed to effect the committee's objective. This large size would give the committee a representative sounding board for debating issues and for criticizing the CCVI program. It would also provide the depth needed to contact the 85 potential investors and allow for dropouts, absentees, and "unreliables." Although 90 percent of the committee's work eventually was done by about 20 members, it would have been impossible to know this in advance. Those with the time and commitment needed to fulfill major roles naturally took on the necessary work load.

Representation   In recruiting more than 50 additional members, the core group attempted to attract representatives from as many of the city's important institutions as possible. They identified 49 "target organizations," including 18 corporations, 6 banks, 4 universities, 9 community organizations, 3 law firms, 2 management consulting firms, 2 advertising agencies, 2 accounting firms, and 3 government agencies. The group believed that, during the planning phase, such a committee would provide the diversity of viewpoints that would be needed to head off major criticisms during the marketing phase. It would also give them internal allies—a fund-raising "Fifth Column"—to sell to the management of their respective corporations when the time came. The committee members were recruited through personal acquaintances and by means of a standard letter that asked the chief executive officer of each target institution to recommend several younger employee volunteers. On balance, sending this letter was probably a mistake. In some cases, it was ignored; in others, several employees were assigned to "check out" the program, but they had no special commitment to participate on the committee. In several cases, the letter was harmful because it led to a premature evaluation of the CCVI idea while it was still in the early development stage; this made the final sale that much more difficult.

Racial Composition   A third strategy decision was to balance the committee membership equally between white and minority representatives. Successful minority entrepreneurs and minority corporate employees, as well as representatives of community organizations, were recruited. The committee membership included blacks, Spanish-speaking Americans, and one Indian. This racial balance gave the solicitations a dimension of breadth, fervor, and first-person experience respected by corporate executives.

Structure   During the planning phase, a deliberate attempt was made to avoid structuring the committee with unnecessary officers, committees, and titles, so that the main objectives would not be sidetracked by issues of status. A strict egalitarianism was maintained in deciding the key issues in the CCVI plan, thereby stimulating identification with the committee's objectives by as wide a group as possible.

Establishing Credibility in the Chicago Business Community

Chicago is the home of more than 80 public corporations, each with annual earnings in excess of $5 million. The key to raising money from this universe—if one can judge from the methods of museums, symphonies, universities, and other leading charities—is to persuade a president of one of those 20 largest corporations to spearhead the campaign with letters, phone calls, and luncheons. A trusted name on the letterhead provides instant credibility to the other executives being approached. Moreover, corporate executives are reluctant to refuse an important company president's request because they are certain that someday they will need *his* company's contribution to *their* favorite cause. Therefore, a top executive had to be found to espouse the CCVI cause. In June, 1970, feelers were sent to several executives who had been considered ideal for this role; in each case the approach was rebuffed. It was concluded that, with the top leaders in the city already committed to other charitable causes, the Chicago MESBIC Planning Committee—without a history, organization, or standing in the community—would be unable to recruit a major civic leader to head up a fund-raising program on its behalf.

Instead, the committee recruited a broader group of top executives to serve on the advisory board, assuring them that the time commitment would be minimal. The board was to lend its names to the committee's work and to open doors, leaving the actual fund raising to the committee members themselves. This group of prominent Chicagoans (see Exhibit 6), whose names were printed on the committee's stationery, gave the committee instant credibility with prospective investors. The advisors also helped to strategize the marketing plan and, later, to make some key follow-up calls to the fence-sitters. Gradually, as they identified increasingly with the committee, their support and friendship became exceedingly helpful to the program.

Relations with Existing Community Organizations

The city's leading civic and community organizations already involved in minority economic development were invited into the committee. Although the full-time staff members of these organizations were often too busy to attend planning sessions, the contact with these groups nevertheless served several important purposes:

(1) It introduced the committee to the most experienced economic development professionals in the city.

(2) The committee became conversant with the local politics, programs, and topography of past efforts to stimulate minority enterprise in Chicago. This familiarity was important in discussing CCVI with corporate decision makers, many of whom were knowledgable about all these groups and had special associations with one or more of them.

(3) The use of these organizations' names helped in fund raising, convincing

Exhibit 6
Organizational Structure
Chicago Community Ventures Corporation

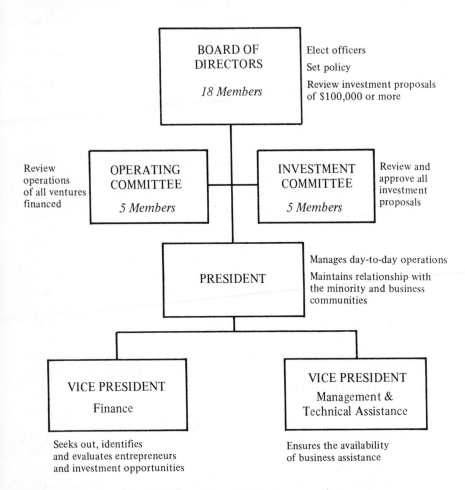

prospective investors that CCVI would not be tied to any splinter group.
(4) Contacts with various community organizations served to prevent them from starting a competing MESBIC. CCVI became *the* MESBIC effort for all these organizations.

In the committee's relationships with these various groups, one notable failure and one special success were achieved. Each merits some additional discussion.

The Chicago Economic Development Corporation (CEDC)   The committee failed in its attempt to merge with the best-known economic development group in the city, the Chicago Economic Development Corporation. CEDC's primary activity is to help minority businessmen develop business opportunities and secure financing from banks and other funding sources in the city. Their full-time staff of more than 20 professionals, operating out of four offices throughout the city, also provides technical and management assistance. Backed by a Model Cities grant, CEDC had set up a funding arm to provide equity seed capital in small amounts. The committee learned early in its existence that CEDC would be starting its own MESBIC to be called Cedco Capital Company. Its capitalization target was $1 million, with $600,000 being provided by the Ford Foundation. Several corporations represented on CEDC's board were providing the primary corporate support, most importantly Borg-Warner Corporation and Meister Brau Breweries.

CEDC's plan posed a threat to the committee in that CEDC would be approaching as many as a dozen of Chicago's most socially conscious firms, reducing the potential market for CCVI investors. Even more significantly, CEDC's existence prevented CCVI from being Chicago's only MESBIC under sponsorship by a consortium of corporations. Therefore, in several meetings with the CEDC principals, the committee officers tried to resolve the differences so that the two efforts could be merged and the business community could be approached with a united front. It soon became apparent, however, that there were some differences in philosophy that could not be reconciled and, moreover, that probably *should not be* reconciled.

Both parties concluded that the two MESBICs' objectives and methods of operation would be sufficiently different to provide a worthwhile comparative test. Cedco Capital would use the existing CEDC professional staff for management assistance, whereas CCVI would rely on personnel from the investing companies and affiliated organizations. CEDC planned to initiate investment opportunities primarily through its own field personnel, whereas it was envisioned that CCVI would use special synergistic relationships with its sponsors whenever possible. Finally, CCVI's commitment to earning a profit would be stronger than Cedco Capital's.

Urban Ventures, Inc. (UVI)   The second object of the committee's persuasion was another organization established to aid minority businessmen, Urban Ventures, Inc. UVI was established in 1969 as a nonprofit foundation to aid inner city entrepreneurs who were unable to obtain adequate capital through normal channels. More than $600,000 in cash and pledges had been raised from corporate and foundation contributors, including about 10 large companies that were an important part of CCVI's target market. A three-man professional staff invested these funds in approximately a dozen small-scale firms during UVI's first full year of operations. Their typical investment instrument was a loan below market interest rates with a maturity of five years or less. By the end of 1970, the UVI board had decided to increase the average size of its investments from under $25,000 to $50,000 and up, in order to have greater impact and higher probability of repayment. This new policy would create a substantial annual fund-raising burden at a time when businesses were under increased pressure from Washington to participate in the MESBIC program.

In the face of this financial squeeze, UVI's board of directors responded with interest when the Chicago MESBIC Planning Committee approached them in late 1970. From the committee's standpoint, an affiliation would provide the benefit of UVI's experience, improve the committee's chances of fund-raising success, and yield operating efficiencies from combining the two staffs and capital pools. The difficulties in negotiating the affiliation stemmed from the inherent legal, organizational, and philosophical differences between a nonprofit foundation and a profit-making enterprise.

After discussions extending over six months, the UVI board and the Chicago MESBIC Planning Committee formulated an affiliation agreement. CCVI would provide complete management services to UVI, including the investment and administration of UVI funds according to the policies and guidelines set down by UVI's board of directors. In return, UVI would pay CCVI a semiannual fee covering the costs of all services rendered. A single management team would report to two boards of directors, each with its own investment policies. The agreement provided for some overlap on the boards, with at least three members common to each. CCVI would take over the employment of UVI's paid professional staff. The two organizations agreed to joint selection of the new chief executive of the combined groups. CCVI would occupy UVI's offices and assume their lease. During the MESBIC start-up phase, UVI personnel provided necessary services, and UVI was reimbursed a reasonable fee.

Under the terms of the affiliation, it was assumed that both UVI and CCVI funds would be invested in the same portfolio companies. CCVI's basic investment objectives would remain unchanged, as would UVI's: both organizations would continue to concentrate on larger minority businesses. With the merger, each organization's efficiency could be expected to improve as less money would be diverted into operating expenses and more would be passed on to minority entrepreneurs. The affiliation agreement also specified that the two organizations would present a noncompetitive fund-raising front to the Chicago community. CCVI would seek capital funds until mid-1971, assisted by UVI, and thereafter UVI would reactivate its own annual fund-raising program, to be assisted by CCVI. The final agreement appeared to benefit both organizations and was accepted with dispatch by their leaders.

Relations with Government

Early in its planning, the Chicago MESBIC Planning Committee established contact with the leading government bodies concerned with minority economic development. These relationships were valuable in cutting through bureaucratic red tape, in keeping the committee informed of nationwide developments, and in gaining assistance in fund raising. Important government contacts were made with individuals in the Washington and Chicago offices of both SBA and the

Department of Commerce, in the State of Illinois Office of Minority Business Enterprise, and in the city administration.

This groundwork reaped rewards when Commerce Secretary Maurice Stans, while on a visit to Chicago, spent several hours meeting with committee members and representatives of a dozen leading Chicago corporations. The meeting and the follow-up letters later sent out over the secretary's signature gave the committee's program an administration endorsement—an assist in urging undecided companies to join in support of CCVI. The visit served as a catalyst to stimulate decisions by several key companies.

Marketing CCVI to Institutional Investors

For an ad hoc group of young, middle-level business and professional men raising $1 million in Chicago for a social purpose is an awesomely challenging task. During the preceding two years, three groups had undertaken to raise a like amount in contributions for programs with somewhat similar objectives. One of these efforts was headed by five leading corporation presidents, another by the chairman of Chicago's largest bank, and the third by the state governor's designee, the head of another large Chicago bank. In each case, the campaigns fell short of the million dollar mark. Being the fourth in a series of programs aimed at stimulating minority economic development, CCVI suffered from others having gotten there first. Throughout this period, moreover, the Chicago Economic Development Corporation continued to seek both annual contributions for CEDC and capital subscriptions for Cedco Capital. In the light of these and other competitive programs, the committee found many companies refusing them because they had made prior commitments to competing programs.

Therefore, the committee decided to base its fund-raising appeal on several distinctive aspects of its program:

(1) CCVI represented a businessman's approach; it used the economic system rather than the welfare system to solve an economic problem.

(2) The company's participation would be in the form of an investment rather than a contribution.

(3) CCVI was to benefit from matching government funds, giving each investor dollar a multiplied impact not available to a firm through other methods of social involvement.

(4) By investing in CCVI, the company would be demonstrating its social commitment to its own employees, while giving them a chance to serve as consultants to fledgling minority businesses.

(5) The investing company would be participating in one of the Nixon administration's highest priority programs for meeting the urban crisis.

While these five points formed the basis for the committee's "unique selling proposition," an implicit sixth point also helped the cause. This effort was a grass roots phenomenon, arising from the initiative of a group of socially committed young men and women—many of them employees of the corporations being solicited.

Developing and Test Marketing the Presentation   To market the program effectively, a standardized half-hour sales presentation was developed to summarize the key points from the prospectus.

After several redraftings based on pilot tests before several receptive firms, the presentation emerged as a much improved selling device, giving prospective investors only the basic information they needed to know.

Establishing the Minimum Unit of Participation   The committee's most difficult and crucial marketing decision was that of establishing the minimum unit of participation at $50,000 per corporate stockholder. The market thus was limited to corporations earning at least $5 million per year, the 2 largest universities, and several foundations, a total of 85 institutions.

Organizing the Marketing Effort   Of the variety of possible approaches for soliciting the 85 target institutions, the committee debated two primary alternatives. Should the presidents of these firms or their representatives be invited to a large luncheon or dinner meeting, where a single presentation would explain the CCVI program, seconded by leading citizens and government representatives? Or should the committee use a low-profile decentralized approach, making dozens of individual presentations to each firm in its own headquarters? The committee finally decided against the mass meeting approach, thinking that it would tend to be ineffective, risky, expensive, and that it would still require considerable follow-up with a larger decision-making group at each company's headquarters.

Instead, it was decided to approach each of the target institutions individually, asking them for a half hour in which to give the presentation to the key executive group. The committee divided into 10 teams, each composed of a minority and majority co-captain and 4 to 6 team members. Each team worked with a single advisor who helped set up an appointment with the eight or nine target companies assigned to that team. From then on, the team was on its own in making the presentation, although the advisors also assisted occasionally with follow-up telephone calls. To minimize the advisor's work, a standard letter, which could be sent out over his signature, was drafted.

Prior to the first presentations, a "sales training" meeting was held for the team captains. A 10-page guide, called "Presentation Tips," was also prepared based on the pilot presentations. It described in detail how to make the presentation and listed common questions that might arise along with sample responses.

Armed with this sales kit, each team proceeded to work independently with its advisor in contacting assigned companies. Monthly progress meetings were held as a follow-up on each team's activities. The entire solicitation period lasted seven months—as opposed to the expected two-months—due to unforeseen difficulties in arranging appointments and in eliciting decisions once the presentations had been made. Frequently, the teams were referred to the company's urban affairs officer, treasurer, or contributions committee, who in turn had to screen the presentation before it was passed up to top management. Furthermore, many firms rejected the proposal, based on the initial letter or phone call, without giving the committee a chance to make its presentation.

The committee's experience indicated that the decision-making process was as varied as the companies it approached, but all favorable responses had one thing in common: the committee succeeded in gaining the ear of the chief executive officer and in furnishing the opportunity to convince him. The committee concluded that social commitments of this magnitude hinge inevitably on such personal decisions.

Publicity   Although committee members made short speeches to several luncheon meetings of business organizations during the fund-raising campaign, publicity was generally avoided. It was reasoned that the managements of large corporations might be less inclined to participate if they had read in the newspaper that CCVI was being spearheaded by four or five smaller firms. Furthermore, it was doubted that any company decision of this magnitude would be meaningfully affected by a newspaper article. The committee never had cause to believe that this low-profile stance was a mistake.

Results of the Fund-Raising Campaign   By the close of the committee's fund-raising campaign in mid-1971, 17 institutions had pledged a total equity capitalization of $1 million for Chicago Community Ventures Incorporated (see Exhibit 5). This level of capitalization made CCVI the largest of all MESBICs licensed as of mid-1971.

The Start-Up of CCVI

The actual creation of the Chicago Community Ventures, Inc.—incorporation, license application, election of the board of directors, and recruitment and hiring of the management team—was deliberately postponed until the solicitations were almost completed and success was assured. This was done to avoid a diversion of attention (and an outlay of cash) during the crucial fund-raising effort.

The committee's general counsel took responsibility for the incorporation, license application, and bylaws. A subcommittee staffed jointly by UVI and CCVI representatives took care of the recruiting, screening, and hiring of management personnel. A special management training program, involving short training stints with several leading venture capital firms in the city, was designed for the president. Selection of the board of directors and other key start-up questions were resolved in meetings attended by representatives of each investing company, which acted in lieu of the board, prior to the latter's election. With the completion of the fund raising and board election, the Chicago MESBIC planning committee, having achieved its sole objective, went out of existence.

AFTERTHOUGHTS

The success of the committee's marketing effort demonstrated that the basic

CCVI proposition made sense to a large number of the corporate executives who heard the presentation; however, the committee decided that, if it had to do the presentation again, it would alter its tactics in several ways. First, a more concerted effort would be made to include an influential young employee from each of the major target companies on the committee, as an inside presentation is the strongest that can be made. Second, the committee would attempt to win the official support and involve the memberships of more existing organizations, both white and black. For example, it might have proved helpful to be able to call upon the resources of the Jaycees and the Harvard Business School Club of Chicago. Third, there should be a more careful sales training system to make certain that each solicitation team masters the complex set of materials describing the program. Several important companies were lost because of poor presentations.

Despite these reservations, the committee concluded that its efforts had succeeded in proving a point of overriding significance: given a good idea, professionally presented and backed by thorough staff work, the executives of leading corporations listened and responded. They showed themselves to be reasonable men, torn by competing pressures, but generally receptive to the need for their companies to play an increasingly meaningful social role.

EPILOGUE

CCVI was incorporated on April 21, 1972 with a capitalization of $1,005,000 and received its MESBIC license June 14, 1972. Thus far it has not been operating for a sufficient period of time to determine its relative effectiveness in providing capital for minority businesses in Chicago.

Exhibit 7
Institutions Pledged to Support Chicago Community Ventures Corporation

---

Arthur Andersen & Co. (Chicago Urban League) (50)*
Armour Dial, Inc. (50)**
Bell & Howell Co. (50)
Central National Bank (55)
Commonwealth Edison (50)
Continental Bank (60)
Field Enterprises*** (Cosmopolitan Chamber of Commerce) (50)
Illinois Central Industries (50)
Illinois Tool Works (50)
Interlake, Inc. (55)
Marcor (100)
National Can Co. (100)
Northern Illinois Gas Co. (65)

Northern Trust Co. (50)
Sears Roebuck & Co. (55)
Trans Union Corporation (60)
Zenith Radio Corp. (55)

---

*Arthur Andersen shares were purchased on behalf of the Chicago Urban League.
**Number in parentheses following the investor's name represent the number of $1,000. shares purchased by the investor, i.e., Armour Dial, Inc. purchased 50 $1,000. shares for a total investment of $50,000.
***Field Enterprises shares were purchased on behalf of the Cosmopolitan Chamber of Commerce (Black run chamber of commerce).

FOOTNOTES

[1] The idea for a consortium MESBIC in Chicago originated six months earlier, in an M.B.A. business environment class at the Northwestern University School of Business. The nucleus group of eight represented a merging of the Northwestern students and their professor with several businessmen who were interested in developing just such a program of expanded corporate involvement in minority economic development.

[2] Small Business Investment Companies (SBICs) were created under the Small Business Investment Act of 1958 as vehicles for providing equity capital and long-term funds for small businesses. The privately owned SBIC is licensed, regulated, and in part, financed by the Small Business Administration. It makes equity investments in, and long-term loans to, small firms for the financing of their operations and for their expansion and modernization.

Since the inception of the SBIC program, more than $3 billion in equity capital and loans has been made available to more than 15,000 small business concerns. In 1970, there were approximately 450 licensed SBICs, with total assets of about $630 million. *SBIC Industry Review*, Investment Division, Small Business Administration, Washington, D.C., December 1, 1970, Appendix I, p. 1.

[3] The rules and regulations pertaining to SBICs are found in the Small Business Investment Act of 1958 (P.L. 85-699) as amended, reprinted in "Small Business Investment Act," Reprint of the Select Committee on Small Business, U.S. Senate (Washington, D.C.: GPO, 1968). The provisions relating to MESBICs are summarized in "Minority Enterprise Small Business Investment Companies (MESBICs), "U.S. Department of Commerce, Office of Minority Business Enterprise, November 3, 1969.

[4] This information comes from a conversation with officials of the Chicago Regional Office of the Small Business Administration.

[5] *Ibid.*, many times the average SBA loss rate of 2.5 percent.

David K. Banner, Samuel I. Doctors

CREATIVE INDUCEMENTS TO PRIVATE INVESTMENT IN THE MINORITY COMMUNITY: THE OFC APPROACH*

THE OPPORTUNITY FUNDING CORPORATION (OFC) STRATEGY

For the American businessman, the major criterion for investment is expected profitability. The high-risk and low-potential reward in poverty areas has historically resulted in minimal business community involvement in poverty-area economic development. OFC is a unique approach for minority economic development. It represents a "third sector" type of institution (neither wholly public nor wholly private), funded by the federal government so that it carries government prestige and economic power. In addition, OFC has the flexibility to remain relatively free of political and civil service restrictions (because of specific charter safeguards).

This combination of attributes can provide substantial leverage in dealing with the difficult problems of minority economic development. OFC's objective is to experiment with various combinations of equity insurance, credit guarantees, rediscount arrangements, and interest incentives in poverty areas to find optimal strategy mixes for poverty-area economic development.

OFC, sponsored by Donald Rumsfeld, director of OEO and counsellor to the president from 1969 to 1970, is a practical embodiment of the theory of "black capitalism" articulated by Theodore Cross in his book, *Black Capitalism*.

HISTORY OF OFC

Early in 1969, Theodore Cross was called to Washington as a special consultant to the Office of Economic Opportunity (OEO) for the express purpose of designing a program to implement his approach for economic development as presented in *Black Capitalism*. Dubbed "Project X," the structure was laid out by Cross and several OEO officials (with the counsel of a large number of businessmen, financiers, community leaders, academicians, and government officials). OFC was to take the form of a nonprofit corporation whose funding would come initially from Title I-D Special Impact OEO funds. OFC was to be relatively independent of the government in order to have more freedom to experiment. To help insure this independence, a highly prestigious board of directors was assembled. The board was initially composed of nine prominent businessmen and community leaders: Dr. David Hertz, director, McKinsey and Co.; Eli Goldston, chairman, Eastern Gas and Fuel Association; Robert O. Delendorf II, president, Arcata National Corp.; John Mabie, vice-president, A.G.

*Excerpted from *Business Perspectives*. Winter (1973), pp. 2-8.

Becker and Co.; Dan Lufkin, chairman, Donaldson, Lufkin and Jenrette; James M. Hall, secretary, State Human Relations Agency, State of California; Dr. Robert Vowels, dean, School of Business Administration, University of Atlanta; Reverend Leon Sullivan, president, Opportunities Industrialization Center; and Alex Mercure, state project director, Project HELP, Albuquerque, New Mexico.

Jack Gloster, formerly head of the economic development thrust at the Urban League, was selected by the board to be OFC's president in the fall of 1970, and subsequently five additional professional staff members were added.

OFC PROGRAMS

In July, 1970, the Opportunity Funding Corporation officially became a $7.4 million OEO-funded experimentation/demonstration program created to test a variety of financial incentives aimed at inducing private investment in low-income communities. The corporation wanted to demonstrate the relative success of different incentive strategies for different economic environments and for different types of development.

The main characteristics of the organization are:

1. *Flexibility*—the ability to seize an opportunity quickly and put business "deals" together that have a high growth potential and a reasonable chance for success.

2. *Creativity*—the ability to try inducement strategies that exploit the sophisticated financial technology of the private sector to build a poverty-area capital base.

3. *Leverage*—OFC, in attracting private funds into low-income communities, is a leveraging device, just like any investment bank.

OFC's success hinges on how successful its inducements are in substantially leveraging private investment to provide a catalyst for minority economic development.

The Banking Program

The first OFC program to be implemented was the banking program. According to Cross, a major impediment to minority business development is the ghetto's inability to attract and maintain institutional credit. This is due to the higher risks and costs associated with ghetto-area business loans, particularly the special credit needs, such as refunding loans and loans to transfer ownership to minority hands. The problem lies in strengthening the lending capabilities of ghetto banks. A five-pronged approach, the banking program seeks to increase deposits in poverty-area banks (direct deposits and incentives to encourage deposits) to stimulate capital infusion, to create a secondary market for SBA-guaranteed paper, and to develop the administrative capabilities of poverty-area banking officers.

Direct Deposit Support.   In this approach, OFC has placed a substantial portion of its uncommitted venture capital (currently around $5.5 million) in time deposits and open demand deposits in more than 40 poverty-area banks. This action dramatically increases the deposit picture for these small banks and gives them funds to pump into the disadvantaged community in the form of business and consumer loans, thereby promoting economic development. One of the requirements for banks accepting OFC deposits is that each bank agree to attempt to invest at least 60 percent of the amount deposited by OFC into new loans to businesses, community organizations, or consumers located in or doing most of their business in the poverty community served by that bank.

Indirect Deposit Support. This approach has two elements: deposit guarantees and interest subsidies. OFC may selectively guarantee that portion of minority bank deposits that exceeds the FDIC insurance limit of $20,000; such guarantees will be made up to a total of $50,000 in any given instance (an OFC exposure of $30,000). The interest subsidy technique will be used in two ways:
1. to compensate investors for gaps that may exist between rates paid by participating poverty-area banks and those paid on comparable investments in competing white banks
2. to provide for the selective payment of *premium* rates to test the effectiveness of such added risk-compensation incentives in attracting deposits.[1]
OFC is planning for the future implementation of its indirect deposit program at selected minority banks.

Capital Support. OFC recognizes three widely differing types of circumstances that often require minority banks to raise capital. The first, particularly common for new banks, occurs when the institution incurs larger-than-anticipated losses through insufficient lending experience, high personnel expenses, or both. The second situation is more often characteristic of older institutions and arises when the bank experiences rapid deposit growth and/or when it needs to expand its facilities (for example, establishment of branch operations). The final situation comes in the establishment of a new bank. In each of these situations, the bank may find it difficult to raise new capital, operating as it does in the capital-poor ghetto economy. Under these circumstances, it will almost certainly find it necessary to introduce some risk-reduction feature to attract outside capital. OFC may provide capital note guarantees or other arrangements (such as interest subsidy payments on capital notes or debentures) to overcome the reluctance of the outside investor to participate in such stock issues.

The Unity Bank Case. There are two specific examples of OFC efforts in the capital support area. By December, 1970, Unity Bank and Trust in Boston had begun experiencing excessive losses through the steady deterioration of its loan portfolio. As a consequence, its capital base became somewhat impaired. A series of negotiations between a group of Boston banks, Unity officials, OFC, and the Massachusetts Bankers Association culminated with an arrangement whereby four large Boston banks put up $450,000 and the Massachusetts Bankers Association infused $50,000. This $500,000 capital support was 80 percent guaranteed by OFC ($200,000), the Cooperative Assistance Fund ($100,000) and the Interracial Council on Business Opportunities (ICBO–$100,000). This led ultimately to the additional infusion of capital notes in the amount of $1,500,000 by the FDIC, with a contingency infusion of another $0.5 million if needed.

OFC's role in this deal was that of a catalyst and coordinator. It helped negotiate the terms and conditions of the total financial infusion to Unity. OFC's guarantee was essentially leveraged to a $2 million capital support, or a 30:1 leverage factor (the actual dollar cost to OFC is only the opportunity cost involved in the maintenance of a $67,000 reserve), plus the time involved in putting the deal together. This deal was consummated on July 27, 1971, and the bank is doing quite well thus far.

OFC has a strategy for loan guarantees that it hopes to use in the future. The following hypothetical example shows how this might work: the stock of a bank will be sold at $30 per share, with OFC giving a "put" at 60 percent of the stock price ($18), the equivalent of a 60 percent guarantee, to the purchases of the stock of, say, a community organization. Also, OFC will take a "call" on the stock at purchase price plus estimated resale, or $32.50 per share. This provision would be handy in the event that the purchased stock was to be resold to the community residents by the organization; the "call" would insure this resale. This rather sophisticated strategy is a potential model for future OFC capital support operations.

The Midwest Bank Case.   The Midwest National Bank of Indianapolis has requested OFC to provide guarantees for loans to facilitate the acquisition of $150,000 of Midwest stock by a local consortium of community residents (to insure community control). This deal is in the final planning stage, and it appears that OFC will provide a 40 percent front-end guarantee. OFC officials hoped to close the deal by mid-April, 1972.

Liquidity Enhancement.   In this approach, the idea is to test the ability of an outside vehicle (OFC) to increase the lending capacity of poverty-area banks by buying the insured portion of SBA or other insured loans and remarketing them. If this can be done successfully with commercial bank paper, OFC may attempt to extend this principle in subsequent programs to loans originated by credit unions, community development corporations, and other poverty-area lending institutions. A subcommittee of the OFC board is exploring ways of creating a secondary market for such discounted paper. Pending the development of such a market (as well as for short periods while arranging placement after the market is developed), it is anticipated that OFC may hold such paper in its own portfolio.

Management Development.   The final banking program segment is the management development approach. Using the interest generated by the direct deposit program certificates of deposit, as well as any net earnings which may accrue from the purchase of loan paper under the Liquidity Enhancement project, OFC plans to develop and implement a management development project for lending officers of minority banks. The program will consist of seminars conducted either at OFC headquarters or at the poverty-area banks themselves. This project is being developed under the sponsorship of the National Bankers Association (the minority banks' professional organization), with the cooperation of the American Bankers Association, certain educational institutions, and others.

Surety Bonding Program

The second major OFC program that has been implemented is the minority contractor's surety bonding program. This is a demonstration project that tests various financial incentives for improving the competitive position of minority contractors within the low-income community. Surety bonding is a formidable obstacle to minority contractors. While racism may be partly to blame, lack of bonding is primarily a reflection of the contractors' weak financial condition and unestablished track record. The technological advances in the construction industry, accompanied by increasing economies of scale, tend to place small minority contractors at a disadvantage. To qualify for bonding and to have a reasonable chance for financial success, minority contractors must overcome racial prejudice as well as problems of insufficient working capital, limited access to a qualified labor force, and minimal expertise in such crucial areas as management, cost accounting, cost estimation, and bidding. To help alleviate these problems, OFC proposes to demonstrate that various financial devices (such as guarantees) can be used judiciously as a means of reducing the perceived risk. OFC hopes to show that these devices will leverage many times their worth in financial and technical assistance from the private sector. In collaboration with the Minority Contractors Assistance Program (MCAP), OFC also plans to supply management and technical assistance to the minority contractor involved, especially in the critical early stages of each project.

Wocala, Inc., of Visalia, California, is a Chicano-owned reforestation firm that employs primarily migrant labor and has both government (U.S. Department of Forestry) and private (Weyerhaeuser) contracts. OFC has issued Wocala a $25,000 letter of credit in favor of surety companies, which have agreed to issue performance bonds totaling $125,000 and bid bonds of $250,000. Thus far, more than $175,000 of work in process has accrued to the $25,000 OFC bond (for which OFC has a $17,000 reserve) for a leverage factor of over 10:1. Other OFC bonding program projects include:

(1) Ogala Sioux ($40,000 reserve commitment for $1.3 million in funds generated, or a leverage of 33:1.)

(2) Glemit Construction Company ($11,500 in reserve has generated $67,000 in business for leverage of 6:1.)

(3) Industrialized Business Systems ($100,000 reserve has generated $1.7 million in funds for leverage of 17:1.)

(4) Equity Development Corporation ($45,000 reserve for $100,000 in initial capitalization, or a leverage factor of 32:1).[2]

New OFC Programs

A third major program, the SBA 502/LDC local injection project, permits OFC to back up local groups by raising the 10 percent local matching contribution for SBA plant and facilities loans. OFC is again acting as a catalyst and leveraging agent, using existing government programs and the resources of different organizations to put the deal together. A major project in New Jersey and New York is in process. The first transaction involves the Presbyterian Economic Development Corporation (PEDCO), which is making $400,000 available (subject to OFC guarantees). Announcement of this new program was recently made in national media.

In theory, this $400,000 could provide up to $14,000,000 in leverage. This OFC support means crucially needed front-end money for several local development corporations. Current PEDCO projects include:

(1) an upholstery manufacturer ($4,750 in OFC reserves has generated $95,000 or leverage of 20:1.)
(2) a dental clinic ($1,300 has generated $26,000 or 20:1.)
(3) a medical clinic ($21,000 has generated $560,400 or 27:1.)
(4) a general contracting company ($3,200 has generated $64,000 or 20:1.)
(5) a photo processing firm ($5,000 in reserve has generated ($100,000 for 20:1 leverage.)
(6) a distributor of paper products ($1,450 has generated $29,000 for 20:1.)

These projects are guaranteed by OFC with reserves of $36,700 and have already generated $848,400 in business for a leverage factor of 23:1.

The Flexible Guarantee Program: Two other programs (flexible guarantee and real estate) were approved by the OFC board of directors at a meeting on February 24, 1972, and have been subsequently approved by OEO officials. In the flexible guarantee program, OFC proposes to alleviate a critical problem regarding the federal guarantee of building projects, that is, the inflexibility of the terms of SBA or other government guarantees. For example, SBA guarantees are all issued at the maximum allowable rate, which is 90 percent of the loan. As explained earlier, this unnecessarily ties up government monies in reserve for guarantees, since many minority projects have smaller risk factors, wherein much lower guarantee levels could be negotiated, and it reduces the leverage factor for government funds by providing lower turnover of money in guarantees.

In addition, SBA loans are restricted as to types of lenders and borrowers that are acceptable. Interminable red tape and delays are the rule rather than the exception. Time-consuming forms must be filled out, sometimes necessitating outside technical assistance. Frequently, SBA will not allow a deal involving more than one type of institution. It often takes the cooperation of several institutions to put a deal together, each with its own bureaucracy. A private lending agency may incur high costs by participating in SBA loans due to the red tape and time involved. The reason SBA inflexibility is so important is because more than half of the $500 million spent in fiscal year 1972 on minority economic development came from SBA, either in the form of loans to MESBICs, loan guarantees, direct loans, or the 8(a) Minority Procurement Program. This is a crucial agency in minority economic development, and in many ways, it is not meeting the needs of the minority community.

This government inflexibility is particularly damaging to minority economic development since fewer projects can be started with a given guarantee pool. The main issue, however, is the fact that 90 percent guarantees are *not* necessary for all poverty-area projects; some are not at all risky and the lender could easily be protected by a substantially lower guarantee. Another factor is leverage: SBA leverage is typically only 4:1. OFC anticipates that, through the use of flexible guarantees, leverage factors of 20:1 and greater will be generated.

Through the use of flexible (negotiable) guarantees, OFC hopes that more poverty-area projects can safely be initiated with a given amount of funds. OFC will have the flexibility to work either alone or with a community organization "partner" to put together financial packages of high complexity that cannot be consummated through existing federal programs. This direct contact with community organizations is a big plus for the OFC approach. SBA can make loans only to profit-making entities, thereby excluding community development corporations (CDCs) and other community organizations closely attuned to community needs and problems. OFC, working through a community "partner," will be able to gauge the pulse of the community and negotiate deals important to the development of the community.

Real Estate Program

The real estate program has interesting potential. In low-income communities, real estate values are disproportionately low; abandoned buildings present an eyesore as well as a hazard for residents. This has a domino effect, resulting in a reduced tax base which adversely affects community services. The development of real estate has high potential for providing immediate income for persons involved in various facets of this activity. Construction and renovation of residences and commercial property would provide many jobs for contractors and laborers. This increase may be obtained with maximum leverage because the collateralized value of real property typically permits very high proportions of borrowed money to be used. Thus, an owner (such as a community organization) may be able to obtain construction of a building with an initial equity that represents only a small fraction of the total building price.

Most of the advantages of real estate development are widely known, yet there are no federal programs specifically designed to facilitate real estate development by low-income community organizations. There are many sources of funds for development—both public and private. However, community organizations find that their "high-risk" status and lack of expertise often prohibit access to these funds. At present, the numerous leveraging possibilities inherent in real estate development serve only to benefit those who understand the intricacies of real estate financing and development, have past experience in the area, and have a large net worth. OFC intends to demonstrate, with the aid of guarantees, that low-income communities can circumvent these "rights of entry" barriers. This demonstration project will then serve as a basis for recommending changes in existing federal programs (for example, EDA, GNMA, SBA), including possible legislation. OFC's experience might also suggest the creation of an operational federal program that would have the flexibility to deal with particular problems of real estate development for low-income communities.

CONCLUSION

OFC represents a viable alternative to the traditional, welfare-style social action program. No money is given to poor people directly. OFC uses the financial principles of leverage and incentive in order to create capital flows into the ghetto, rather than the more typical outward flow. It might be argued that the OFC funding of $7.4 million is just a drop in the bucket compared with what is needed to accomplish its lofty ambitions; however, many other social action programs have raised this cry as a palliative for failure. With a rigorous evaluation design, it should be possible to isolate effects of OFC programs and make recommendations for appropriate administrative and legislative actions.

OFC programs can provide numerous opportunities for the creative use of business investment and expertise. There were some initial problems with OEO red tape in the approval of operational programs, but this is traceable to OEO's evaluation orientation; OFC programs must lend themselves to evaluation in a scientific way so that generalizations for future legislative action may be made. With experience in working together (OEO and OFC), so that OFC's proposals satisfy this evaluation criteria, OFC's flexibility to seize the financial opportunity should be preserved.

Because of its nonwelfare orientation, the flexible and businesslike OFC approach to poverty-area economic development is anathema to traditional government agencies. The issue then becomes one of whether, through strong business support, such a program can be shown to provide a viable and even superior method of building the economies of our disadvantaged communities. With a powerful demonstration of the effectiveness of OFC-type incentives, government agencies with the traditional "poverty" approach might be willing to try new strategies.

Finally, it might be wise to state explicitly what we have been saying implicitly throughout the article: *the real purpose of OFC is to alter economic power relationships.* OFC seeks to provide ghetto communities with economic leverage so that they can deal from an equal position with their white counterparts, thereby enhancing their ability to enter into more normal economic bargaining relationships. As we have shown, poverty areas lack the resources for economic development because of unequal economic power; in other words, these areas lack the ability to reward capital (make it safe) and are consequently in an unequal situation in terms of competing for resources. OFC is therefore one model seeking to redress this basic economic power imbalance.

FOOTNOTES

[1] There is a legal question involved here. *Regulation Q* of the Federal Reserve System states the Federal Reserve Board has the right to set maximum interest rates for savings accounts at participating banks; offering an interest subsidy may therefore be illegal. OFC is exploring this problem before implementing the program.

[2] Equity Development may prove to be OFC's first bonding program loss. The Corporation is showing year-to-date expenses in excess of revenues. Bankruptcy proceedings are a possibility, according to an OFC official.

*Richard W. Barsness, Richard A. Mayer**

HERMAN KNOCKWURST & COMPANY

Herman Knockwurst & Company began in 1883 in a small store front in Midwest City. About five years later, the butcher shop and sausage-making facility moved to a location five blocks away. At that time, the location was in the midst of a proud German neighborhood filled with many immigrants starting their own businesses in America.

Eighty years later, Herman Knockwurst & Company was still at the same location, meanwhile having grown to national importance in the sale of processed meats. This manufacturing activity differs from the packing of fresh meat, the latter being dominated by such giant firms as Armour, Swift, and Wilson & Company. By way of contrast, Herman Knockwurst & Company has long been noted for its degree of integration of operations. After slaughtering and dressing operations, it goes on to process most of its raw meat into scores of convenience meat products. In fiscal 1967, the company's sales totaled $402 million, while net income after taxes was over $9 million. In fiscal 1971 sales rose almost 60 percent to $652 million, while net income also increased sharply to over $22 million.

*This case was prepared by Professor Richard W. Barsness, utilizing in part material from a student report by Richard A. Mayer. Professor Barsness is an Associate Professor of Management History at Northwestern University's Graduate School of Management.

Since almost two-thirds of company sales are derived from branded processed meats selling at premium prices, Herman Knockwurst & Company has
consistently had the best profit margin on sales in the entire industry. For
example, when its after-tax margin on sales was 2.33 percent, the next best
margin in the industry was 1.6 percent. Other competitors had 0.9 percent, 1.0
percent and 1.2 percent profit margins. In addition to high-quality branded
products with good profit margins, Herman Knockwurst's skillful management
has emphasized large expenditures for research and development in both manufacturing and packaging techniques, a "distribution center" marketing concept,
and a recent commitment to national "prime time" radio and television advertising. The administration of the firm has remained in the hands of the Knockwurst
family, although the recently named president, Randall Forrest, is one of four
nonfamily directors on the firm's 11-man board. About 200 members of the
family own 80 percent of the firm's stock. In addition to the Midwestern
facility, Herman Knockwurst & Company has seven other manufacturing locations and 29 wholly-owned distribution centers throughout the country.

In contrast to the original character of the neighborhood at the major site,
this area today is one of the worst ghettos in Midwest City. During the riots of
April, 1968, a shooting took place across the street from the plant. A large
public housing project, which is a major center of disorder, is located nearby.

Although the neighborhood became a ghetto several years ago, the widespread violence is a relatively recent phenomenon. Thus far, Herman Knockwurst & Company itself has experienced little in the way of violence, but the
severity of the problem is underscored by the fact that the area is regarded as
unsafe for anyone, black or white.

COMPANY INVOLVEMENT WITH URBAN PROBLEMS

The increasing urgency of the nation's urban problems, as illustrated by conditions around Herman Knockwurst & Company's Midwest plant, has caused top
management to conclude that the firm should commit some effort and resources
toward the alleviation of these problems. However, management has limited its
urban involvement (other than token donations) to Midwest City and has not
extended these activities elsewhere. National expansion is a relatively recent
development—during most of the firm's history, it had facilities only in Midwest
City, Madison, Wisconsin, and Davenport, Iowa. Top management believes it
unwise to leap head-first into the turbulence of urban problems elsewhere, since
neither the company nor most other private corporations possess much expertise
in this field.

Although Herman Knockwurst's response to urban problems has been
limited to Midwest City, where the crisis literally lies on its doorstep, some key
management people hope that activities in Midwest City will serve as a useful
test of concepts and programs of urban rehabilitation that may have applicability to other cities. More specifically, the company's involvement with the

urban environment relates to three key problems: (1) air and water pollution, (2) social welfare for the disadvantaged, and (3) plant location and community welfare.

Air and Water Pollution

Although Herman Knockwurst & Company complies with present laws, management realizes that pollution problems do exist. For example, in the absence of any dramatic new municipal solutions to the problem of solid waste disposal, Herman Knockwurst continues to burn all combustible waste matter by incineration. The company has given some study to this operation, including the possibility of using compressing devices instead, but it appears unlikely that incineration operations will be changed significantly or terminated until government pressure requires it.

The company's boilers are also a serious source of pollution. The firm has installed afterburners on all chimneys to its boilers, reducing the visible pollutants being released into the atmosphere, but these devices offer no relief from the emission of sulfur dioxide. Notwithstanding this fault, to date the system is still in compliance with governmental requirements. The company also has a problem in connection with the smoking of meats, which is a necessary process in its manufacturing operations. Vacuums have been installed in all smoking chambers to help keep the smoke confined within the plant; new seal and duct work has recently been completed to help prevent smoke leakage. Nonetheless, the smoke must eventually be evacuated from each chamber after every smoking operation. Company efforts to devise a method to burn off the smoke rather than release it into the atmosphere have not yet been successful.

The problem of grease is the only major water pollution problem confronting Herman Knockwurst's Midwest City plant, which is primarily a sausage-making facility. The company has installed processing tanks which skim the grease off the water, then treat the water sufficiently with chemicals to comply with the local pollution requirements before discharging the water into the public sewage system. Elsewhere in plants which conduct animal slaughtering operations, the firm has installed more complex sewage treatment systems. The original need for such a system arose at the Madison, Wisconsin plant, which used Lake Mendota for waste disposal. The susceptibility of this lake to pollution caused Dane County to adopt strict regulations which necessitated the complete treatment of slaughterhouse wastes before any water was released. The treatment system designed for the Madison facility has been installed in Herman Knockwurst's other slaughtering plants.

Social Welfare for the Disadvantaged

For years the Herman Knockwurst Foundation has been making cash contributions to local Midwest City agencies such as churches, YMCAs, schools, and clubs. Until 1967 these donations followed the pattern of noncontroversial corporate philanthropy. Then the company's board of directors and the trustees of the foundation decided that just being a "good neighbor" was not an adequate response. They concluded that they would have to go beyond traditional philanthropy and make a greater commitment to black urban welfare. In keeping with this philosophy, the trustees of the Herman Knockwurst Foundation allocated $100,000 per year, 20 percent of the total foundation budget, exclusively to black problems.

Herman Knockwurst is not going aimlessly into this program. The commitment is frankly directed toward the priority goal of building black "economic power." The firm's management believes that widespread progress for the black community will come only when money begins to flow *into* the ghetto and remains there.

As Herman Knockwurst's management perceives the situation, blacks who become successful must be encouraged to stay in the ghetto, where they can help provide both the incentives and means for others to succeed. The firm has become involved in various projects intended to improve the opportunities available to black workers and black entrepreneurs in inner city areas. These projects range from helping to develop student talent at a local high school to seeking out social workers to provide consumer education for ghetto residents.

On its own, the Herman Knockwurst Foundation has undertaken two projects directed toward improving the economic well-being of the black community. The foundation is helping a group of blacks purchase a large department store. A second venture is the organization of a small black-owned firm near the Herman Knockwurst & Company plant, which will supply certain essential goods for sausage-making operations. The corporation will help the firm get started by providing money, expertise, and a dependable market for the firm's products.

The company has also become involved in hiring hardcore unemployed workers. Four top executives carefully surveyed the corporation's relationship with the changing urban environment and concluded that, in addition to expanding the firm's general commitment to improve neighborhood conditions in metropolitan Midwest City, the company would seek a Department of Labor Manpower Administration Program Contract.

With high-level executive backing, the Manpower Administration (M.A.-2) contract was obtained. At that time, Herman Knockwurst & Company was one of four firms in the Midwest City area to be awarded this type of contract. James Dunn, a black who has worked in every one of the city's major ghettos, was hired from the neighborhood YMCA to coordinate the program and take responsibility for the company's various neighborhood social welfare projects. Dunn supervises a staff of five employees and reports directly to Philip Kane, director of personnel in the Midwest City plant.

Under the M.A.-2 contract, Herman Knockwurst & Company guarantees the federal government 50 jobs established solely for the training of "hardcore disadvantaged" residents of the community. In keeping with the recommendations of the Presidential Commission on Civil Disorders, the company was careful not to displace any existing workers in order to create these 50 new job opportunities. The M.A.-2 program aims to guarantee disadvantaged people a job after they have completed their training. The major deficiency of a previous governmental program (M.A.-1) was that disadvantaged workers who underwent skills training did not always find a job when they completed their training.

In addition to their responsibilities regarding the M.A.-2 program and the company's involvement with various ghetto-oriented organizations, Dunn and his staff are also working for internal employment reforms. One objective is to change the employment test given to all potential employees. This test has not been validated by the Government Contracts Compliance Board for use by minority groups whose education and aptitude level is lower than average. The company also plans to alter and liberalize screening procedures for prospective employees, encourage the recruitment of black salesmen (eight are currently employed), and increase the proportion of nonwhite office personnel from its present level of 10 percent. Total employment at the Midwest City facility is presently 1,300 people, approximately 1,100 of whom are plant workers. Of the latter, 50 percent are black, 46 percent white, and 4 percent of Spanish-American descent.

PLANT LOCATION AND COMMUNITY WELFARE

One major consideration ultimately affecting Herman Knockwurst & Company's commitment to improving the economic and social welfare of ghetto communities in Midwest City will be the response of the disadvantaged blacks whom the company is seeking to help. Another crucial factor is the changing economics and geography of the meat-packing industry, coupled with the relative obsolescence of the company's Midwest City facility.

In recent years the meat-packing industry has undergone a virtual revolution, the results of which have been extremely trying for the entire industry, especially the major firms. Slaughtering and packing operations, historically highly centralized in a few large cities, have been decentralized into small, modern plants located in rural areas near the supply of animals. This shift has made it possible for many aggressive new firms to enter the industry and has whittled down the market shares of the traditional industry leaders.

Although it is not clear whether previous economics of size in the industry are no longer economical, there is no doubt that most of the leading firms (which had assumed an institutionalized character not unlike the railroad industry) have found it financially painful to adapt to this new environment. In addition to the heavy costs involved in disposing of old facilities and building new decentralized plants, firms have been forced to undertake increased vertical integration. The thin profit margins associated with the slaughtering and dressing operations, which historically have been the essence of "meatpacking," have caused many firms to expand their processing and marketing activities in order to improve their overall financial performance.

These general industry developments, coupled with the desire of certain firms to emulate the strategy that has given Herman Knockwurst & Company a secure market niche and the best profit margin in the business, indicate that Herman Knockwurst & Company will face much more direct competition in the future. Production costs as well as marketing efforts will be crucial to the outcome of this intensified competition. As part of their efforts to cut costs and become more efficient, Swift, Armour, Wilson, and other firms that made Midwest City the meat-packing center of the world recently have abandoned their facilities on the Southwest side of the city and have moved their operations elsewhere. Thousands of people lost their jobs when these companies left, and the city was left with dozens of vacant buildings and an idle neighborhood that has yet to be revived.

In its efforts to remain competitive within the context of a changing industry, Herman Knockwurst & Company is rapidly approaching the point when it must decide the fate of its sausage-making facility in Midwest City. Three alternatives are available to the company:

(1) modernize the increasingly obsolescent plant and expand its capacity to accommodate the growing demand for the company's products

(2) build an entirely new, large plant on an excellent site which the company has optioned in a western suburb of Midwest City near the state highway

(3) build one or more plants in a downstate area or in a neighboring state.

If the Midwest City plant were modernized and expanded, it would cost approximately $4 million and would create about 200 additional jobs. Company studies indicate that, depending upon business conditions, such an investment would satisfactorily accommodate Herman Knockwurst's short-run needs for about 8 to 10 years, at which time another thorough reappraisal of production capacity, efficiency, and capital investment would be required. Present evidence *tentatively* suggest that, regardless of modernization, the Midwest City facility will be inadequate for the company's long-run needs, and it will have to be supplemented or replaced by new facilities elsewhere within about 10 years.

However, even in the short run, the economic validity of additional investment in the Midwest City plant requires that no further serious deterioration occur in the already violence-prone neighborhood surrounding the plant. Any significant increase in property damage, insurance costs, or employee turnover arising from neighborhood conditions would cast grave doubt on the wisdom of investing any additional funds in the Midwest City facility.

If Herman Knockwurst & Company decides to leave and move its sausage-making operations to a new suburban plant or to one or more small plants elsewhere, the short-run capital outlay would be between $12 million and $15 million, depending on the rapidity with which the present plant would be closed down, the exact extent of integration incorporated into new facilities, and capacity for future expansion. Even though relocation would require considerably more capital in the short run, it would, of course, permit Herman Knockwurst & Company to optimize all aspects of its sausage-making operations, instead of remaining committed to what will still be a relatively obsolescent plant.

Yet in seeking to resolve the dilemma of plant location, top management is aware that the firm's shareholders are not the only group that will be directly affected by the outcome. Departure from Midwest City will deprive the area of adjoining neighborhoods of literally hundreds of jobs while the city government will lose valuable tax revenues and will have to bear the burden of still more hardship and discontent among the blacks left behind. This will be true even if Herman Knockwurst builds a single large facility near the state highway since many of the company's black employees do not own cars and the suburban location is difficult, time consuming, and expensive to reach by public transportation.

On the other hand, three academic consultants recently engaged by the firm point out that private business firms in the United States historically have served society best when they concentrated on maximizing their own economic performance and left the task of individual and community social welfare to government. One consultant even suggests that the company should keep its commitment to "social responsibility" in perspective by remembering that if plant relocation would make the firm more viable economically, ultimately this would mean *more* jobs and *more* income for society. In the long run, society's well-being would be enhanced, according to this consultant.

The consultant also points out that if it were economically sound to build one or more plants away from Midwest City's urban and suburban areas, society's welfare might be served by providing the kind of attractive employment opportunities that will discourage younger people from leaving rural communities to seek jobs in metropolitan areas such as Midwest City. The consultant reminds the company that the federal government itself has acknowledged that the eventual solution of the nation's urban problems will depend in part upon making economic opportunities and life in small and medium-sized towns and cities sufficiently attractive to stop (and perhaps reverse) the continuing migration of people from these locations into metropolitan agglomerations that are fast becoming ungovernable.

Given the numerous variables and apparently conflicting considerations involved in the plant location issue, top management at Herman Knockwurst & Company is presently wondering what move to make next. Can the company's desire to remain an efficient, highly profitable industry leader be reconciled with its desire to provide meaningful, tangible assistance for Midwest City's black neighborhoods and the urban community?

Fred C. Allvine, Alvin D. Star*

THE ROLE OF WHITE-OWNED BUSINESSES
IN THE INNER CITY* *

The flight of white residents from the inner portions of major American cities is so well known a phenomenon in our recent history that it need not be detailed here. A related question that does require assessment is whether white-owned businesses will and/or should join the migration, thus leaving the inner city solely to blacks and other minority groups. Also, what role should white-owned business enterprises play in the distribution of goods and services in the "ghetto?" This article will direct itself to that question, limiting itself to blacks living in inner-city minority group residence communities.

Businessmen who were interviewed were quite concerned with "The Role of White-Owned Businesses in the Inner City." Unfortunately, it was often necessary to promise not to disclose sources because of the sensitive nature of the information. Conversations with businessmen indicated that their point of view varied according to whether they were retailers, who required direct contact and financial investments in the black community, or manufacturers who could carry on large-scale marketing in the black community without direct contact or sizable investment there. As a result of these differences, the roles of white-owned retail businesses and manufacturing businesses will be examined separately.

WHITE-OWNED RETAIL BUSINESSES

For analytical purposes, a retail store matrix, which divided retail enterprises into meaningful groupings, was developed. Our conversations with retailers showed differences along two dimensions: convenience goods stores versus shopping goods stores, and corporate chain stores versus independent and franchise stores.

With respect to the first grouping, stores classified as selling mainly convenience goods and services are supermarkets, drug stores, restaurants, liquor stores, service stations, hardware stores, and banks. Generally, these are the stores with merchandise and services that shoppers do not wish to go far out of their way to purchase. On the other hand, those stores classified as selling mainly shopping goods and services include large general merchandise operations— department and discount stores—and specialty operations such as clothing stores, accessory stores, appliance outlets, and car dealers. These are stores that shop-

---

*Fred C. Allvine is an Associate Professor of Marketing at Georgia Tech University and Alvin D. Star is an Associate Dean at the University of Illinois, Circle Campus, College of Business Administration.
**Revision of paper prepared for Inner City Marketing Conference, SUNYAB, June 4-6, 1970.

pers may go out of their way to reach and in which they may make more competitive comparisons. The reason for this distinction lies in the degree to which the inner city resident can be served by retail facilities outside the ghetto. For shopping-type goods and services, such operation is possible; for convenience-type goods and services, location in the inner city presumably is mandatory.

The second grouping of the retail store matrix is the type of business organization. Changes in black communities have a different impact on corporate chain stores than on independents (including franchisees and small chains operating exclusively in the black community), and this dichotomy is used to further structure the problem. The reason for this distinction lies in the degree to which white-owned businesses are vulnerable to pressures generated within the black community. To most chain store operators, such as A & P, Sears, and Walgreens, the inner city represents an important but relatively small proportion of total chain sales. However, independents operating in minority communities derive most, if not all, of their revenue from this market. As a result, these independents (and small chains) are more vulnerable in the short run to pressures from black activists.

Matrix for Studying White-owned Retail Businesses in the Inner City

	Convenience Goods and Services Stores (Supermarkets, drug stores, restaurants, liquor stores, service-stations, hardware, banks)	Shopping Goods and Services Shores (Department stores, discount houses, specialty apparel and shoe stores, auto dealers)
Corporate Chains	Examples: A & P, Hillmans, Walgreens	Examples: Marshall Fields, Lerners, Thom McAn
Independents and Franchisees	Examples: Red Rooster, McDonalds	Examples: Independent apparel stores, auto dealers

Chain Stores Selling Convenience Goods and Services

In a recent speech, Donald Perkins, President of Jewel Companies, stated that supermarket chains are having difficulty earning a profit from their inner city stores. Basically two factors contribute to this poor profit performance:

(1) Many operating costs are higher in the inner city. These include such items as high rent, unproductive guard costs, high pilferage rates, larger insurance costs, and lower labor productivity.

(2) A policy of near-uniform pricing for stores both inside and outside the inner city is followed. This pricing practice, adopted during the last few years, has been a response to private and public concern because *The Poor Pay More.*[1]

If supermarket chains continue to experience unprofitable inner city business, a gradual withdrawal from this phase of their operation can be expected. However, it seems unlikely that most chains with substantial inner city operations are going to withdraw without first making a real effort to overcome these problems. Since supermarkets specialize in convenience goods, they could expect only marginal success in locating outside the inner city with the hope of attracting a larger proportion of their customers from the inner city. Another reason why chains with substantial inner city positions are not ready to give up is that the black and minority market in many metropolitan areas simply is too large to write off. For example, in the black belt of Chicago, the chains operate approximately 150 supermarkets. From the perspective of the black community, in the intermediate future it would not be to their benefit to lose the white chain stores, because the black community does not yet have the managerial skills to run supermarket chains. Therefore, if the white-owned chains were to withdraw, black consumers will still pay more.

However, even if white-owned food chains retain their inner city stores, it is possible that black consumers will have to pay more for food than they do under current "uniform pricing" policies within metropolitan areas. *From an economic viewpoint*, a policy of charging uniform prices in high-cost inner city stores and low-cost suburban stores is ludicrous. Nevertheless, *from a political viewpoint*, such a policy is essential for the contemporary supermarket chain. Imagine the furor if even the appearance of price discrimination by a supermarket chain were uncovered by minority group residents, as in the Red Rooster incident which will be detailed later.

Yet it is not clear whether uniform pricing policies are wise for the chain operator in the long run, advantageous for the ghetto inhabitant, and desirable for society. In the long run, a uniform pricing policy will limit profit and will prevent investment in inner city stores, thus leaving the supermarket chain with outmoded, deteriorated, and innefficient inner city facilities. Since corporate chain uniform pricing will tend to drive out inner city independents, the minority group community will have to shop in antiquated chain facilities or else will have additional transportation costs in order to shop outside the inner city. For convenience goods, the latter costs would be substantial.

While, in the long run, chains must receive a fair price for the goods and services they are providing in the inner city, the white-owned chains, in turn, have a responsibility to the black community. The days of white-owned businesses in the inner city being both *operated by* and *managed by* whites with no black participation except as customers inevitably must end. It is an affront to black dignity and says to black people, "You simply don't have what it takes." White-owned chains with inner city operations must have a conscience. One of the principal reasons why blacks do not operate and manage inner city stores is because they have not been given the chance.

In talking with both "black militants," who are doing the agitating, and with operators of supermarket chains with inner city locations, the conflicting points of view come through. Militants want jobs, especially management positions, and some of the chains appear reluctant to grant these demands. The stumbling block seems not so much the demand for jobs and management positions but the next step. Some blacks look forward to the day when they not only ask for jobs but are in a position to grant them. Some whites seem afraid that, when blacks get the management jobs and learn to run large-scale organizations, confiscation by blacks will be the next step; this thesis has yet to be proven. In fact, it might be argued that unless whites hire blacks as employees and managers, virtual confiscation will inevitably occur because the white-owned company will be unable to continue business.

With apparent reluctance, some chains are giving in and permitting blacks to manage and operate white-owned stores in the inner city. Chicago appears a mecca for such tests—it is no coincidence that Chicago serves as the headquarters of Operation Breadbasket, economic arm of the Southern Christian Leadership Conference. Following Philadelphia Reverend Leon Sullivan's technique of "Don't shop where you can't work," Reverend Jesse Jackson, then National Director of Operation Breadbasket, used the economic boycott as leverage to implement many of his programs.

A classic case in Breadbasket's confrontations with supermarket chains was the boycott of A & P's inner city Chicago stores. In October, 1968, after 16 weeks of boycotting, A & P signed a covenant with Operation Breadbasket calling for 268 new jobs for blacks within a year. In addition, A & P agreed to stock products of 25 black manufacturers (milk, ice cream, orange juice, lemon juice, sausage, cosmetics, floor waxes, drain openers, pine oil, and oven cleaner) and to use a similar number of black-owned services (trash collection, extermination, and others). Similar covenants also were signed by seven other Chicago chains.[2]

It is important to observe the Operation Breadbasket experiment in Chicago. It is not known what effect entering a covenant will have on a company's cost and price structure. It is difficult to "hypo" blacks into management positions without adequate training and background. Some blacks have created problems by becoming belligerent as they gain more and more control. For example, a general superintendent visiting one of his stores was confronted by one employee who said "Whitey, what do you want in here?"

In contrast to A & P, another major chain with inner city stores has made few blacks store managers. This chain seems to believe that black demands for store managers are unjust and would rather invite confrontation pressures than be stampeded into putting unqualified and untrained people into store management positions. A program in operation for five years which is designed to develop blacks for management has resulted in only 2 black store managers—a ratio of less than 1 in 10.

The experience of the Hillman supermarket chain in Chicago tends to be somewhat more favorable than that of other major chains. Hillman's operates 16 large volume supermarkets, 4 of which are inner city stores. According to Hillman's president, Gardner Stern, Jr., inner city stores are gaining in sales and are making a good profit. Hillman's has always had uniform chain prices. An adequate gross margin is obtained because of good movement of longer margin house brands and ethnic foods. Running high volume stores is another key factor in Hillman's successful operation. Hillman's was one of the first to hire black clerks in Chicago's downtown area, and 10 years ago the company began hiring black managers. Stern's formula for survival of white-owned inner city stores is:

(1) Be sensitive to what customers want—you can't run inner city stores from the suburbs.

(2) Stores must be well run, in good condition, clean, and well lighted.

(3) Stores must be run and managed by the indigenous population.

(4) Where possible, black products and services should be used.

(5) You must have close working relationships with community leaders and organizations to help them solve their community problems.

Also, Hillman has entered an agreement to operate a supermarket in Woodlawn Gardens, a housing development being built in Chicago's black ghetto by The Woodlawn Organization (TWO), a nonprofit black community development group. The ownership of this store, named TWO-HILLMAN'S, is shared two-thirds by TWO and one-third by Hillman's, while being managed by Hillman's under a management contract. It is too early to venture an opinion on the feasibility of this working arrangement, but the agreement does offer a possible alternative form of ownership which, through black participation, might potentially reduce some of the high costs of inner city operation.

Drug stores are the second most important type of chain operation selling commercial goods in the inner city. In the Chicago area, Walgreen's alone has approximately 20 stores that sell predominantly to black customers. During the April, 1968, riots, several Walgreen stores were damaged. Walgreen's repaired all damaged stores and has plans to open new stores in black areas where demand suggests the need.

Walgreen's reports that the black area stores are relatively high volume and are reasonably profitable. The same quality of products is sold both in and outside the inner city, and a uniform pricing policy is followed. Black personnel are used extensively, and Walgreen's has 20 black store managers and 50 black assistant store managers. A recent Operation Breadbasket boycott has resulted in a signed covenant promising more jobs for blacks at Walgreen's.

One adaptation made by Walgreen's and others in areas subject to disturbances is the elimination of windows. One such store at 87th Street and Cottage Grove in Chicago had burned and was reopened. Outside steel doors seal off entranceways when the store is closed. The roof is made of a fireproof substance. The fortress-like store is also being tested by a supermarket chain and by a discount house operation to determine community reaction and to ascertain what effects such stores may have on sales.

The experience of white-owned chains points to the establishment of what can be called a CRASH program for business survival in the inner city. The elements of this program are:

(1) communicate with and become part of the local community.

(2) run a clean, modern, and well-lighted store.

(3) add minority-group-manufactured products to store (and chain) assortments and use minority group services.

(4) stock a product-service mix desired by local community (for chains at area-wide uniform prices).

(5) hire minority group employees, store managers, and executives.

Although uniform prices are recommended in the short run for chains in this program, it is recognized that some consequences of uniform pricing are undesirable. Further research is necessary in this area as well as on the benefits of joint ventures (such as TWO-HILLMAN'S) or corporate associations, and on the cost effects of retail chain-minority group covenants before definite appraisal of these practices or policies can be undertaken.

No consideration has been given here to the concept of government subsidy of white-owned chains in order to induce the latter to enter or remain in the ghetto. Although such proposals have been made by Perkins[3] and Sturdivant,[4] they are considered politically unfeasible by most retail executives surveyed.

Independents and Franchisees Selling Convenience Goods and Services

Independent white-owned retailers of convenience goods in the inner city do not have the market diversity of the chains behind them. As a result, they must directly absorb the pressures from the black community and must make their own appropriate responses. Some information is available as to what is happening in the grocery field, and much the same thing seems to be occurring in the retailing of other types of convenience products.

Two examples illustrate what has been happening to a large number of white-owned independent grocery retailers. Mr. Mizruchy's store was located in an area of Chicago torn by extensive rioting after the assassination of Martin Luther King. His store was looted but was not burned, supposedly because the white proprietor was considered a "fair" man. After the store reopened, Mizruchy sold it to several of his black employees, and he purchased another store in an all-white community. Mizruchy believes that a white man can not presently operate a retail establishment in a black neighborhood. Milton, formerly an operator of four stores, has retrenched, but has not withdrawn totally. He has closed one of his stores and has sold two others to black employees. He intends to continue to operate the fourth store, which is located in a high-density public housing project that is exclusively black.[5]

The gradual withdrawal of independent white-owned grocery businesses from the inner city is illustrated by statistics of the Certified Grocery Company of Chicago, a large cooperative wholesale organization. The number of black-owned inner city stores almost tripled from July, 1967 to April, 1970, increasing from 10 to 29 with estimated weekly store volume up from $170,000 to $400,000. In comparison, white-owned businesses have decreased approximately 40 percent, from 81 to 55, with estimated total weekly store volume down from $1,230,000 to $725,000. These figures indicate that the turning point in black ownership was the riot that followed Martin Luther King's assassination.

Even though a white organization may operate a substantial chain of food stores in the inner city, it is not immune to ownership pressures from the black community. The Red Rooster Food Stores in Chicago became the center of such a controversy. This seven-store supermarket chain operated in predominantly black areas and was nominally owned by Bernie Hahn, a white. A recasting of the major events that occurred should provide insights into the problems that a white organization has in responding to confrontations with the black community.

At the March 1, 1969, Breadbasket meeting, Reverend Jesse Jackson told some three thousand people that a boycott of the Red Rooster chain was to begin. This protest did not center around employment, as more than 98 percent of Red Rooster employees were black. The issues in this boycott were of a qualitative nature—the blacks alleged that the Red Rooster chain was operating dirty and unsanitary stores, selling poor quality merchandise, giving poor service, using misleading advertising, and overcharging. The chain had had numerous problems with local government officials, adding some credence to the charges against Red Rooster. Charges of consumer fraud had been brought against the chain, and five convictions had been obtained while several remained pending. In addition, court proceedings had been instituted in January for revocation of the licenses of four Red Rooster stores.

Following the Breadbasket boycott announcement, picketing started at the seven Red Rooster stores. As a result, the stores were closed. Addressing the boycott leaders, Hahn was quoted as saying that the people they (the boycott leaders) were putting out of work were those they claimed to represent. Hahn added that he thought that those workers would want to talk with Breadbasket. Later in the day, a caravan of cars carried a large number of the 300 Red Rooster employees to Breadbasket headquarters where they demanded an audience with Reverend Jackson. Violence was barely avoided as blacks confronted blacks. Jackson agreed to call off the boycott temporarily.[6]

On March 5, 40 black organizations united to form The Coalition for United Community Action Against Consumer Fraud. The new group vowed to continue the boycott and picketing until abuses by Red Rooster ceased. To relieve the pressures from blacks who might be laid off, the coalition announced that 150 jobs were available for immediate placement. Meanwhile a new confrontation of blacks was taking place: the picketing was interrupted by members of a powerful street gang. Supposedly, the gang had been led to believe that if the demands of the Coalition were met, jobs promised by Red Rooster would be seriously jeopardized. However, the gang leader was persuaded to join forces with the Coalition for the good of the black community. Picketing resumed with gang members swelling the ranks of the boycotters.

The boycott ended dramatically on March 15, when Hahn became ill and resigned as Red Rooster president. Richard Kay, newly appointed black president of Red Rooster, announced that his company agreed to all demands. An 18-point covenant between The Coalition for United Community Action Against Consumer Injustice and the Red Rooster Supermarkets was signed that evening at a "victory" celebration.

The agreement reached on March 15 did not end the Red Rooster incident. In a letter dated March 28, 1969, Red Rooster informed the coalition that 22 blacks employed by the chain were gang members. In addition, 15 of the 22 were members of the ruling body of the gang and had accumulated records and charges pending against them that ranged from aggravated battery to murder.[7]

The street gang members were fired 10 weeks after being hired, and Red Rooster sought police protection. The chain charged that padding the payroll with black gang members was helping to put Red Rooster out of business. In September, 1969, Red Rooster stores closed, claiming in their bankruptcy petition that depressed financial conditions had forced them out of business.

Any inference drawn from the Red Rooster drama must be tempered by the experience of another white businessman. Mr. X operates four large-volume supermarkets in a big city black belt and has just celebrated his thirty-eighth anniversary of doing business there. Even before recent black militancy existed, X employed blacks primarily, and today 99 percent of his employees are black. Two of his store managers are black, one is Puerto Rican, and the other is white. According to Mr. X, it has not been burdensome to use black service companies and products. He is glad to stock black products that move: "The market takes care of inferior products." Mr. X places considerable emphasis on giving customers quality products at fair prices. Furthermore, he claims it is essential for a white operator to maintain good relationships with his black customers. He has no present plans to sell his stores, but he does not rule out the possibility. An executive of a major chain told the author that Mr. X's stores had been offered to his firm.

To summarize, it would appear that the CRASH program applies to convenience goods independents as well as to chain organizations. Two points must be noted with respect to the difference between the two cases. First, the smallest independents cannot be expected to hire black managers. The creation of an extra layer of management could put the white owner out of business. The most that can be expected is that he will hire black employees. Second, no matter how well he is doing, the white owner would be well advised to *prepare* to move, sell out, or take in a minority group partner or partners, because he is so vulnerable to community pressures.

While it is possible that white independents operating in the ghetto would welcome government guaranteed loans, investment protection, or outright subsidy, it is most likely that the greater number of beneficiaries of such programs would be minority group entrepreneurs. What many white owners would like is a government program designed to help them sell out to government-trained-and-financed black capitalists (see discussion of Project Transfer below).

Chain Stores Selling Shopping Goods and Services

The nature of shopping goods and services is such that most people will travel farther to obtain them than they will travel for convenience goods and services. Examples of shopping goods include apparel, merchandise, appliances, and automobiles. Such purchases are made less frequently than convenience goods—they can quite often be postponed and usually involve comparison shopping.

As a result of the characteristics of shopping goods, a large proportion of the market demand can be attracted from residents of poverty-stricken areas. This is particularly true for mass merchandisers such as department stores and discount stores where individuals can shop for a wide range of household and personal items in one store. Because of the violence in many black communities during the past six years, blacks have been going outside their own communities to purchase shopping goods. The burning and looting of retail stores from Watts to Newark permanently closed many stores. The blatant disrespect for law and order by toughs and street gangs has caused the closing of still more specialty stores, and the exodus is not over. Conversations with chain executives who asked not to be quoted suggest that they will be opening no new stores in black communities and that they will be closing existing ones when the leases run out. They believe that business will make new financial commitments in the inner city ghettos only as a result of government pressure, or very strong financial aid programs.

Central business districts in major metropolitan areas seem to be attracting an increasing proportion of the shopping goods business from black and minority communities. During the early 1960s, whites were estimated to constitute 80 percent of the shoppers in the Chicago Loop area with its six major department stores—Sears, Ward's, Marshall Field's, Wieboldt's, Carson Pirie Scott, Goldblatt's. However, the proportion of black customers has increased until today it is estimated at 40 percent of all shoppers. An informed estimate for Carson's department store is that 60 percent of the shopping trade is black and Goldblatt's purportedly has an even higher proportion of black customers.

Furthermore, Frederick Sturdivant's hope that, as a result of investment insurance and tax incentives, large department stores could be persuaded to locate stores in the black community was greeted with skepticism by several retail executives.[8] One executive worries that the federal government, using fear of adverse public relations as a lever, might pressure his company into such actions.

Before the government acts, research should be undertaken into the mobility and transportation opportunities of the inner city resident. It is far from clear whether the inner city resident is able or desires to leave the ghetto to shop. Government intervention of the type suggested by Sturdivant is feasible only if minority groups want to shop in the inner city.

Department store chain executives report that one urgent problem in dealing with stores in neighborhoods changing from white population to minority group population is creating merchandise assortments desired by the new residents. At least one large chain has established a special merchandise office for inner city stores, and it reports that this step has helped alleviate the problem.

To summarize, the experience of white-owned chains selling shopping goods indicates that new investment in the inner city should be avoided. Consideration should be given to servicing inner city residents from central business districts or outlying shopping centers. When shopping goods chains are tied to inner city locations, either by lease or public relations necessity, the CRASH program outlined previously is endorsed by chain executives for retailer adoption.

Independents Selling Shopping Goods and Services

All sources surveyed are in agreement that, for all but the shortest run, there is no future for the white-owned independent retailer of shopping goods in the inner city. High operating costs, harassment of white owners by street gangs, fear of loss of property—all of these have reduced business opportunity for the white store owner to the vanishing point, particularly when his customers may prefer to shop elsewhere and can do so.

An example is provided by the experience of merchants of East 63rd Street, a secondary shopping area on the South Side of Chicago. Before the assassination of Reverend King, the 63rd Street area was a reasonably successful business area. However, during the last four years a psychological transformation has taken place in this area, and gangs have gradually obtained the upper hand. One merchant explains, "When gang members walk three abreast down the sidewalk and force legitimate customers to step aside, this hurts. Ladies have been accosted on the streets and young people harassed. As a result, they stop coming on the street." Traffic is, of course, essential for shopping goods stores.

A primary factor contributing to the problems of the East 63rd Street merchants is a reduction in the effectiveness of the police force. The police purportedly have turned their backs on gang activities; this has led to a worsening of conditions. Regardless of the cause, the facts indicate that merchants are moving out. Three shoe stores have closed; Mayson's, a local clothing chain store, has closed and so have several independent operators. A few white-owned women's clothing stores still are trying to make a go of it, but several remaining stores are said to be for sale.

Other sources suggest that conditions are not much better in primary inner city shopping areas. Even so, it is widely believed, although this is not proven, that black owners, who are not the focus of pressure that white owners are, could operate profitably in inner city locations. If this is true, then some way of easing the transition from white to black ownership is needed. As suggested previously, governmental financing and training could be beneficial. Perhaps an Operation Transfer sponsored by government, community organizations, and the business community, and employing the methods of the Urban Renewal program, can be formulated. Certainly here is another area that needs study.

To summarize, *the preponderance of opinion is that opportunities for white-owned independents are minimal*. White owners should move out, sell out, or take in a minority group partner or partners. In the shortest run, the CRASH program described previously may help alleviate community pressures and is recommended.

Overall, the evidence in regard to selling shopping goods in the black communities does not look favorable. The poverty of these problem-laden communities is forcing blacks to go out of their own communities to purchase shopping goods. Unless the atmosphere in the inner city becomes more amenable to white-owned businesses, or unless the government provides massive financial and training support for black-owned businesses, a gradual void of shopping goods facilities in the inner city will be created.

WHITE-OWNED MANUFACTURING AND FRANCHISING BUSINESSES

Since white-owned manufacturers and franchisors typically do not have substantial investment in fixed assets in the inner cities (the flight of the white-owned factory to the suburbs is well known), they do not face the direct threats to property experienced by retailers. However, some white-owned manufacturing operations have experienced pressures of a different kind—"selective product boycotts." Reverend Leon Sullivan used this technique against several of Philadelphia's largest companies. Tasty Bread was chided from black pulpits because the company did not have enough black salesmen.[9] Similarly, Reverend Jesse Jackson called a boycott against Country Delight Milk in Chicago after the company had refused to disclose employment records. On the following Sunday, 100 black churches announced the boycott to their congregations. Three days later, the dairy agreed to offer 44 new or upgraded jobs so that blacks would comprise 20 percent of employees.[10]

Franchisors have had similar boycott problems. Since franchisors are interested in maintaining market representation, they have a vested interest in the survival of franchisees. They also maintain control over what franchisees can and cannot do. As a result, the franchisor often becomes involved with his operators in problems of major significance.

McDonald's Problems in Cleveland

One of the major confrontations between a black community and a franchised operation involved the world's largest hamburger operation, McDonald's. The controversy centered around franchises in Cleveland's black community; these franchises were among some of the better McDonald's units in the country. The confrontation went on quietly for many months and then exploded. Before it was over, two men had been killed and another shot, the mayor had become involved, and the McDonald units were shut down for several months. The entire episode gives further insight into the black frame of reference and the problems white-owned companies have in making adjustments.

The catalyst of this emotion-charged confrontation with McDonald's was David Hill. Hill, "ex-hustler, con-man and priest, now a self-styled rabbi," and arrested more than 30 times, had for several years been developing a plan for blacks to gain control of white businesses in the ghetto.[11]

Early in 1968, Hill told McDonald's that it would have to sell its four white-owned franchises in the ghetto to blacks. McDonald's scoffed at this man who had walked in off the street with loud demands. After all, the franchisees' employees were almost exclusively black and three of the four managers were black. McDonald's, nonetheless, decided to encourage the franchisees to sell out to qualified blacks and promised to give those franchisees selling to blacks first priority for new units. To implement this decision, McDonald's unilaterally set out to locate qualified blacks who had or could borrow adequate money and who could be properly trained. However, Hill and his militant followers wanted none of that "qualified nonsense."[12]

At a meeting attended by McDonald's personnel, Mayor Stokes, and "Rabbi" Hill (with bodyguards), a local preacher named Ernest Hilliard known as "prophet Thomas," was proposed as a buyer. After finding Hilliard an associate with a strong financial background, McDonald's agreed to move ahead with the deal. However, early on the morning of July 5, the day the deal with McDonald's was to be consummated, Hilliard was shot to death in the driveway of his home.[13]

In a manner resembling the aftermath of the assassination of Reverend Martin Luther King, Jr., Reverend Hilliard became a martyr in the Cleveland ghetto. Rumors spread that Hilliard was murdered by a white man because he was attempting to purchase the McDonald's franchise. Fourteen community organizations closed ranks and formed "Operation Black Unity" with McDonald's as the target. Picketing, boycotting, demonstrations, and pray-ins at the McDonald ghetto units ensued. The units were closed off and on for six months, and business was reduced to a small fraction of what it had been previously.[14]

To end the boycotting, McDonald's negotiated with the blacks. McDonald's and their franchisees thought the selling price should be near $200,000 per unit because of the high volume nature of the units. However, Hill considered the price far too high, and said that it included "goodwill," which McDonald's certainly wasn't able to supply in the ghetto. Hill figured the right price to be around $100,000, while "Operation Black Unity" wanted McDonald's to make a $150,000 contribution to aid ghetto residents and improve living standards. Also, each of the white franchisees was to contribute $2,500 per unit plus 2 percent of the purchase price.[15]

McDonald's underestimated Hill's power in asking to negotiate with "more responsible" members of the black community than Hill. This move failed when organizations such as the NAACP, CORE, the Urban League, and various church groups announced their support of Hill.[16]

After two months of picketing, moderate blacks did force Hill to step down from the head of Operation Black Unity and attempted to negotiate with McDonald's. However, McDonald's demanded that picketing stop before negotiations reopened. Thereupon, Hill urged the boycott to continue. Because of the continued boycott, McDonald's refused to negotiate, even though the parties were close to agreement. As a result, the moderates were forced to call Hill back. Hill returned stronger than before saying, "No negotiations for 60 days." McDonald's, which had wanted to work with the moderates, lost the opportunity.[17]

In the next occurrence in this sequence of events, Hill was arrested and charged with blackmailing McDonald's. Allegedly, he had threatened to harm McDonald's properties unless several demands were met. Hill was jailed pending a psychiatric examination; he had been committed to a state mental hospital in the past. However, McDonald's received bad publicity when the prosecutor investigating the indictment called the charges irresponsible. When Hill was released a few days later, he was a bigger hero than ever. He was mobbed by large crowds of blacks as he went through the ghetto.[18]

A few days before an election, former Cleveland Mayor Carl Stokes personally interceded and asked Hill to stop the dispute. Hill thereupon ended the boycott. McDonald's announced that since Hill had yielded to its demand, negotiations could resume.[19]

Early in 1970, the year-old battle with McDonald's ended. The agreement involved four existing units and one under construction. With Hill's approval, the Hough Area Development Corporation, a nonprofit black-controlled organization, which aims to provide economic aid to ghetto residents, purchased two McDonald's units. The units are to be operated by qualified blacks who will buy large minority stock interest. A third unit was purchased by a black who had spent a year attempting to buy one of the McDonald's units but had been unable to obtain the necessary SBA guarantee. A bank granted this individual the loan without the government guarantee. Two other units were expected to be sold to individual blacks.[20]

Who was the winner in the battle for ownership of the McDonald's franchises in Cleveland's black community? The costs in this apparently unnecessary confrontation were high for everyone involved—the city, the black community, the franchisee, and McDonald's. Hopefully, others will learn from the McDonald's experience. The McDonald's agreement should establish some precedent for solving other disputes that might arise between white-owned franchises and the black community.

BLACK PERSONNEL AND WHITE PRODUCTS

In addition to avoiding a selective product boycott, white manufacturers must maintain the goodwill of personnel in the inner city stores. Some manufacturers already employ black representatives who carry out the detailing and missionary sales work in the inner city stores. These representatives improve sales by straightening their products on store shelves, juggling for more shelf space, setting up displays, placing point-of-sale materials, and suggesting quantities of products that should be reordered. The extent to which white companies are successful in such efforts depends on the relationships they are able to develop with store personnel and managers. Black manufacturers' representatives are gaining an edge over their white counterparts because of their ability to win favors due to the growing importance of black employees and store managers.

Manufacturers have a problem other than those of avoiding a selective product boycott and maintaining support for their products in retail stores: the proliferation of black-manufactured products designed to compete directly with those of white manufacturers. In the Breadbasket group alone, more than 20 companies produce a number of edible, cosmetic, and chemical products for the consumer market. These companies feel they have been excluded from business opportunities far too long. As a result, they ask, and at times demand, that retailers stock their products.

The impact of these three problems on white-manufactured products tends to vary according to the strength of brand preference for a category of products. Those white-manufactured products having strong brand preference are less vulnerable to the changes taking place in the inner city. Also these products are typically supported by heavy advertising. Examples of categories of products with strong brand preference include beer[21] many cosmetics, and household detergents. In contrast, those white-manufactured products with relatively weak brand preference include such products as milk, orange juice, and bread. The inroads made by black manufactured products are likely to be much greater for such products.

Budweiser Beer

An example of what a company selling a product with strong brand loyalty is doing to maintain its leading position is provided by Anheuser Busch, brewer of Budweiser Beer. Budweiser and Schlitz, the two leading beers, have a stronger position in the black community than in the white community.

In August, 1969, Budweiser established its first black distributorship on the turbulent West Side of Chicago. The black distributor is Art White, who has been with Budweiser for fifteen years, and has experience ranging from brewing through marketing. He worked on Chicago's West Side and has exercised leadership in that community. According to White, Budweiser has made available more help than he has needed to get established, and he can quickly get assistance merely by picking up the phone.

Budweiser is determined to maintain its position in the black community and has taken steps to insure this. They have picked a man with an excellent background and experience, and they have backed him with all necessary support. Budweiser has also had to consider the potential threat of Black Pride beer,[22] bottled for a black business that was hoping to take advantage of increasing black pride and consciousness. Schlitz and Hamm's have followed Budweiser's lead and established black distributors.

Automobile Dealerships

Automobile manufacturers have responded to the changing nature of the inner city by establishing a number of black dealers. One source of information indicates that during the past two to three years 26 black dealers have been franchised by the big U.S. automobile manufacturers. The black dealers are facing a variety of problems which are contributing to their failure:

(1) Many of the dealerships were marginal or unprofitable before the blacks took over.

(2) Few blacks had strong backgrounds for managing automobile dealerships with the many facets of business involved.

(3) The training and other assistance prior to and after taking over franchises has not been adequate to compensate for the limited business background of the black dealers.

(4) The poor level of credit in the black community has made financing, a key aspect of the car business, extremely difficult.

As a result, with only a few exceptions, the black automobile dealers are said to be failing.

Black-Distributed Products

For those categories of products where brand preference is relatively weak, black companies have made, and should continue to make, marked gains on products of white businesses. Distribution is a key aspect in marketing products with low brand preference. With the black power movement of recent years, black businessmen for the first time have been able to get distribution for their products in their own communities. In Chicago, thriving businesses have been built in this manner in sausage, milk and orange juice—Parker House Sausage, Joe Louis Milk, and Grove Fresh Orange Juice. However, the black-owned milk and orange juice companies do not manufacture their products. They are operating distribution and marketing businesses and are purchasing products under their own label from white manufacturing and processing businesses. For those white manufacturers who are not fearful of jeopardizing relations with existing customers, an opportunity exists to sell to black distribution and marketing companies.

Companies with low-brand-preference products can try to strengthen the demand for their products among black customers. To the extent that they are successful in such programs they will reduce the likelihood of being replaced by a black-manufactured or distributed product. There are indications that this strategy soon may be tested in the bread business. In recent years Continental Baking Company, which sells Wonder Bread, has exerted considerable effort to strengthen its consumer franchise in the black markets. Continental was the first baking company to hire black sales representatives and supervisors. Wonder Bread products are donated to black ladies' groups, clubs, and churches, and the company receives a great deal of good publicity in return. In addition, Wonder Bread advertises heavily on Chicago's WVON, an all-black programmed radio station. Black disc jockeys continually plug Wonder Bread as bread for black people.

The test as to how successful Wonder Bread has been in developing a strong consumer franchise is provided by the Silvercup Bakery. Supposedly, Silvercup Bakery was sold to black owners in the latter part of 1969. The idea seemed to be that Silvercup could take advantage of being black owned to improve its position in the black community. While Silvercup attracted some business on this basis, it did not penetrate the black community to the extent necessary to sustain the bakery operation, and in 1971 it was forced to file for bankruptcy.

To summarize, white-owned manufacturers and franchisors face three problems: selective product boycotts, support of store personnel, and competition of black products. These effects can be minimized by strengthening the brand preference for the manufacturer's products and by pursuing a program roughly equivalent to the CRASH program prescribed for retailers:

(1) communicate with minority groups and participate in their activities
(2) resort to minority group services and supply sources
(3) appoint minority group distributors and franchisees
(4) design products especially for minority groups if and when necessary
(5) hire minority group employees and managers.

SUMMARY, CONCLUSIONS AND RECOMMENDATIONS

The rapid changes occurring in the inner city are affecting the activities of white-owned businesses that derive revenues from this market. Hopefully other businesses will learn from the successes and failures reviewed here and will make appropriate adjustments before minority group community pressures, that may prove harmful to these businesses, are applied.

Problems of four categories of white-owned retail stores were analyzed and an adaptive strategy for each category was recommended. These strategies are summarized below, along with unresolved problems (marked with an asterisk) that require further investigation and research:

(A) Chain Convenience Goods Stores
   (1) CRASH program
      (a) communicate with and become part of the local community
      (b) run a clean, modern, and well-lighted store
      (c) add minority group manufactured products to store (and chain) assortments and use minority group services
      (d) stock a product-service mix desired by local community (for chains at area-wide uniform prices)
      (e) hire minority group employees, store managers, and executives.

(2) study possible corporate associate and/or joint venture possibilities*
(3) investigate effects of signing covenants with minority group organizations*
(4) investigate consequences of area uniform pricing.*
(B) Independent and Franchised Convenience Goods Stores
   (1) CRASH program
   (2) prepare to move, sell out, or take in minority group partners
   (3) investigate possibility of Project Transfer program*
(C) Chain Shopping Stores
   (1) CRASH program
   (2) minimize inner city investment
   (3) study feasibility of serving inner city from outside the area*
   (4) investigate mobility and transportation opportunities of inner-city resident
(D) Independent and Franchised Shopping Goods Stores
   (1) move, sell out, or take in minority group partner(s)
   (2) CRASH program
   (3) investigate possibility of Project Transfer program.* support of store
White manufacturers and franchisors of goods being sold in inner city stores face three problems: selective product boycotts, support of store personnel, and competition of black products. The effects of these problems appear to be much greater for products having low brand preference as opposed to products having a strong customer following. As a result, companies producing products with low brand preference may expect to lose sales in the inner city. However, there are steps that they can take to preserve their position in the inner city market:
(1) strengthen brand preference.
(2) adopt modified CRASH program
   (a) communicate with minority groups and participate in their activities.
   (b) resort to minority group services and suppliers.
   (c) appoint minority group distributors and franchisees.
   (d) design products especially for minority groups if necessary.
   (e) hire minority group employees and managers.

Of course, white-owned businesses have another course of action open to them. They can write off as potential customers the minority communities of the United States. The authors feel strongly that such an alternative strategy is, except for independent retailers, neither a good long run business policy nor a morally defensible action.

FOOTNOTES

[1] Donald S. Perkins, "The Low Income Consumer—A Human Problem and a Selling Problem," *Executive Lecture Series* (University of Notre Dame, March 2, 1970).

[2] "Blacks Wrap Up Slice of Action at Food Chains," *Business Week* (April 26, 1969), p. 162.

[3] Perkins, *op. cit.*

[4] Frederick D. Sturdivant, "Better Deal for Ghetto Shoppers," *Harvard Business Review* (March-April 1968), pp. 130-139.

[5] Frank Solton, "Blacks Especially Like a Squareshooter," *Supermarket News* (December 22, 1969), p. 5.

[6] "Breadbasket Halts Pickets," *Chicago Tribune* (March 3, 1969), pp. 1 and 7.

[7] William Jones, "How Blackstone Rangers Helped Scuttle Red Rooster Food Chain," *Chicago Tribune* (March 8, 1970), p. 2.

[8] Sturdivant, *op. cit.*

[9] "Tower of Strength in the Ghetto," *Business Week* (November 2, 1968), p. 103.

[10] "Jesse Jackson: One Leader Among Many," *Time* (April 6, 1970), p. 16.

[11] Ken Sandler, "Legacy of the Long McDonald's Battle: New Ground Rules for Ghetto Business," *Nation's Restaurant News* (March 2, 1970), p. 25.

[12] *Ibid.*

[13] Ken Sandler and Noel Wical, "Black Power Battle Closes 3 McDonald's," *Nation's Restaurant News* (August 4, 1969), pp. 1 and 10.

[14] *Ibid.*

[15] Ken Sandler, "McDonald's Rejects Payoff; Blacks Cry War," *Nation's Restaurant News* (September 1, 1969), pp. 1 and 10.

[16] *Ibid.*

[17] Ken Sandler, "Blacks Split, Reunite; Pledge to Finish McDonald's," *Nation's Restaurant News* (October 27, 1969), pp. 1 and 28.

[18] Ken Sandler, "Jail Boycott Leader on Blackmail; Pickets Gone but McDonald's Business Slow," *Nation's Restaurant News* (October 27, 1969), pp. 1 and 14.

[19] Sandler, "Legacy of the Long McDonald's Battle," *op. cit.*

[20] *Ibid.*

[21] See Fenster and Director, "Black Pride Beer." In this volume.

[22] *Ibid.*

SECTION FIVE:
COMMUNITY ECONOMIC
DEVELOPMENT

The term "community development" has come into international usage to connote the processes by which the efforts of community people are united with those of government agencies to improve: the economic, social, and cultural conditions of countries; to integrate their communities into the life of the nation; and to enable communities to contribute fully to national progress.[1] This complex of processes is then made up of two essential elements: (1) the participation by the people themselves in efforts to improve their level of living with as much reliance as possible on their own initiative; and (2) the provision of technical and other services in ways which encourage and effectuate initiative, self-help and mutual help, and make endeavors more effective.

Minority groups in many parts of America have concluded that equality is as much a matter of economic power as it is of political rights. They also have recognized that in economics, as in politics, there is strength in numbers. They are pooling their talents, their meager resources and their knowledge in organizations called "community development corporations" (CDCs). CDCs are similar to many private corporations, but they have one major difference—their stated objective is not the enrichment of private stockholders but the enrichment of the people of poor neighborhoods.

So far, the accomplishments of CDCs have been modest. Nevertheless, the CDC idea has spread. Despite resistance from bureaucrats, politicians, social scientists and some capitalists—black and white—CDCs are operating or are being established in almost every ghetto and barrio in the nation. Foundations and government agencies are besieged with demands for aid to community economic development programs, and legislation has been introduced in Congress to make community development organizations the primary focus of a national urban development program.

The concept of the CDC is new. It seems to violate much conventional wisdom. There is confusion as to what community development corporations are and what their potential is for resolving problems of urban poverty and powerlessness. Many view them as either socialistic or as a threat to other antipoverty programs; others claim that they represent the best traditions of free enterprise or view them as a panacea that would make existing programs unnecessary.

Community development corporations can not by themselves cure the sickness of the cities. There is no single cure. Neither development, nor dispersal, nor a family assistance plan, nor any one of a dozen other programs alone is the answer. All of these programs are needed and are needed now. Unless the nation can offer hope to the determined inner city residents who are working against great odds to build economically sound communities in the inner cities, they too will eventually abandon their efforts and there will be little to build on.[2]

Minority economic development need not be only an employment or an entrepreneurial strategy. Community economic development is also an alternate and complementary strategy that attempts to include more than just a few selected individuals in the ghetto in a program of employment or to make possible a few successful businesses. Its intent is to involve a community in a self-help program that utilizes a variety of approaches to remove the blight of poverty.

Section five of this book is devoted to exploring this alternative for minority economic development. First, an overview of the various types of community economic development projects is considered.

Programs of expanded participation, as delineated in Robert Duncan's paper, "Minority Economic Development Through Community Participation," range from CDCs to cooperatives, credit unions, and employee stock ownership arrangements. Cooperatives have long existed on a large scale in rural settings for economies of scale in processing, promoting, and distributing farm products, but they have recently become more widespread in urban areas, particularly for economies of scale in purchasing basic commodities. Often promoted by employees or unions to provide a convenient method of saving and borrowing for persons with little collateral, credit unions have a long history in this country. The use of stock ownership as a vehicle for broad-based economic development has only recently received great impetus with the various publications.of Louis Kelso. Stock participation plans have long been limited to high ranking executives or professionals in most of the leading corporations, but now various plans have been put forward to broaden such participation to virtually the entire workforce.

The remaining three articles of the section concentrate on specific areas of concern for the newest form of community endeavor, the CDC:

(1) With its complex mix of economic and social goals, the success of a CDC is difficult to evaluate. This concern is examined and several indicators of success are presented.

(2) The federal government along with its financial support for CDCs has developed a bureaucracy to monitor CDC activities. The bureaucracy, its politics and its evolving role with the CDCs are explored in the context of understanding the current state of CDC development.

(3) The actual blend of social, political, and economic activities of a CDC are analyzed in a case study of a Chicago-based CDC, the West Side Organization.

Michael Brower, in "The Criteria for Measuring the Success of a Community Development Corporation," contends that community economic development is hampered by lack of criteria by which to judge the usefulness of such development. The operation of the marketplace is the judge of the ability of corporate activity. Professor Brower argues that such a single criterion for success foregoes the production of social benefits for society. The CDC is deliberately designed to produce *both economic* and *social* goods and services. Thus our standard yardstick for measuring performance falls short when we seek to determine the success of the CDC.

CDCs in need of government backing find themselves in a conflict situation —they are torn between the need to produce simple and easy-to-count successes and the need to develop complex interrelated development programs. Mr. Geoffrey Faux, in "Politics and Control in Community Controlled Economic

Development," raises questions as to how the government maintains control of CDCs by use of multiple levels of bureaucracy, political pressure, and funding. Faux states that "where there is no constituency there is no power": minorities lack a constituency because few of them have money or political "clout." For a CDC to get off the ground, it must tap the federal and private involvement of those with a constituency to act as backers.

The final article is a case study which discusses one CDC's response to the political pressures of government sponsors and the local city hall machine. David Banner, in his case study of the West Side Organization (WSO), presents an example of a truly indigenous community development organization. The case shows how WSO is able to combine its social programs of welfare counseling and employment with its business enterprises—a McDonald's hamburger franchise, a Shell service station and a paper stock recycling company. The organization is not very popular outside the community since it is engaged in building a political organization with which to challenge the Daley political machine. Also it seeks to maintain its independence by avoiding grants or contracts from sponsors who might seek to control its policies or operations, further arousing the distrust of the Daley organization.

FOOTNOTES

[1] *Community Development and Related Services.* (New York: United Nations Department of Economic and Social Affairs, 1960), p. 1.

[2] Twentieth Century Fund Task Force on Community Development Corporations, *CDCs: New Hope for the Inner City* (New York: Twentieth Century Fund, 1971), pp. 27, 28, 15.

Robert Duncan

MINORITY ECONOMIC DEVELOPMENT
THROUGH COMMUNITY PARTICIPATION*

COMMUNITY DEVELOPMENT CORPORATIONS

The community development corporation (CDC) is an increasingly common form of an expanded participation organization in minority communities.[1] Generally, the CDC can be identified by four characteristics:

(1) Community. The activities of the CDC, particularly in the benefits it dispenses, are associated with either a specifically defined geographic or ethnic community. In large cities, this area is usually an enclave (for example, black ghetto, barrio, Appalachian neighborhood, or white ethnic community). In rural areas, the community is more likely to be defined by racial lines, as in multicounty areas in the Deep South.

(2) Broad Support. The CDC is based on broad support from the people of the community. The support may take the tangible form of shareholding, or of a block club federation, church group, or association of various community groups. The efforts by a few residents to generate business, whatever the attendant benefits to the community, are not generally considered a CDC.

(3) Revenue. Either the CDC or one of its subsidiaries or affiliates must aim at generating revenue through the sales of products and/or services. An organization that subsists only as an intermediary for private or public agents and does not aim at generation of revenue through broad participation in the community does not qualify as a CDC.

(4) Comprehensive Activities. The CDC has purposes and activities that go far beyond the mere generation of business revenues. Comprehensive social and economic activities must be initiated, because the CDCs must provide broad benefits for many. Thus, a group whose sole funtion is to package loans for small businesses, although a potentially useful element in a community economic development program, would not be a CDC.

Underlying these basic characteristics is the importance of the CDC as a basis for institutional development in the minority community. Minorities have suffered not only from a debased status within this society, but also from the

*This paper is excerpted from the President's Advisory Council on Minority Business, *Minority Enterprise and Expanded Ownership: A Blueprint for the Seventies*, Appendix C. ed. by Robert Duncan (Washington, D. C.: U. S. Government Printing Office, August, 1971). Professor Duncan is Associate Professor of Organization Behavior, Northwestern University, Graduate School of Management.

absence of their own institutional resources through which they could assume their rightful place in society. The CDC provides an institutional base upon which the minority community can enter and influence the economic sphere.[2] Business development in the minority community is not simply an economic necessity; of equal, or greater importance, are the psychological, institutional, and political impact that such development provides. Kenneth Clark has emphasized the demoralizing impact that affects minorities blocked from the normal channels of economic opportunity and mobility.[3] This often leads to a feeling of alienation and helplessness that causes withdrawal and apathy. Private profit-seeking organizations, whether minority or majority owned, can make some contributions to the development of minority communities, but they alone can not accomplish this development. Michael Brower has indicated that, given the conditions of minority communities today, multi-purpose corporations are needed that will dedicate themselves to the overall development of their respective communities.[4] Specifically, Brower has indicated that CDCs can:

(1) Concentrate scarce outside resources and use them to develop leverage from banks and insurance companies; concentrate scarce minority managerial talent together with these resources; and put together a group of development projects that individual minority businessmen alone could not put together.

(2) Help to promote organizational and social skills among the minority population, in both the CDC itself and other community institutions.

(3) Provide jobs in the minority community with an opportunity to get maximum community benefits from scarce minority M.B.A.s and other persons with managerial knowledge and ability.

(4) Make business decisions guided by the goal of profitability, but which also takes into account the many social benefits required by the community. The CDC can take into account, much more than can the private businessman, the wishes and feelings of the community in deciding where to locate a new business.

For working purposes, the CDC will be assumed to perform some or most of the following functions:[5] A corporation, profit or nonprofit in structure, is organized by community (that is, poor or minority) representatives to marshall both indigenous and outside resources (such as venture capital, short- and long-term loans, and technical assistance) which will be coordinated in developing the economic, human and physical makeup of the community. The corporation can then proceed to operate its own businesses, invest in or grant loans to a variety of subsidiary profit-making businesses, and maintain a policy of financial support for the specific needs of particular enterprises in poor communities. The umbrella ("holding company") CDC can retain control of subsidiary businesses through a variety of stock and financial arrangements and can deliver business and technical assistance to aspiring minority businessmen. A CDC can make more specific contributions to community development than simply helping individual entrepreneurs by encouraging and helping businesses that offer tangible rewards to community residents. Some of the profits from these sponsored enterprises can be used both to create new businesses and to provide needed social services for members of the community.

Although there are many variations on this theme, each project is responsive to specific local needs as well as to funding sources. Some of the similarities in organizational structures are indicated below.

First, a word should be said about why the CDC concept relies on the corporate form, and why this form is particularly responsive to the multiple processes required in community economic development. The corporate form provides a particularly good link between business enterprise and democratic control; it ensures that the functions of the institution will be a suitable blend of economic, social, and political development. Both individual and community needs will be satisfied. The belief that the corporate model can be adapted to the economic development problems of minority communities is based on the assumption that one organization may simultaneously fulfill various roles as a legitimate public corporation, as a progressive economic institution, and as a responsive source of social services.

As mentioned above, there are a number of structural configurations which a CDC could assume, depending on the community in which it operates and on funding sources available to it. Some important factors in this respect are:

(1) profit versus nonprofit status
(2) resident or community participation structure
(3) business development versus community development
(4) reinvestment versus dividends versus community service expenditures
(5) capital structure and relationship with subsidiaries.

In isolating the fifth variable, relationship with subsidiaries, potential and existing CDCs can be constructed on the premise that the development corporation's relationship with other economic enterprises in the minority community is critical to the CDC concept. Under this classification, there are three main types of CDCs.

1. Sponsor: This type of CDC does not take an equity position in businesses being developed in the area. Its primary function is to provide grants, loan guarantees, technical assistance, and other services that assist and stimulate business development. The only opportunity for community participation lies in allowing residents to purchase stock in the individual firms. In a case such as this, the CDC is able to exert informal influence through its discretion about the type of assistance to be given; resident members of the CDC would presumably have control over some of these decisions. In this type of arrangement, no profits from the businesses flow back to the CDC, except from loans or fees for its technical assistance.

This type of relationship with developing enterprises usually characterizes the formative stages of most CDCs. But it is not a desirable arrangement because it is oriented more toward economic development than community development. It dilutes the control that the community has in determining the direction of businesses. Due to a lack of equity participation control of businesses, it may fail to concentrate and localize the benefits from such business development.

Examples of this kind of relationship can be found in CDCs such as the Bedford-Stuyvesant Restoration Corporation (Brooklyn). In most cases, however, these CDCs anticipate moving into other relationships with businesses by taking an equity position in the near future.

2. Shared Ownership: This type of CDC takes a limited equity position in its business subsidiaries and shares the remaining equity with other community businessmen or with outside investors. Shares of such subsidiaries are offered to community residents, in some cases, with preferential riders or voting options. Under these circumstances, profits flow both to the community resident owners as well as to the umbrella CDC (or outside investors).

Some of the advantages of this type of relationship are fairly obvious. First, it increases the control of the CDC over the subsidiary business so that there is more community input and consideration in determining future business policies. The individual entrepreneur or other investor is offered the incentives needed to manage a business and attract the necessary capital. Second, assuming the subsidiary is operating profitably, this type of arrangement returns to the CDC funds which can be channeled into other business investments and/or educational, recreational, social, and other community development services. Examples of this pattern can be found in existing CDCs such as Progress Enterprises, Inc. (Philadelphia), which provides that profits be split 40 percent for the shareholders, 20 percent for the employees, and 40 percent for the CDC.

3. Sole Ownership: This type of CDC models itself after the modern-day large corporation, or the modern-day conglomerate, with a series of coordinated subsidiaries. While community residents do not hold stock in any individual business under this type of relationship, they do purchase stock in the parent or umbrella CDC. The CDC, in effect, acts as a layer of insulation between the community and the control of the individual subsidiaries. All profits from the individual subsidiaries flow directly back to the CDC. Stockholders may decide to reinvest the profits in other community enterprises, to distribute them to employees of the subsidiary, or to channel them into needed social services or other community activities.

This purest form of "community capitalism" is the type of relationship chosen by such CDCs as Fight On (Rochester) and Action Industries (Los Angeles).

All three categories of CDCs may exist alone or in conjunction with other for-profit or nonprofit structures. The most common arrangements seem to involve (for historical reasons, tax advantages, and so on) a nonprofit parent organization (since there is no flow of capital back to the parent, and since much of the present capitalization for profit-making subsidiaries is being squeezed from government grants or gifts from foundations) with a profit-oriented holding company actually setting up the business subsidiaries. This nonprofit parent usually holds all or a majority of the stock (although in some cases, preferred, nonvoting stock is issued to outside investors), and looks only to the dividends for a return flow of funds from its profit-oriented development corporation or individual subsidiaries.

The possible arrangements of all of these structures are nearly as endless as the number of communities needing assistance and the number of conditions to which a development unit in one of these communities must respond. All have different distributions of power, benefits, functions, profit flows, and capital resources.[6] These organizations may also include other forms of community ownership such as cooperatives, credit unions and/or share ownership.

COOPERATIVES[7]

Operational Attributes

At the heart of any cooperative are the cooperative principles, which include the democratic control of the cooperative by its membership. This does not change in the case of low-income cooperatives and, in fact, provides an important reason why this form of economic development should be encouraged today in our ghetto communities.

Our nation's urban centers are undergoing a period of great stress; pleas abound for community control and better distribution of political and economic power.[8] The cooperative can be a welcome response to these pleas. The one man/one vote principle equitably distributes power throughout the cooperative membership regardless of the individual investment. The community that participates in a local cooperative will own and control it—control not only its administration, but also the profits that result from the venture. In some cases, these profits could be used to benefit the broader community by investing them in the maintenance of community programs such as recreational facilities or job training programs.

The main principles, which apply to all cooperatives and distinguish them from business corporations, are:

(1) open membership. Membership in a cooperative is open to all, regardless of race, color, class, or creed, the only prerequisite being that the members share the common interests of the cooperative.

(2) one man/one vote. Control of a cooperative is in the hands of its members. Regardless of the number of shares he may have, each member has only one vote.

(3) limited interest on invested capital. The member receives a fair but limited return on his investment. This is to discourage speculation and to encourage real cooperation.

(4) patronage refunds. Surplus profits are distributed each year in proportion to the members' use of the services of the cooperative. Those members who utilize

the cooperative more receive a larger refund.

(5) cash sales. Cooperatives do business for cash. When members need credit, arrangements are sought with a credit union or some other lending institution.

(6) sales below market prices. Cooperatives sell to their members at lower prices than those charged by other businesses.

The simplicity, adaptability, and practicality of cooperatives have allowed them a new role in modern society: implementation in the economically depressed communities of the United States as a form of economic development. For many low-income communities, the cooperative seems to fit the needs of the people. Because the community cooperative allows a low-income person to own, manage, and control the business that serves him, it provides for somewhat greater community control and participation than do typical small one-owner business ventures.

THE COOPERATIVE VERSUS THE CORPORATION

The cooperative supermarket is a good example of the differences between cooperatives and business corporations in this country. The consumer who shops in a cooperative store and owns shares in it can have a strong say in its policies. It might seem that a shareholder in a large supermarket chain would be on equal footing, but there is little comparison. The shareholder in the large supermarket has one vote for each share he owns and is therefore easily outvoted by the large shareholders, who probably do not patronize the supermarket chain. The differing cooperative principle here is basically that of one man/one vote. No matter how many shares he owns, a co-op shareholder has only one vote at shareholders' meetings.

The distribution of profits is another important difference. Business corporations distribute their profits equally among all shareholders. Cooperatives utilize the "patronage refund," so named because those shareholders who patronize the co-op receive a refund in proportion to the amount they have spent there. Of course, another difference is the fact that a cooperative is considered a nonprofit corporation, and its profits can be distributed as patronage refunds to its shareholders without being taxed as corporate income. (Cooperatives are taxed, however, at regular corporate tax rates on any earnings retained by the business.) On the other hand, while the returns on money invested in an investor-owned corporation can be unlimited, the dividends on user-owned cooperatives usually are limited to maximum of five to eight percent.

Problems of Minority Cooperatives

As a result of the newness of cooperative ventures to urban communities, many problems have had to be overcome, the most obvious being:

(1) Most of these organizations are community-service oriented rather than profit oriented.

(2) The lack of management experience and the shortage of capital has hindered the low-income businessman's ability to expand this investment.

In order to succeed, it has been necessary for such organizations to become competitive by setting prices that will allow them to pay expenses and salaries, provide for expansion, and receive a profitable return on their investment. A successful cooperative must be capitalistic in the sense that it must function as a corporation or business venture in order to endure the changing cycles of the economy.

Additional obstacles to low-income cooperative development have been defined in these specific areas:

(1) pre-organizational Problems:
    (a) understanding the concept of a cooperative
    (b) definition of market and service
    (c) potential membership
    (d) management capabilities
    (e) location
    (f) operating costs and financing
(2) Incorporation[9]
    (a) articles of incorporation and bylaws
    (b) legislation to allow flexible operation
    (c) insurance
(3) roles of board and management versus membership
(4) distribution of earnings
(5) initial capital and capital for growth.

Future Improvements for Minority Cooperatives

Local or regional cooperative associations can open new areas of endeavor for the cooperative.[10] By expanding on the successes of the three most common types of cooperatives (consumer, producer, and service cooperatives), such associations can become more capitalistic and, thus, participate in new industries and utilize new concepts. Such activities would not only provide for new investments, but they would also provide ownership opportunities and jobs for the minority community.

Another problem confronted by cooperatives in minority communities is the lack of understanding about cooperative ventures. For example, the idea of giving five hard-earned dollars to a cooperative and getting back merely a service may not seem an appropriate investment to the poor. Even though the poor benefit from the low prices and patronage refunds, people are often skeptical because there is no immediate tangible transaction; this seems to be a major obstacle to the development of cooperatives. The following suggestions may help in eliminating these problems:

(1) To aid in understanding and identifying with a cooperative, informative community meetings or seminars explaining the concepts and benefits of a cooperative should be made available to minority individuals prior to their financial commitment.

(2) A symbol, such as those used by foreign cooperatives and corporations, should be created for all cooperatives so that the general public—especially the

poor—will immediately recognize what cooperatives mean and represent.

(3) Another marketing and promotional vehicle that should be used is the encouragement of some active minority cooperative members to sell shares to other residents of the community. Payment of additional shares to the soliciting members would be an incentive.

(4) Cooperatives could request technical assistance from large businesses and corporations in developing a guaranteed market program for their products.

Sources of Funding

Sources of financing ostensibly are available to cooperative associations from conventional institutions and federal agencies. However, when "cooperative association" (agricultural or nonagricultural) is understood to mean a low-income or minority enterprise without financial backing, the apparent sources of finance rapidly decrease in number.

Farmers Home Administration.   The Farmers Home Administration (FHA), an agency of the Department of Agriculture, is presently the best source of funds for financing poor, rural cooperatives. The only qualification needed for obtaining a loan is the inability to obtain credit elsewhere. The purposes for which FHA may loan its funds are presently rather limited, although for these purposes the repayment terms and interest rates are very liberal.

During the Ninety-first session of Congress, Senator Frank Moss introduced a bill[11] that would significantly expand the FHA's lending power by authorizing loans or the insuring of loans to

> local cooperative associations furnishing to farmers and rural residents services and facilities for harvesting, storing, processing (including preservation or preparation of edible products for market), transporting or marketing agricultural commodities or products of farmers or rural residents. Such loans may include funds for the organization and establishment of the association, necessary land, buildings, and equipment, or for the repair, expansion, or enlargement of such services or facilities for operation capital and for refinancing.

The FHA also administers loan funds under Title III of the Economic Opportunity Act. These loans may be used for nearly any purpose related to processing, purchasing, or marketing services, supplies, or facilities by poor, rural cooperatives. As in the case of FHA's own loan funds, the only security required is a reasonable assurance of payment based upon a plan of operation. Loans under Title III are limited in amount only to the extent adequate to assure completion of the loan's purpose. Repayment terms and interest rates are also very liberal.

Small Business Administration.   The Small Business Administration (SBA) has loan funds authorized for a number of low-income and minority small business developments. Loan recipients are defined as "small business concerns," and this is interpreted by the SBA to mean business concerns operated for profit. Therefore, the Small Business Administration can be used at the present time neither as a source or financing for cooperatives nor for businesses owned by cooperatives.

SBA is, however, a primary source of debt capital for small business corporations. Its stated purpose in the Employment and Investment Incentives title of the Economic Opportunity Act of 1964 is "to assist in the establishment, preservation, and strengthening of small business concerns and improve the managerial skills employed in such enterprises, with special attention to small business concerns (1) located in urban or rural areas with high proportions of unemployed or low-income individuals, or (2) owned by low-income individuals; and to mobilize for these objectives private as well as public managerial skills and resources." SBA programs include direct loans, participation in loans, and guarantees of loans to low-income individuals or enterprises in low-income areas. SBA is also providing technical assistance, management training, and government contracts to eligible small businesses.

Office of Economic Opportunity.   The Office of Economic Opportunity (OEO) is authorized to make loans to local cooperative associations furnishing essential processing, purchasing, or marketing services, supplies, or facilities predominantly to low-income rural families. OEO and EDA (the Economic Development Administration of the Department of Commerce) are both authorized to make financial assistance grants for organizing, operating, training, and securing technical assistance to "poor" co-ops and small business corporations.

Banks for Cooperatives.   Although Banks for Cooperatives are agencies of the Farm Credit Administration and as such would seem to be the obvious and best source of financing for low-income cooperatives, they are not. The reasons for this are fourfold: First, only farmer cooperatives meeting certain eligibility requirements may be borrowers. This immediately eliminates a significant number of cooperatives engaged in nonagricultural activities. Second, the basic criterion for obtaining a loan is that the applicant be credit-worthy; this requirement eliminates a very large number of marginal cooperative associations that have not exhibited well-documented success.

Third, the cooperatives must supply some capital in order to receive a loan. Banks for Cooperatives usually limit facility loans to not more than 50 percent of the value of the security offered by the cooperative, and they expect the balance to be financed by the members' investment in the association's permanent or long-term capital. The banks require that seasonal commodity loans are secured by warehouse receipts by third parties, covered by eligible commodities, or merchandise in storage. The bank usually limits such loans to 75 percent of the net market value of the commodities.

Fourth, most Banks for Cooperatives arrange their long-term facility loans to be repaid in ten years or less and their operating loans for periods of usually one year, but not longer than five years. This is an unattainable standard for many low-income cooperatives. Thus, since small corporations are obviously ineligible due to practical considerations, Banks for Cooperatives are an unacceptable source for the needs referred to in this report.

Commercial Banks and Other Conventional Financial Institutions.   Commercial banks and other financial institutions (savings and loan companies, finance companies, credit unions, insurance companies) have by far the greatest financial resources of the groups considered, have the most flexibility in that they can lend for almost any purpose, and have offices in virtually every community. Ultimately, they must be the principle source of loan capital for low-income cooperatives.

Outside Investors and Control.   To attract investors, the organization that presents the most attractive securities offerings will probably be most successfully based on such traditional investment considerations as return on investment, security or risk involved, and, in the case of large investors, safeguards such as participation in management or representation on the board. However, with the trend toward greater "national conscience," the social purpose of the project may draw additional investors from private foundations, local and national church groups, and profit-oriented corporations.

If based only on traditional motivations, however, the flexibility of the corporate form and its frequent use of a number of classes of unrestricted and more easily transferable stock make it a preferable vehicle to attract outside investors. Utilization of large-investor safeguards by cooperatives, such as allowing participation in management or representation on the board of directors, are concessions that are available but should be considered only if very large monetary investments are involved or no alternative source of funds are available.

Assessment of Funding Prospects.   In the financing and investment spectrum detailed above, the FHA-administered Economic Opportunity funds are most readily available to cooperatives, while SBA funds are most readily available to small corporations. However, even these funds are inadequate to meet the present and anticipated needs of low-income business development. In order to fill the gap which presently exists, and which can easily continue to exist or widen, new methods of financing low-income business development must be devised or drawn from current institutions.

The cooperative venture is not a new idea; it has operated successfully in other countries for a number of years. The question of most concern, however, is whether or not the cooperative concept can be successfully implemented as a means of expanded economic participation on a more global scale.

CREDIT UNIONS

Organization of Credit Unions

Credit unions are cooperative thrift and credit associations organized among groups of people having a common bond of occupation, association, or residence. They are nonprofit, voluntary membership organizations authorized by either federal or state credit union law, operating under standard bylaws and procedures. Credit union leagues are statewide associations of credit unions that are nonprofit, dues-supporting, voluntary membership organizations of individual credit unions.

The Role of Credit Unions in Alleviating Poverty

Credit unions have the potential for playing a major role in alleviating poverty in this country. Several reasons for this potential are outlined below:

(1) Credit unions can be utilized in the fight against poverty because of their unique ability to provide people with a device to wisely manage their income, no matter how meager, irregular, or unpredictable this income is. This ability has the potential of accumulating capital, among persons whose income is by definition quite limited, sufficient to meet their credit needs.

(2) Credit unions have certain aspects that make them particularly suited to the programs and objectives of the government's efforts to combat poverty. Each member of a credit union becomes one of its owners. Officials of the credit union are elected by the members. This arrangement provides an unusual opportunity for the practice of citizen participation in an economic institution. Credit unions also often make family participation a special objective, with emphasis on participation by young people.

(3) Because of the lack of economic expertise that is so prevalent among the poor, credit unions are good devices for management of family income available to people who might otherwise be locked in their poverty.

(4) Credit unions provide secondary services that also go straight to the heart of the money management problems of the poor. Because credit unions are service-oriented, they are in a position to become true "learning by doing" schools in providing consumer education and family financial counseling to its members. The direct result, then, is that minority group members become a better resource for further economic development.

(5) Credit unions aid in creating the stability required for economic development. On an individual basis, the effective credit union can help solve many of those financial problems that keep an employee frustrated and cause high turnover and reduced performance. On a group basis, a credit union can stabilize an area since it represents a concentration of purchasing power.[12]

Problems with Credit Unions

Credit unions that experience a spurt in growth tend to assume that the growth will continue and therefore curtail further efforts on their part,[13] even though self-sufficiency has not been achieved. A credit union that rises from $10,000 to $60,000 in one year will tend to see this growth as sufficient, which it may not be. Many credit unions are often unable to handle the managerial and administrative duties necessary for continued growth and success. Credit unions must provide adequate training and technical assistance in order to deal adequately with these problems.[14]

SHARE OWNERSHIP

Profit sharing can be defined as any method of raising output and lowering costs through human cooperation by a system under which the employees receive a part of the profits of the enterprise.[15] The distinguishing mark of profit sharing is that the organizational contributions to the plan fluctuate with current profit levels.

Dual Advantages of Share Ownership

Most community-oriented organizations, especially corporations with a large employee population from the minority sector, enthusiastically sponsor activities that will lead to a broader base of ownership for the minority employee. A major difficulty, however, is that since the employee is not financially capable of participating in the stock option plans normally sold to the public, the employer must assume high risks and a large percentage of the contributions when creating such profit-sharing plans for minorities. Therefore, consideration should be taken not only of the disadvantaged minority, but also of the profit or nonprofit organization that must make a substantial return on its investment for the benefit of the organization, board, stockholders, and others. A corporation may have considerable sympathy for this type of program, but overwhelming financial needs may force it to seek value of one kind or another (for example, a guarantee) for a substantial interest in a business.

Any successful share ownership plan, therefore, must be structured to benefit the employer as well as the employee. The ownership of shares of capital stock involves three basic rights: (1) the right to vote upon various matters specified in the corporate charter and state corporation law, (2) the right to participate in earnings and profits of the corporation, largely through payment of dividends, and (3) the right to participate in distributions of corporate assets upon dissolution and liquidation of the corporation.

FOOTNOTES

[1] For a discussion of the legal background of CDC's pending legislation, see John McClaughry, "The Community Corporation Act of 1971," *Law and Contemporary Problems*, (Summer, 1971).

[2] See Stewart Perry, "A Note on the Genesis of the Community Development Corporation," Unpublished paper (Cambridge, Massachusetts: Center for Community Economic Development, 1970).

[3] Kenneth B. Clark, *Dark Ghetto: Dilemmas of Social Power* (New York: Harper and Row, 1965).

[4] Michael Brower, "Why Do We Need Community Development Corporations for Ghetto Development?" Unpublished paper (Cambridge, Massachusetts: Center for Community Economic Development, 1970).

[5] The material in this section is drawn from *The Role of Expanded Participation Organizations in Promoting Minority Business and Economic Development*, Report prepared for the National Advisory Council on Minority Business Enterprise (Boston, Massachusetts: Circle Associates, 1970), pp. 62-66.

[6] For an excellent discussion of one CDC, see David K. Banner, "The West Side Organization" in this volume.

[7] Nicolaus Retsinas, "Working Paper: Notes toward an Evaluation of Community Development Corporations," Unpublished paper (Cambridge, Massachusetts: Cambridge Institute, 1970).

[8] Sterling Tucker, *Beyond the Burning: Life and Death of the Ghetto* (New York: Associated Press, 1968). See also Alan Altshuler, *Community Control: The Black Demand for Participation in Large American Cities* (New York: Pegasus, 1968); Kenneth Clark, *Dark Ghetto, op. cit.*; and Howard Oleck, *Non-Profit Corporations, Organizations.*

[9] Local statutes should be consulted as these requirements vary from state to state. Also Oleck, *op. cit.*

[10] See Richard Rosenbloom and Robin Marris, eds., *Social Innovation in the City: New Enterprises for Community Development* (Washington, D.C.: National Training Laboratories, Institute for Applied Behavioral Science, 1968).

[11] Senate Bill S-305, Ninety-first Congress was resubmitted in 92nd Congress.

[12] Contract No. 4069: *A Report on Credit Unions Sponsored by Community Agencies.* Prepared by the Organization of Limited Income Groups (Madison, Wisconsin, CUNA International, Inc., 1970), pp. 22-23.

[13] *Ibid.*, p. 21.

[14] Useful sources here are CUNA International, Inc., *People Power Through Credit Unions* (Madison, Wis.: CUNA, International, Inc., 1970); CUNA International, Inc., *Credit Union Pilot Guaranty Program* (Madison, Wis.: CUNA International, 1970); *The Credit Union Magazine* (Madison, Wis.: CUNA International, 1970).

[15] B. C. Metzger, *Profit Sharing in Perspective*, 2nd ed., (Evanston, Illinois: Profit Sharing Research Assoc., 1966).

Michael Brower *

THE CRITERIA FOR MEASURING THE SUCCESS OF A COMMUNITY DEVELOPMENT CORPORATION IN THE GHETTO

INTRODUCTION

Our society lacks widely used and accepted criteria for judging the social utility of private corporations. Our nominally private profit-seeking corporations are, in a basic sense, social institutions. They fulfill a variety of important social functions including product development, production and distribution, employment, skill training, and income distribution. But despite the multiple functions they fulfill, we have traditionally consigned the judging of the success or failure of our corporations to the private marketplace and, in the long run, to the overburdened single indicator of private profitability. This reliance on the marketplace and, basically, on profitability as the sole standard of success brings with it severe problems. Many social benefits that corporations might provide us go unproduced, because the private marketplace will not reimburse them for their costs in producing these benefits. Profit-seeking corporations produce or contribute to a host of expensive social costs such as water and air pollution, the alienation of some employees, and the rise of central city ghettos with few jobs and many people. Decisions as to location and whether or not (usually not) to install antipollution equipment are (or until very recently were) based almost solely on the calculation of private profitability. Thus society as a whole misses out on the potential benefits corporations might provide, and it bears the burden of these social costs.

By choosing to judge our corporations in the marketplace and not in a central government, which theoretically could take into account all these benefits and costs, we have been spared the great cost and threat to freedom of giant bureaucracy for total planning of the economy. And we have put off until now the need to develop a complex set of criteria by which to judge the overall performance of corporations. Increasingly, as these excessive social costs and the missed social benefits become larger and more obvious, local communities, citizen organizations, legislatures and state and national governments, together with the vanguard of private corporate executives, are seeking ways to build such social concerns and criteria into corporate decision processes.

And with the advent of community development corporations in the past

*This paper was written while the author was a consultant to the Center for Community Economic Development, Cambridge, Massachusetts, which was supported by the United States Office of Economic Opportunity. Much of the field research on which it is based was conducted while the author was on the faculty of the M. I. T. Sloan School of Management, with travel supported by the M. I. T. Urban Systems Lab using funds provided it by the Ford Foundation.

few years, it has not become crucial and unavoidable that we determine criteria for judging their success, since their goals are far broader than those of private profit-seeking corporations. In fact these CDCs are typically chartered as not-for-profit corporations. They are usually owned and controlled by residents of poor communities, set up to promote the overall development of festering urban slums and decaying rural areas left behind by profit-seeking private corporations moving to more lucrative locations. Since the CDCs have economic objectives, they assist in setting up and expanding individual businesses, and many also seek to develop larger new businesses (especially manufacturing) in their communities, with all or part of the ownership in the hands of the CDC itself. And the CDCs also have a range of other human and social goals.[1]

To understand the multiple objectives of the community development corporations, it is necessary to understand that development is a complex human, social, and political, as well as an economic, process. It involves growth in experience and ability in social interaction, social participation, and social organization. It is also a process of human development. This depends upon the early home environment of the child, the school, the culture of the street corner and neighborhood in which he learns from his peers, the nutrition and health or lack thereof provided at home and in school, the role models set by adolescents and adults of his own race and social class as he sees them in his daily life, the employment experiences he acquires in early youth, and the resulting set of values, attitudes, hopes, ambitions, expectations, and overall identity which he develops as a result of these and thousands of other inputs during his formative years.

Development is also a political process. Ghetto residents lack power. Individually, the male ghetto resident lacks the power to provide a steady, adequate income for his family; he has no power to protect his family from either open violence or the covert violence of racial and class discrimination. Collectively, the ghetto community lacks the political power to insist that the city provide it a fair share of municipal services, such as street repairs and cleaning, street lighting, trash and garbage collection, police protection, and high-quality schools. This powerlessness is undesirable both because it inevitably results in the ghetto receiving fewer basic services than higher income, better-organized, more politically powerful neighborhoods, and because it is humanly corrupting. Because ghetto residents are powerless, they become apathetic, despairing, unambitious, and drug-prone. This human corruption can also lead to a total alienation, which can then erupt in an explosion of fearless, almost pointless, violence from those who have nothing to lose.

Economic development thus represents only one part of a complex web that also involves social, human, and political development. And over the last decades worldwide efforts to promote economic development alone, relying on strictly economic analysis, decisions, tools, and incentives often have failed. Time after time, a too narrowly economic analysis has led to the construction of a road or factory or the adoption of an economic plan or policy that did not end up functioning as planned and did not make the expected contribution to development because important human and social elements and developmental needs were not recognized and achieved at the same time.

If they are to succeed in promoting successful development of America's ghettos, the community development corporations must have a multiple set of goals, including but not limited to economic development. And to measure their success or failure we must therefore use a broad range of economic, social, human, and political indicators. Section II of this paper offers a variety of possible indicators for consideration. Of course, no one CDC can hope or be expected to achieve improvement in every one of these indicators; indeed, some of these indicators are no doubt in conflict with others, at least in the short and intermediate run, and hard choices and trade offs will be necessary. Section III discusses the question of time, of how long it will take for reasonable changes to take place in the community of a CDC that is receiving sufficient outside funding and support and is effective in promoting development, and how long that outside support will be necessary for the continued survival and effectiveness of the CDC.

POSSIBLE INDICATORS FOR MEASURING CDC SUCCESS

Economic

Since some of the figures can vary tremendously with the size of the CDC and with the amount of OEO money provided, each of the following economic indicators might be used directly, or on a per unit basis, depending on the kind of outside resources provided. Some possible indicators are:

(1) Number of dollars raised from governmental sources other than OEO.

(2) Number of dollars raised from nongovernmental grants.

(3) Number of bank loans negotiated for CDC projects or for assisted businesses.

(4) Total dollar volume of bank loans negotiated.

(5) Number of employees hired directly by the CDC. (This may not be regarded in all cases as a positive, beneficial indicator.)

(6) Number of new employees in subsidiary organizations of the CDC and in businesses aided by the CDC.

(7) Number of employees given special training programs and courses.

(8) Number of new businesses started either wholly or partially owned by the CDC, and number not owned but aided by the CDC.

(9) Number of white corporations convinced to provide a market for ghetto-produced goods and services, or to place a facility of their own in the ghetto community, or to collaborate in other ways with the CDC in supporting development of the area.

(10) Number of units of low-income housing produced by the CDC, or in collaboration with the CDC, or by promotion and instigation of the CDC.

(11) Number of units of rehabilitated housing for low-income people produced.

(12) Changes in average per capita or per family income in the community.

(13) Changes in community unemployment and underemployment rates, compared to previous levels and with concurrent citywide and nationwide changes.

Social and Organizational Development of the CDC and the Community

A basic objective of most of the CDCs is (or should be) the development of social and organizational participation among people of the community, development of their experience and skills in forming and building organizations, and in leadership and management abilities. The CDC must also build its own organization by developing the leadership and management skills of its employees and by increasing its ability to expand into additional and more complex areas, to replace key men who go on to other challenges, and to survive when its founder and prime mover leaves the organization, as he most likely will at some point.

How are these organizational and social skills measured in the short run? The following considerations may provide a rough guide although exact or objective measurements will be virtually impossible to obtain.

How solid, stable, and viable is the CDC itself as an organization? Do all decisions flow through and from one man? Or is there a beginning of delegation of authority, division of labor, and development of independent decision centers? Has the CDC attracted and held men who are potential replacements for the original leader? Do these men show signs of personal growth, increasing ability to lead and to organize the work of others, to delegate and train employees under them? Is the top individual supportive of his subordinates?

How broad is community participation in the organization and control of the CDC? To what degree was the CDC organized by the people of the community? Or was it largely the product of outsiders? What is the legal-organizational structure of the CDC with regard to who holds ultimate authority? Does the CDC have members, or owners who live in the community and with whom ultimate authority rests? Is membership open at little or no cost to all adults in the community? Does this membership/ownership meet at least once a year to elect the board of directors or top executives of the CDC? Or are there some other processes whereby new community leadership, from outside the CDC, can emerge, convince the community that the CDC requires a change, and win an open election to replace the existing management? Or, is there instead a closed, self-perpetuating board of directors that names its own replacements? If so, how representative of the community is this board? What access to the board do the community members have? In sum, what mechanisms, if any, are there to give the community residents some degree of control, some ultimate power over the management and policies of the CDC?

How broad is ongoing community *participation* in the operations and activities of the CDC as distinct from ultimate community *control* over the CDC? Some meaningful participation can obviously be obtained through direct paid employment; this can not and should not be the form of participation for most community members. How many additional members of the community, beyond the full-time paid employees, does the CDC employ in a part-time activity, whether paid or unpaid? How many people are involved in gathering information for the CDC on community needs, desires, and priorities? How many are active in planning or advisory councils? Has the CDC organized special volunteer action groups for one or another community project—whether it be day-long clean-up campaigns, visits to hospital wards, or assistance to the elderly and infirm? Has the CDC, if it operates in a large area, made an effort to set up neighborhood sub-bodies, with their own boards of directors or councils to carry out activities in the local neighborhood and to channel requests, information, pressures, and perhaps also representatives to the board up to the CDC? How many people from the community come to the CDC headquarters on randomly selected days? Does the CDC try to make space available for a variety of community activities both because that activity needs space and because this may help build identification with the CDC?

Is growth of social particiation and of other organizations in the community taking place and is it influenced by the CDC? Has the number of voluntary community organizations, clubs, and activities increased? Has the number of community members participating in such activities shown noticeable signs of increase? Are there signs of greater effectiveness of the activities of any other organizations? Any or all of these changes *may be* indirectly or in part due to the existence and activities of the CDC, although a direct causal link or influence may be difficult or impossible to verify.

What is the degree of recognition of the CDC, knowledge about it, and identification with it? Survey research can be used to determine what percentage in the community have heard of the CDC. What percentage knows its general purposes? How many know something about its structure?

Psychological Changes

The conditions of life in an urban nonwhite ghetto—extreme overcrowding, decaying housing, poverty, massive unemployment and underemployment, individual and institutional violence, and daily evidence of class and caste status in the prejudiced outer society—these produce debilitating psychological effects in many ghetto residents. If development of these ghettos is to take place and is to be considered a success in human terms, there must be a dramatic measurable change in both these objective destructive conditions and forces and in their psychological consequences. Over the years, if development, and the CDC, are to be termed successful, we should find among community members involvement replacing apathy, courage and confidence conquering fear, pride replacing feelings of inferiority, potency and efficacy driving out helplessness and fatalism, hope replacing hopelessness, independence instead of dependence, and a strong racial, group, and community identity in place of isolation, loneliness, and alienation.

Other Indicators of Human Development

Many other indicators of human development, of utilization of health and educational services, of reduction in alienation and antisocial behavior might be utilized. The following is merely a list of suggestions. Most of these changes probably would not be taking place in the earliest years of a CDC's work, and again improvements could not be attributed solely or perhaps even primarily to the influence of the CDC:

(1) percentage of children continuing in school
(2) infant mortality rate
(3) crime rates for various crimes
(4) arrest rates
(5) sale of alcohol in the community
(6) rates of drug addiction
(7) enrollment in adult education programs
(8) incidence of illegitimate births
(9) incidence of malnutrition symptoms.

Political Development

The final and in some respects most important result of a successful CDC and its community development program should be improved political participation and organization by the community members, with a resulting greater degree of political power wielded by them and their organizations. Since the CDC itself is usually a nonprofit organization eligible for tax-exempt status, it cannot engage in open political activity, but it can and should help create the climate and the organizations for more effective political activity.

Below are listed some indicators of exercise of political power. As with other kinds of changes and developments, improvements in these indicators should not be attributed solely or even primarily to the existence and activities of a CDC. Nor should the absence of improvement in these indicators in the short run (three to five years) be taken as evidence of the failure of the CDC. But if marked improvement in political participation is noted, it may well be an indirect result of activities by CDC personnel and CDC projects, of growing community economic resources, of an increasing sense of purpose and hope, and growing organizational and political sophistication on the part of community residents. These are some indicators of exercise of political power:

(1) Has registration to vote increased as a percentage of those eligible?
(2) Has actual voting increased in absolute numbers or as a percentage of those eligible?
(3) Does the CDC community now have, or share with contiguous areas, representatives on the city council, in the state legislature, and/or in congress who more accurately represent their community than in previous years?
(4) Are there more community members involved in the local branches of the political parties, in political clubs, and other political organizations?

(5) When issues of importance to the CDC community are being discussed and voted at the city council or the state legislature, are there more spokesmen for the community who show up to present community views?

(6) Whether or not there are newly elected representatives from the CDC community serving in city, state or national bodies, are community members increasingly presenting themselves as candidates in elections and in primaries?

(7) Is there an increased flow of municipal funds into programs of the CDC or into other community action and development programs in the area? Of state funds? Of funds from federal agencies other than OEO?

(8) Finally, are the established centers of power (individuals and institutions) beginning to notice, to take account of, or to complain about the rising power of the community around the CDC or of its leaders and spokesmen?

If most of these questions can be answered *yes*, there exists a growing political ability and sophistication on the part of community members and organizations, perhaps due in part to existence of the CDC.

HOW LONG DOES IT TAKE?

In making estimates of how long it will take for a CDC to be successful, a number of separable questions arise. These involve:

(1) The time span necessary before business activities of the CDC can be expected to provide a significant income to the CDC.

(2) Whether or not local community residents can be expected to make voluntary contributions to the CDC, or purchase its stock, in sufficient amounts to make it self-sufficient.

(3) How long the CDC will require and should benefit from nonrepayable grants from the federal government or from foundations and churches.

(4) The time needed before important measurable community benefits are obtained.

(5) The number of years one might expect a CDC to function before closing down, after having created a successful community endeavor in self-development.

The following estimates are more optimistic than conservative; they assume adequate funding, good leadership, and a highly successful CDC. These are of course highly personal and subjective judgments, but they are based on many years of study of development problems and programs in our cities and in other countries, and on conversations with many CDC leaders.

How long will it take for the businesses organized and fully or partly owned by the CDC to show a continuing profit and to return a significant flow of net income to the CDC?

This will take a considerable time. From the time of establishment and funding of the CDC, it will take at least a year or two for the CDC leadership and staff to:

(1) survey a range of possible business opportunities

(2) select a few of them for intensive further studies

(3) recruit people or organizations to carry out feasibility studies and have them done

(4) decide which project or projects to push first and find the men needed to organize and manage them

(5) secure the financing

(6) pick the best location, incorporate the new businesses, purchase or lease the necessary machinery and equipment, hire and train employees, purchase raw materials, secure contracts or other marketing mechanisms and start into production.

Next there is the delay involved from the start of production until the time when the new business finally begins to show a net profit. This may take another year or two at least and may easily take longer.[2]

These delays add up to from two to four more years, except in very rare cases, between the founding of the CDC and the first *month* when a subsidiary business established by the CDC begins to show a profit. These time lags are by no means solely or largely due to the ghetto location or the inexperience of the CDC leadership and of the managers and employees of the new businesses; time delays of this sort before showing a profit are common for most new business, nonghetto as well as ghetto.

It must be noted that the new business enterprise can not be expected to turn much money back to the CDC for several years after that first profitable month. This is especially true of a manufacturing operation which, if successful, will be in continuous need of capital for expansion and which must build up reserves for setbacks and difficult times which are almost certain during the early years.

Some businesses set up by the CDC will surely fail and die as is of course generally true of new businesses, which have a high failure rate in our economy. And some businesses started by CDC's will survive, but they will never show much if any net annual profit. Some of them may even show a small net loss, year after year, and they would be judged a failure by traditional business standards. But if they generate enough total social benefits to the community to justify their continued operation at a financial loss or by breaking even, the CDC and the country should subsidize their continued existence. One such social benefit that should be generated by ghetto corporations, including unprofitable ones, is steady employment and income to ghetto residents who otherwise might be on the welfare roles at best and, at worst, turn into dope addicts and criminals—with large costs to society. These businesses also should provide continuous training for new employees and managers; their increased skills and abilities to produce and earn should enable them to move on to better paying jobs with other organizations. Ghetto businesses also might lower the costs or raise the quality of goods purchased by community residents, or in other ways contribute to improving the physical, economic, and psychological neighborhood. To summarize, some CDC businesses will not survive, some should survive with subsidies even though they do not provide a net financial profit, and some should return a share of their profits to the CDC—but only several years after the startup process begins.

The widely touted franchise is sometimes a short cut to quicker profits. Starting a new gasoline station or hamburger stand franchise in a good location in the ghetto or purchasing an existing profitable franchise has been shown to be a successful road to earlier profits for a CDC. Such opportunities should certainly be taken after careful study of their feasibility and profitability. Only a limited number of such operations can be picked up and turned into profit makers in the first years, and our ghettos may soon be saturated with franchise operations.

It will thus be many years before most CDCs have created enough new wholly or partially owned businesses that are successful enough in financial terms so that the CDC can expect to receive all or even a major portion of its income from its own business operations. A few CDCs might reach self-sufficiency in 5 to 10 years, others in 10 to 15 years, and others may never generate sufficient income to cover all their programs.

How many local community residents can be expected to make voluntary contributions to, or buy membership shares in, the CDC?

How much will they pay, and for how long? The only successful example is Philadelphia Reverend Leon Sullivan's 10-36 plan. With the income from the first few hundred of his 10-36 club members as a basis, multiplied by grants and loans from outside, Reverend Sullivan and his colleagues built what has become a network of housing, business, and training operations. Seven thousand people are said to have participated or are now participating in this program. If this is so, more than $2.5 million dollars will be raised over seven years, if everyone completes his pledged $360 payment. This is a remarkable achievement, certainly the most successful of any ghetto nonprofit corporation in the nation. But it is still only about $350,000 per year on the average, and only a fraction of the funds needed to support the administrative staff and promote and finance the business and other programs needed to effectively develop a big city ghetto.

Can this performance be duplicated in other minority areas? It is doubtful. For one thing, the average income level of the parishoners appealed to by Reverend Sullivan and his fellow preachers is higher than that of many other ghetto areas. Furthermore, Reverend Sullivan is not only an extraordinary man and leader, but also an extraordinary orator. He had first exercised these and other unusual qualities to promote a highly successful series of selective boycotts of Philadelphia companies until each agreed to hire a given number of additional black employees. This was followed by his initiation of the first of the Opportunities Industrialization Centers to provide prejob training and preparation for Philadelphia unemployed black people. Together, these activities gave him great acceptance, credibility, and support in the black community, and they undoubtedly have contributed to his success in obtaining 10-36 club members. It is unlikely that either black or white leaders in other cities will approach the rare mixture of qualities, opportunities, and achievements of a Leon Sullivan. Perhaps the best evidence of this is that such a performance has not to date been duplicated or even approached in other cities. This does not mean that other community leaders and CDCs should not try; it does mean that the American people and the federal government should not expect voluntary contributions, or membership purchases, by poor ghetto residents to bear the full or even the major cost of operations of CDCs.

How long will the CDCs need outside aid grants, partly or largely from federal sources such as OEO?

In the author's judgment, some of those CDCs that are strongly supported in their early years (and most CDCs are at present receiving very little or no support at all) might be able to develop enough profit-making businesses and other local sources of income to become largely self-sufficient in 5 to 10 years at the earliest. But the majority of the CDCs cannot become independent of sizable outside grants in less than 10 years from the date of their first major funding, and for some it will be even longer.

How long will it take for the CDCs, together with other community organizations and activities, to produce important measurable benefits to the community?

Here again the answer must surely be tentative, and what follows is only one possible scenario.

Some of the most direct and easily measurable economic benefits should be occurring but in a very limited degree, within the first year or two of the CDC's life. Likewise within its first year or two the CDC should be showing some of its ability to involve the people of the community as members, stockholders and participants in a variety of ways. By the end of the first year or early in the second, the CDC should be able to produce some visible "showpieces" to demonstrate its presence and capability to the community. If a public opinion survey were taken, it should show at least a significant percentage of community members who have heard of and have hopes for the future of the CDC, even if they do not have much knowledge of it. By the third and fourth year a variety of social activities and organizations stimulated or organized by the CDC should be well founded and operating without the fear that each month will be their last. There should be a variety of smaller economic projects, and a few larger projects should be coming into being and beginning to produce income. The CDC itself should be a more stable organization, showing itself capable of developing new leadership.

After the fourth year, one would expect to find a greater knowledge about the CDC among community members and a significant degree of positive identification with the CDC, its purposes, projects, and leaders. There should be a wider variety of participation in CDC activities underway, a growing number of voluntary and part-time affiliations with it, and a noticeable growth in other social and organizational activities in the community. The cumulative impact of activities of the CDC and of other organizations working in the community may have brought about a noticeable change in some of the personal attitudes of a significant number, although probably still a minority, of the residents of the area.

In the fifth and sixth years, the impact of the CDC should be really measurable, if financial support throughout this period has been adequate and if the CDC has been effective. A number of CDC-owned businesses should be producing income, but some of them will be expanding rapidly and therefore will not be able to send much if any income back to the CDC. Perhaps an effort has been made to attract outside corporations to invest in the community, perhaps in partnership with the CDC, or under some form of turn-key contract, whereby after setting up a successful business the outside corporations, by previous agreement and contract, sell it to community members or institutions. If such an effort has been made, by now such projects should be underway, already successful. By the seventh or eighth year, total unemployment and underemployment in the community of a successful CDC should be shrinking, and incomes should be rising, provided that the overall economy of the nation and city has been functioning adequately. Hopefully, attitude measurement by now would indicate that a considerable number of ghetto residents show significantly different attitudes towards themselves, their race, their community, and their future. And by now, if not before, some of the indicators of political development should show significant positive change.

If all goes well, we might hope for a really measurable major impact on the functioning of the community and on its economic, social, psychological, and political development after about a decade has passed and perhaps in the most successful cases in a few years less.

How long should it take before the CDC demonstrates that success has been so great that it ought to go out of business—and does so?

Some CDCs will fall by the wayside after one, two, three or more years—not through great success, but through failure of one kind or another, either of the CDC, the people of the community, or of the federal government in not supporting it adequately. On the success side, 15 years seems to be the minimum time, and 20 to 30 years is a more likely period in which to hope for so much development in the community, or other changes so great, that a highly successful CDC would be needed no longer. It seems unlikely that such total changes in the ghetto environment could occur in less than two to three decades, and some CDCs might endure and continue to make important contributions for even longer periods.

We must not repeat in the United States our post-World War II mistakes with Latin America, Asia, and Africa, when both our taxpayers and the leaders of some of those poor countries were led to believe that development might be obtainable in a few years or a decade, quickly and cheaply, with a bit of outside capital and a lot of technical assistance. We should have learned by now that development is a slow, tedious process because it is economic; that it cannot be imported but must instead grow up within a country or community; that outside technical assistance sometimes does more harm than good, and at best it can only make a marginal contribution and then only when it is wisely used; and that sizable amounts of outside capital will be needed over a considerable period of time.

FOOTNOTES

[1] For more information on the nature and origins of community development corporations, see the Twentieth Century Fund Task Force Report, *Community Development Corporations: New Hope for the Inner City* (171), and especially the detailed history and analysis of CDCs by Geoffrey Faux published by the Twentieth Century Fund in the same volume. A directory of the larger CDCs is available from the Center for Community Economic Development, 56 Boylston Street, Cambridge, Massachusetts.

[2] For further discussion of ghetto business start-up problems, see Michael Brower and Doyle Little, "White Help for Black Business," *Harvard Business Review* (May-June 1970).

*Geoffrey Faux**

POLITICS AND BUREAUCRACY IN COMMUNITY CONTROLLED ECONOMIC DEVELOPMENT

A basic dilemma for those who have been struggling with community-controlled economic development programs is that government support is essential, but the bureaucracy that accompanies such support often dooms the program to failure.

There are three essential ingredients to effective economic development in poverty areas:

(1) *social investments*, which require government, usually federal, resources
(2) *community control*, which requires local organization
(3) *business organization*, which requires freedom from bureaucratic constraints.

*Geoffrey Faux was a fellow of the Kennedy School of Public Administration, Howard University during the 1970-71 academic year and prior to that was acting head of the Economic Development division at OEO. Reprinted with permission, from a symposium Community Economic Development appearing in *Law and Contemporary Problems* (Volume 36, No. 2, p. 277, 1971) published by the Duke University School of Law, Durham, North Carolina. Copyright, 1971 by Duke University.

The ghettos, barrios, and poverty-stricken rural areas of this country are poor areas for investment. Their labor forces are not competitive, their management talent is thin, and in urban ghettos, physical safety is uncertain. Furthermore, the resident population is often black or Mexican-American which in itself is an obstacle to attracting white-controlled investment. Effective economic development of these areas requires that someone cover the costs of developing the labor force and management, of providing for the organization of community support and ownership, and for making long-term investments to improve the economic infrastructure of an impoverished area. Only when these largely social investments make the area and its institutions attractive places in which to invest will private sector funds flow. Since these investments benefit society as a whole (higher tax revenues, lower welfare costs, and so on), society as a whole should pay for them.

Public investment alone, however, is not a sufficient condition for the economic development of poverty areas. Experience with domestic programs over the past decade shows that the benefits of a program flow primarily to those who control it. With some temporary exceptions, Urban Renewal, War on Poverty, Manpower Training, and Model Cities programs have been put in the hands of local politicians and social scientists who have been the primary beneficiaries. If the social investment necessary to stimulate poverty area economies is to be effective in helping poor residents, poor residents must control it. Only they have the motivation to insure that benefits flow in their direction. To be of lasting value for the poor, economic development must be self-development.

To public investment and community control must be added a third item: the set of techniques and organizational forms that have proven effective in producing economic development in the private sector. Organizational effectiveness requires freedom from entangling bureaucratic red tape and interference. The great advantage private businesses have over government institutions is the freedom to act decisively in their own interests. A developer must be able to take immediate advantage of sudden opportunities that cannot wait for approval from myriad bureaucratic chieftains. A piece of land may become available, and it must be bought immediately or be lost forever; a chance to invest in a good business having cash flow problems may appear and disappear within a few days; a talented potential manager must be offered a job when he becomes available or he will go elsewhere.

FREEDOM VERSUS ACCOUNTABILITY

A natural tension exists between those who finance and those who manage. Any financier, public or private, requires some degree of control to assure that funds are used as intended, while any business organization is concerned with having as much freedom as possible.

If financing comes from the public sector, the tension increases because of the natural tendencies of bureaucracies towards caution and delay. In order to protect himself from being held personally accountable, the bureaucrat spreads the risk through systems of coordination and multiple review of decisions. Where everyone is responsible for a decision, no one is responsible for it. Thus delay, obstruction, and interference ensue.

The power to delay, to obstruct, and to interfere is directly related to the power of the program's beneficiaries or constituency. The private contractors who deal with the Defense Department, the farmers who deal with the Agriculture Department, the banks which deal with the Federal Reserve Board, the airlines which deal with the Federal Aviation Agency or the Civil Aeronautics Board all experience a level of bureaucratic frustration that is minimal compared to that of poor people who deal with the local welfare department, or the community organizations which deal with the Office of Economic Opportunity (OEO) or the Model Cities program.

The Defense Department is more responsive to the needs of its contractors than OEO is to its grantees, not so much because defense contractors have the power to override Defense Department decisions, but because the defense contractors have the power to defend Defense Department decisions. People who form the permanent labor force of a government agency generally identify with its constituency. As the constituency grows in importance, promotions and status rewards flow faster to the government officials responsible for dealing with that constituency. Therefore, an important function of an organized constituency is the protection of its interests through protection of the bureaucracy that is fighting for its interests. The constituency must constantly watch to see that the bureaucracy continues to protect those interests. Where the constituency does not play this role, the bureaucracy will try to protect itself, sometimes at the expense of its own constituency.

THE ANTIPOVERTY CONSTITUENCY

The history of the War on Poverty is an example of a weak constituency that could neither protect its bureaucracy nor prevent its bureaucracy from exercising self-protective devices of delay and interference. The creation of the Model Cities which placed the program firmly in the hands of the mayors in 1966 was the handwriting on the wall. In 1967, the power of the constituency to defend itself against local governments was tested and found deficient with the passage of the "Green Amendment" to the Economic Opportunity Act. This amendment gave local governments the power to control community action procedures, thus creating a dramatic expansion in federal rules and regulations as well as a marked increase in the exercise of government power over recipients of antipoverty money.

The crumbling of the antipoverty constituency's power over the bureaucracy caused many people to look for new means of financing independent programs. The possibility of generating independent funds for antipoverty programs was a partial reason for the attractiveness of community-based economic development. Frustrated antipoverty workers grasped at the notion that profits from economic development programs could generate funds for social programs. From the same frustrated sources came the idea that the private sector could finance such development with a little bit of prodding from Uncle Sam. This idea was encouraged by both the Johnson and Nixon administrations whose budgets were being depleted by the Viet Nam War.

Political weakness could not, however, be wished away. The political failure of the antipoverty constituency also led to a search for new allies and for a path that would skirt mounting congressional opposition to OEO programs. A partnership between big business and the impoverished community financed through incentives which would not require annual congressional appropriations was the cornerstone of the Community Self-Determination Act introduced in the Congress in 1968. The bill had many defects, but most liberals who opposed it missed the point that it was an attempt to continue to finance community organization in an increasingly conservative atmosphere.

The first OEO-funded community-based economic development programs quickly became vulnerable to political pressure and to the increasing power of the bureaucracy in relation to the community organizations they were dealing with. Crawfordville Enterprises in Georgia, the Southwest Alabama Farmers Cooperative Association, and the Harlem Commonwealth Council all were subject to political pressures and bureaucratic abuse. The first two, being in the South where the political power of the minority antipoverty interests was weakest, were particularly battered. Demands that the projects become self-sustaining in unreasonable periods of time, changes in directives from Washington, visits by consultants and OEO staff members each with conflicting authority and advice, added to the initial burden of being black-controlled projects in hostile Southern surroundings.

The history of OEO's Special Impact Program illustrates the ways in which the power of bureaucracy can expand with crippling effect on a program where the general constituency is weak. It also illustrates the importance of the careful cultivation of local political alliances to the process of community based economic development.

THE SPECIAL IMPACT PROGRAM

The Special Impact Program was written into the Economic Opportunity Act under Title I-D in 1966 in order to support a specific economic development project in the Bedford-Stuyvesant section of Brooklyn. The late Senator Robert F. Kennedy was the principal motivating force behind the amendment and the project. To finance the program, Senator Kennedy and Senator Jacob Javits introduced an amendment to Title I of the Economic Opportunity Act.

The Kennedy-Javits Amendment to the Economic Opportunity Act authorized "special impact programs" for urban areas with high concentrations of low-income people. Programs were to be designed "to arrest tendencies toward dependency, chronic unemployment, and rising community tensions." They were to be carried out in poor neighborhoods, and they were to be of "sufficient size and scope to have an appreciable impact."

The language of Title I-D was intentionally imprecise. The structure of the program implied that decisions should be made at the local level and that the business/community alliance should be as free as possible to respond to needs and opportunities.

Partially reflecting the desire of Kennedy and his staff to keep the program out of the hands of the local Community Action Program and the New York City bureaucracy, the senate committee saw to it that the program was administered initially by the Department of Labor.

The Special Impact Program was based upon the following assumptions:

(1) The War on Poverty, particularly its major component, the Community Action Program, was insufficiently concerned with jobs and economic development.

(2) The squabbling and politicking that inevitably accompanies a program run by city hall prevents accomplishment of the program.

(3) The approach of the War on Poverty was piecemeal, and a comprehensive strategy was required. "We must grab the web whole," Kennedy said in a 1966 speech on poverty.

(4) The business community must play a major role in solving poverty problems.[1]

Robert Kennedy perceived, as did Lyndon Johnson afterwards, that the Viet Nam War would drain away the funds that had been promised for major domestic programs, and he wanted the private sector to take up the slack. In addition, the presence of influential businessmen in a ghetto development program might free the community organizations from dependence on local politicians. The Special Impact Program embodied an alliance of business and ghetto residents and minimized the influence of city and antipoverty bureaucracies.

This alliance was reflected in the structure of the Bedford-Stuyvesant program. Two separate corporations were set up to run the project. The Restoration Corporation, made up of 26 leaders chosen from the Bedford Stuyvesant community, and the Development and Services Corporation composed of 12 white establishment figures. In addition to Kennedy himself and his fellow New York senator, Jacob Javits, the Development and Services board included Thomas Watson of IBM, C. Douglas Dillon, former secretary of the Treasury, William Paley of CBS, George Moore of the First National City Bank and Benno Schmidt of J. A. Whitney Company.

Twenty-five million dollars was appropriated for the Special Impact Program in fiscal year 1967. Of this sum, $6.9 million went to the Bedford-Stuyvesant program, and the rest was scattered in various projects throughout the country as a supplement to the Labor Department's Concentrated Employment Program.

Such a scattering of funds was not what the Senate Committee had intended. The committee criticized the Labor Department in its report on the 1967 Amendments to the Economic Opportunity Act and strengthened the language of the legislation to eliminate a special focus on youth employment, to concentrate on economic development programs, and to include rural areas in the program. The report stated:

> "Experience of the first year's operation demonstrates that successful program operation, including the participation of business, requires and depends on the utmost cooperation of community residents. That cooperation, in view of the committee, will best be achieved through effective and substantial participation of the residents in program decisions, responsibility, and benefits. Community and community-based corporations, which have demonstrated their potential utility as vehicles for such participation should be encouraged by the Secretary of Labor to undertake sponsorship of programs under this part."

There was great resistance to implement Title I-D within the Johnson administration. Part of the resistance was programmatic. Officials in the Office of Economic Opportunity and the Labor Department wanted to concentrate on education and manpower training programs which would encourage the poor to disperse from impoverished areas, and they felt that the development of inner city ghettos and poor rural areas would defeat that purpose. Part of the resistance was political. The White House under Lyndon Johnson was not anxious to build up a program with Robert Kennedy's stamp on it.

At the same time, some middle-level bureaucrats in the Office of Economic Opportunity had developed and analyzed the ills of the antipoverty program, and their findings paralleled those of Kennedy. They concluded that growing interest in black ghettos for building up community-controled economic institutions could be a constructive movement. They thought that ghetto development could be a surer stepping stone to social and economic integration than could an instant "dispersal" approach. They argued that dispersal as a short-term solution was neither politically realistic nor economically sound, and concentration on dispersal was becoming a political excuse for not financing the immediate, practical needs of the poor. Despite the importance of the "dispersal and development" issue to urban strategy, the only national political dialogue on the subject occurred during the Kennedy-McCarthy television debate preceding the 1968 California primary. Kennedy argued for the development strategy.

After a great deal of bureaucratic tugging and hauling, the fiscal year 1968 Special Impact appropriation was finally split up among four federal agencies: the Departments of Labor, Commerce, and Agriculture, and OEO. OEO received the smallest part of the pie—$1.6 million out of $20 million—to implement the ideas of some of its staff.

The OEO program aimed to promote economic development of the poverty area under the control of indigenous institutions. It was based on the assumption that, if institutions were to evolve, they had to have control over resources, that is, real power. Without such power the institutions could not attract the talented albeit cynical and alienated males who held the key to strengthening ghetto life.

The emphasis on alienated males led to another assumption—the election process was not necessarily the best means of establishing leadership. Elections under the Community Action Program had produced disappointing turnouts. People were elected to CAP and neighborhood boards with less than five percent of eligible voters participating. Many boards were dominated by women and members of the clergy who tended to have a strong social welfare orientation. The young alienated males did not participate.

The economic assumptions of the program were also based on the experience of the past. The OEO staffers felt that attempts to induce existing businesses to move into the poverty areas had failed and would fail because of the unattractive economic environment and racial fear. They also concluded that economic development could not be built on the small marginal ghetto entrepreneur because of the need for planning and for large interrelated projects that could make an impact on the poor population.

The OEO staffers did not attempt to replicate the Bedford-Stuyvesant model. They felt that in most places such a formal partnership would result in the "community" partner being the junior one, which would restrain its growth and development into a strong institution. In addition, the unusual circumstances of having a powerful and prestigious senator who put time and energy into a program in order to get just the right balance between forces and personalities could not be replicated in many other places, if at all.

Rather than have the federal government or the local government attempt to affect the business/community alliance, the OEO program left it to the community organization itself. As a requirement of the grant, the community organization had to negotiate its own arrangement with the local business community. The program was to build upon existing neighborhood institutions, not set up new ones. The degree to which the community organization had the respect of the local business community would serve as a measure of its strength and ability to run an effective economic development program.

The grants were to be made directly from Washington to avoid the multiple levels of bureaucracy in OEO regional offices as well as in the local community action agencies (CAA's). The grants themselves called for maximum flexibility and could be used for seed/equity money in the establishment of businesses and housing projects.

The question of political acceptability was left to the strength and political abilities of the community organization. No formal approval rights were given either to the local government or to the local CAA. However, it was understood that the local CAA would be told of the program in advance, and it would be up to the CDC to draw up sufficient political strength to overcome any objections.

In June of 1968 the OEO program began with a grant of $1.6 million (the total OEO allocation) to the Hough Area Development Corporation in Cleveland. In the winter of 1968-69, Bureau of the Budget officials under the out-going Johnson administration determined that the OEO program (as opposed to the Fiscal Year 1968 Agriculture, Commerce and Labor programs) was the only one that met the intentions of Title I-D and recommended that the entire program be run by OEO. The incoming Nixon administration concurred, and the Special Impact Program became the first and only program to be "spun in" to OEO. OEO spent $11.4 million in Title-I-D funds on community development corporations in 1969, and peaked with $31 million in Fiscal Year 1971* ($39 million was projected for FY 1974).

The freedom and flexibility of community development corporations financed by the Special Impact Program became restricted as a result of three separate, but interrelated forces:
(1) political pressures arising from local opposition to specific projects in specific localities
(2) bureaucratic pressures arising from the natural tendency of the bureaucracy to protect itself by delay and obstructionism
(3) ideological pressures arising from the basic philosophy of the administration representatives who controlled the program.

POLITICAL PRESSURES

In April, 1969, three months after the Nixon administration had taken over the Office of Economic Opportunity, a Special Impact grant was made to the Foundation for Community Development, a nonprofit corporation in Durham, North Carolina. The grant was intended for the use of United Durham, Inc., a profit-making CDC which the Foundation for Community Development had helped establish. The grant raised a political storm among Republicans in North Carolina because of the presence on the staff of the nonprofit corporation of a controversial "black militant."

The bureaucrat in charge of the Special Impact Program was called to the White House to explain. After listening to the rationale for the grant, a prominent White House aide reportedly said, "Oh, I understand, all right. But now you have to understand that the South is very important to this administration. I know that OEO money had been used to start riots and elect Democrats, and it is going to stop. The President wants that grant killed."

The CDC had the involvement of a number of highly respected businessmen, black and white. It was however in the South and was aimed at putting almost a million dollars of investment capital under the control of poor black people who were not part of the Republican constituency. And where there is no constituency there is no power. For example, a White House assistant who was the only black on the staff had personally intervened with the OEO staff to support the grant while it was being considered. However, after the political storm broke, he could not be reached for weeks by those who were trying to save the program.

The grant was not killed, primarily because of the determination of some of the OEO staff to save it. However, it was held up for about a year. Legally, the grant could not be terminated "for cause," but the Republican administration did not want to release funds to a project so clearly in conflict with its Southern Strategy. Finally, as a result of the intervention of a white Durham businessman, OEO permitted the release of funds for a specific business project on condition that the grant not be channeled through the controversial nonprofit organization.

The delay was costly. A site for the location of a modular housing business had to be given up. Committed orders for two hundred units of housing were lost, and a potential manager had to be kept on the payroll. It cost the organization approximately $20,000 of scarce foundation money just to negotiate with OEO.

Political pressure took another twist in Cleveland where the Hough Area Development Corporation (HADC) was attacked by the *Cleveland Plain Dealer* for what the newspaper strongly implied was a mishandling of public funds. While the attack focused on the CDC, the obvious target was black Mayor Carl Stokes of Cleveland. The *Plain Dealer's* case turned out to be so weak that a number of prominent citizens and businessmen came to HADC's defense.

However, HADC's funds were frozen by the OEO, and negotiations between the Small Business Administration and HADC over the financing of a shopping center were halted. After an exhaustive investigation and "evaluation" by the OEO and the General Accounting Office (the FBI and the McClellan Committee had previously investigated HADC), funds were released, but with a significant tightening in the power of the government to control program decisions.

Where community development programs survived political pressures without much damage to their programs, they had strong establishment allies. One program in the South was funded by the Nixon administration because a major corporation and its president were involved. Before the corporation became involved the program was considered too controversial by Democratic appointees. The program had not changed, but the political support had.

Bureaucratic Pressures

In many ways, bureaucracy-generated pressures on CDC freedom were more damaging than were political pressures. Bureaucratic pressures pushed against the entire program rather than against specific projects. They affected the day-to-day workings of the community development corporations and, in the long run, had a great effect upon the performance of CDCs.

The freedom of the first OEO Special Impact grantee, the Hough Area Development Corporation, initially was to be limited only minimally. Accounting and auditing procedures were to be established, evaluation visits were to be made, and reports on the progress of the program were to be filed. In addition, a number of legislative prohibitions, such as those prohibiting the use of federal funds for political activity, had to be observed.

The first issue to arise concerned the degree to which CDCs would be able to make independent investment decisions. The designers of the program proposed that CDCs have the freedom to make any investment decision they chose without approval from OEO as long as the decisions met some general criteria as to benefits going to the poor and disadvantaged, and as long as the CDC could give reasonable evidence that the business or housing venture's feasibility had been established. Accountability was to be determined by a periodic review of the program. The plan was denied by the acting director of the agency because it did not fulfill OEO's responsibility toward public funds. As a result OEO insisted upon approval rights on all investment decisions.

There were no serious restrictions on the freedom of the Hough Area Development Corporation in the first grant. However, by the winter of the following fiscal year (1968-69), the program had gained some prominence in OEO, and the noose of bureaucracy had begun to tighten.

There were many hands on the rope: lawyers who lacked precedents, administrators who saw a need for a multitude of forms and procedures and who wanted the rights to approve anything going into "their territory," and researchers and planners concerned that CDCs should produce simple programs that could be evaluated easily.

Lawyers

Some of the lawyers' problems were understandable. OEO had been set up to provide the poor with services, not to give them independent economic power. Conventional service programs, such as recreation or manpower training, did not generate permanent income: producing assets would be free from federal control after the 24 month grant period was over. How could OEO be sure that the poor community would always benefit from the successful investments made with the federal funds?

The question was an important one. Assuming that a community development corporation was responsive to the needs and interests of the poor area to begin with, what was to assure that it would always be so? The argument centered on projects with self-selected boards. Despite the history of meaningless elections, the poverty lawyers were satisfied that elected boards were always "representative."

Out of the arguments and discussion over this point, there emerged the notion that a CDC had a choice as to how it would be accountable for the income and assets it controlled after the federal grant had expired. On the one hand, the CDC could establish a structure whereby the board would be chosen in a neighborhood election or by future low-income shareholders. On the other hand, OEO could retain the right in the future to step in and take over the CDC if OEO felt that the CDC was no longer responsive. All but one of the CDCs with self-selected boards chose the first arrangement.

In negotiations between OEO and the CDCs over the CDC structures, OEO lawyers postulated every conceivable contingency which in turn required that there be a provision to counteract it. The result was often a legal monstrosity that was impossible for most poor people to comprehend, much less utilize if they had to. The negotiations over the structure of one grant took more than six months to complete after the grant had been made.

Of course, precedents exist for federal investment grants to be made without going to such length. The subsidizing of private business in the name of national interest is rooted in the nation's economic history. Railroad, shipbuilding, and airline subsidies, land grants to farmers, and tax subsidies for oilmen and real estate developers, are but a few examples of the use of public funds to achieve social goals through private institutions. But there are no influential interest groups to argue the cause of the poor, no congressional committees eager to please a powerless constituency.

Government lawyers often take for themselves the responsibility for preventing agency decisions that may be politically controversial. After the Durham episode, the General Counsel's office began to monitor the program more closely, often getting into program areas in which they had no competence. One such instance occurred in connection with a CDC project in Chicago. The proposal called for the renovation of a four block area in North Lawndale for a commercial and housing program. The proposal was developed by a community organization assisted by a number of established Chicago banks and businesses. This was one of the most competently written proposals that OEO had received. During the last two weeks of the fiscal year, however, the project almost fell through when one OEO lawyer demanded that the precise calculations involved in projecting what would eventually be a $10 million program be explained in detail. A half-dozen experts had to fly in from Chicago to explain such points as the projected costs of maintaining the white lines in the parking lot over a 20-year period.

Such absurdities and indignities would have never been suffered by a business applicant. In fact, only when the nature and depth of business involvement in the Chicago project became apparent did the politically sensitive OEO General Counsel's office back down.

Administrators

The increase in the number of forms that accompanied the growth of the Special Impact Program was simply a special case of a familiar bureaucratic phenomenon. Each week the program staff was notified of another obscure agency regulation or Bureau of the Budget request which required another form.

At first the program staff consciously resisted. However, as the program came under political criticism, the bureaucrats in charge of the program had to spend their time and energy in other battles, and the forms and complicated procedures grew relentlessly. When complaints were made, those responsible for the increase in paperwork would reiterate their devotion to principles of efficiency and speed. But each form seemed to have a reason—although all together they were an irrational burden, and they continued to pile up.

This paper snowstorm had two results. First, it added to the things a CDC had to do in order to get and to keep a grant. Failure to fill out each form and otherwise fulfill the new requirements put the CDC in violation of its agreement with OEO. Therefore, the CDC spent more staff time filling out forms and less time doing economic development. The second result was delay. Failure to fill out all the forms properly and in the right order meant that funds could not be released. These delays were in addition to those caused by an overworked staff which had to approve every CDC investment decision.

The delays in approving projects lengthened from weeks to months. CDCs made business deals on which they had to renege because OEO could not process all the papers in time. The CDCs experienced a serious erosion of their credibility among neighborhoods and local business communities.

Jurisdictional disputes were perhaps inevitable. Regional offices wanted the right to approve and monitor all programs in their regions—another layer of bureaucracy. The state Offices of Economic Opportunity also wanted to approve programs. Topping it all off were interagency committees, administrative offices, advisors to the director, and "liaison" offices.

In most cases the result was more delay. However, in some instances the programs and their objectives were arbitrarily changed and even thwarted completely. In the rural South, for example, one project was stopped and several seriously hampered by the opposition of the local community action agencies which preferred that the poor be denied a project rather than have that project controlled by an independent organization.

The first grant to the Hough Area Development Corporation required the approval of three separate offices within OEO. Two years later, the number was ten and rising.

Social Scientists

The program was also subject to pressures from that part of the bureaucracy interested in research and planning. Primarily the people involved were social scientists who were spending a few years at OEO away from the university or from the RAND Corporation.[2] Their complaint was that the objectives of the program did not fit into neat categories. Employment was not, for example, the chief goal. It was one of several goals which included developing the economic base of the poverty area, spreading ownership and control of enterprises, and developing community institutions.

Quantitive analysis, which the planners felt should be the major determinant of a program's value, could not handle such multiple objectives and interrelated goals. Although such goals reflected the needs of the community as seen by the community, they could not easily fit an academic frame of reference for Washington planners. The program planning and budget system required simple "inputs" and simple "outputs". There is nothing simple about organizing people for economic development or anything else in a place like Hough or Bedford-Stuyvesant.

At OEO, the planners had great influence on the budget. CDCs were pressured to concentrate on projects that maximized one goal. Thus such a project as a combination shopping center/public housing project in Cleveland, which was the single most important project insofar as the Hough community was concerned, became much harder to justify quantitatively than a project to create a few unskilled jobs with no future and no impact upon the community. The multiple benefits of a shopping center/public housing project on employment, ownership, community services, and the economic base were hard to quantify; it was easy to quantify the number of people passing through a training program.

Another result was a narrowing of the concept of economic development. Rather than a broad comprehensive program such as that originally envisaged by Robert Kennedy for Bedford-Stuyvesant, and by those who put together the Hough Area Development Corporation, in some areas the Special Impact Program became closer to the small business-oriented "minority capitalism" program of the Nixon administration. The concept of using public funds for basic investment in the infrastructure gave way to an objective of creating individual small businesses, *which had been rejected originally by the designers of the program as doomed to failure.* But individual businesses were easier to count.

The final and politically most tragic limitation imposed by the social scientists was the insistance that all Special Impact Programs be judged on their direct impact upon the poor, *as defined by OEO*, whose definitions were kept deliberately low for political reasons.[3] Although this limitation made some sense as a device for maximizing the delivery of *services* to those most in need, it was a destructive notion in an economic development program which required the involvement of many skilled individuals. Moreover, a large portion of the key target population—adult males—could not be drawn into a program with arbitrarily low income standards.

The demand that the benefits and advantages be limited to such a small segment of the population also defeated the notion of developing community institutions, and it had the effect of limiting the constituency for the program. The insistance of the social scientists/planners that OEO funds be used only for the poor in the interests of program efficiency, combined with the decision to keep the income definition unreasonably low, cost the poor and their programs the chance to broaden their base of support.

Ideological Pressures

The ideological pressures on the Special Impact Program reflected the way in which OEO's leadership looked at the problem of poverty. While these pressures had political implications, their source was not so much specific political problems as a desire to operate programs according to a general political philosophy.

In the last year of the Johnson administration, the ideological opposition to the Special Impact Program centered upon two points:

(1) Development programs, particuarly in the cities, would lead to racial separatism.

(2) The development of businesses would necessarily mean concentration on the nonpoor.

As previously indicated, the designers of the program had argued that development would lead to integration and not separatism. The second point was answered by arguing that the benefits of an economic development program in large part was a function of who controlled the program. If the poor controlled it, they would benefit. The differences between those who designed the program and the OEO leadership were not completely resolved, but the ideological concerns of the latter were recognized by the designers as reasonable concerns and were addressed with sufficient seriousness to gain approval for a limited number of projects.

The new Republican OEO Director and his staff brought an entirely new set of objections to the program. Shortly after he assumed the directorship, a report to Donald Rumsfeld written by one of his assistants recommended that the program be terminated immediately and all outstanding funds be returned to the Treasury. Another report to Rumsfeld stated that the primary question was whether or not the program *was consistent with the Protestant ethic*. Rumsfeld declared that making such grants without very tight controls was irresponsible. "What happens," he asked, "if ten years from now the Black Panthers are chosen by the stockholders to run one of these CDCs? How are you going to prevent that?"

The program staff replied that businesses could not be run effectively under government controls. But that argument was brushed aside. "They" were using "our" money and "we" had to control its use. Thus it was that the party of business, advocate of local control and freedom from government regulation, gave the final shove which pushed the Special Impact Program into the bureaucratic quicksand.

The lawyers set to work to create still more restrictions. Ironically, it was a point the lawyers previously had insisted upon, electoral response to the neighborhood, that most concerned Republicans. But there was no attempt to defend the program from the General Counsel's office. The theme was *control*—control over staff, control over investment decision, control over strategies.

The concern for controls, however, was selective. Those projects which had strong establishment support, such as the original Kennedy program in Bedford-Stuyvesant, were not questioned. In fact, so that Rumsfeld might have something to "deliver" on a trip to New York City, he announced the $10 million refunding of the Bedford-Stuyvesant program before the basic documents had been approved for reasonableness or legality.

Another example of the selective concern for accountability for federal monies was the creation of the Opportunity Funding Corporation (OFC). The OFC was the creation of Theodore Cross, author of a book on black capitalism who was hired by Rumsfeld to come up with innovative business-oriented programs.[4] Cross proposed that the OFC be formed by a small group of financiers and businessmen and be supported by OEO for the purpose of experimenting with new ways to encourage investment in poverty areas. While no one could quarrel with the general goals of the program, none of the ideas were spelled out in detail. Still Rumsfeld agreed to terminate the entire CDC program and to use the funds for the OFC, sight unseen, programs undefined, and relationship to the poor unclear. The important thing to Rumsfeld was that the OFC would be run by reliable, white businessmen. So anxious was Rumsfeld to shift resources from control by the poor to control by the rich that he announced the OFC program to the press before it had been reviewed for legality.

The Opportunity Funding Corporation was modified only after the community development corporations themselves organized to fight the plan and several members of Congress joined in their protest. The monies for the support of OFC that were to come out of Title I-D were decreased considerably. Two CDC leaders, one of whom was a Special Impact grantee, were added to the board.

Despite the Republican party's rhetoric against federal controls, particularly economic controls, OEO managers favored central state control for programs in which the poor participated. Freedom and independence were reserved for the higher social orders.

THE NEED FOR AN EFFECTIVE CONSTITUENCY

The history of the Special Impact Program illustrates that the tension between a community economic development organization's need for freedom and the bureaucracy's need for accountability are directly related to the political support that the former can muster. Individual community development corporations successfully defended themselves against political and bureaucratic pressures only when they were able to secure influential allies. The Bedford-Stuyvesant program with its built-in alliances with the business community has been most successful. The Hough Area Development Corporation's program was saved by supporters in Cleveland's business and political community. Where such allies have been absent, the going has been much rougher, particularly in the rural South and in Appalachia.

Most support has come from the business community. Thus the original hypothesis of the Kennedy-Javits Amendment, which established that businessmen could act as effective guards against political and bureaucratic interference, has proven correct. However, business support is of uncertain stability. It is a commonplace observation that as the memory of urban riots fade and business conditions deteriorate, the interest and enthusiasm of businessmen in assisting community organizations begin to sag. The assumption of many that the business community would provide massive resources to develop rural slums and urban ghettos has not proven correct.

Businessmen can not be expected to give the kind of political attention to the needs of poor people that they give to their own needs. It has been estimated that it will cost the U.S. Treasury $6 hundred million to rescue the Lockheed Corporation from its mismanagement of the C5-A Program. This figure—to help *one corporation* recover from its own mistakes on *one project*—is more than ten times the total federal resources devoted to supporting community-based economic development in the entire nation.

The private business sector has been of help primarily in the large urban areas where local self-help organizations pose no immediate threat to the establishment. The histories of both the Community Action Program and the Special Impact Program have demonstrated how thin the support is for social and economic change on the part of those who control the destinies of small towns and cities and rural areas. When the relationship between the economic facts of poverty and the structure of political influence becomes clear, the mere existence of a semi-independent organization with the responsibility to "eliminate poverty" is enough to cause uneasiness at city hall and the county courthouse.

The rhetoric of community-based economic development often tends to emphasize the conservative aspects of self-help. And indeed, the notion of people organizing for their own economic improvement is in the best traditions of American business. But it would be a fatal mistake for those who were interested in strengthening the movement for community economic development to forget that, on the national level, their cause is linked to the cause of antipoverty efforts in general. The notion that political conservatives who oppose social welfare programs would support local control and economic independence for the poor and disadvantaged has been tested for three years by the Nixon administration, and it has failed. Community economic development organizations will gain the scale of resources and degree of freedom they need only as part of a reconstituted and revitalized antipoverty constituency which crosses racial as well as programmatic lines.

To begin playing this role, community economic development organizations will have to organize themselves. Even now, most of these organizations define themselves nationally in terms of their financiers—rather than in terms of what they themselves do. A network that cuts across such lines is needed to share experiences and to provide mutual protection and reinforcement.

Efforts also should be made by those concerned to encourage the expansion of the community development corporation idea to groups that thus far have not been much involved, such as the white urban poor and near-poor. To the extent that these groups are more concerned with *community development* than with *economic development*, it may require a broadening of the concept of community economic development. As the history of the Special Impact Program shows, a social scientist's concern for definitional purity can be detrimental to the building of a political constituency. If efforts at community control of an area's economic development are to be taken seriously, they must be seen as applicable to disadvantaged people generally and not simply as a program just for minority people or minority businessmen.

Outside alliances should be maintained and strengthened. At present, businessmen will play an important role in any economic development program. But other players must also be drawn into the game, including the more progressive elements in the labor movement who in some areas (Los Angeles is a primary example.) have given financial support to community economic development organizations.

A Washington consultant with long experience in the economic development field recently noted that when people come to Washington to lobby for urban programs, they concentrate on such programs as education, welfare, and housing. The issue of economic development programs rarely comes up. Therefore, senators and congressmen assume that it is not very important.

If community economic development is to claim public funds, community organizations will have to talk to congressmen and senators and those who influence them. And if community organizations are to use economic development funds to respond to the needs of officialdom in Washington or city hall, the process of building political strength can not begin too soon.

FOOTNOTES

[1] Kennedy and his staff presumably also hoped that by championing the role of business in solving urban problems, the hostility to him among businessmen would be somewhat moderated.

[2] In fairness it should be pointed out that another group of social scientists also primarily interested in research were the prime movers in establishing the Special Impact Program in OEO.

[3] As of this writing the OEO poverty line for a family of four is one-half the income estimated by the U.S. Bureau of Labor Statistics as minimal for health and decency.

[4] See David K. Banner and Samuel Doctors, "Creative Inducements on Private Investment in the Minority Community," in this volume, for a discussion of the OFC concept.

David K. Banner

THE WEST SIDE ORGANIZATION

The West Side Community Development Corporation (WSCDC), in Chicago, was incorporated in February, 1969, as a nonprofit corporation to sponsor minority entrepreneurship, educate residents about economic needs, and seek financial and technical expertise from outside sources.[1] This corporation serves a geographic area of 20 square miles with 400,000 people. The first goal of WSCDC is profit generation: it plans to use business profits from sponsor firms for the economic development of the neighborhood and its residents. In other words, the income will be used to provide capital for other resident-owned enterprises for the improved community services.

WSCDC is commonly called "The Hand" because it is essentially an umbrella agency for five West Side groups which consist of:

(1) The West Side Organization (WSO), which deals in job placement and welfare grievances, has a Shell Oil gas station franchise, a McDonald's hamburger franchise, and is a co-partner in the West Side Community Paper Stock Company.

(2) The Garfield Organization, whose specialty is political education.

(3) Student Afro-American group, specialists in neighborhood health services and owner/operators of a hot dog restaurant.

(4) The Egyptian Cobras, Inc., a former street gang turned welfare organizer, which has a Standard Oil gas station franchise.

(5) The Conservative Vice Lords, Inc., another former gang, which now operates the Teen Town Restaurant, a security guard service, a pool hall, two ice cream franchises, and a fashion shop.

While a review of the organization and strategy of the other WSCDC groups would be illuminating, this case will concentrate on the activities of the West Side Organization.

Unlike some other black community organizations which are often led by women, Chicago's WSO is run by men, and the organization is not very popular outside the community. The group's main focus is jobs and welfare. The organization operates in Chicago's famous first ward, Al Capone's old headquarters, where the crime syndicate still runs a protection racket. There are one hundred thousand people in the area that WSO considers its neighborhood. About 80 percent are black and 15 percent are Spanish. Of the total population, about 25 percent are unemployed, and one-third of the families are on public assistance.

In 1964, five clergymen and theological students were sent by the Urban Training Center, the Chicago City Missionary Society and the Meadville Theological Seminary to work on developing a community organization on the Near West Side. Initially, these men thought all that was necessary to help the chronically unemployed in this area was to tour local bars and pool rooms, and interview and find jobs for the individuals they found there. However, the social distance between these "outsiders" and members of the community was so great that their attempts were rebuffed.

Undaunted by this failure, these men sought to secure help from such traditional well-established organizations in the community as labor unions and churches. With the help of these agencies, they formulated a list of 250 unemployed men in the area. Each of these men was invited to an open meeting to discuss conditions in the area. Four men showed up at the meeting—yet another failure. The clergymen were at a loss to explain this rebuff. At the suggestion of the four community residents, eight men (four clergy and the four from the community) decided to live together on a one-to-one basis in the community to give the clergymen a close-in view of the culture and its natural distrust of "outsiders."

With this initial socialization process into the black subculture, the clergy, utilizing the help of the four community people, undertook the task of generating interest in further neighborhood meetings. The size of the group gradually increased as interest was sparked. In the fall of 1964, the group secured an office storefront on West Roosevelt Road. Financed by a grant of several thousand dollars from the Urban Training Center, the office proved an immense help in recruiting new members. However, the problem of being viewed as "neo-colonialists" still remained; a catalyst was needed to solidify and legitimatize the organization.

This catalyst came in the form of a confrontation between WSO and a local laundry which had been practicing discriminatory employment practices by not hiring blacks for other than menial jobs. By demanding that this policy be changed, WSO was thrust into the community limelight. After picketing and negotiating, culminated by a presentation of the case to the Illinois Supreme Court, the laundry acquiesced, agreed to change its policies, and recruited black applicants for all available jobs in consultation with WSO.

This event established WSO as a tough-minded organization able to get results, and people began coming to the storefront to seek help with their problems.

Since these early beginnings, the organization has grown steadily. Most programs of the organization have emerged from staff member evaluations of the most recurrent and urgent requests of community residents. The office is now manned by four key full-time staff members and many part-time volunteers. Some of the achievements of the organization from 1964-1969 include:

(1) processing more than 25,000 job applications and placing more than 1,000 people

(2) reaching an agreement with National Tea Company for employment of community personnel

(3) convincing the Illinois State Employment Service to station personnel to work at WSO

(4) successfully processing 1,300 welfare grievances

(5) instituting basic education in math, reading and typing for community residents

(6) entering into a joint, share-the-profits agreement with Shell Oil Company to operate a gas station in the community which is selling large amounts of "Freedom Gas"

(7) publishing a financially self-sufficient, free newspaper (*West Side Torch*) with a circulation in excess of 40,000.

In July, 1966, West Side residents seeking relief from the oppressive heat turned on a fire hydrant on Roosevelt Road, a few blocks from WSO headquarters. After police closed the hydrant and teenagers reopened it several times, an altercation began. Violence quickly spread throughout the West Side. After the riots, Chicago papers stated that the police had insisted on closing the hydrant (even though they had apparently allowed others in nearby neighborhoods to stay on). The WSO acted as an agent of pacification and as an information source. WSO leaders went into the streets at great personal risk to persuade their fellow citizens to stop the rebellion.

In 1968, on the evening Martin Luther King was assassinated, a crowd of a thousand young blacks gathered outside WSO headquarters, questioning organization leaders as to what shops and businesses in the white suburbs should be burned in retaliation. The leaders of the organization talked the angry crowd out of its mission.

ENVIRONMENT OF WSO

Life in Chicago's West Side is different from that of other sections of the city. The South Side is largely black but many middle class Negroes live there, a factor that distinguishes it from the West Side which is almost all poor and black.[2] It represents a way of life that is unknown to most people who have not lived in a poor black ghetto.

Poverty is endemic to the West Side; in 1969 the median annual family income in the area was $4,000 compared to nearly $7,000 for the city as a whole. Those people making more than $10,000 per year represent only 5 percent of the population as compared with 20 percent for the city as a whole. Approximately 45 percent of the housing units are substandard, compared with 15 percent for the city as a whole.[3] More than one-quarter of the families in the area are on public assistance. Unemployment averages 25 percent of the total population. Schools provide inferior education, machine politicians exploit the people, public services are few and shoddy, and neighborhood-owned businesses are virtually nonexistent. The West Side is an ugly and stagnant place. It is physically unattractive; its people are poor and unhappy, and efforts to improve it have been largely ineffective.

The West Side is geographically distinct; in fact it has often been characterized by residents as an "island ghetto." Based on conversations with WSO leaders, it appears to have few economic, social, or political ties with other sections of the city. Also, as witnessed by the deteriorating environment and large number of welfare recipients, the economic base of the area is rather small. For this reason, one might question the development of "black capitalism" solely in the ghetto since no significant "multiplier effect" may accrue with such a limited money supply. On the other hand, it can be argued that black people can not develop an ethnic pride without the power that comes with material success and control over their own economy. This means the building of a ghetto economy, and that is the goal of the WSO leadership.

ORGANIZATION OF WSO

As stated earlier, the work that led to the establishment of the West Side Organization was initiated by people from outside the community. The beginning efforts were conceived, financed and carried out by Protestant clergymen. There were many people involved in the early organizational activities, but the three prime movers were the Reverends Archie Hargraves, Robert Strom, and Donald Benedict.

Reverend Hargraves is a middle-aged black minister born in North Carolina. Reverend Strom, a white man born in Elyria, Ohio, is the key implementer and critic of Hargraves' theories. It was Strom who went into the West Side, engaged its people, and encouraged them to work with him in developing the concept of WSO. Reverend Benedict, the white executive director of the Community Renewal Society known as the Chicago City Missionary Society at the time WSO was organized, provided most of the financial resources necessary for the organizational work.

However, four black men (Chester Robinson, William Darden, William Clark and John Crawford) became the operational leaders of WSO. Robinson was at the original 1964 meeting with the clergymen, and the other three men joined soon thereafter.

In 1971, WSO's program was guided by a cadre of 12 men from the neighborhood; the 4 full-time staff members (Chester Robinson, executive director of WSO, William Darden, William Clark, and John Crawford) and 8 volunteer organizers. Metropolitan Consulting Associates Inc. (MCA), headed by Bob Strom, provides technical assistance for the organization.

The Leaders of WSO

Chester Robinson, executive director, was born into a large rural family in Tucker, Arkansas, in 1931, and first came to Chicago's West Side in 1933. He attended various vocational schools through the eighth grade. During his teens, he participated in juvenile gang activity and engaged in petty thievery. Arrests and convictions resulting from illegal activities caused him to spend most of the late 1950s in jail.

During his last period of imprisonment, he completed two years of high school, attended barber college, and read extensively. After his release, he "went straight," working as a barber before joining the West Side Organization as a full-time worker in late 1964.

Important in the organization from its beginning, he is presently its executive director. In this role, he has had extensive dealings with many of the most important public and private organizations in Chicago and has developed impressive skills of negotiation and administration.

William Darden, assistant director, was born in 1935 into a small family in Franklin, Tennessee. He started school late and lost a year because of illness, but was finally graduated from high school at the age of 20. Darden did well in school, earning an overall B average and, coupled with his outstanding participation in athletics, his performance produced several offers of college scholarships at graduation. However, he was unable to attend college because of family responsibilities.

After high school he joined the Air Force in 1955 and was discharged as an "undesirable character" in April, 1956, as the result of an altercation with one of his superiors. Soon after his discharge, he managed to get a job, which he held for more than six years, at a local bottling company in Chicago.

Throughout most of his adolescence and into early adulthood, he was a semi-professional and professional gambler. These activities resulted in many fines and a number of brief periods in jail on convictions for gambling and armed assault.

In March, 1965, he went to work for the West Side Organization and eventually became second in command as director of the Welfare Union. He is thus involved in almost constant negotiations with the Cook County Department of Public Aid, as well as with other public agencies. He has developed excellent administrative and bargaining skills, in addition to technical expertise in welfare law.

John Crawford, treasurer and director of the Welfare Union, was born in Arkansas, but he has lived much of his life on Chicago's West and South Sides.

Having to change schools as his family moved, he attended a number of schools. In 1957, he dropped out of the final one, a vocational school, before graduation. His life until his 1964 association with the West Side Organization was a patchwork of jail, brief periods of work, unemployment compensation, and welfare.

His work as director of one of the West Side Organization Welfare Unions locals has been excellent. And, as is the case with others in the organization who have specialized in welfare matters, he is an expert in public assistance.

William Clark, vice-president, was born on the West Side of Chicago in 1932, the youngest in a family of nine children. Clark quit school when he was in the sixth grade (this was at the age of 15 or 16). From that time until he joined the West Side Organization, his history was one of almost constant "hustling" (gambling, playing pool for money, and so on), an occasional menial job, armed robbery, and jail. He served his first term in prison in 1954, serving two years for assault, robbery, and illegal possession of narcotics. After his release, he was subsequently arrested and spent additional time in jail.

Clark went to work for the West Side Organization in 1965 and he eventually became one of the few paid staff members and head of one of the Welfare Union locals. Through his work with WSO he has become acquainted with local businessmen and has met and worked with them and with other local public and private figures who have had dealings with the organization.

Funding

From its inception, no funds have been accepted for the work of the organization except those funds free from outside control. WSO is supported by the following sources: the Stern Family Fund (a New York-based foundation), Chicago City Missionary Society, Urban Training Center for Christian Mission, United Church of Christ Board for Homeland Ministries, United Church of Christ Fund for Racial Justice Now, and community donations.

Wary of the dangers of co-optation but realistic in its need for increased funding, WSO has sought and had loans guaranteed by Container Corporation of America, McDonald's Corporation, and Shell Oil Company. In addition, the Illinois Housing and Development Authority and the Federal Housing Administration (FHA) have jointly funded a housing development corporation owned by WSO. The W. Clement Stone Foundation granted $10,000 to WSO for collection of paper from inner city sources to supply the Paper Stock Corporation. WSO also gets all profits from the sale of Professor William W. Ellis' book, *White Ethics and Black Power.*

Meetings

WSO holds public meetings every Wednesday night, and special meetings are held to discuss matters of great urgency. These special meetings have been few in number.

The regular Wednesday meetings, with an average attendance of 50 to 100 persons, consist of the singing of "freedom songs," followed by a scheduled speaker. (On separate occasions, Martin Luther King and Stokely Carmichael spoke to crowds of more than 500 people.)

The speeches usually stress self-help and responsible social and political action. Heated exchanges often occur. These debates clarify WSO positions and allow useful feedback from the community to be weighed in policymaking. The organization claims between 2,000 and 3,000 members.

The organization holds two kinds of "strategy meetings": "inside" and "outside." At the "inside" meetings the high-level members of WSO meet frequently to deal with immediate and long-range problems. Common topics include alternatives for action in immediate crises, questions of finance, and problems of relating to other organizations in Chicago. The "outside" meetings with other black leaders in Chicago offer an opportunity to share viewpoints and frames of reference for viewing common problems. WSO has always taken an independent tack at these meetings, since the organization is wary of forming coalitions that may result in an outsider developing substantial influence over future WSO policy.

WSO ACTIVITIES

Job Locating and Placement

The most important factor in recruiting and placement of the unemployed is the development of a community organization staffed and directed by the poor within which the unemployed can receive counceling, can voice their real aspirations and fears about employment, and can plan realistically for a program of economic upgrading within a structure which will be effective in fighting discrimination. Because WSO from its beginning realized the importance of the community-organizing process as motivation for employment, the initial organizing thrust centered around the issue of employment for the thousands of jobless persons on the Near West Side. "Full Employment Now" emerged as the organizational slogan almost three years ago.

As the program of the WSO developed, full responsibility for continuing the organization of unemployed persons and job-finding and placement was assumed by the director of WSO, Chester Robinson. The employment program of the WSO has proceeded in the following ways:

(1) contacting businesses to determine market needs;
(2) recruiting the unemployed and underemployed of the Near West Side through word-of-mouth and through articles in the *West Side Torch*, listing available jobs with salary ranges and minimum qualifications
(3) determining applicants' job skills (realized or potential)
(4) emphasizing the need for training to meet job market demands and to upgrade employability potential
(5) assisting in securing and comprehending the necessary documents needed for job application and employment.

Results of this procedure included:
(1) five hundred job placements in one year, 80 percent of which were successful
(2) agreement with National Tea Company in which their official job applications could be used in WSO
(3) conducting job interviews by the University of Illinois at WSO
(4) placing Illinois State Employment Service personnel in the WSO to recruit job applicants
(5) continuing communication as to placement and job follow-up between the director of the WSO and at least four major companies in Chicago.

Follow-ups on job placement, initiated through volunteer help and feedback as to employer/employee experience, is becoming helpful in locating new placement possibilities and in developing more adequate recruiting techniques of the unemployed. Emphasis is also given to finding summer jobs for youths.

Education and Development Program

There are many educational programs presently available to undereducated, low-income people including a variety of Manpower Development Training Act (MDTA), and Job Corps programs. WSO leaders consider these programs ineffective at upgrading the educational level of Near West Side residents because poor persons did not participate in curriculum planning, and teaching is carried out through structures alien to many undereducated West Side residents. These residents see little functional relationship between the improvement of basic educational abilities and the daily problems of living in an urban poverty area.

After some months of work at job placement for the unemployed, WSO began a program of basic education in reading and mathematics, as well as a program in typing. These programs were advertised as having a functional relationship to the problems of the unemployed and as holding the possibility of job placement for those who lacked a basic education. Despite the fact that classes were staffed by volunteer teachers and tutors who had little money available for teaching materials, more than 300 persons enrolled.

Beginning with this attempt to provide basic education courses for community residents, WSO has progressed to the development of working relationships with such educational institutions as the University of Illinois (Chicago Circle), Malcolm X Community College, and various community public schools. WSO encourages its youth to continue their education, and it provides vehicles for such growth. An example of this is the Educational Assistance Program at the Illinois Circle Campus, a program to aid educationally deficient applicants through college.

Welfare Administration Program

The WSO Welfare Union is proving that hardcore welfare recipients can be mobilized to act in their own behalf to eliminate welfare abuses and to push for a federally guaranteed income program. In one year, this organization attracted a membership of more than 1,500 welfare recipients and successfully processed nearly 1,000 welfare grievances.

Action in this area began when members of WSO recognized that efforts to mobilize people solely around the issue of jobs would not be sufficient for the West Side community. One-quarter of the area's population was on public assistance, and most of these were young children and their ADC mothers who could not be rallied by the promise of employment. In analyzing community leadership, it was learned that these people looked to their precinct captains, who gained support for various political candidates by processing individual welfare grievances. These candidates, once in office, often divorced themselves from the people and would not work to achieve their constituents' long-range goals.

Challenging these politicians, WSO began handling welfare complaints. An article in the *West Side Torch* points to the fact that politicians have been "peddling fear for years . . . threatening that they'll take you off welfare or cut your checks if you don't do what they want." West Side welfare recipients soon learned to push for their own restitutions once they had a supporting group which had explored a public welfare manual and could assure them they were only asking welfare to "obey its rules." Daily complaints against welfare were handled in this way until a WSO member rebelled after struggling six weeks to have a large supplemental check released to her. Thirty WSO members accompanied her to the welfare office and this check was issued "at once." This was the beginning of the WSO Welfare Union. A formal grievance procedure has been perfected so that there are few problems arising from the welfare administration that cannot be dealt with through negotiation with WSO personnel and appropriate bureaucrats at the Cook County Department of Public Aid.

Business Development

Residents of urban poverty areas regularly expend larger sums of money for necessary goods and services than do residents of more affluent neighborhoods.[4] Yet, due to the lack of neighborhood-owned businesses, the flow of capital is almost entirely out of the community with no profit accruing to residents either in increased income or in quality of goods and services rendered.

At the same time many community persons have the potential business ability and technical skills to provide certain goods and services required; the difficulty lies in finding the necessary capital to begin such businesses and in locating business advisors with prior experience to assist small business developments. WSO has pioneered in the development of such community-owned businesses as:

(1) WSO Shell Station, a profitable operation with 15 employees, including an excellent mechanic.

(2) West Side Hamburgers, Inc., a McDonald's franchise with 50 employees. Gross sales have risen to more than $400,000 a year, with net profits to WSO in excess of $25,000.

(3) West Side Community Paper Stock Co.

In addition to these going concerns, the West Side Community Development Corporation is planning the formation of West Side Dry Cleaners, Inc., a large Norgetown dry cleaning center to be located in Forest Park, a western suburb. This full-service dry cleaning franchise will cost the West Side Organization $120,000. The W. Clement Stone Foundation has agreed to guarantee a loan of $60,000 toward this end, to be borrowed from either the Hyde Park National Bank or the First National Bank of Chicago. If the West Side Community Development Corporation can arrange the remaining $60,000 in financing, yet another potential business will join the list of "black capitalism" ventures on the Near West Side.

The WSO venture into the paper stock business is an exciting one. Representatives from Container Corporation of America (CCA) and directors of the West Side Community Development Corporation met to discuss the feasibility of developing a paper grading and packing plant to be owned by WSCDC. The plant would collect, bale, sort, and pack old newspapers to be reprocessed into newsprint, most of which would be sold to Container Corporation of America at agreed-upon prices and in agreed-to quantities, thus providing a protected market. Container Corporation along with Metropolitan Consulting Associates (MCA), a consulting firm headed by Bob Strom, provided the technical assistance necessary to set up a paper reclaiming operation.

As a result of these actions, the West Side Community Paper Stock Corporation was formed. A loan of $300,000 guaranteed by Container Corporation was made by the First National Bank of Chicago, and the plant became operational. The plant employs 8 community people and, at full capacity could employ 12 to 15 persons. Product output began at 100 tons of paper stock per month; the break-even point was projected at 500 tons. At optimum capacity, the plant could process paper at a rate of 1,000 tons per month. On an annual basis, at an average monthly rate of 650 tons at agreed-upon prices, WSDC could earn between $25,000 and $30,000 before taxes on gross sales of approximately $225,000, and WSO will receive a percentage of this profit.

The West Side Community Development Corporation owns 100 percent of the company. It is anticipated that the community development corporation will make a private offering of up to 49 percent of the stock to finance additional enterprises. The president of the company is Chester Robinson, also president of WSO.

West Side Organization Community Health Center

Located directly above WSO headquarters, the West Side Organization Mental Health Center is an expanded community service program of the WSO. With the assistance of the Illinois State Psychiatric Institute, the center provides counseling services for troubled area residents. The Institute refers outpatients to the clinic for help in solving their emotional problems. However, the staff does not rely on referrals alone; it seeks out persons and families in the community who are displaying signs of emotional illness or mental anguish. The informal ghetto communications process greatly aids the clinic in identifying potentially disturbed people; the people's trust in WSO helps to make this program a success. Included in the staff are a consulting psychiatrist, a social worker, and group and individual therapy leaders.

Youth Group Recreational Activities

WSO has been an instrumental force in forming a number of neighborhood youth groups which exist for the purpose of steering young people away from street activities toward constructive pursuits. WSO is responsible for securing community use of Circle Campus recreational facilities, including a new athletic center recently constructed on the campus. WSO has organized Little League baseball teams, football teams, basketball teams, and track squads. These activities enable WSO to influence the development of future members of WSO and its potential leaders.

Community Communications

The residents of the WSO urban poverty area have no vehicle within public housing projects or blocks of private dwellings for articulating their concerns for community development. They have no structure for small group planning to create neighborhood programs addressed to the problems of greatest concern to residents. WSO has attempted to create block clubs, public housing councils, and teen gang federations as structures to enable Near West Side residents to participate more fully in community action programs. However, lack of adequate staff has resulted in formation of *ad hoc* groups from all points in the community which are concerned about specific issues. This style of organizing has enabled WSO to mobilize large numbers of persons for specific action projects. It has not, however, involved the great number as yet untouched by the possibility of democratic participation in problem solving.

Some examples of specific community communications programs currently in progress designed to increase community impact on matters relating to the community are given below.

Police/community relations.   In the ghetto neighborhood of the Near West Side of Chicago, resident difficulties with the police and with the complicated system of civil and criminal justice are numerous. WSO has established a reputation for quick action in processing civilian complaints, aiding local police in more effective law enforcement, and providing access to excellent legal service for residents through contact with public aid, private agencies, and individuals willing to provide legal representation for a nominal fee.

Community planning.   WSO is constantly available to area residents for their input into the community planning process. This includes businessmen interested in moving a plant, renovating a business, individual residents interested in improving the number of pedestrian walkways, and so on. WSO, in conjunction with members of the Chicago Associated Planners and Architects, who donated more than $19,000 of their labor, began developing a plan for upgrading the environment of the Near West Side. Several items were jointly decided upon: (1) to reduce crime and increase pedestrian access, the alleys of the Near West Side were to be converted into scenic pedestrian malls; (2) Roosevelt Road was to be the focus of industrial development of firms owned by community residents—a commercial strip, and (3) major access routes were to be constructed between the residential area and the northern institutions (the Medical Center and the University of Illinois) and the southern institutions (mostly small wire companies, salvage companies and the paper stock plant). This design has been completed and WSO believes work will begin shortly, pending acquisition of funding.

West Side Torch.   This weekly paper is an attempt to fill the communications gap between downtown newspapers and community news. Available in the Near West Side, Garfield, and Lawndale communities, the *Torch* has reached a circulation of 35,000 to 45,000 papers per publication. The *Torch* has been a device for advertising community services to residents by WSO, Garfield Organization, and other indigenous community groups. It has also been a source of communications concerning the businesses of the area. Long a marginal operation, the *Torch* is now reportedly a profitable, on-going concern.

Low-Income Housing.   WSO, located in the heart of the ABLA/CHA housing project, and adjacent to a deteriorated neighborhood south of Roosevelt Road and west of Ashland Avenue, is cognizant of the numerous problems associated with the need for adequate low-income housing by area residents. WSO has effectively dealt with community landlords and planned with residents for the construction of new housing for present community residents. The organization was instrumental in organizing the Resident Development Corporation, headed by Bob Condas, a resident of the community. This corporation has begun a $20 million land use program, funded jointly by the Illinois Housing Development Authority and the FHA, to build housing on a 26 acre site within the community (see Exhibit II). More than 900 units are to be constructed, 20 to 30 percent of which are to be rent subsidy housing for public aid recipients. The remaining 70 percent will be FHA housing for incomes in the low to middle ranges.

Institutional Relationships.   WSO as a community advocate has developed relationships with the University of Illinois, the Medical Center, Presbyterian St. Luke's Hospital, Cook County Hospital and other area institutions. In addition, working relationships with the Democratic party political machine and with syndicate leaders have been established, since the realities of political life in this area must take into account these two major power centers. The organization has built extremely valuable coalitions (without co-optation) in order to upgrade the quality of life of the area residents.

Child Care

Representing a great number of community working mothers in need of adequate day care for their children, WSO has applied for a grant from the State of Illinois to provide community child care services. This represents a major step forward in increasing the income-earning potential of area residents. The facility will be located in a small building in the rear of the proposed drug abuse center.

WSO Drug Abuse and Rehabilitation Project

This plan is an outgrowth of the community health center. In providing mental health services to area residents, WSO has found that drug addiction and drug-related problems are the most pervasive sources of social and psychological deviance. WSO estimates that 70 percent of community residents aged 17 to 25 are on some form of drugs. The incidence of drug-related crimes is rising daily. In 1970, 207 drug deaths by overdose were recorded in Cook County, many of them occurring on the Near West Side. Because of this crisis, WSO has submitted a comprehensive proposal to the Department of Health, Education and Welfare (HEW) for a grant of $210,000 to fund a rehabilitation program in the community. A building has already been secured and potential staff contacted and committed, pending approval of the grant.

THE FUTURE OF WSO

Executives of such community social institutions as WSO can make substantial contributions to changing its community. But without expanded participation of community residents in new programs, little progress will be made no matter how generous these institutions are with their resources. WSO provides a nucleus of leadership and an image that could catalyze needed social change—a rallying point for community cohesion.

To accomplish this goal, WSO needs to increase its budget and extend its outreach into the community. For the first few years of its existence, it was understaffed and underfinanced. Only about half of the full-time staff received any salary at all, and the few salaries that were paid ($75 to $100 per week) were woefully inadequate. With the McDonald's, Shell, and paper stock profits, the picture has improved. Office space still is inadequate, and the transportation facilities spotty. It is difficult for WSO to manage its current work, much less the West Side and its people within the constraints of its current budget.

One obvious source of funding is the federal government. The proposal to HEW concerning the drug abuse program is an attempt to secure federal funds. Other sources might include local merchants, private foundations (Ford, Rockefeller, and others), revenues from WSO-owned companies (the paper stock company), and others. In this regard, the obvious question must be asked: Can the critical need for funding balance out the inevitable co-optation of policy making by the funding agency? WSO apparently feels that it can develop links with the bigger, "outside" world without being co-opted.

FOOTNOTES

[1] "First Venture at 'Hand'," *Urban Enterprise*, Vol. 1, No. 6, (December 5, 1969), p. 6.

[2] U.S. Department of Labor, Bureau of Labor Statistics, Urban Employment Survey (Chicago), "Poverty—The Broad Outline," (Washington: USPO, March 1970), p. 3.

[3] *Idem.* No statistics are yet available from the 1970 census, but it does not appear that the relative income pattern on the West Side has changed significantly since the last census.

[4] See Frederick Sturdivant, *The Ghetto Marketplace* (New York: The Free Press, 1969), pp. 14-157, for evidence of the higher prices paid by black consumers.

EPILOGUE

Beginning in 1964 with the Poverty Act and accelerating after the Kerner Commission Report in 1967, a number of programs have been initiated to promote minority economic development. The various articles and case studies in this book have discussed many aspects of this national program including various employment, enterprise, and community development programs. As much as $3 billion per year has been spent on such programs, primarily through OEO funding. This is a *very minimal* expenditure. This amount is less than one-sixth the yearly cost of servicing the debt created by previous wars, or about one-eighth the average yearly cost of the Vietnam War. To put the cost of minority economic development another way, it has amounted to less than $100 per year investment for each disadvantaged individual. In 1973, the Nixon administration has proceeded to dismember OEO and to curtail or eliminate many of its programs altogether.

What of the results? The policy makers have thus far labeled all of the programs as "experimental" and "demonstration" because of their limited size. Neither the Johnson nor Nixon administrations have attempted to educate Congress or the general public as to the essentially experimental nature of these programs. Thus, many members of the general public as well as many congressmen have thought that these programs were in fact operational and have judged their results or lack thereof accordingly.

The bulk of the money expended has been in the manpower area, much of it spent with private sector firms to pay the costs of recruiting and training the "hardcore" unemployed. Due to the wartime economy of the middle and late 1960s. overall unemployment reached very low levels. The disadvantaged took part in this employment "boom," primarily through lower level entry jobs. However, as the Vietnam War has been wound down, overall unemployment has gone above six percent, with minority unemployment almost twice that figure. Thus, the historical pattern of minority economic advancement occurring only during wartime periods has continued into the present era, and the impact of the various job training programs has been quite minimal. Since little effort has been made to provide for upward mobility from entry level jobs, many, if not most, of the jobs provided have been dead-end jobs in low-growth industries.

The other major thrusts in economic development have been in the fields of community development corporations and minority capitalism. Thus far, 1973 has been the peak year for spending in these areas—$31 million has been expended for CDCs, and over $1.5 billion has been programmed for minority enterprise development. (The $31 million is included in this $1.3 billion plus figure.) Most of this $1.5 billion has been provided in the form of 90 percent SBA-guaranteed small business loans (about $600 million), procurement of goods and services from minority businessmen (about $700 million) and technical assistance to these same businessmen ($100 million).

Given the magnitude of the problem, these sums are obviously too small to have any significant national impact. Their importance lies in what they might teach us about structuring larger scale programs in the future. We have gained increased understanding about economic development through these programs, and we can learn much more, provided that adequate evaluation is built into each program. Such evaluation is not provided today nor have funds been made available for research to support these operational efforts. More important, very little money has been made available for business/management education for minority managers and entrepreneurs.

The President's Council on Minority Business Enterprise (PACMBE) recommended in its final report (February, 1971), that business education and training be made a high-priority part of any national program of minority enterprise development and that $170 million be made available in the succeeding three years to support this recommended educational program.[1] As of the end of fiscal year 1973, less than $2 million had been made available for educational programs by all federal agencies engaged in the minority enterprise program. This $2 million is out of total federal program funding in the minority enterprise area of over $3 billion during FY's 1969 to 1973. The only response to these PACMBE recommendations was the establishment, in 1972, of a joint HEW/OMBE Task Force for Minority Business Education and Training. This task force will issue its report early in 1974, *still little or no money for education and training* has been forthcoming.

We know that the majority of successful new businesses are today based on the educational, technical and management skills of its founders. We know that the majority of small business failures are due to a lack of these skills and yet very, very little has been done to support this critical area, so important for economic development. We know, moreover, that our highly educated workforce has been our principal strength in our overall economy and that educational opportunities for minorities have been very limited (most limited in business and management).

For the effect of educational expenditures on business development and on overall economic development to be felt requires a relatively long period. Symptomatic of the problems of present minority economic development programs is a lack of funding for such areas as business/management education which have a relatively long lead time. There has been no attempt to establish the overall, long-term goals of such programs, nor has there been any attempt in present program funding to foster fundamental economic change which could, ultimately, lead to economic parity for our disadvantaged population. Thus existing programs have focused largely on short term injections of loan capital, contracts or technical assistance in the hope of fostering some small business development, but to what end?

When we speak of bringing minority groups into the economic mainstream, we are obviously speaking of a major socio-economic program requiring a national commitment over at least several decades. Time and money are key ingredients in any such effort, but the *will to allow change* by those people with the power to effect change is a key element. Thus far, none of these ingredients has been supplied in sufficient quantity to effectuate appreciable change. Of course, the lack of will is indicated by the small sums expended and by the impatience when miracles are not wrought overnight with these small sums. We have raised the expectations of our minority population so that they anticipate meaningful and large-scale economic change. Yet aside from increases in the minority enterprise program, other development expenditures in employment, health care, education and social welfare for the disadvantaged are being cut back or cut off.

Massive socio-economic change does not lend itself to quick and easy answers. Many worthwhile programs have no doubt been aborted prematurely, simply because of our penchant for short-run demonstration of effectiveness. Political expediency and budgetary constraints have placed an unreasonable "get results quickly" criterion on social action programs. Using a different perspective, our short-run orientation has most likely produced program designs of sub-optimal long-run quality. Knowing full well the "produce or bust" constraints, policymakers have opted for programs with questionable long-run impact. We must learn to stick with promising programs until their fruition; at the same time, we need to develop more sophisticated evaluation processes to measure both quantitative and qualitative program results. Only with a comprehensive, well-integrated strategy for minority economic development can parity be achieved—and the sooner we realize this, the less strain we will feel on the societal fabric.

FOOTNOTE

[1] PACMBE, *Minority Enterprise and Expanded Ownership: A Blueprint for the Seventies* (Washington, D.C.: U.S. Government Printing Office, December 1971).

SELECTED ANNOTATED BIBLIOGRAPHY

I. DEFINITION OF THE PROBLEM

Banfield, Edward C. *The Unheavenly City.* Boston: Little, Brown, and Co., 1970. A conservative political scientist's view of the nature of our urban dilemma and his proposed solutions for its amelioration.

Banfield, Edward C. and James Q. Wilson. *City Politics.* New York: Vintage Books, 1963. The classic book on how city government operates, using Daley's Chicago as one example of a type of political governance and, to a lesser extent, other prototypes such as Dallas and Los Angeles.

Bell, Carolyn Shaw. *The Economics of the Ghetto.* New York: Pegasus Books, Inc., 1970. An economist's view of the questions of income and poverty, housing, consumers and markets, employments and education. A good primer on the subject.

Blaustein, Arthur and Geoffrey Faux. *The Star-Spangled Hustle.* New York: Doubleday, 1972. An excellent, if somewhat biased, critique of the growth of the federal minority enterprise program, written by two former OEO staff members.

Bradley, Schiller. *The Economics of Poverty and Discrimination.* Englewood Cliffs, N.J.: Prentice-Hall, 1973. An interdisciplinary analysis of poverty and discrimination.

Carmichael, Stokeley and Charles V. Hamilton. *Black Power.* New York: Vintage, 1967. A classic explanation of the sources of black rage and what blacks should do to "take care of business."

Clark, Kenneth. *Dark Ghetto: Dilemmas of Social Power.* New York:

Harper and Row, 1965. This book's emphasis on the pathologies of American ghettos attempts to describe and interpret what happens to human beings who are confined to depressed areas and whose access to the normal channels of economic mobility and opportunity is blocked.

Cleaver, Eldridge. *Soul on Ice.* New York: Bantam Books, 1968. This eloquent book is one of the best statements of white racism's impact on the black man's personality and self-concept.

Downs, Anthony. *Urban Problems and Prospects.* Chicago: Markham Publishing Co., Inc., 1970. A radical view of alternative futures for the American ghetto with some insightful suggestions on how to achieve racial harmony.

Elkins, Stanley. *Slavery.* Chicago: University of Chicago Press, 1968. A brilliant dissertation on the effect of slavery on the historical reluctance of black Americans to assert their rights. Compares the psychology of slavery to concentration camp studies. This book recently fell into disrepute because Daniel Moynihan drew upon it to argue that "Negro family pathology" was at the root of race problems.

Elman, Richard M. *The Poorhouse State: The American Way of Public Assistance.* New York: Dell, 1966. A horrifying description of poor persons caught in bureaucratic welfare machinery with its systematic humiliation.

Farmer, Richard and W. Dickerson Hogue. *Corporate Social Responsibility.* Chicago: Science Research Associates, Inc., 1973. General overview of the role of large corporations in social problems with a number of specific case examples. The focus is on the corporation's role in dealing with its major constituencies—management, employees, stockholders, creditors, consumers, suppliers, the public and governments.

Ferman, Louis, Joyce Kornbluh and Alan Haber, eds. *Poverty in America.* Ann Arbor: University of Michigan, 1968. A book of readings about the problem of poverty in its broader, societal context, and of how that problem meets the issue of the great society.

Frazier, E. Franklin. *Black Bourgeoisie.* New York: Collier Books, 1968. An interesting look at the black middle class; Frazier contends that, once a black "makes it" in the white world, he looks down on his former brothers in typical white middle-class disgust.

Grebler, Leo, Joan Moore and Ralph Guzman. *The Mexican-American People.* New York: The Free Press, 1970. The most complete overview of the history of the Mexican-Americans, including a historical perspective of migration patterns, socio-economic conditions, the individual in the social system, the role of churches (especially Catholic) and political interaction.

Grier, William and Price Cobbs. *Black Rage.* New York: Basic Books, 1968. The book focuses on the problems forming one's personal identity in a white-dominated society and provides a survey of mental illnesses and symptoms directly traceable to racial oppression.

Hannerz, Ulf. *Soulside: Inquiries into Ghetto Culture and Community.* New York: Columbia University Press, 1969. Like William Whyte's classic study,

Hannerz depicts urban ghetto society in graphic detail from the vantage point of an observer living in such a society. An excellent study of modern ghetto society and culture which provides an important framework for any economic solutions to the problems of urban poor.

Henderson, William L. and Larry C. Ledebur. *Economic Disparity.* New York: The Free Press, 1970. An overview of the problems of economic inequity with a comparison of moderate and militant solutions.

Kain, John F. (ed). *Race and Poverty.* Englewood Cliffs, New Jersey: Prentice-Hall, Inc., 1969. Readings on the economic condition of the Negro, the labor market and discrimination, the housing market, attitudes toward race and police alternatives for solving the problem.

Kerner Commission Report. Washington, D.C.: U.S. Government Printing Office, 1967. The shocking report of the causes of urban unrest with some excellent, definitive strategies for correcting the underlying problems.

Malcolm X. *Autobiography of Malcolm X.* New York: Grove Press, 1964. The white press greatly minimized the significance of Malcolm X. His vision and prose are gradually achieving recognition.

Marris, Peter and Martin Rein. *Dilemmas of Social Reform.* New York: Atherton Press, 1967. A scholarly, dispassionate and thorough report of the frustrations and entanglements into which specific federal reform projects have fallen.

Meir, Matt and Feliciano Rivera. *The Chicanos.* New York: Hill and Wang, 1972. This book provides a fairly detailed history of Mexican-American history in the U.S. from the Spanish conquest to the present.

Myrdal, Gunnar. *An American Dilemma.* New York: Harper & Row, 1944, 1962. The monumental study of black/white relations in the United States prepared on the eve of the many changes that were about to be wrought on this relationship in the aftermath of World War II, the Korean War, and the riots of the sixties. This is must reading for anyone who wants to gain historical perspective on the cultural problems created by our dual society.

Peren, Francis and Richard Cloward. *Regulating the Poor.* New York: Pantheon Books, 1972. This is an excellent description and analysis of the development of public welfare during two periods of "explosive" growth—the depression era and 1960's.

Rainwater, L., and William Yancy. *The Moynihan Report and the Politics of Controversy.* Cambridge: the M.I.T. Press, 1967. An excellent case study of how "custodial liberalism" operates and how angry it makes black leaders. In this case, Moynihan used "mental health" perspectives to argue that the Negro family was often pathological. True? possibly, but the road to hell is paved with research findings; you emancipate people with perspectives that label them inferior? Book consists of the report, rebuttals, and comments.

Silberman, Charles E. *Crisis in Black and White.* New York: Vintage, 1964. Probably the best popular account of race relationships written by a white man. One of the first books to advocate "Poor Power" and praise the Woodlawn Organization for its fight against the expansion of the University of Chicago.

Spear, Allan. *Black Chicago.* Chicago: University of Chicago Press, 1967. An in-depth statistical and psychological examination of Chicago's black population and its characteristics.

Sturdivant, Frederick ed. *The Ghetto Marketplace.* New York: The Free Press, 1969. This book contains a collection of articles about the "incongruity created by the ghetto environment for the consumer." It is a marketplace in which the unwary poor are often victims of unethical or illegal merchandising ". . . (and in which) retailers who do try to serve their customers are faced with such problems as high operating costs and, often, community resentment."

U.S. Bureau of Census and Bureau of Labor Statistics. *The Social and Economic Status of Negroes in the United States, 1970.* Washington, D.C.: U.S. Government Printing Office, 1971.

"Which Way Black America?" *Ebony Magazine*, August 1970. A broad presentation of a cross section of contemporary black ideologies; this represents must reading for the uninformed white.

Willhelm, Sidney M. *Who Needs the Negro?* Cambridge: Schenkman Publishing Company, Inc., 1970. This author explodes many myths about the causes of urban unrest and, in so doing, develops a clearer understanding of the black power movement. This book is a heavy indictment of white America.

Wright, Nathan, Jr. *Ready to Riot.* New York: Holt, Rinehart and Winston, 1968. A highly statistical and thorough description of Newark on the eve of the "rebellion." Wright has drawn criticism for using the term "riot," which is a "white term." He writes ponderously about very dramatic events.

II. EMPLOYMENT

Bakke, Wight. *The Mission of Manpower Policy.* Kalamazoo, Michigan: The W.E. Upjohn Institute for Employment Research, 1969. An excellent analysis of federal manpower policy pointing up inherent weaknesses of lack of focus, duplication, and ambiguous objectives; he then offers some viable strategies to get back on the right track.

Bolino, August. *Manpower and the City.* Cambridge: Schenkman Publishing Co., 1969. This book attempts to discuss the many manpower laws, their effectiveness, and their relationship to the broader society.

Chalmers, Ellison and Gerald Cormick. *Racial Conflict and Negotiations.* Ann Arbor: Institute of Labor and Industrial Relations, 1971. Some good case studies on perspectives of racial negotiations are presented showing the dynamics of the actual bargaining sessions.

Diamond, Daniel E., *et al. Industry Hiring Requirements and the Employment of Disadvantaged Groups.* New York: NYU School of Commerce (in cooperation with the Labor Department), 1970. This book represents an in-depth study of both unemployment and underemployment, the role of hiring requirements, and implications for manpower policy programs.

Doeringer, Peter B., *et al. Low Income Labor Markets and Urban Manpower Programs: A Critical Assessment.* Cambridge: Harvard University, 1969. A research report on the dynamic relationship between manpower programs and the economic and social environments in which they operate; originally intended to be only an evaluation of the CEP (Concentrated Employment Program).

────── ed. *Programs to Employ the Disadvantaged.* Englewood Cliffs, New Jersey: Prentice-Hall, 1969. A collection of case studies of various businesses with formal programs to employ hardcore unemployed is presented.

Epstein, Edwin and David Hampton, eds. *Black Americans and White Business.* Belmont, California: Dickenson Publishing Co., Inc., 1971. This reader gives a social and economic perspective on the black condition in America, plus the social and psychological implications of contemporary racial attitudes; these two theoretical contributions are then used to analyze the relationship of business institutions and the black community.

Ferman, Louis, Joyce Kornbluh, and J. A. Miller. *Negroes and Jobs.* Ann Arbor: University of Michigan Press, 1969. This book gives a well-rounded account of Negro worker's economic position in the contemporary American labor market. It is a compendium of more than 30 articles, all written since 1960, dealing with various aspects of Negro employment.

Jacobson, Julius, ed. *The Negro and the American Labor Movement.* New York: American Management Association, 1969. This research study demonstrates that the hard-core unemployed are employable, and profitably so. It shows how 43 companies are organized for employing the hard-core successfully. Emphasis is placed on stumbling blocks that may be encountered and how the companies studied have overcome them.

King, Carl and Howard Risher. *The Negro in the Petroleum Industry.* Philadelphia: University of Pennsylvania Press, 1969. This study is concerned with the development, status, and problems involved in racial employment policies in the petroleum industry.

Lebergott, Stanley, ed. *Men Without Work.* Englewood Cliffs, New Jersey: Prentice-Hall Inc., 1964. An excellent explanation of the problem, a definition of who is unemployed, and a review of recent programs (here and abroad); design to relieve the problem is presented.

Lecht, Leonard. *Manpower Needs for National Goals in the 1970s.* New York: Praeger Publishers, 1969. The author gives a summary of extrapolations and trend analyses of manpower requirements to meet national goals in the 1970s; one of the best of its kind.

Mangum, Garth L. *MDTA: Foundation of Federal Manpower Policy.* Baltimore: The Johns Hopkins Press, 1968. Mangum presents an evaluation of the Manpower Development and Training Act (MDTA), to include the legislative evolution of the program.

_____. *The Emergence of Manpower Policy*. New York: Holt, Rinehart and Winston, 1969. A historical perspective of manpower policy evolution is presented, with emphasis on the problems that stimulated its development; a good section on issues for the future in manpower policy.

Marshall, F. Ray and Vernon Briggs, Jr. *The Negro and Apprenticeship*. Baltimore: The Johns Hopkins Press, 1967. In this study, the authors provide us with an objective analysis of the factors that influence the low rate of Negro participation in apprenticeship.

Nathan, Robert. *Jobs and Civil Rights*. Washington, D.C.: U.S. Commission on Civil Rights, 1969. A comprehensive look at antidiscrimination legislation and its impact on opening up job opportunities for minorities. Nathan gives very low grades to present federal enforcement policies in the fair employment area.

Northrup, Herbert R. *The Negro in Aerospace Industry*. Philadelphia: University of Pennsylvania Press, 1968. This study is concerned with the development, status, and problems involved in racial employment policies in the aerospace industry, and in the principal companies therein.

_____. *The Negro in the Automobile Industry*. Philadelphia: University of Pennsylvania, 1968.

_____. et al. *Negro Employment in Finance*. Philadelphia: University of Pennsylvania Press, 1970. The authors describe how these once almost all-white industries (banking and insurance) are now seeking to employ larger numbers of Negroes, and what problems remain to be solved before equal opportunity can be attained.

_____. *The Negro in the Paper Industry*. Philadelphia: University of Pennsylvania Press, 1969. This study examines the paper industry's current racial policies after describing the structure of the industry and the extent of Negro participation as an employee prior to 1960.

_____. *The Negro in the Rubber Tire Industry*. Philadelphia: University of Pennsylvania Press, 1969.

_____. et al. *Negro Employment in Land and Air Transport*. Philadelphia: University of Pennsylvania Press, 1971.

Pearl, Arthur and Frank Reissman. *New Careers for the Poor*. New York: The Free Press, 1965. This is an excellent treatment of potential strategies for hiring and training the "unemployable" in higher growth areas to promote minority economic development.

Regan, Barbara. *Mexican-American Industrial Migrants*. Dallas: Institute of Urban Studies, Southern Methodist University, 1971. The author presents her research on the adjustment process and measures of economic progress, including changes in level of living, of disadvantaged Mexican-American families in Texas who accepted retraining for industrial jobs, with emphasis on rural/urban migrants.

Rees, Albert and George P. Schultz. *Workers and Wages in an Urban Labor Market*. Chicago: University of Chicago Press, 1970. A research of the Chicago-Northwestern Indiana Standard Consolidated Area as defined in the census of

1960, to include mobility, commuting patterns, wage differentials, information channels and various spatial characteristics is presented; a solid job by the "Chicago school."

Reissman, Frank and Hermine I. Popper, eds. *Up From Poverty*. New York: Harper and Row, 1968. A collection of readings is presented, with emphasis on the public view of social reform, social implications of the new careers movement, and some innovative ideas for new careers for the poor.

Sovern, Michael. *Legal Restraints on Racial Discrimination in Employment.* New York: Twentieth Century Fund, Inc., 1966. A thorough look at the development of state and federal antidiscrimination (in employment) statutes; written in a style that the layman can understand.

U.S. Department of Labor. *Job Patterns for Minorities and Woman in Private Industry*. Washington, D.C.: U.S. Government Printing Office, 1967. A good statistical analysis of minorities and women involvement in industrial work paths (including relative status of jobs) is presented.

Weber, Arnold R., Frank H. Cassell, and Woodrow L. Ginsburg, eds. *Public-Private Manpower Policies*. Madison, Wisconsin: Industrial Relations Research Association, 1969. This is a readings book with a number of good articles on manpower planning methods for evaluating social programs, OJT programs, and manpower policies of the federal government and business.

III. MINORITY ENTERPRISE AND THE MINORITY ENTREPRENEUR

ABA National Institute. "Business in the Ghetto." (A special issue) *The Business Lawyer*, **25** (September 1969). This collection of essays by practitioners represents early thinking on minority enterprise development.

Baumol, W. J. "Entrepreneurship in Economic Theory," *American Economic Review*, Vol. 58 Supplement (May 1968), pp. 64-71. The paper examines the grounds on which entrepreneurship should concern economists, seeks to explain why economic theory has failed to develop an illuminating formal analysis of entrepreneurship and argues that economic theory can contribute to understanding of entrepreneurship.

Berry, Brian, Sandra Parsons, and Rutherford Platt. *The Impact of Urban Renewal on Small Business*. Chicago: Center for Urban Studies, University of Chicago, 1968. A case study of the Hyde Park/Kenwood area of Chicago and the impact of federal renewal projects on small businessmen, including an analysis of the mortality experience of the displacees.

"Black Capitalism: Problems and Prospects," (a special issue), *Saturday Review*, August 23, 1969. These articles focus on the need to intensify ghetto economic development while maintaining momentum toward integration; how ghetto capitalism has served succeeding waves of ethnic groups but so far has failed black Americans; evaluates possible government-business programs of "compensatory capitalism"; and on "The New Black Businessman."

Brimmer, Andrew and Henry Terrell. "The Economic Potential of Black

Capitalism." A paper presented before the 82d Annual Meeting of the American Economic Association, New York Hilton, New York, December 29, 1969. Brimmer stated black capitalism intending to better the black economic position might do the opposite. He said most black capitalists—defined as self-employed businessmen serving ghetto areas—could probably do better by taking salaried jobs with larger, white-controlled chains or companies.

Brimmer, Andrew F. "The Black Banks: An Assessment of Performance and Prospects." A paper presented to the American Economic Association, December 28, 1970. A rather conservative black man's analysis of the black banking industry. He concludes black banks serve little or no economic function in our society.

Business and the Development of Ghetto Enterprise. New York: The Conference Board, 1970. A review of corporate participation in ghetto enterprise from mid-1966 to mid-1970; examines why companies have gone into the ghetto, the problems they have encountered, and the results they have achieved.

Coles, Flournoy, Jr. *An Analysis of Black Entrepreneurship in Seven Urban Areas.* Washington, D.C.: The National Business League under the sponsorship of The Booker T. Washington Foundation, 1969. A survey of 564 black enterprises in seven cities to determine what resources and assistance are necessary to make these enterprises—and black enterprises in general—productive and self-sustaining. The study considered the characteristics of both the enterprises and the entrepreneurs who operate them, and is one of the very few empirical studies in this area.

Cross, Theodore. *Black Capitalism: Strategy for Business in the Ghetto.* New York: Atheneum, 1969. This book is concerned with a different face of poverty—not the view that proclaims that almost everyone in the ghetto is poor—or rather the reverse face of poverty that states that almost nobody in the ghettos of America is rich, or even affluent. The author's thesis is that the ghetto economy operates at the threshold of anarchy. Therefore, it must be completely reshaped and stabilized.

Doctors, Samuel and Anne Huff. *Minority Capitalism and the President's Council.* Boston: Ballinger, 1973. A detailed analysis of the work of the President's Council for Minority Business Enterprise and the effects of its recommendations on federal policy development.

Durham, Laird. *Black Capitalism.* Washington, D.C.: Arthur D. Little, Inc., 1970. An incisive little book which attempts to explode some prevailing "myths" concerning why black capitalism has failed. The author then discusses his ideas for making black capitalism a viable strategy.

Foley, Eugene. *The Achieving Ghetto.* Washington, D.C.: The National Press, Inc., 1968. This book by a former SBA administrator is written about a subject which is of increasing importance; the economic development of the black ghetto.

Harris, Abraham. *The Negro as Capitalist: A Study of Banking and Business Among American Negroes.* Glouchester, Massachusetts: Peter Smith, Inc., 1968. An examination of black banking and other businesses in the United States, pinpointing the huge gap in deposits, capital, size and other variables between these enterprises and their counterpart white firms.

Hund, James. *Black Entrepreneurship.* Belmont, California: Wadsworth Publishing Co., 1970. A good overview of the problem of black entrepreneurship and possible future directions for minority economic development.

Galbraith, John Kenneth. *The New Industrial State.* New York: Bantam Books, 1967. A theoretical treatise on the nature and exercise of business power in the United States, which includes causal analysis concerning the reasons for the decline of the small entrepreneur and the growth of giant corporations.

Haddad, William and Douglas Pugh, eds. *Black Economic Development.* Englewood Cliffs, New Jersey: Prentice-Hall, Inc., 1969. This book provides a number of opinion papers on the problems of black economic development by leading authorities and is one of the early works in the field.

Mayer, Kurt and Sidney Goldstein. *The First Two Years: Problems of Small Firm Growth and Survival.* Washington: School of Business Administration, University of Washington, 1961. This study is based on the detailed study of 81 small retail and service firms over a two-year period. It analyzes the problems of small business during the founding period. The study was begun without rigid hypotheses, and covers areas of motivation, location, financing, development, closures, and survivals.

McClelland, David. *The Achieving Society.* Princeton: D. Van Nostrand Company, Inc., 1961. This book shows how one human motive, the need for achievement, appears with great regularity in the imaginative thinking of men and nations before periods of rapid economic growth. The way in which a strong need for achievement promotes successful entrepreneurs is also explored. It is suggested that economic growth can be accelerated by increasing the motivation needed for success.

————, **and David Winter.** *Motivating Economic Achievement.* New York: The Free Press, 1969. The report of an original attempt to apply achievement motivation training in the field. The theory was tested, and a period of exposure to psychological inputs did increase the achievement motivation of businessmen and entrepreneurs in India and the United States. The authors conclude that economic achievement can be stimulated by psychological education.

McLaurin, Dunbar. "Ghediplan: Ghetto Economic Development Plan." Testimony before the Select Committee on Small Business, U.S. Senate, 90th Congress on the Role of the Federal Government in the Development of Small Business Enterprise in the Urban Ghetto, 1968. This plan is designed to generate up to $200 million for the economic development of New York City's ghettos.

"Minority Enterprise." Special issue, *Journal of Small Business*, April-June 1969. These articles discuss ways businessmen and educators can assist new business formations in the minority community through corporate spinoffs, private consortiums to finance and advise new enterprises, ways to organize business and educators to provide know-how, much needed in minority business formations, and how business schools can support all of these activities.

Reiss, Albert. *Minority Entrepreneurship.* Washington, D.C.: Small Business

Administration, Office of Planning, Research, and Analysis, June 1969. The most comprehensive study until the 1970 census on the state of minority business enterprise in the United States.

Report of the President's Advisory Council on Minority Business Enterprise. *Minority Enterprise and Expanded Ownership: Blueprint for the Seventies.* 2 vols. Washington, D.C.: U.S. Government Printing Office, August 1971. The findings of the presidential commission appointed to study minority business enterprise include comprehensive recommendations in the areas of national strategies and goals, finance, business opportunities, expanded ownership and management and technical assistance, as well as proposed legislative and administrative action.

Roberts, Edward and Herbert Wainer. *Some Characteristics of Technical Entrepreneurs.* Cambridge: Research Program on the Management of Science and Technology, 1966. The study explores the question of entrepreneural motivation and also those factors which seem to contribute to success in an entrepreneural venture.

―――. *Technology Transfer and Entrepreneural Success.* Cambridge: Research Program on the Management of Science and Technology, 1966. An examination of the ways by which technology is transferred; out of government, university, and industrial laboratories into the general economy and an analysis of how this transfer aids entrepreneural ventures.

"The Negro in Business," *Ebony Magazine,* September 1963. This historic survey of the initially integrated but later segregated role of the Negro in American business is part of an anniversary issue.

U.S. Department of Commerce, Office of Minority Business Enterprise. *A Piece of the Action: Report to the President on Minority Business Enterprise.* Washington, D.C.: OMBE, 1970. OMBE's annual report on the state of minority enterprise development for fiscal year 1970, including all public and private sector activities.

―――. *Special Catalogs of Federal Programs Assisting Minority Enterprise.* Washington, D.C.: OMBE, 1971. A comprehensive listing of federal programs, by agency, that either directly or indirectly assist minority business enterprises.

IV. OTHER FORMS OF ECONOMIC DEVELOPMENT

Boyer, Ralph E. *Non-Profit Corporation Statutes: A Critique and Proposal.* Ann Arbor: Michigan Legal Studies, 1957. The study is directed first to a careful, accurate appraisal of the nonprofit corporation statute of Michigan. The author states a framework of statutory and case law of various states which can be used to appraise nonprofit statutes. The author's aim is to ascertain the sufficiency of the corporation's statutes in view of nonprofit organizational operations, and to suggest appropriate changes.

Cohn, Jules. *The Conscience of the Corporations.* Baltimore: The Johns Hopkins Press, 1971. This book provides a chronicle and analysis of big business' efforts to relieve urban problems, includes both positive action and public relations gimmicks.

Hack, S. *Legal Aspects of Small Businesses' Use of Cooperative Arrangements.* The University of Wisconsin, (Madison): Office for Small Business Administration, 1964. The report describes relevant statutes and cases, indicates the actions which cooperative arrangements are permitted or prohibited to take, and suggests possible legislation that may permit them to extend or expand their functions.

Oleck, Howard. *Non-Profit Corporations, Organizations, and Associations* 2nd edition. Englewood Cliffs, New Jersey: Prentice-Hall, Inc., 1965. Oleck attempts to cover the entire area of nonprofit organizations. The area of the law is too broad to cover in a one-volume treatise and therefore the work is over simplified, but it provides the only comprehensive attempt to treat the subject.

Roy, Ewell P. *Cooperatives: Today and Tomorrow.* Interstate Printers and Publishers, Inc., 1964. This is a college text for teaching cooperative associations in a business program. This book is a good beginning place for researching cooperative problems.

Voorhis, Horace J. *A New Look at the Principals and Practices of Cooperatives.* Published by the Cooperative League, 1966. A good discussion of the institutional characteristics of cooperatives is presented.

Walker, Charles T. *The Cooperative Experience.* Washington: ABA National Institute, 1969. This author predicts an increasing trend toward nonprofit forms of corporations in minority communities to build an economic base.

V. COMMUNITY ECONOMIC DEVELOPMENT

Altshuler, Alan. *Community Control.* New York: Pegasus Books, Inc., 1970. A sociological treatment of the black demand for political participation in large American cities is presented, with a focus on realistic options at this point in time.

Bonjean, Charles, Terry Clark and Robert Lineberry, eds. *Community Politics.* New York: The Free Press, 1971. This is a collection of readings on the structure of mass participation in community politics, elites and power structures, attitudes and values of community leaders, and the multiplicity of local governments.

Bruyn, Severyn. *Communities in Action, Pattern and Process.* New Haven: College and University Press, 1963. What can be accomplished by aroused citizenry—four variously successful cases of community "democracy" solving social problems—but communities are mostly white and prosperous. Book has an "optimistic" flavor.

CDCs: New Hope for the Inner City. New York: The Twentieth Century Fund, 1971. This report of the Twentieth Century Fund Task Force on Community Development Corporations contains a condensed, easily understandable summary of findings and recommendations.

Clark, Kenneth and Jeanette Hopkins. *A Relevant War Against Poverty*. New York: Harper Torchbooks, 1969. The authors offer a prophecy of the future concerning the Johnsonian War on Poverty and other such programs based on their analysis of the planners' naïveté in not understanding the nature of power and its use. Community participation is an ideal goal, but when thrust upon people unfamiliar with principles of participation democracy, it is unachieveable.

Clark, Terry. *Community Structure and Decision Making*. San Francisco: Chandler, 1968. This book may become the standard sociological and descriptive treatise on the structural organization of communities. Not easy for the amateur sociologist to read.

"Community Development Corporations: A New Approach to the Poverty Problem," *Harvard Law Review*, (Note), Vol. 82 (1969). This is a good general treatment from a lawyer's viewpoint of the Community Self-Determination Bill. There is an examination of the bill's main provisions for forming and operating a CDC, as it relates to three goals: a political institution, a service organization, and an economic institution.

Ellis, William. *White Ethics and Black Power*. Chicago: Aldine Publishing Co., 1969. A case study of Chicago's West Side Organization, a community development organization in the Near West Side; shows how an organization controlled by community residents is responsive to the people's needs.

Kotler, Milton. *Neighborhood Government*. New York: Bobbs-Merrill, 1969. This author argues for community control of all institutions that directly affect the lives of the residents; decision making on the economic structure of the community (localism) should emanate from the community.

Minar, David and Scott Greer, eds. *The Concept of Community*. Chicago: Aldine Publishing Co., 1969. This is a reader on the concept of community, the different kinds of communities, the relationship of politics and community, community and social change and the social and personal consequences of change.

Moynihan, Daniel P. *Maximum Feasible Misunderstanding*. New York: The Free Press, 1969. A discussion of the dynamics related to community action and participation in the War on Poverty. This conservative theorist argues that the poor may never be ready to assume power in an advanced society.

Polsky, N. W. *Community Power and Political Theory*. New Haven: Yale University Press, 1963. A classic academic treatise on community decision making—supports the plurastic view against centralized planning.

Rosenbloom, Richard and Robin Marris, eds. *Social Innovation in the City: New Enterprises for Community Development*. Cambridge: Harvard University, 1969. Economic and political interests, ideological presuppositions, institutional rigidities, and old habits and attitudes are found to dilute and even defeat what may be a genuine public desire to do something about urban housing, racial tensions, and poverty. The various authors suggest a variety of programs and different types of organizations to help resolve many of the present urban problems with the major emphasis on community controlled economic development.

INDEX